Routledge Revivals

A. E. Housman

First published in 1992, *A. E. Housman: The Critical Heritage* brings together the most important and significant critical response to the poetry of A. E. Housman from the time of his writing to 1951. It contains ninety-four items —articles, reviews, and comments which provide an accurate picture of how Housman the poet was seen during his lifetime and for some years beyond it. The picture which emerges is of a poet not only of popular appeal, but of great literary distinction, who was admired by the majority of reviewers and critics who discussed his work. Among those quoted are J. B. Priestley, Edmund Gosse, Cyril Connolly, T. S. Eliot, George Orwell, Cleanth Brooke, Stephen Spender, John Sparrow, and E. M. Forster.

A. E. Housman
The Critical Heritage

Edited by Philip Gardner

First published in 1992
by Routledge

This edition first published in 2024 by Routledge
4 Park Square, Milton Park, Abingdon, Oxon, OX14 4RN

and by Routledge
605 Third Avenue, New York, NY 10017

Routledge is an imprint of the Taylor & Francis Group, an informa business

© 1992 Philip Gardner

All rights reserved. No part of this book may be reprinted or reproduced or utilised in any form or by any electronic, mechanical, or other means, now known or hereafter invented, including photocopying and recording, or in any information storage or retrieval system, without permission in writing from the publishers.

Publisher's Note
The publisher has gone to great lengths to ensure the quality of this reprint but points out that some imperfections in the original copies may be apparent.

Disclaimer
The publisher has made every effort to trace copyright holders and welcomes correspondence from those they have been unable to contact.

A Library of Congress record exists under LCCN: 91038327

ISBN: 978-1-032-88814-9 (hbk)
ISBN: 978-1-003-53980-3 (ebk)
ISBN: 978-1-032-88816-3 (pbk)

Book DOI 10.4324/9781003539803

A. E. HOUSMAN

THE CRITICAL HERITAGE

Edited by
PHILIP GARDNER
Professor of English
University Research Professor
Memorial University of Newfoundland

LONDON and NEW YORK

First published in 1992 by
Routledge
11 New Fetter Lane, London EC4P 4EE
Simultaneously published in the USA and Canada by
Routledge
a division of Routledge, Chapman and Hall, Inc.
29 West 35th Street, New York, NY 10001

Compilation, preface, introduction, notes, bibliography and index
©1992 Philip Gardner
Typeset in 11/12pt Bembo by
Thomson Press (I) Ltd, New Delhi
Printed in Great Britain by
T J Press (Padstow) Ltd, Padstow, Cornwall

All rights reserved. No part of this book may be reprinted or reproduced or utilized in any form or by any electronic, mechanical, or other means, now known or hereafter invented, including photocopying and recording, or in any information storage or retrieval system, without permission in writing from the publishers.

British Library Cataloguing in Publication Data
A catalogue record for this book is available from the British Library.

Library of Congress Cataloging in Publication Data
also available.

ISBN 0 415 03298 9

In Memoriam

Arnold Trevor Owen
John Desirée Berbiers
Ethel Mary Steuart

General Editor's Preface

The reception given to a writer by his contemporaries and near-contemporaries is evidence of considerable value to the student of literature. On one side we learn a great deal about the state of criticism at large and in particular about the development of critical attitudes towards a single writer; at the same time, through private comments in letters, journals or marginalia, we gain an insight upon the tastes and literary thought of individual readers of the period. Evidence of this kind helps us to understand the writer's historical situation, the nature of his immediate reading-public, and his response to these pressures.

The separate volumes in the *Critical Heritage Series* present a record of this early criticism. Clearly, for many of the highly productive and lengthily reviewed nineteenth- and twentieth-century writers, there exists an enormous body of material; and in these cases the volume editors have made a selection of the most important views, significant for their intrinsic critical worth or for their representative quality – perhaps even registering incomprehension!

For earlier writers, notably pre-eighteenth century, the materials are much scarcer and the historical period has been extended, sometimes far beyond the writer's lifetime, in order to show the inception and growth of critical views which were initially slow to appear.

In each volume the documents are headed by an Introduction, discussing the material assembled and relating the early stages of the author's reception to what we have come to identify as the critical tradition. The volumes will make available much material which would otherwise be difficult of access and it is hoped that the modern reader will be thereby helped towards an informed understanding of the ways in which literature has been read and judged.

B.C.S

Contents

PREFACE	xiii
ACKNOWLEDGMENTS	xvii
INTRODUCTION	1
NOTE ON THE TEXT	57

A SHROPSHIRE LAD (1896)

1	THOMAS HUMPHRY WARD, unsigned notice, *The Times*, March 1896	58
2	HUBERT BLAND, unsigned review, *New Age*, April 1896	58
3	O.O., review, *Sketch*, April 1896	61
4	'CLAUDIUS CLEAR' (WILLIAM ROBERTSON NICOLL), *British Weekly*, April 1896	62
5	A.M. (ANNIE MACDONELL?), review, *Bookman*, June 1896	65
6	Unsigned review, *Guardian*, June 1896	67
7	NORMAN GALE, review, *Academy*, July 1896	68
8	LOUISE IMOGEN GUINEY, review, *Chap-Book* (Chicago), February 1897	70
9	Unsigned notice, *Literary World* (Boston), April 1897	73
10	Unsigned notice, *Citizen* (Philadelphia), November 1897	74

A SHROPSHIRE LAD (1898)

11	WILLIAM ARCHER, review, *Fortnightly Review*, August 1898	75
12	Unsigned notice, *Outlook*, September 1898	81
13	Unsigned review, *Academy*, October 1898	81
14	Unsigned notice, *Bookman* (London), October 1898	86
15	Unsigned notice, *Athenaeum*, October 1898	86
16	'The Funereal Muse', *Literature*, October 1898	87
17	Unsigned review, *Saturday Review* (London), November 1898	90

CONTENTS

18 CHARLES SORLEY on *A Shropshire Lad*, May 1913   93
19 JAMES ELROY FLECKER, from 'The New Poetry and Mr. Housman's "Shropshire Lad"', undated, pre-1915   98
20 HOLBROOK JACKSON, 'The Poetry of A.E. Housman', *To-day*, August 1919   102
21 HAROLD MONRO on Housman, 1920   109

LAST POEMS (1922)

22 'The "Shropshire Lad" again', *Times Literary Supplement*, October 1922   112
23 EDMUND GOSSE, 'The Shropshire Lad', *Sunday Times*, October 1922   114
24 D.C.T., 'Professor Housman's Last Poems', *Cambridge Review*, October 1922   120
25 B.S., review, *Manchester Guardian Weekly*, November 1922   122
26 J.C. SQUIRE, review, *London Mercury*, November 1922   124
27 AMABEL WILLIAMS-ELLIS, review, *Spectator*, November 1922   126
28 Unsigned notice, *English Review*, December 1922   129
29 JOHN FREEMAN, 'Hail and Farewell', *Bookman* (London), December 1922   129
30 Unsigned review, *Outlook*, December 1922   132
31 LEE WILSON DODD, 'The Stoic Muse', *Literary Review*, December 1922   134
32 J.B. PRIESTLEY, 'The Poetry of A.E. Housman', *London Mercury*, December 1922   136
33 H.J. DAVIS, 'An English Poet', *Canadian Forum*, January 1923   153
34 STEWART MARSH ELLIS, review, *Fortnightly Review*, January 1923   154
35 G.H.C. (GEORGE HERBERT CLARKE), review, *Sewanee Review*, January 1923   159
36 WALLACE B. NICHOLS, 'Mr. A.E. Housman's Return', *Poetry Review*, January–February 1923   160
37 CLEMENT WOOD, 'The Shropshire Corydon: Opus II', *Nation* (New York), February 1923   162
38 WILLIAM A. NORRIS, review, *New Republic*, February, 1923   165

CONTENTS

39 WILLIAM ROSE BENÉT, 'The Book of the Month: A.E. Housman's "Last Poems" ', *Bookman* (New York), March 1923   168
40 O.W. FIRKINS, 'Living Verse', *Yale Review*, July 1923   172
41 EDWARD SAPIR, 'Mr. Housman's Last Poems', *Dial*, August 1923   174

42 F.L. LUCAS, 'Few, but Roses', *New Statesman and Nation*, October 1923   178
43 J.C. SQUIRE, 'Mr. A.E. Housman', 1923   186
44 J.F. MACDONALD, from 'The Poetry of A.E. Housman', *Queen's Quarterly*, Fall 1923   191
45 OSBERT BURDETT on Housman, 1925   206
46 IOLO WILLIAMS on Housman, 1927   208
47 H.W. GARROD, 'Mr. A.E. Housman', 1929   213
48 CHARLES WILLIAMS, 'A.E. Housman', 1930   226

THE NAME AND NATURE OF POETRY (1933)

49 LASCELLES ABERCROMBIE, 'A.E. Housman on Poetry', *Manchester Guardian Weekly*, June 1933   234
50 G.W. STONIER, 'Professor Housman on Poetry', *New Statesman and Nation*, June 1933   236
51 J.C. SQUIRE, editorial note, *London Mercury*, June 1933   238
52 D.W. HARDING and L.C. KNIGHTS, 'Flank-Rubbing and Criticism', *Scrutiny*, September 1933   239
53 S. GORLEY PUTT, review, *Scrutiny*, September 1933   241
54 R.R. (RICHARD REES), review, *Adelphi*, July 1933   243
55 BASIL DAVENPORT, 'The Terrier and the Rat', *Saturday Review of Literature* (New York), July 1933   244
56 KARL SCHRIFTGEISSER, from a review, *Boston Evening Transcript*, July 1933   251
57 R.P., 'Exponent of Pure Poetry', *Christian Science Monitor*, July 1933   252
58 T.S. ELIOT, review, *Criterion*, October 1933   254

59 EDITH SITWELL on Housman, 1934   257
60 CHAUNCY BREWSTER TINKER, 'Housman's Poetry', *Yale Review*, September 1935   261

CONTENTS

OBITUARY COMMENTS (1936)

61	From 'Death of Professor A.E. Housman', *Manchester Guardian Weekly*, May 1936	272
62	E.L. WOODWARD, 'Les Lauriers Sont Coupés', *Oxford Magazine*, May 1936	273
63	F.L. LUCAS, 'Mithridates: The Poetry of A.E. Housman', *Cambridge Review*, May 1936	277
64	CYRIL CONNOLLY on Housman, *New Statesman*, May 1936	282
65	RICHARD REES, 'The Modernism of Housman', *Adelphi*, June 1936	288
66	JOHN ERSKINE, 'What is Contemporary Poetry?' *North American Review*, Autumn 1936	292

MORE POEMS (1936)

67	RAYMOND MORTIMER, 'Housman Relics', *New Statesman and Nation*, October 1936	300
68	IVOR BROWN, 'Poet and Scholar: the Last of the "Shropshire Lad" ', *Observer*, October 1936	304
69	PETER MONRO JACK, 'The Shropshire Lad's Farewell: A Distinguished Final Volume by A.E. Housman', *New York Times Book Review*, October 1936	307
70	JOHN SPARROW, 'A.E. Housman', *Spectator*, October 1936	310
71	CONRAD AIKEN, 'A.E. Housman', *New Republic*, November 1936	313
72	E.M. FORSTER, 'Ancient and Modern', *Listener*, November 1936	316
73	EDWIN MUIR, review, *London Mercury*, November 1936	321
74	GEOFFREY GRIGSON, review, *New Verse*, Christmas 1936	324
75	ROBERT HILLYER, review, *Atlantic Monthly*, December 1936	326
76	WILLIAM EMPSON, 'Foundations of Despair', *Poetry* (Chicago), January 1937	328
77	EARLE BIRNEY, 'Swan Song', *Canadian Forum*, January 1937	330

CONTENTS

78	JACOB BRONOWSKI, review, *Criterion*, April 1937	335
79	EUGENE DAVIDSON, 'The Span of Housman's Poetry', *Yale Review*, Winter 1937	338
80	NEVILE WATTS, 'The Poetry of A.E. Housman', *Dublin Review*, January 1937	341
81	LOUIS KRONENBERGER, 'A Note on A.E. Housman', *Nation* (New York), December 1937	355
82	LAWRENCE LEIGHTON, 'One View of Housman', *Poetry* (Chicago), May 1938	360
83	CARL and MARK VAN DOREN, 'A.E. Housman', 1939	365

COLLECTED POEMS (1939, London; 1940, New York)

84	BONAMY DOBRÉE, 'The Complete Housman', *Spectator*, January, 1940	369
85	PETER MONRO JACK, 'A.E. Housman's Lasting Art', *New York Times Book Review*, March 1940	372
86	STEPHEN SPENDER, 'The Essential Housman', *Horizon*, April 1940	376
87	LOUIS MACNEICE, review, *New Republic*, April 1940	381
88	JOHN PEALE BISHOP, 'The Poetry of A.E. Housman', *Poetry* (Chicago), June 1940	384
89	MORTON DAUWEN ZABEL, 'The Whole of Housman', *Nation* (New York), June 1940	392
90	BENJAMIN GILBERT BROOKS, 'A.E. Housman's Collected Poetry', *Nineteenth Century*, July 1940	399
91	CLEANTH BROOKS, 'The Whole of Housman', *Kenyon Review*, Winter 1941	405
92	GEORGE ORWELL on Housman, 1940	410

TWO POST-WAR SUMMINGS-UP

93	' "A Shropshire Lad" at Fifty', *Times Literary Supplement*, March 1946	415
94	JOHN CROWE RANSOM places Housman, 1951	424
	SELECT BIBLIOGRAPHY	426
	INDEX	428

Preface

Much the meatiest of all the books on A.E. Housman was published by Oxford University Press in 1941. Entitled *Housman 1897–1936,* it was by his publisher, Grant Richards, and described in copious detail the professional and personal relationship the two men had had from the republication of *A Shropshire Lad,* under Richards's imprint, in 1898, to Housman's death nearly four decades later. In the opinion of its author it was neither a biography nor a critical study; yet it partook generously of the attributes of both, and what was not fully supplied by Richards was added in ten appendices by other hands, which considered not only Housman's life and personality but such matters as the dating of his poems, the many reminiscences of other writers to be found in them, and their attractiveness, as lyrics, to a number of English composers. Though some later studies of Housman have been more methodologically rigorous and of greater critical acumen, none has offered such a wealth of information or such a warmth of personal response.

Two of Grant Richards's chapters, entitled 'Eulogy' and 'Detraction', provided a commentary, necessarily brief but richly illustrated by quotation, on many of the responses provoked in his lifetime by Housman's poetry. At the end of the latter chapter Richards looked forward, in effect, to the series of which this present volume forms a part: 'As a publisher I have always had in mind the fact that a series in which the ebb and flow, the reverses, the successes, of the great figures in our literature were chronicled from contemporary books and journals would be of more than usual interest and here, however imperfectly, the thing is done for A.E. Housman.' Whether, some fifty years later, the fuller documentation I have attempted to provide in this book 'does the thing' any less imperfectly is for the reader to decide; but I hope that the ghost of Grant Richards, if not of A.E. Housman, will be glad that at least an attempt has been made.

Though it is a longer attempt, it is not the first since Richards wrote. Norman Marlow made another necessarily brief one in 1958, in a book published by Routledge & Kegan Paul now unjustly neglected, *A.E. Housman: Scholar and Poet*. Marlow devoted his eighth chapter to 'Contemporary Criticism of Housman'; making no attempt to conceal his partisanship for the virtues of Housman's poetry, he took the view that 'the early critics' (among whom he named only Hubert Bland, who had reviewed *A Shropshire Lad*, and J.B. Priestley, who had reviewed *Last Poems*) were 'vastly superior to the later'. Their efforts, mostly produced in the two decades since Housman's death, Marlow roundly dismissed as 'splenetic and ill-considered outpourings'.

A year before Marlow's book appeared, John Wain had published in *Preliminary Essays* (1957) a brief and grudging essay on Housman which concluded with the remark that 'even today any disparagement of [Housman's] work is certain to be greeted by a chorus of protests.' Perhaps Marlow's hostility to critics who disparaged Housman will seem, with its air of proprietorial outrage, only to justify Wain's view – which, at that point in his essay, appeared to assume some largely unbroken critical ascendancy for Housman's poems into the 1950s. The opening sentence of Wain's essay, however, had suggested a very different situation: 'I have been expecting – but not, so far, seeing – a resurgence of interest in Housman; if not as a poet, then at least as a case-history.' Set against an assumption like this – of Housman's poetry as a spent force – Marlow's comment may be read more sympathetically, as a necessary piece of polemical defensiveness, intended to restore Housman's poetry to the critically favoured position it had once held.

I should read it so myself, having first encountered Housman's poetry as a schoolboy, then remained devoted to it as an undergraduate in the decade when Marlow and Wain were writing. On the one hand, I sensed more than a 'faint neglect' of Housman in the critical atmosphere of the time; on the other, I felt myself responding to both the emotional poignancy and the verbal distinction of Housman's poetry, and was unwilling to disparage them in order to be thought intellectually respectable. My admiration was certainly shared, however naïvely, by some of my contemporaries: I remember a fellow-student giving me a handwritten copy of 'Loveliest of Trees' as an example of what real poetry still was, however assertive the takeover bid then being mounted by 'the Movement'.

PREFACE

But if, in 1957, John Wain looked in vain for 'a resurgence of interest in Housman' and felt some pleasure in not finding it, the situation thirty years later is very different. Not only is Housman's poetry, as I was told in 1988, gaining ground (which perhaps it had never lost) among Cambridge students, it has again become a topic of study for scholars and for influential critics. In 1988 Christopher Ricks brought out his extensively annotated compendium, running to over 500 pages, of Housman's *Collected Poems and Selected Prose*, thus adding to the service he did to Housman's memory twenty years earlier by his compilation of essays (one of them his own) in the *Twentieth Century Views* series. John Bayley has recently completed that rare thing, a critical study of Housman's poetry; and an authoritative Oxford edition of the poems is currently in preparation by Archie Burnett.

The beginning of the 1990s seems thus an appropriate time for the appearance of a reasonably full-scale collection of critical responses to Housman, especially since we are approaching the centenary of the first publication of *A Shropshire Lad*, in 1896. Completing my work on this book in 1990, I had not aimed at the numerical exactitude which has resulted: ninety-four years since then, ninety-four items here. But I am happy to leave it so, feeling that the items I have chosen to include (selected from a number more than half as large again) provide an essentially accurate picture of how Housman the poet was seen during his lifetime and for some years beyond it. To have added more items from the period I have delimited for myself – 1896 to 1951 – would have been to lengthen the book unduly, without the compensation of significantly increased and varied insights into Housman's poetry. I am sure that Housman himself, as the author of only three small volumes of poems, however good, and one illuminating lecture on poetry, would have reprehended any such prolixity.

Nor have I wished to go beyond my 'cut-off' date and reprint more recent essays already available in Christopher Ricks's collection published in 1968, when there existed so much published in Housman's lifetime which it was the more proper province of a *Critical Heritage* volume to retrieve. Whether or not the reader will agree that the 'later' criticism castigated by Norman Marlow in 1958 and the detraction recorded by Grant Richards in 1941 (most of both reprinted at length in his book) are less persuasive

xv

than that larger number of essays and reviews which consent to Housman's high poetic status, I cannot predict. All I can say is that, as so often happens when one delves into a 'critical heritage' to resurrect the opinions of the past, I have emerged from my survey with no less respect for the acuity of the often long-dead than for that of the living. Those who consider the reputation of A.E. Housman as a poet might well keep in mind what he himself said – in that other capacity, of classical scholar, which this volume does not address – in the closing sentence of his Cambridge Inaugural Lecture of 1911: 'Do not let us disregard our contemporaries, but let us regard our predecessors more; let us be most encouraged by their agreement, and most disquieted by their dissent.'

Acknowledgments

I acknowledge with great pleasure the help given me by numerous individuals and institutions while I was compiling and editing the material presented in this book. I am grateful for the kindly co-operation of members of staff at the following libraries: Cambridge University Library; the Harry Elkins Widener Memorial Library of Harvard University; the Queen Elizabeth II Library of Memorial University of Newfoundland; the Periodicals Division of the British Library. My research was financially supported by Memorial University of Newfoundland, first by means of funds, locally administered, supplied by the Social Sciences and Humanities Research Council of Canada; then by its appointment of me, in 1988, to a University Research Professorship. I am grateful to Ms Laura Taylor, departmental secretary, for her exemplary typing of a long and arduous manuscript; and, as always, to my wife, colleague and (from 1987 to 1990) head of department, Professor Averil Gardner, for her continuous help and understanding. My research was made the more pleasurable during the summer of 1988 by the Provost and Fellows of King's College, Cambridge, who made me a Visiting Member of High Table; I particularly wish to thank two senior Fellows of King's, Dr George Rylands and Mr Christopher Morris, for the light they were able to shed on A.E. Housman as a person. I also gratefully acknowledge the help of Professor Kenneth Muir.

I am indebted to the following institutions, publishers, periodicals and individuals for allowing me to reprint a number of the items published in this volume: *The Atlantic Monthly* for No. 75 (©1936 by Robert Hillyer), first published in *The Atlantic Monthly*, December 1936, and used by permission; Faber & Faber Ltd for No. 58; The Johns Hopkins University Press for No. 94; King's College, Cambridge, and the Literary Estate of F.L. Lucas for No. 63; *The Listener* for No. 72; *The New Republic* for Nos. 71 and 87; Oxford University Press for Nos. 47 and 48; the Editor of *Poetry* for No. 76 (Copyright 1937, *Poetry*), No. 82 (Copyright 1938, *Poetry*) and No. 88 (Copyright 1940, *Poetry*), reprinted by permission; the Editor of *The Poetry Review* for No. 36; Prentice-

ACKNOWLEDGMENTS

Hall, Inc., Englewood Cliffs, New Jersey, for No. 83, from Carl and Mark Van Doren, *American and British Literature since 1890* (©1925, renewed 1953), pp. 166–70; Mr S. Gorley Putt for No. 53; the Estate of the late Sonia Brownell Orwell and Martin Secker & Warburg Ltd for No. 92; *The Spectator* for Nos. 27, 70 and 84; The Statesman and Nation Publishing Company Ltd for Nos. 42, 50, 64 and 67; Times Newspapers Ltd for No. 93 (© Times Newspapers Ltd); *The Yale Review* for Nos. 60 and 79.

Every attempt has been made to obtain permission to reproduce copyright material. If any proper acknowledgment has not been made, we invite copyright holders to inform us of the oversight.

Introduction

I

Just a month into his seventy-eighth year, A.E. Housman died on 30 April 1936. Two days later Virginia Woolf, in a letter to her nephew Julian Bell, made a comment on his contemporary literary status that is all the more telling for being indirect: 'I get the most astonishing elaborate letters from poet Eliot, who is now titular head of English-American letters since the death yesterday of Houseman.'[1] The notion of T.S. Eliot being elevated to that honorific pinnacle in his late forties will, one may conjecture, be less surprising today than the realization that, even for a novelist who misspelled his name, Housman was still felt to have been its occupant up to the time of his death, which had outdistanced by fourteen years the publication of only his second book of poems. It may be, of course, that Virginia Woolf's remark was a tacit acknowledgment, not of the chorus of praise which greeted *Last Poems* in 1922, but of the much more recent stir provoked by Housman's Leslie Stephen Lecture, 'The Name and Nature of Poetry', given at Cambridge in May 1933. Whereas Eliot's self-appointed champions at *Scrutiny* (Nos. 52 and 53) had seen this as putting back the literary-critical clock by a decade,[2] Eliot himself had reviewed it (No. 58) with notable circumspection and possibly sincere respect, having waited a full six months for the dust to settle. Virginia Woolf was Leslie Stephen's daughter; but, with her husband Leonard, she was also the publisher of *The Waste Land*, whose first English edition appeared from the Hogarth Press in September 1923, nearly a year after *Last Poems*.[3] Her sense, in 1936, that the former, and the new kind of poetry it represented, had not succeeded in displacing the latter, and its distant predecessor *A Shropshire Lad*, was an eloquent if unintended tribute to the hold that Housman's poetry had maintained for four decades and across generations of readers.

Its hold on Virginia Woolf herself, however, was far from total, and in going on to ask her nephew his opinion of Housman's poetry she reeled off a list of its properties which, though accurate enough in substance, was casually reductive in tone: 'Did you know him? Do you like his muse? I don't altogether; why, I can't say. Always too laden with a peculiar scent for my taste. May, death, lads, Shropshire.' Clearly enough, Virginia Woolf's glancing acknowledgment of Housman's high reputation as a poet was accompanied by some puzzlement about it. In 1915 she seems to have felt more than puzzlement, confiding to her diary how annoyed she had been, when attending a concert in the Queen's Hall, to find that a couple sitting next to her were taking advantage of the music to press hands, read *A Shropshire Lad*, and look at some 'vile illustrations'[4] – presumably the eight water-colour plates of Shropshire landscapes which appeared in the first illustrated edition of the poem, published in 1908.[5]

No devotee of music (though surprisingly often he gave reluctant permission for his poems to be set, most notably by Vaughan Williams in 'On Wenlock Edge' in 1908), Housman might have been amused, even gruffly touched, by such evidence of his popularity, particularly in wartime. In 1916 he half-joked to Grant Richards about the 'advertisement to which I am always looking forward: a soldier is to receive a bullet in the breast, and it is to be turned aside from his heart by a copy of *A Shropshire Lad* which he is carrying there.'[6] Though the fact cannot be documented by reviews, it was during World War I that Housman's poetry came to be widely read and appreciated: in 1915 he agreed to the suggestion of Sir Walter Raleigh that poems from *A Shropshire Lad* be included in a broadsheet printed by *The Times* for distribution in the trenches,[7] and his refusal (until 1922) to accept any royalties from the volume was intended to subsidize the sale of at least some editions at as low a price as possible. From 1907 onwards, copies of *A Shropshire Lad* were regularly issued at prices varying between sixpence ($2\frac{1}{2}$p) and 7s. 6d. ($37\frac{1}{2}$p), so it is just possible that Housman's hope for physical proof that the pen is mightier than the sword, the printed word than the bullet, might have been vindicated. 'May, death, lads, Shropshire' remained a prepotent combination well into the 1920s, and by the end of 1922 the first printing (4,000 copies) of *Last Poems* had been more than quadrupled to keep pace with public demand.[8]

Virginia Woolf's sense of a 'peculiar scent' in Housman's

poetry, which kept her from wholehearted admiration, did not blind her to his perceived stature even in 1936: her comment to Julian Bell, however oblique, is a considerable tribute to an 'ancient' from a 'modern'. In 1930, the death of the Poet Laureate, Robert Bridges, had prompted a tribute of another kind and from a very different cultural quarter, a tribute which gives some indication of Housman's appeal to his own generation. Though the Laureateship passed to the 52-year-old John Masefield, and though King George V had wished to appoint Rudyard Kipling (who was thought likely to refuse), the poet favoured for the post by the then Prime Minister, Ramsay MacDonald, was Housman. By that time (and indeed up to the time of his death) Housman was known to readers as the author of hardly more than a hundred short poems. Without needing to propose Ramsay MacDonald as a literary critic, one may take his wish that Housman should become Poet Laureate (an honour which Housman, too, was expected to decline) as acknowledgment of poetic distinction of a very high order.9

II *A SHROPSHIRE LAD* (1896)

In 1928 Housman was asked, through his publisher Grant Richards, to give permission for some of the poems in *A Shropshire Lad* to be included in an anthology. Housman gave such permission extremely rarely, and was especially adamant on this occasion, since the anthology in question was *A Book of Nineties Verse*, edited by A.J.A. Symons. His reply (whose nice combination of accuracy and disingenuousness must have given him considerable satisfaction) is a *locus classicus* of Housmanian wit, though it is not known whether Richards passed it on to Symons verbatim: 'to include me in an anthology of the Nineties would be just as technically correct, and just as essentially inappropriate, as to include Lot in a book on Sodomites; in saying which I am not saying a word against sodomy, nor implying that intoxication and incest are in any way preferable.'10 Only a biographer of Housman could do full justice to the ironic nuances of this; here it is sufficient to render a précis, to the effect that Housman felt he was a 'poet of the Nineties' only by an accident of timing, and wished to avoid any misconception consequent on being juxtaposed with those who were 'poets of the Nineties' in spirit, by reason of their use of symbolism, their 'decadence' of attitude or subject matter, their concern with the atmosphere and life of the metropolis, and anything else that might be attributable to French influence. 'My name is Housman, not Huysmans', the affronted poet (whose sexual orientation was his own concern) might almost have said.

It is not difficult to agree with Housman's own view of his poetry. Thirty-four years after his death, when it was too late for him to make a second protest, another anthologist, Kelsey Thornton, included eight poems from *A Shropshire Lad* in his collection entitled *Poetry of the 'Nineties*. Admittedly, though it was not the purpose of this anthology 'to get rid of the 'nineties myth',[11] the poems in it were 'chosen to illustrate not a thesis but a period'; thus the inclusion of poems by Housman (and by Kipling and Newbolt too) was perhaps intended to show that a particular historical decade was not exclusively filled with the kind of poetry pre-emptively associated with it. Even so, in its wish, or need, to include poems concerned with the arts, London and its denizens, religious longing and doubt, 'Love and Death', the sense that all comes to an end, and (in Section 6, entitled 'Fire from France') poems in English translation, the anthology strongly suggests that the 1890s was not just a period but an atmosphere – a rather overheated, introverted atmosphere from which the eight poems by Housman, with their freshness and simplicity of diction, their almost faultless ear, and their unpretentious distinction of form, seem effortlessly to escape. In this anthology Housman opens a welcome window in a room still occupied for the most part, given the inclusion of a far larger number of their poems, by John Davidson, Ernest Dowson, Lionel Johnson, Arthur Symons and W.B. Yeats, whose famous verdict on *A Shropshire Lad* – '[it] is worthy of its fame, but a mile further and all had been marsh'[12] – communicates the wry admiration of a fellow-practitioner for Housman's skill in avoiding dangers ('a facile charm, a too soft simplicity') which he himself, in the 1890s, had not always escaped.

Yeats did not air his view of Housman until 1936, in his introduction to *The Oxford Book of Modern Verse*, where with Housman's reluctant permission he had included five poems, all of them from *Last Poems*. But his late acknowledgment of its predecessor's well-merited 'fame' is not a tactful redrafting of the record; though Yeats was not among the volume's reviewers on its appearance in March 1896, those who did review it were almost unanimous in their response to it as something well out of the common run. Yeats's contemporary (and fellow member of the Rhymers' Club) Richard Le Gallienne wrote of its 'delightfully fresh and spontaneous note',[13] and the epithets 'fresh', 'spontaneous' and 'original' figure constantly in the volume's reviews. That these were many, and largely favourable, it is as well to emphasize here, since a snowball of statements by later commentators on Housman can easily mislead readers unable to begin at the beginning into thinking that *A Shropshire Lad* went largely unnoticed on first publication. This was true neither in England nor in the United States, where copies exported by Kegan Paul made their appearance under the imprint of John Lane early in 1897.

Housman had originally offered his volume to Macmillan. There, however, to use the phrasing of its last poem, 'the hue was not the wear'; apparently on the advice of their reader, the journalist and biographer John Morley,[14] the book was rejected, though the reason may have been no more than Macmillan's difficulty in finding a market for poetry. But Housman did not bring his flowers home unheeded; through his Oxford contemporary A.W. Pollard he was put in touch with the firm of Kegan Paul, by whom (but at Housman's expense) the book was published. It was Pollard who was responsible for its title. Housman's own had been, variously, 'Terence' or 'The Poems of Terence Hearsay' – a title which, though rather flat, accurately placed Housman inside his poems yet at a distance from them. Pollard's suggestion of 'A Shropshire Lad' met with Housman's quick approval, perhaps because it seemed to offer not only a saleable atmospheric ring but a *persona* he could conveniently disavow, as he did in 1933: 'The Shropshire Lad is an imaginary figure, with something of my temper and view of life. Very little in the book is biographical'.[15] There is no doubt that the title was worth the risk; but it is arguable whether the Professor of Latin much relished, over the years, being himself described as 'the Shropshire Lad' by overfamiliar critics, and being caricatured, however laudatorily, in this guise in *Punch*, on the appearance of *Last Poems*.[16]

Though their author was himself neither a lad nor from Shropshire, the fact that Housman's first collection had 'a local habitation' did not go unnoticed by some of its reviewers. One of them (No. 3) even risked the ridicule of critics yet unborn by saying that 'Shropshire may be proud that its fields and streams have been sung by this genuine and individual poet'. Such a formulation, though made by a reviewer fully responsive to Housman's 'fresh, spontaneous, vigorous poetry', mistakenly suggests that a topographical emphasis might have been Housman's own intention. More accurate was the comment of the volume's first reviewer, Matthew Arnold's nephew-by-marriage Humphry Ward: 'The mere mention, here and there, of Ludlow, Wenlock and Shrewsbury, of Wrekin and Severn, gives a pleasant element of local colour' (No. 1). But though this element was clearly part of *A Shropshire Lad*'s charm for Ward (and for other reviewers, and surely many readers of the volume, then and since), its true distinction lay elsewhere: the local colour 'would be nothing if the essentials of thought and music were absent. Happily they are there in no niggardly measure'. For William Robertson Nicoll, who granted Housman to be 'a writer of true refinement and originality' (No. 4), the topographical element in *A Shropshire Lad* hardly signified at all. 'Local colour', for him, was an ingredient to be judged according to standards variously set by the novels of Thomas Hardy[17] and the Dorset dialect poems of William Barnes: though Housman's poems from time to time mentioned 'the names of Shropshire towns and hills' (and rivers, Nicoll failed to add), his volume, such passing references apart, 'might have borne the name of any other English county', since Housman described neither the landscape nor the rustic inhabitants of Shropshire with any pretensions to particularity.

Probably Housman would not have been downcast at Nicoll's rather purist view on this peripheral matter. In 1933 he disposed of it thus, in a letter to a French admirer of his poetry, Maurice Pollet: 'I had a sentimental feeling for Shropshire because its hills were our western horizon. I know Ludlow and Wenlock, but my topographical details – Hughley, Abdon under Clee – are sometimes quite wrong'.[18] That 'sentimental feeling' was certainly apparent to many of Housman's earliest readers, and *A Shropshire Lad* would, *pace* Nicoll, be a very different book without it; but, in justice to Nicoll, and to place Housman's topographical concerns in perspective, it should be pointed out that only fifteen of the sixty-three poems in *A Shropshire Lad* contain references to

Shropshire places, and of the rest of his published poetry (another 114 poems) only two, both of them in *Last Poems*. It was, and is, for other elements than its specific rendering of place that Housman's poetry gained, and retains, its high critical reputation.

'Every poem is quotable', said Richard Le Gallienne of *A Shropshire Lad*.[19] In his view – that of a poet six years younger than Housman, but with already two volumes of verse in print and a third soon to appear – such a statement was 'rare praise'; but then, Housman's book was 'a quite notable exception'. An exception to what, Le Gallienne did not say – presumably to the general run of poetry of the 1890s. Since his own work was a fair but not outstanding example of this, Le Gallienne's praise was generous. It may also be felt to convey a craftsman's admiration for effects of sound and rhythm at which Housman was more skilled than himself. In 'A Ballad of London' Le Gallienne could quite creditably write:

> Ah, London! London! our delight,
> For thee, too, the eternal night,
> And Circe Paris hath no charm
> To stay Time's unrelenting arm.[20]

But this hardly compares for euphony with four lines from the only poem of Housman's (*A Shropshire Lad*, No. XXVI) which Le Gallienne had space to quote in his short review:

> And sure enough beneath the tree
> There walks another love with me,
> And overhead the aspen heaves
> Its rainy-sounding silver leaves.

This is, as Le Gallienne pointed out, 'delightfully fresh and spontaneous'. It also possesses an unobtrusive dexterity for which the earliest reviewers of Housman could find no adequate terminology, certainly not the dry exactitudes with which academe was later to make readers so familiar. But even the vagueness of Annie Macdonnell (No. 5) suggests, in however muddled a fashion, that Housman's attributes as a stylist did not go entirely unperceived: 'Mr. Housman's technical merits might easily be surpassed, but his rhythms and forms call for no criticism. They are simple, sometimes rough, never subtle, save with the subtlety that catches and reflects the mood, and sets the matter to the right tune.' In what areas (other than rhythm and form) Housman's 'technical merits' might be surpassed, and by whom, is never made clear; but the granting to Housman's poetry of a kind of 'subtlety' appropriate to its mood and material is a sizeable concession. All in all, one senses in this passage, and in many reviews by others, an awareness that Housman's poetry was not like that of his contemporaries, and a considerable pleasure that this should be so. Indeed, Annie Macdonnell's review itself begins by making that very point, quite unequivocally: 'Here is a writer who stands outside all the poetical vogues of today.... I have seen no book of verses for years that breathes at least more spontaneity, and very few with as much individuality.' In more measured tones, the anonymous reviewer in the Anglican paper the *Guardian* (No. 6) – one of the very few who took issue, at this stage, with Housman's 'sombre vein' – expressed much the same view: 'It is pleasant, after all the books of art-poetry that are now the fashion, to come upon a poet who sings with a natural note, and is not too concerned to be clever. Mr. Housman's muse may not be a nightingale, but neither is it a garden-warbler setting up to be a nightingale.' A critical vocabulary like this – whose metaphors the reader of 1896 could perhaps decode into human names – conveys little now but a qualified approval; but approval it does convey, as does Norman Gale's over-simple attribution to Housman of 'bird-like unconsciousness' and his simile for 'the abounding presence [in Housman's poems] of verbal felicity' : 'Arresting phrases are as numerous as sparrows in ivy at night' (No. 7).

Housman's letters contain very few references, even, to reviews of his work, so it is not easy to know how many of them he read. Of the handful on which he actually commented, Hubert Bland's review of *A Shropshire Lad* (No. 2) was his clear favourite: ten days after its appearance he described it, to his brother Laurence, as 'very nice'; writing to his young American admirer Houston Martin, forty years later and a week before his death, he called it 'the best review' of his poems.[21] It is doubtful whether Bland's especially favourable verdict alone accounted for Housman's preference: one who, as a classical scholar, notoriously failed to suffer gladly the mistakes of fools would have been unlikely as a poet to rest easy under foolishly undiscriminating praise. That of Bland combined strong general approval with a shrewd and precise sense of where Housman's power really lay – in a 'perfect simplicity' which those accustomed to the 'pretty', 'pleasing' and 'derivative' poetry of the day might mistakenly take for baldness, and in an absence not of 'art' but of 'artifice'. Though Housman deplored Bland's 'disparaging the other chaps' in his first paragraph, he must surely have been pleased by Bland's recognition in *A Shropshire Lad* of an 'individual voice' which 'rings out true and clear', and which expressed 'elemental emotions' with the directness of Heinrich Heine, who had died three years before Housman was born and a compendium of whose poems had appeared in English translation when he was a young man.[22] He would also, I feel, have approved of Bland's refusal to overstate: though Housman's poetry appeared to him 'little short of consummate' and 'astonishingly near the highest', it operated 'within narrow limits' and lacked – an essential element, for Bland – the 'note of gladness'. Housman was quite able to admit as much himself, in the short poem printed by his brother Laurence as preface to the posthumous *More Poems* (1936):

> They say my verse is sad: no wonder;
> Its narrow measure spans
> Tears of eternity, and sorrow,
> Not mine, but man's.

In later years, many of the most eloquent and perceptive – though not always the best-disposed – responses to Housman's poetry came from the United States; but with one outstanding exception American reviews of *A Shropshire Lad* were summary and even grudging. Anonymous commentators in Boston (No. 9) and Philadelphia (No. 10) clearly found the absence of 'gladness' from the volume a major stumbling block to their appreciation of what was present, either in terms of subject matter or stylistic felicity. The Philadelphia reviewer assuaged his qualms by taking the gloom as a solemn practical joke; the one in Boston, who admitted the virtues of a single poem, 'The Recruit', would doubtless have been more pleased if the whole volume had been what Spencer Blackett, the manager of Kegan Paul, had apparently first wished it to be – 'a romance of enlistment'.[23] Even William Morton Payne, who noticed *A Shropshire Lad* in the *Dial*, unintentionally undermined the credibility of such praise as he gave ('a collection of short poems, extremely simple in diction, which strike a thin but pure lyric note') by comparing Housman's volume with one by A.C. Benson (*Lord Vyet, and other Poems*), which he described as 'almost equally simple, but now more animated, now informed with a deeper passion'. Such qualities were hardly in evidence in the poem, 'Envoi', whose conclusion he approvingly quoted and whose last stanza ran:

> But I can sing as sings the prudent bee,
>   As hour by patient hour he goes and comes,
> Bearing the golden dust from tree to tree,
>   Labours in hope, and as he labours, hums.[24]

The balance of American criticism, however, was more than redressed by the Anglophile poet Louise Imogen Guiney, whose appreciation of Housman (No. 8) was expressed equally by a handsome rhetoric and by a perceptiveness which anticipated that shown eight months later by William Archer. Louise Guiney was the first reviewer to see through the rustic mask of *A Shropshire Lad* to the sophisticated and learned poet behind it: far from being an unlettered versifier, like the collier-poet Joseph Skipsey, Housman had much in common with – though far more 'native freedom and power' than – the poet and Eton master William Johnson Cory, the author of *Ionica* (1858), with its famous epigram translated from Callimachus which begins 'They told me, Heraclitus, they told me you were dead'. In recognizing this classical strain, this 'moan as of Thessalian seas' underlying Housman's poetry, Louise Guiney was also the first reviewer to show an awareness of its almost-Miltonic 'grandeur', not merely its clear simplicity. For her, Housman was more than a poet significantly different from his contemporaries; just as Shakespeare was greater than Spenser and Beaumont, Housman was superior to the 'minor bards' around him, and it was for them to 'touch their rusty lances to the rim of his shining shield'.

III *A SHROPSHIRE LAD* (1898)

One of the reviewers of the 1896 *A Shropshire Lad* was Grant Richards, who concluded his brief notice in the *Review of Reviews* by describing Housman as 'a distinct acquisition to the body of young men who are worthily doing their utmost to keep alive the traditions of English song'.[25] Since Housman was 37 at the time, and Richards 24, the comment is unintentionally amusing; but it had behind it a devotion to Housman's poetry which was to lead to a long and profitable association: in 1897 Richards set up as a publisher, and in the following year Housman become 'a distinct acquisition' to his list. After negotiations with Housman and with Kegan Paul, whose 1896 edition was not yet sold out, Richards published *A Shropshire Lad* under his own new imprint in September 1898; and though this single action did not generate reviews where none had existed before (as has sometimes been supposed), Richards's assiduity over the years contributed greatly to the sales of the volume: between 1898 and 1940 more than 138,000 copies were printed, the years 1920 to 1924 accounting for over a quarter of this number.[26]

But if the reviews of the 1898 edition were no more numerous than those which had greeted Housman in 1896, some of them were considerably longer, and nearly all of them responded to the conscious artistry of the poet, rather than to the rural simplicity of his material. 'It is that sort of easy reading which is hard writing,' said the *Athenaeum* (No. 15); and the *Saturday Review* (No. 17) made a similar point a month later: *A Shropshire Lad* was a 'remarkably successful dramatic experiment', in which 'the very finest art' could quickly be discovered behind an 'apparent artlessness' of presentation. So much, in fact, does this *aperçu* (already made across two thousand miles of North Atlantic by Louise Imogen Guiney) repeat itself from mid-September to early November 1898 that one almost suspects an orchestrated response, assisted perhaps by the persuasion of the publisher; though that, if true, would not invalidate the accuracy of the perception. It may, however, have had behind it simply a growing awareness of who A.E. Housman was. The London *Bookman*, as well as reviewing *A Shropshire Lad* in June 1896, had published two months later a piece on Housman, illustrated by a photograph of him taken in a Regent Street studio, which fully described his academic career and his contribution to classical scholarship:[27] it would surely have seemed unlikely, *prima facie*, that the Professor of Latin at University College, London, would be naïve as a poet.

But considerable influence on critical opinion certainly came to bear from another quarter. A month before Richards's edition was published, much the longest commentary on *A Shropshire Lad* had appeared in the *Fortnightly Review* (No. 11), from the hand of the highly regarded drama critic William Archer. Indeed, it was Housman's awareness of this article, in advance of its publication, which in part persuaded him that Richards's proposed new edition might be timely.[28] There is no evidence, however, to suggest that the 'review', late as it was in relation to the 1896 edition of *A Shropshire Lad*, was a prearranged 'puff' or Richards's reissue of it; in fact Archer added, on publication, a footnote to the effect that, at the time of writing, he 'knew nothing of Mr. Housman save his name'. Thus his view that the 'Shropshire Lad' was 'a mere mask' could stand as an example of native intelligence rather than as evidence of inside information.

The degree of Archer's commitment to making a strong case for Housman's excellence is indicated not only by his generosity with illustration – seven poems quoted in full, three sets of sequential stanzas, and twelve lines from 'Terence, this is stupid stuff' (*A Shropshire Lad*, No. LXII) – but also by what he added in a final paragraph four years later, when reprinting his article in a volume of his essays: 'I have a curious feeling of having quoted the wrong things. Not that I admire these things less, but that I admire others more. One may safely say, at any rate, that every poem here singled out could be replaced by another of equal merit without by any means exhausting the wealth even of so small a book.'[29] His show-casing of Housman was accompanied by an unusually high concentration of perceptive critical comments, as well as by one of the earliest attempts to summarize, not so much the subjects of Housman's poems, but the 'cast of thought' of their writer, which Archer described as 'a stoical pessimism; a dogged rather than an exultant patriotism; and what I may perhaps call a wistful cynicism'. It was a very fair opening shot in the long-lasting struggle of critics to pin down the tone of a deceptively simple, fascinating and elusive poet.

Particularly shrewd was Archer's recognition, not of melancholy in Housman, but of 'melancholy vitality', and of the related combination in his poetry (which gave it an affinity with Hardy's novels) of 'rapturous realisation' of life and 'bitter resentment' of it. The language through which these feelings were expressed was both vernacular and also 'classical in the best sense of the word' – terse, reticent and pregnant. And though 'his metres are of the homeliest', Housman's sensitive and masterly handling of them revealed 'the touch of the born metrist'. All in all, despite his passing references to Hardy, and to Heine (the latter repeated without elaboration by a number of reviewers later in 1898), Archer found Housman to be a poet who owed nothing to others, whose 'diction and ... methods are absolutely his own'.

Few of the reviewers proper dissented from Archer's high estimate. Less than three weeks later, most of it was reprinted in the *Academy*, with an explanatory note: 'When a discerning critic, a lover of poetry (to use a misused phrase) happens upon a poet altogether new, reads him with avidity, and writes about him enthusiastically, the result is good reading'.[30] The result was also that, well before *A Shropshire Lad* was reissued, the stereophonic availability of Archer's opinion created a climate highly favourable to Housman. A number of the autumn reviews (which included a further one by 'O.O.' in the *Sketch* for 9 November 1898, emphasizing the unusually 'direct appeal to the heart' of Housman's poems) referred back to the volume's original appearance in 1896, and one of them (No. 13) twice mentioned Archer's article deferentially in the course of its own painstaking and largely favourable assessment, which was able to come to terms with Housman's 'grim and pessimistic philosophy' because it was 'made impressive by the downright sincerity of the poet and his power of expression'.

Two important *caveats*, however, were entered by reviewers in 1898. For the one in *Literature* (No. 16) – who nevertheless obliquely apologized for the magazine's failure, since it did not exist then, to welcome *A Shropshire Lad* in 1896 – Housman's poems, though of undoubted power, were overmuch occupied with mortality, death and the grave. Such themes were legitimate, but the mood which led to their expression was 'only a mood like another', and its too frequent occurrence – involving what the reviewer felt to be an unduly schematic harping by Housman on the opposition of death and life – ended by producing tedium in the reader. For a poet to stir the reader deeply was one thing; for him to risk becoming 'a bore' was quite another, and Housman would be well advised 'to stop before reaching the Styx'. And if 'the tragic side of life' was only one of its aspects, so, in the view of the *Academy* (No. 13), was Housman's poetry not the 'only wear in song': in quite properly extolling the directness of Housman as 'an excellent thing for Mr. Housman's aims', there was no need to assert that such a style was the only one for all poetry.

Presumably this anonymous reviewer had been irritated by the emphasis given by some of his predecessors of 1896 to Housman's pre-eminent originality, even though they had criticized none of Housman's 'fellow-singers' by name; perhaps, too, the period between 1896 and 1898 had seen Housman's reputation rise too steeply. It is easy enough, especially since the *Academy*'s reviewer valued Housman's contribution to poetry, to sympathize with his wish – expressed in terms of violin virtuosi – not to see the rest of it undervalued as a fashionable consequence: 'we do not cry down Joachim, because we cry up Sarasate; we admit a pantheon in music – why not in poetry?'

The view is obviously sensible, and Housman would have agreed with it. Nevertheless, that the appeal was being made at all argues the very high place in poetry which Housman had remarkably quickly attained and which the reappearance of *A Shropshire Lad* had consolidated. The *Saturday Review*, speaking a week later than *Literature*, and praising Housman's achievement in producing 'in this jaded age a little volume of perfectly original verses' (No. 17), may fairly be allowed to have the last word: 'If Mr. Housman should write nothing more, this little book of his is yet likely to keep his name fresh in the history of poetry'.

IV

Over the next twenty-four years Housman published only eight more poems – one in an anthology entitled *Wayfarer's Love* (1904), five in publicly available magazines, between 1900 and 1917, and two in magazines of very limited circulation: *Blunderbuss*, published for and by the 5th Officer Cadet Battalion, quartered at Trinity College, Cambridge, where from 1911 onwards Housman was a Fellow; and the *Edwardian*, the magazine of King Edward's School, Bath, where one of Housman's nephews, killed in action in World War I, had been a pupil. It must therefore have seemed that Housman, though active and illustrious as a classical scholar, had virtually spoken his last word as a poet. But *A Shropshire Lad*, constantly reprinted, kept his name fresh in the mind of the public, though there is little to record by way of criticism in this period other than a few comments by fellow poets and, between the Great War and 1922, a handful of articles in journals.

Although, in the autumn of 1928, Housman expressed his unwillingness to be included in an anthology of 1890s poetry, a letter he wrote in the spring of that year to an American collector suggests that he was not necessarily ill-disposed to the 'jaded age' in which *A Shropshire Lad* had appeared. Its greatest luminary was Oscar Wilde, imprisoned for homosexual practices in 1895; when he was released from Reading Gaol in May 1897, Housman sent him a copy of the volume[31] – an action on whose mixture of kindness, fellow-feeling, admiration and self-advertisement it is unnecessary to speculate here.[32] The only indication of Wilde's response was given by Housman's brother Laurence, who quoted 'almost the exact words' of a letter he had received from Wilde, thanking him for a similar gift: 'By the same post that brought me your book of *All Fellows* I received from your brother A.E.H. a copy of his poems, *A Shropshire Lad*. So you two brothers have between you given me a taste of that rare thing called happiness'.[33] Perhaps, in view of Wilde's new directness and simplicity in *The Ballad of Reading Gaol*, published in 1898, 'happiness' had been accompanied by admiration for Housman's style; that, however, can be no more than inference.

But it is hard to be sure of Laurence Housman's accuracy in remembering, not only because he was writing more than fifty years after receiving Wilde's letter, but also because his recollection of another response, that of the 75-year-old George Meredith, can be shown to be at fault. According to Laurence Housman's memoir *A.E.H.* (1937), Meredith had 'received a copy [of *A Shropshire Lad*] from an enthusiastic friend', and had called it 'an orgy of naturalism'.[34] Since one of Housman's recent biographers has not only quoted this phrase without comment but has also attributed to it Housman's very real distaste of Meredith, expressed in August 1903,[35] it is worth pointing out what Meredith really wrote, to the minor poet Herbert Trench, in March of that year: '*The Shropshire Lad* is a revelry of naturalness'.[36] Neither phrase conveys any very precise intellectual meaning; but Meredith's actual words surely express approval rather than dislike.

In view of the frequent – if usually sketchy – comparison made by reviewers and critics between Housman and Thomas Hardy, the latter's opinion would be of considerable interest; but the record is disappointing. Grant Richards sent Hardy a copy of *A*

Shropshire Lad in 1898, and Hardy met Housman the following year, first in London and two months later in Dorchester; but, according to Housman in 1935, 'Hardy and I never talked about my poems', and it was Florence Hardy who told Housman that her husband's favourite poem was 'Is My Team Ploughing?' (*A Shropshire Lad*, No. XXVII).[37] But Hardy was clearly an admirer of Housman's poems in general: just before meeting Housman in Cambridge in 1913, after an interval of some years, Hardy said in a letter to Sydney Cockerell: 'I should like to compel him to write some more "Shropshire Lad" verses; but he won't'.[38] 'Is My Team Ploughing?' was also the favourite Housman poem of Hardy's exact contemporary, the poet, traveller and Arabist Wilfrid Scawen Blunt, at whose home in Sussex Housman spent a weekend in November 1911. Blunt found Housman 'prim in his manner, silent and rather shy', but with the help of Francis Meynell he was able to persuade him to talk about his poems; he confined his diary entry, however, to his own view of them: 'I have a great admiration for his "Shropshire Lad", on account of its ballad qualities and the wonderful certainty of his choice of exactly the right word'.[39]

So much – one wishes there were more – from the older generation of Housman's readers. But a younger generation, destined for distinction as poets, had begun to respond to the varied attractions – verbal, topographical, philosophical – of *A Shropshire Lad*, and was reaching out to proselytize those who might not have heard of Housman. In 1906, on the verge of leaving Rugby School, the 19-year-old Rupert Brooke gave a very comprehensive paper on modern poetry to his fellow sixth-formers, in which he spoke of the 'undeniable ring of poetry' given out by Housman's 'little countrified songs in a vein of pessimistic but healthy quietism', even though 'in form they incline towards doggerel, being generally of the utmost simplicity of phrase and metre'. What Brooke felt to be their essential quality was expressed by his suggestion of the most appropriate circumstances in which to read them for the first time – 'on an autumn morning when there is a brave nip of frost in the air and the year is sliding quietly toward death'.[40] There is an element of understated coaxing about these remarks to a school audience. The following year, writing to an undergraduate contemporary at King's College, Cambridge, Brooke spoke out unequivocally: 'I met Laurence Housman the other day. His brother is the only poet in England'.[41] Housman's influence on Brooke is clear enough from the latter's poem 'The Chilterns', written in the stanza form of 'Bredon Hill' (*A Shropshire Lad*, No. XXI); Brooke's regret that Housman seemed to have dried up as a poet was expressed, however ironically and parodically, in 'A Letter to a Shropshire Lad', written in 1911 on hearing that Housman had been elected to the Latin chair at Cambridge:

> Latin? So slow, so dull an end, lad?
>   Oh, that was noble, that was strong!
> For you'd a better wit to friend, lad,
>   Than many a man who's sung his song.
>
> You'd many a singer's tale to show it,
>   Who could not end as he began,
> That thirty years eats up a poet,
>   And the muse dies before the man.[42]

Rupert Brooke died in the First World War, before Housman could prove him wrong. He died in the same year, 1915, as Charles Sorley, who in 1913 had followed Brooke, but at much greater length and with a wealth of quotation, by introducing Housman's work to his own schoolmates, at Marlborough College. Sorley valued Housman less than John Masefield, to whose work he was devoted and on whom he had spoken to the Marlborough College Literary Society the year before; but his piece (No. 18) is nonetheless highly appreciative, showing an even-handed awareness of the strengths and limitations of Housman's view of life, and valuing particularly Housman's 'earthiness', localized in Shropshire, as a necessary antidote to the 'essential falseness and shallowness of the mid-Victorian court-poets', Tennyson included. A dourer personality than Brooke (of whose 'sentimental attitude' to war he later spoke harshly in a letter), Sorley did not mind sounding iconoclastic; on the other hand, for one of his earnest, active temperament Housman's emphasis on 'rest' as the end of life was an insurmountable obstacle to poetic greatness. But there is no doubt that Housman's work had impressed him deeply, and his thumbnail sketch of Housman's 'essential features' is remarkably perceptive: they were 'primitive impulses and emotions, purged and civilized, as it were, but never essentially altered or improved, by a restrained and balanced intellect'. This intuition of an 18-year-old schoolboy may profitably be set beside words which Housman, conversing in his seventies, proffered as an apt inscription for his gravestone: 'Here lies the only member of the middle classes who did not fancy himself a gentleman'.[43]

That Brooke and Sorley, of the generation of poets who died in the First World War, approved of *A Shropshire Lad* it is possible to demonstrate from their comments on it. What Wilfred Owen thought of it appears nowhere in his letters; all that can be said is that he bought a copy in August 1916, shortly after being commissioned.[44] Ivor Gurney's response can be documented, though only briefly: *A Shropshire Lad* seems to have been a book he was anxious to keep by him on active service, and in 1917 he threw light on its general popularity when speaking in a letter of his own first volume, *Severn and Somme*, published that year: 'A friend of the Hunts tried in London – at the Times Book Club – for Severn and Somme. Out of print it is! Harvey's two books, a "Shropshire Lad" and mine are selling like hot cakes, they told her!'[45]

A Shropshire Lad was enjoyed by soldiers, as well as soldier-poets; this was attested to well after the war by St John Adcock in his book The Glory that was Grub Street (1928). In a short and otherwise unremarkable section on Housman, Adcock spoke of the sixpenny edition of the volume, published in 1907 and small enough to fit into a waistcoat pocket, and added: 'I know that when I was on a visit to France and Belgium, during the war, the three volumes of verse that were greatly in demand among the soldiers of the new army, down at the rest camps, were Browning's "Men and Women", Omar Khayyám, and that excellent edition of "The Shropshire Lad".'[46] Holbrook Jackson (No. 20) reported the same interest at second hand in 1919, mentioning a friend who had been reading *A Shropshire Lad* to soldiers at 'a military encampment near London': 'By gad! don't they love it!' he had said. Jackson's article, with its emphasis on those poems of Housman's concerned with soldiers, soldiering and soldierly attitudes, shows one of the reasons; another, advanced by Adcock, was that their 'wry, whimsical, indomitable realism' chimed with the mood of soldiers, who had no illusions about the war. A further reason for the popularity of *A Shropshire Lad* was its sheer 'Englishness', a point reiterated by the music critic Ernest Newman in 1918, writing about the unsuitably over-dramatic music to which its poems had been set by Ralph Vaughan Williams in his song cycle 'On Wenlock Edge'.[47]

In 1900 Grant Richards had issued *A Shropshire Lad* in his series entitled *The Smaller Classics*, to Housman's considerable annoyance. When Richards went bankrupt in 1906, and his firm was bought up, Housman took the opportunity of withdrawing his book from the series, since he thought it 'unbecoming that the work of a living writer should appear under such a title'.[48] Nevertheless, it is clear enough that by 1920 Housman's slim volume had achieved the status of a classic, both with the public and, by and large, with the critics. From 1902 onwards considerations of his work had appeared in the few books surveying new poetry, and although in 1920 Harold Monro (No. 21) expressed the reservation that Housman was 'not a genius', he also felt that the 'new intellectual folk-poetry he has so deftly invented' had had a great influence on younger poets in their reaction from the 'bulky pomposity of late Victorianism'. That same year a two-page article by John Freeman in the London *Bookman*, generously illustrated by quotation and by no fewer than three photographs of the poet, summed up his position without reserve. Widely imitated, yet 'inimitable', Housman was a poet to be grateful for, whose 'perfect stanzas and phrases' were fixed by the dozen in the minds of many readers. While his small output was 'a subject for constant regret', that regret could not 'mar our thankfulness for what we have received'.[49]

V *LAST POEMS* (1922)

One American critic expressed no thankfulness for what he was about to receive. In March 1922, Howard Mumford Jones began a long article on Housman with this pronouncement: 'I heard not long since a rumor that A.E. Housman was intending to publish another book of verse, and I can not compliment him more than by hoping it is not so'.[50] For Mumford Jones the virtues of *A Shropshire Lad* — its inheritance of the 'Roman manner', its rootedness in a particular soil, its supreme embodiment of the period in which it was written and (to invert a phrase of Professor Frank Kermode's) the loquacity of its reticence — combined to make it 'a man's entire product, not fragmentary but sufficient'.

It was a volume 'at the fountain-head of the contemporary movement in poetry', and among other things it had profoundly influenced 'modern war poetry'. The details of Mumford Jones's argument are sometimes obscure; what underlies them is the wish that Housman, already made immortal by his art, should neither repeat himself nor cause disappointment by perhaps falling short of his own 'flawless and passionless perfection'.

How, though, could Mumford Jones have come by his rumour? *Last Poems*, which appeared on 19 October 1922, was not officially announced until a month or so before, and though Housman had mentioned a possible new volume to Grant Richards two years earlier (only to deny the possibility in January 1921) he gave strict instructions that no one should be told. A request for poems from Harriet Monroe, editor of the American magazine *Poetry*, elicited on 30 November 1921 a reply from Housman which was less than frank: 'I have no poems by me which I wish to see in print'.[51] Not until the April of 1922, when a sudden resurgence of poetic energy enabled him to finish half a dozen poems long left incomplete and to write a handful of new ones, was Housman sure that he had 'a volume of poems ready for the autumn'; but, again, he adjured Richards 'not [to] mention it to anyone until you are obliged to mention it'.[52]

However Mumford Jones had come to hear of Housman's new volume, his reluctance to have it was not shared by its reviewers, and especially not by the *English Review* (No. 28), which not only welcomed Housman's return (in foolish and gushing terms, admittedly) but begged that his ominously titled volume should not in fact be his swan-song as a poet. The extreme regard in which Housman was held, and the delight – indeed relief – with which his poetic resurrection was greeted, were splendidly if irreverently summed up by a cartoon by Bert Thomas, published in *Punch* a week after *Last Poems* appeared: a Muse in classic garb reaches out her arms in welcome to a smock-frocked, heavy-booted Housman, who carries a knapsack oddly heavy with his two slim volumes and capers towards her playing on a pipe. The caption (in a familiar Housman metre) reads: 'Oh Alfred, we have missed you! My lad! My Shropshire lad!'[53]

Nearly all the reviews, too many and too long to comment on here in any detail, were essentially footnotes to this cartoon. Richard Le Gallienne, welcoming *Last Poems* as he had welcomed its predecessor twenty-six years before, and taking a very different view from that of Howard Mumford Jones, summed up the expectation that had preceded its arrival: 'Probably had most of us been asked to name the literary event which we would care best to have happen, our choice would have been a new volume of poems by the author of *A Shropshire Lad*'.[54] But it was not simply Housman's old admirers from the tail-end of the nineteenth century who turned out to applaud him. Whereas the reviewers of *A Shropshire Lad* had been Housman's seniors or near-contemporaries, since 1900 those who commented on his work had been considerably younger than him, and of those whose reviews of *Last Poems* were signed, all but Edmund Gosse (aged 73) were very much his juniors, from John Freeman, aged 42, down to J.B. Priestley, who was only 28. These had come to *A Shropshire Lad* in the process of growing up (in Priestley's case, on the Western Front), and that they should have greeted the *Last Poems* of a sexagenarian with such enthusiasm is a powerful testimonial to Housman's enduring vitality, particularly when one considers that 1922 was also the year, and its autumn the season, in which *The Waste Land* first made its impact.

A recurrent concern of reviewers was the extent to which *Last Poems* was, on the one hand, a continuation and a rounding-out of *A Shropshire Lad* and, on the other, a volume different in emphasis and atmosphere from its solitary predecessor. For Edmund Gosse (No. 23) it was 'a continuation of the old theme' in 'the same voice', any change being 'in the direction of a completer technical excellence'; for the *Times Literary Supplement* (No. 22) it was the same and yet subtly different – a loss of 'vividness', perhaps, an alteration in 'the pitch and quality of the writer's feeling'; for the *Cambridge Review* (No. 24), it was the repetition of 'a triumph', but not 'a mere sequel', the 'inevitable complement' to *A Shropshire Lad*, yet 'more thoughtful, more hopeless, more mature'. Part of the reviewers' difficulty was in finding a precise enough language for their varying intuitions; but part of it came from their simply not being sure, from style and content alone, which poems were written nearer 1895 and which nearer 1922. Housman's prefatory note is likely to have teased them, in baldly stating that 'about a quarter of this matter' – but not, one notices with the sharpness of informed hindsight, a quarter of the poems – 'belongs to the April of the present year, but most of it to dates between 1895 and 1910'. It was hardly surprising that many reviewers fell into their trade's besetting temptation, the urge to compare volumes and perhaps discover 'development' or the lack of it. Their problem was accidentally but nicely encapsulated in a question posed by the reviewer in the *Outlook* (No. 30): having quoted the first stanza of *Last Poems*, No. XIII ('The Deserter'), he went on to say: 'Who will swear, without exact and careful reference, that was not first published nearly twenty years ago?' The poem, in fact, had not been published at all, but it had been started in either 1901 or 1905, and had not been finished until April 1922; and that Housman did not always begin his poems at the beginning is shown by No. XXXVI, whose first stanza ('West and away the wheels of darkness roll') was written last, in 1922, and the other two at some unspecified earlier date.

Nearly all the reviewers, however, went on from their tentative weighing of the two volumes to a decided commendation of *Last Poems*, not by comparison but for itself; though for William A. Norris (No. 38), a Harvard instructor whose review carries an echo of Mumford Jones, *Last Poems* was redundant to a reputation already well-won. But only an anonymous notice, signed 'Recorder', in Harold Monro's magazine *Chapbook* dismissed the volume out of hand, as showing Housman as merely 'a pupil in his own school', the 'school of English poetry' he had founded with *A Shropshire Lad*; for this reviewer only 'Epitaph on an Army of Mercenaries', first published in 1917, was worth mentioning – indeed, it was 'worth all the other poems in the book'.[55] But for most commentators it ultimately mattered little whether a poem was new or old: Housman's style, tone and matter, settled on when he was about thirty, gave a remarkable unity to nearly all he had written in the thirty years since then, as is apparent from the two supreme instances of 'this poet's peculiar excellence of mode and meaning' singled out by the American critic George Herbert Clarke (No. 35). One was 'The West', written before 1899; the other was the widely admired 'Hell Gate', begun in 1905 but not completed until April 1922.

Much the longest response to the publication of *Last Poems* was a thirteen-page article in the *London Mercury* (No. 32) by the young J.B. Priestley, not a novelist yet but an aspiring essayist with a taste for eloquent turns of phrase. It was hardly a review:

for Priestley, distinctions between *Last Poems* and *A Shropshire Lad* – 'a little more of this and a little less of the other', as he cavalierly referred to efforts in this direction – were not worth making, and though his essay quoted frequently from Housman's poems, the new volume accounted for only a couple of the quotations. The likeness between the new and the old, for him, was such that 'there is no reason why these two volumes, with the poems kept in their present order, should not be bound up together to form the two sections of one complete volume'. Housman expressed much opposition to this idea in various letters of 1924 and 1925, and summed up his attitude pungently in a letter to Houston Martin ten years later: '*A Shropshire Lad* and *Last Poems* will never be joined together while I am here to prevent it, and I think it a silly notion'.[56] Clearly Housman himself felt the two books to be essentially different, less in style and content, perhaps, than in their use and non-use, respectively, of a rustic *persona*.

Nevertheless, Housman liked the article – which Priestley sent him on its republication two years later in his collection *Figures in Modern Literature*[57] – and it has much to recommend it, despite its imperceptive treatment of Housman's metrical skill, with which J.F. Macdonald rightly took issue in the Canadian magazine *Queen's Quarterly* in 1923 (No. 44). Priestley was the first critic to point to Housman's employment in his work of three distinct poetic 'kinds' – the ballad, the lyric, and the epigram – to his masterly handling of each of them, and to the remarkable amalgam of the three which his poetry represented. (To express the sure instinct which lay behind Housman's ability to reach 'nearer and nearer to perfection', Priestley coined a remarkably Housmanian phrase: 'The difficulty is not in merely taking trouble but in knowing what kind of trouble to take'.) Perceptive too was Priestley's discussion of Housman's use of language, with its preference for the concrete over the abstract, the noun and the verb over the unnecessary adjective, which could lead to his appearing 'positively brutal to some of his readers': Priestley's own adjective, only partly pejorative, is very telling.

Perhaps most illuminating, however, was Priestley's capturing of a coexistence of attitudes central to Housman's response to life: on the one hand Housman saw life as lovely but short, with death as its 'enemy'; on the other he felt life to be a misery, from which death was 'the deliverer'. Yet the contradiction (if, indeed, there was a contradiction) between these two positions was only noticed when the reader intellectualized the content of what had been read; in the poetry itself, during the act of reading, the two views worked powerfully and harmoniously together. The conclusion of Priestley's article introduced a further new note into responses to Housman's work. Earlier critics had sometimes spoken of similarities (rarely perceived as strong, and never as detracting from Housman's originality) between Housman and Heine, Housman and R.L. Stevenson, Housman and Edward Fitzgerald. For Priestley, Housman's poetry rated an altogether higher level of comparison: 'A line from A.E. Housman is as unmistakable as a line from Milton, Shelley or Wordsworth, and bears the same impress of the poet's individuality; and to me the difference between the modern poet and these three Titans, on this count of original force, is one of degree alone, for I hold him to be of the same imperishable kind'.

John Squire, the *London Mercury*'s editor, was similarly in no doubt that the cumulative achievement of Housman's two volumes had earned him a permanent 'place among the most illustrious of English poets' (No. 26). Vital to this success was the flawlessness of Housman's poetic technique, both verbal and rhythmical, which made him 'at once the example and the despair' of his contemporaries in the practice of verse; the despair too, one feels, of many of his reviewers, who perceived and admired the 'magic' of his poems – the term was used by Le Gallienne in the *New York Times* and by Wallace Nichols in the *Poetry Review* (No. 36) – but were unable to define its secret. But whatever it was, it would be strong enough, in the opinion of John Freeman (No. 29) to survive any superannuation of Housman's philosophy; though for Amabel Williams-Ellis (No. 27), who felt *Last Poems* to be peculiarly English and likely to arouse the 'incomprehension' of foreign readers, that philosophy, with its 'poignant tone of realistic stoicism', was an equally important ingredient of its 'great popularity'.

Precisely where the deepest appeal of Housman's poetry lay – in the subtlety of its technique, in some rapport between the poet's feelings and those of its readers, in some elusive combination of these two elements – became a recurrent concern of many commentators on Housman from 1922 onwards. Housman's long absence from poetry was an additional source of fascination:

an anonymous review in the *Nation and Athenaeum* bore the title 'The Silent Singer',[58] and Wallace Nichols (No. 36) made the reasonable point that *Last Poems* would not have been bought in such large numbers 'if it were its author's sixth or seventh volume'. For Edmund Gosse, who first defined the essence of Housman's poetry by the Latin term *desiderium*, 'the unconquerable longing for what is gone for ever', there was something 'mysterious' at the heart of his work: 'Nothing is told right out; the emotion is veiled and discreet; we are left to conjecture what is the exact nature of it' (No. 23). Stewart Marsh Ellis, though himself eschewing a search for the man behind the poems, rightly foresaw that later readers would 'want to know more', since 'all sincere poetry is the conscious or unconscious expression of momentous personal experience' (No. 34).

Only one reviewer, however, actually presumed at this time to draw aside the curtain of Housman's poems and reveal the picture, not biographical but psychological, behind it. This was R.W. Postgate, in a review entitled 'A Defeated Poet'.[59] Postgate felt Housman to be 'a fine poet', but found behind the 'marvellous perfection' of *Last Poems* a 'dead soul', the soul of one so worn down by his awareness of human defeat that he had abandoned his struggle to right the wrongs of the world, and had turned away from poetry 'to editing and studying the obscurer Latin poets' — specifically Manilius, 'whom few do read and none desire to read'. Postgate's thesis was not very plausible: Housman's concern for classical scholarship started early in his life, and neither his poems nor his letters suggest him to have been a man weighed down by social conscience (as distinct from metaphysical consciousness), or capable of feeling crushed by an 'industrial machine' whose operations he seems not to have noticed. Yet it is possible to agree that Housman's prefaces to his volumes of Manilius, extensively quoted by Postgate, display a degree of 'violence and savagery' which suggests a deeply frustrated spirit, and Postgate's regret that Housman's absorption in classical scholarship may have deprived the world of much fine poetry is not difficult to sympathize with. Describing Housman as 'the great poet that we lost', Postgate ended by giving his own reason why Housman, in the prefatory note to *Last Poems*, was right in forecasting no likely successor to it: 'Weapons go rusty in so long a time: the mind that has spent more than a quarter of a century on Manilius can not, if it would, turn to anything else'.

Most of the American reviews of *Last Poems*, appearing a couple of months later than the English ones, welcomed the volume in the same spirit, if not at the same length, as J.B. Priestley, and did not indulge in any of the socio-psychological speculations developed by Postgate to account for Housman's production of, apparently, only forty or so poems over a quarter of a century. But if it is hard to believe, as Postgate did, that the 'machine' of modern capitalism had squeezed Housman's output so small, 1922 had nevertheless been the year of *The Waste Land* and *Ulysses*, and in that post-war watershed of style it would have been surprising if no critics had felt any reservations about the work of a writer already in his sixties. Had not T.S. Eliot suggested that poetry, in a complex society, would of necessity be 'difficult' if it were to encompass the whole truth about life?[60] Two of the American reviewers, though neither mentioned Eliot and both were appreciative of Housman, turned politely but distinctly in a new direction and summoned up the first breaths of a colder critical wind.

One was Clement Wood (No. 37), who was not quite content to call Housman 'a great minor poet', and whose absurd distortion of him – into a poet who 'must talk of ... the wild-duck flight of airplanes raining death upon a countryside, in terms of Corydon and Thyrsis' – was an attempt to draw attention to what he saw as a basic immaturity in Housman's poetry, a 'beauty ... of brainlessness', 'a voice out of an impossible youth of the race'. For Clement Wood, himself at 35 about the age Housman had been when *A Shropshire Lad* appeared, 'the morbid wisdom of nineteen' was no longer adequate to comprehend the sterner necessities of the contemporary present. Six months later the anthropologist Edward Sapir (No. 41), who himself wrote poetry in a lushly old-fashioned vein, simply felt that Housman's work, despite being possessed of an 'admirably simple and clear, classical' style superior to that of any younger poet, 'will not go'. Whatever his virtues, Housman did not speak vitally to the emerging generation, whose pessimistic 'zero' was 'cultural' rather than 'personal'. There was 'room for a new Shropshire Lad'; but Housman, 'serene and bitter where we are bitter and distraught', was not he.

VI

The reluctantly negative verdicts of Wood and Sapir were far from typical responses to Housman in the 1920s; indeed, it was really not until after Housman's death in 1936 that a significant number of critics began to express dissatisfaction with his work, and even then there were more who defended it or simply found hostility off the mark. Even Sapir, in 1923, felt Housman's technique to be decidedly superior to that of his unnamed juniors who seemed closer to the spirit of the age; in the opinion of Stephen Gwynn, writing six months later in the Canadian university journal *Dalhousie Review*, no poet had given the world more 'beauty', or had captured more of 'the savour of life', than Housman, whose stanzas, 'often simple and hackneyed in their form, yet always subtle in their cadences', had a memorability which seemed clearly destined to outlast 'any of the *vers libres* now in fashion'.[61]

Sapir's article appeared in the *Dial*, with which T.S. Eliot and Ezra Pound were both connected, and which had not only published 'The Waste Land' in the autumn of 1922 but had awarded Eliot its annual prize of $2,000. Given the absence from Eliot's letters of any response to the publication of *Last Poems*, and his statement to his brother, at the end of 1922, that 'there is very little contemporary writing that affords me any satisfaction whatever',[62] it is tempting to suspect some link between the tone of Sapir's review and a wish on the part of the *Dial* to push older poetry aside in favour of new. But, if so, a substantial redressing of the critical balance took place just over a year later, when the *Dial* reprinted in September 1924 an article by F.L. Lucas (No. 42) which had originally appeared in England in the autumn of 1923. Lucas, who resembled Rupert Brooke in being a Fellow of King's College, Cambridge, and an expert on John Webster, but who differed from him in having survived active service in the first World War, was a determined opponent of anything in poetry that seemed needlessly complex and obscure. For Lucas, Housman's two slim volumes were 'this shadow of a great rock in the weary land of modern verse, so boundless and so bare', and his admiration for their technique, on which he commented with particular astuteness, was accompanied by approval for 'the essence of their being', that pessimistic outlook on life which, Lucas felt, had been cravenly deprecated, or side-stepped, by most reviewers. For Lucas, the style of Housman's verse could no more be separated from its content than a building from its foundations; to take them together was to appreciate Housman's poetry at its true worth, as a brave and passionate secular substitute for religious belief. Such a view of it could hardly be shared, of course, by one possessed of that belief. Both Lucas and Housman might well have found more impertinent than touching the hope with which a Catholic priest, H.E.G. Rope, concluded a short piece on Housman published in 1931: 'That the author of *A Shropshire Lad*, with its haunting unforgettable romance and beauty, may come at last to seek and find revealed Truth will be the earnest prayer of all his Catholic readers'.[63]

But few critics felt a pressing need either to identify themselves with, or to detach themselves from, Housman's 'pessimism' – a term which, incidentally, Housman felt to be an inaccurate description of his attitude to life, since by his own account he was 'not a pessimist but a pejorist (as George Eliot said she was not an optimist but a meliorist)'.[64] The small distinction was important to Housman, as was his statement – again in response to critical usage he felt to be inexact – that he was not a Stoic but a Cyrenaic. Most commentators on his work, however, used neither term in any strict sense, but rather as shorthand to convey the poignant grimness of the world Housman depicted and the brave, sometimes sardonic, endurance with which he faced it. John Squire, in an essay of 1923 (No. 43) which functioned as a sort of postscript to his review of *Last Poems* (No. 26), provided for the term 'pessimism' a context of credible and frequent responses to Housman's poems which makes it neutral and disperses much of the fuss: 'It is a strange quality in him that his very pessimism attracts those who like pessimism nowhere else. He is honest and courageous; he incites, in the end, to honesty and courage; he stimulates enjoyment even while he laments; and his music is so beautiful that whatever he says must delight'. Housman's real excellence, that superiority of expression which made him 'a standard' for other poets, was for Squire 'a matter apart from philosophy'.

That excellence was difficult to rank, however, though it provoked a spirited attempt to do so on the part of J.F. Macdonald, who published the longest article to appear on Housman in the 1920s, in the Canadian university magazine *Queen's Quarterly* in 1923 (No. 44). Macdonald, who wrote appreciatively – almost as if introducing the subject to Canadian readers – of a number of earlier critics of Housman, notably William Archer, had been very annoyed by two reviewers of *Last Poems*, though it is doubtful if they ever had the benefit of his comments. One was J.B. Priestley, whose lack of appreciation for Housman's metrical skill and stanzaic diversity led Macdonald to produce a valuably detailed analysis of Housman's real performance in these areas; the other was Clement Wood, whose use of the term 'great minor poet' to describe Housman had about it, for Macdonald, an offensive condescension. Not that Macdonald felt able entirely to dismiss the term 'minor poetry'; but in so far as it suggested mere prettiness, and not the 'passion' which characterized Housman's work, it misrepresented a writer who, though deficient 'in sheer bulk, in range and breadth', nevertheless wrote 'genuine poetry' and was in the good company of Pindar, Sappho, Burns, Blake and Thomas Gray – the last a poet beside whom, perhaps oddly but with no pejorative intention, Housman was often to be placed from this point on.

For Macdonald, clearly enough, comparison with Gray was meant as a considerable compliment, as was the general statement, made by Osbert Burdett in 1925, that Housman 'is perhaps the only poet, technically a minor, who seems too great for such a term' (No. 45). But just as the term 'minor poet' was given different weights and meanings by different critics, so the placing of Housman in relation to other poets depended not only on what was variously thought of him but also on what was variously thought of them. One of the poets beside whom, in Macdonald's opinion, Housman definitely could not be placed was Keats, on the grounds of 'bulk, range and breadth'; but to another critic, looking at both Housman and Keats from a different angle, the comparison seemed entirely appropriate. George McLean Harper, writing in *Scribner's Magazine* in 1925, had these glowing words to say: 'For poetic beauty in the strictest sense of the term, beauty that in this case depends almost wholly on sound and on those suggestions, now vague and again vivid, which are produced by sound, we must go back to Keats to find an equal quantity of verse by any one poet which excels them'.[65] It was presumably to this passage that Housman was referring when, a month before his death, he wrote to Houston Martin: 'The American who called them (I do not know where) the best poetry since Keats is endeared to me by his amiable error'.[66]

What Housman thought of H.W. Garrod's lecture on him (No. 47), given during the latter's tenure of the Oxford Chair of Poetry and published in 1930, is not recorded. 'His conjectures were singularly cheap and shallow', Housman wrote that same year, in the preface to the last volume of his edition of Manilius;[67] but he meant Garrod's treatment of the second volume of Manilius in 1911, and not, one must presume, what Garrod had said of him a few years before. Garrod's admiration for Housman is made abundantly clear by two comments: 'Of this beautiful elegy I am ashamed to qualify the praise', he said of 'To an Athlete Dying Young'; and there was 'no gainsaying perfections of [the] order' of *A Shropshire Lad*, No. XII. Nevertheless, Housman's rustic paraphernalia, which Louise Imogen Guiney and William Archer had seen as no more than a permissible concealment for Housman's poetic sophistication, was reproved by Garrod as 'false pastoralism' and 'sham masculinity', these elements serving as 'veils and pretences' adopted to disguise, 'out of some mercy to himself and others', the true emotional basis of Housman's poetry.

It is unlikely that Garrod's many hints and guesses would have appealed to Housman, but they are an early and far from obtuse example of that interest in Housman's personality which Stewart Marsh Ellis had predicted in 1923. More plausibly than R.W. Postgate, Garrod saw Housman's classical scholarship as 'an anodyne for the wounds which poetry has wrought in him', or rather, perhaps, for the disappointments of which so much of his poetry was the record. Garrod went too far, in asserting that Housman 'hated' poetry; and yet, with a poet who wrote so well when he did write, some such explanation of his long silences might have seemed no less likely than failure of inspiration. At any rate, a poet who 'could say all that he had to say in verse by biting his lip' was the sort of 'enigma' likely to provoke conjecture, and Garrod's last, dramatic sentence – 'It is his fault if we stare' – was surely echoed, *sotto voce*, by many of those 'contemporaries' who heard Garrod's respectful yet provocative lecture.

VII LAST YEARS AND *THE NAME AND NATURE OF POETRY* (1933)

Few but his Latin students ('an audience ... unworthily sparse', F.L. Lucas said in 1923) had had an opportunity to stare, literally, at Housman. Only his London University Introductory Lecture of 1892 and his Cambridge Inaugural Lecture of 1911 had made him visible to a more general public, and in 1925 he declined his own college's offer of the Clark Lectureship, saying that 'literary criticism' was 'a high and rare accomplishment and quite beyond me'.[68] On 9 May 1933, however, he made the last of his very few appearances before a large audience to give the Leslie Stephen Lecture at Cambridge. Although in one letter Housman spoke of 'The Name and Nature of Poetry' as 'that infernal lecture', and in others as written 'unwillingly' and 'against my will',[69] it is hard to believe that a man of 74, who shunned the limelight, would have taken on such an arduous task had he not wished to communicate something that mattered to him. According to one who was present (and who, over four decades later, described Housman's lecture as one of the two most impressive he ever heard), Housman was clearly moved by what he was saying;[70] to read it now, in the knowledge that it was spoken only three years before Housman died, is surely to feel that, among other things, it was Housman's long-delayed *apologia* for the kind of poetry he chiefly valued, and for the poetry he himself had written.

That Housman was regarded as a literary figure of great, if cloudy, eminence is indicated by the profusion of response, of which no more than a quarter is included here, to his solitary incursion 'into the foreign territory of literary criticism'. The day after Housman's lecture was delivered, *The Times* reported on it in detail, and devoted to it a leading article entitled 'What is Poetry?'; the reactions to its publication, a few weeks later, lasted on both sides of the Atlantic from the beginning of June until well into October, and in a few instances beyond. It was the view of Gerald Bullett, writing in the *Week-end Review*, that 'when one of the very few living poets whose work bears the mark of immortality delivers himself of a pronouncement on the nature of poetry it behooves us to hear him with a more than ordinary attention',[71] and this was the working assumption of most commentators on the lecture, James Southall Wilson going as far as to say, in the *Virginia Quarterly Review*, that 'as the matured speech of the author of "A Shropshire Lad", "The Name and Nature of Poetry" will be garnered up with the essays by poets on poetry, with Sidney's, with Coleridge's, with Arnold's.'[72] It would, even so, have been strange to find all the reviewers agreeing in detail with all Housman's general pronouncements and particular preferences: a number engaged vigorously with Housman's disparagement of the Metaphysicals and the Augustans, and some were dismayed by his apparently exclusive regard for the emotional and verbal elements in poetry, rather than the intellectual. Nevertheless, the critical views of one who had made such a notable contribution to the art which he discussed were not easy to put aside, and Housman's nicely calculated revelations of his own poetic practice were greeted by most commentators with the gratitude of desert travellers at last stumbling on an oasis.

For Professor Chauncy Brewster Tinker, who expressed grave reservations about many of its 'critical assertions', Housman's lecture was yet 'a draught of blood and iron', inasmuch as 'it asserts once more the inalienable power of the poet to elude the theorists and the law givers'.[73] Tinker, at Yale University, could afford to be detached; in certain quarters of Cambridge, however, Housman's lecture provoked a smouldering, embattled irritation which finally surfaced in the pages of *Scrutiny*, founded the year before. Leaving the Cambridge Senate House, I.A. Richards was heard to say 'It will take us at least a year to undo all that'[74] – 'all that' being, essentially, Housman's preference for the direct emotional appeal of the Romantics, and of verbal magic generally, over the intellectual complexities of the Metaphysicals, elevated to recent prominence by both the critical efforts and the poetic practice of T.S. Eliot. Tinker had noticed in Housman's lecture what he took to be a 'deliberate exclusion', its total lack of reference to 'that phenomenon known as modern poetry'. So, it would seem from his editorial in the *London Mercury* (No. 51), had John Squire, who rushed in to emphasize the comfort which Housman, telling 'the straight truth about poetry', had given to all those increasingly dismayed by the poetic and critical trends of the previous ten years. That these were the years since the publication of *The Waste Land* Squire did not need to say, but his mention of 'dons, who would have been better employed ... in psychological laboratories' and 'critics, dull and solemn ... who test poems by their intellectual content' referred clearly enough, at the time, to Richards and to F.R. Leavis, the latter of whom had in 1932 declared Housman to possess a talent which, though 'original', was 'of a minor order' and 'apt to exert a disproportionate influence'.[75]

Whether intentionally or not, Housman had disturbed a hornets' nest, as was demonstrated by the September 1933 issue of *Scrutiny*, which contained not just one piece, but two, in reaction to his lecture. F.R. Leavis, presumably leading from the rear, left the protests to be made by two of his *Scrutiny* lieutenants, and by an undergraduate in his last year at Cambridge. But though the latter's denial of the likelihood of 'lively criticism of English poetry from a professor of Latin' came close to impudence, both short essays seem, in relation to Housman himself, 'willing to wound but yet afraid to strike', confining themselves essentially to covert sneers at 'cultured people' who thought well of *A Shropshire Lad* and the views of its author (No. 53), and to a defence, almost as much in sorrow as in anger, of T.S. Eliot, the setting aside of whose poetry and criticism by Housman's supporters only proved that group's 'shoddiness of thought and feeling' (No. 52). The accusing finger of *Scrutiny* pointed explicitly at the recently knighted John Squire, editor of the *London Mercury* and leader of the Neo-Georgians; but Leavis could hardly have been any less displeased by Sir Richard Rees, editor of the *Adelphi* (No. 54), who pronounced the achievements of Housman, 'severely restricted' though they were, to be 'the very flower of humane culture' when set beside the 'bastard science of literature' which had grown up in Housman's adopted university. Nor, had they seen them, would the Scrutineers have relished, though they would undoubtedly have patronized, the views expressed in the *Boston Evening Transcript* (No. 56) by Karl Schriftgeisser, who saw in Housman's lecture 'fifty pages of everlasting truth' which reasserted the importance of feeling and at last superannuated 'the essays of T.S. Eliot and those who cringe at his feet'.

Eliot himself might have read this; he certainly knew of the *Transcript*'s unfavourable review, published in April 1920, of his *Poems*.[76] But, of course, his attitude to that newspaper had already been expressed in 1915, in his poem which spoke of evening 'wakening the appetites of life in some/And to others bringing the

Boston Evening Transcript;[77] so perhaps he could easily set Schriftgeisser's opinion aside. His own review of Housman's lecture (No. 58), published in the *Criterion* in October 1933, was an olympian performance which revealed neither irritation with those who were, or might be considered, hostile to him, nor partisan support for those who had sprung up to defend what they took to be his position. In fact, Eliot conducted himself as though no controversy had been raging, and one is hard put, finally, to decide whether his essay (which opened by praising the excellence of Housman's prose style) is a masterpiece of evasion; or whether (ending as it did with a mixture of hyper-cautious critical disagreement and tentative poetic empathy) it offers proof that, though their disciples may quarrel, one master can find grounds for respecting the gifts of another.[78]

For the reviewer in another Boston paper, the *Christian Science Monitor* (No. 57), any hypothetical disagreement between Housman and Eliot was outweighed by the fact that 'for distinction of manner and a discreet exercise of the most refined sensibilities, Mr. Housman's criticism ranks with Mr. Eliot's – a high honor, whatever its analytical shortcomings'. Such a pairing of the two writers only adds weight to what is already suggested by the volume of response, favourable and unfavourable alike, to *The Name and Nature of Poetry*: that Housman in old age was still a name to be reckoned with and a voice to be heard. Though Edith Sitwell – vexed perhaps by his undervaluation of Pope – could in 1934 (No. 59) find Housman's handling of the octosyllabic line inferior to Eliot's, Chauncy Brewster Tinker, in a long essay (No. 60) published the following year, had no doubt that Housman was '*par excellence*, the poet who has produced nothing poor', and that his poetry possessed a 'power to pierce the breast with unutterable emotion' which the reader would 'seek in vain among other living poets in England'.

VIII DEATH AND *MORE POEMS* (1936)

At the end of April 1936, eight months after these words appeared, Housman died. Nine days before his death, he responded thus to the new editor of the *London Mercury*, R.A. Scott-James, who had asked for a contribution: 'I am obliged by your letter, but my career and it is to be hoped my life are so near their close that it is to be hoped they will concern neither of us much longer'.[79] Not a single poem by Housman, in fact, was published in the fourteen years between *Last Poems* and his death; but the event to which Housman had looked forward at least since 1925 and the writing of 'For My Funeral' (*More Poems*, No. XLVII) did not bring about a cessation of concern in others with Housman's career. 'Death of a Great Poet', announced the *National Review* in June 1936, assigning to Housman 'a place in English literature which neither time nor criticism can ever take from him'.[80] Nor was such a view of Housman confined to England, despite the feeling of Amabel Williams-Ellis in 1922 that Housman's poetry might have some difficulty crossing the Channel. Between June 1936 and September 1937 no fewer than four highly appreciative pieces on Housman, the man and his poetry, appeared in important French literary magazines, that by René Elvin in *Le Mois*[81] describing him as 'un grand poète pessimiste', comparable in England to Byron and in France to Alfred de Vigny, who had been a professor of Latin at the Sorbonne. For Elvin, Housman had a wider readership than any contemporary poet in England, 'not excepting W.B. Yeats, Rudyard Kipling, or twenty others who spring to mind', and the reason was this: 'his public consists not only of the cultured, who admire in him the artist combining supreme verbal felicity with a power of emotion unsurpassed by any English lyric poet, but also of all those who discover or recover in his poems the simple and musical expression of their true youthful emotions, of those impressions and feelings of childhood which are as profound as they are difficult to reveal'.

Richard Rees (No. 65) differed from Elvin, and from the *National Review*, in finding Housman neither 'a great [nor] a very original poet'; nevertheless he was, 'after the deaths of Hardy and Lawrence, the best and most original poet in England'. Whether – since Hardy and Lawrence died, respectively, in 1928 and 1930 – Rees literally meant that Housman had held his pre-eminence for only six years, is unclear; what is clear is Rees's conviction that Housman was no tired survivor of a superannuated poetic age, but a live presence, a very definite 'modern' in cast of mind despite his 'resolute conservatism of style'. This view of Housman, the more weighty in coming from someone born at the start of the century, is expressed by John Erskine (No. 66) with a rather different emphasis appropriate to a critic twenty years older than Rees, and thus twenty years nearer Housman's generation. For Erskine, Housman's value lay in his reinterpretation of old themes, 'the themes which occupy our common fears and hopes', in the language 'of our own day': thus his work had remained, through the four decades since the publication of *A Shropshire Lad*, 'as true to the time as a mirror', and its acceptance 'by the readers of our time' served to highlight the dangers risked by more obviously experimental poets, who in seeking both new themes and a new language might well 'throw away all chance of securing an audience'.

Admiring and regretful as were the obituary responses of London, Manchester, Paris and New York, they lacked the note of personal threnody to be found in the university magazines of Oxford and Cambridge where Housman had begun and ended his career as a classical scholar. F.L. Lucas (No. 63), who had been acquainted with Housman and whose article of 1923, 'Few, but Roses' (No. 42), had given him pleasure, rose to the occasion of Housman's death with an essay which blended clear-headed treatment of his poetry's weaknesses and far-outweighing strengths with a plangent feeling of loss, expressed most eloquently in the elaborate yet graceful articulation of its final paragraph. As from Cambridge, so from Oxford, one day earlier, came the sense that with the death of the author of *A Shropshire Lad* and *Last Poems* a whole generation had fallen silent. The point made by the historian E.L. Woodward (No. 62), thirty years younger than Housman yet moved by the disappearance of 'this England of the white main roads, with a dust on the wild roses in early summer', was no mere rhetorical flourish decently indulged at a funeral but a true perception of the relationship between good poets and their readers: 'When a poet dies, an element in his humbler contemporaries dies with him ... they have lost their herald. They are dumb.'

Appearing little more than a week after these two deeply felt tributes – and thus little more than three weeks after Housman's death – Cyril Connolly's debunking essay in the *New Statesman* (No. 64) might perhaps have fulfilled his intention of bringing some 'comfort to those whose ideas about poetry are the opposite of Professor Housman's, and whose success also varies inversely to that of the Shropshire Bard', but it certainly gave great offence to Housman's admirers, four of whom were quick to respond with corrections of Connolly's matter and animadversions on his poor manners in publishing 'his dissent from popular opinion at a time when that display would attract the maximum of attention'.[82] In September 1935, Chauncy Brewster Tinker (No. 60) had asked a question which in its context was intended to be rhetorical: 'What scoffing Mephistopheles has pointed his critical finger to Housman's worthless lines, and caused them to be blotted out forever?' Now, nine months later, Connolly had risen to attempt that role, and not simply as the theoretical 'advocatus diaboli' he claimed to be in his largely unrepentant response published at the end of the controversy, in June 1936.

Spirited Connolly's essay undoubtedly is; one may even, in some moods, feel that it let some necessary fresh air into an unduly holy hush. But the mockery with which Connolly assailed his chosen brief quotations from 'bad poems' (and for Connolly only half a dozen poems by Housman were any good) does not hold up when the lines are returned to their contexts, and his attempt to embarrass Housman's admirers by accusing them of incorrectly (and 'unanimously') labelling Housman a 'classical poet' cut no ice either with John Sparrow, who happily agreed that he was not classical but 'romantic' in spirit, and none the worse for it; or with F.L. Lucas, who had already written, only eight days previously, that Housman's strength as a poet sprang from the blend in his work of both elements – a view which the record of Housman criticism up to 1936 demonstrates that Lucas was far from alone in holding. Behind the semantic wrangling, however, lay an obvious dislike of Housman's poetry on the part of Connolly, whose tactlessly timed attack essentially conveyed a resurgence of the irritation provoked in pro-Eliot quarters by *The Name and Nature of Poetry*. But Connolly was very much in the minority, and the July–August 1936 issue of the *Poetry Review* was largely given over to a two-part 'Tribute to A.E. Housman' consisting of an essay by Daphne Binny (entitled 'The Spirit of Poetry') prompted by Housman's Leslie Stephen Lecture, and a detailed essay by Alicia C. Percival on 'The Art of A.E. Housman', in which his 'simplicity' and 'fastidious correctness' of word-choice came in for particular praise.[83]

'The title of the next volume will be *Posthumous Poems* or *Chansons d'Outretombe*,' Housman drily informed his friend Robert Bridges in the summer of 1923.[84] A decade later he told an enquirer that *Last Poems* was 'not necessarily the last, but the last volume which will appear in my lifetime'.[85] The promise of both comments was borne out, six months after Housman's death, by the appearance of *More Poems*, a volume of forty-nine poems (including one, unnumbered, printed as an epigraph) assembled by Laurence Housman in accordance with the terms of his brother's will, which had specified that, if a posthumous collection were issued, it should include 'any poems which appear to him to be completed and to be not inferior to the average of my published poems'.[86] Thus, though the poems themselves were written by Housman (and a very few published) approximately between 1880 and 1925, and though he had discussed possible inclusions and exclusions with his brother in 1934,[87] the internal ordering of the volume, both as to text and to total shape, was done by Laurence Housman. Though clearly not averse to his own literary resurrection, A.E. Housman himself had nothing to do with the preparation of *More Poems* for the press (Jonathan Cape, this time, not Grant Richards). A result of this was that the American text of the volume, published by Knopf, differed in some of its readings from the British edition; furthermore, when the volume was incorporated into Housman's *Collected Poems* three years later a number of changes were made, notably the elimination from No. II of its last, and perhaps most beautiful, stanza.[88] *More Poems*, therefore, is as a collection not quite 'canonical' in the sense that *A Shropshire Lad* and *Last Poems* are; but this was not a problem for the vast majority of its reviewers, nor was it expected to bother that large audience which, it was clear from his obituarists, still regarded A.E. Housman as a poet of pre-eminent importance: even before the publication of its first British impression, of nearly 9,000 copies, a further 5,000 copies of *More Poems* were in the press,[89] and nearly 10,000 copies were printed in America.[90]

'This book has been eagerly awaited,' wrote the anonymous reviewer of the *Times Literary Supplement*[91] – a claim backed up by the large number of reviews (only a third of them reprinted here), by the extreme promptitude of many of them, and by the favourable response of most. Only the 24-year-old poet John Gawsworth, whose belief in Housman's 'happy spontaneity' was upset by seeing in print what he termed 'workshop material', went so far as to say that 'one cannot but regret the publication of at least half the matter'; nevertheless, even for him, the whole book was worth buying if only to possess Housman's 'superb translation' of Horace's 'Diffugere Nives' (*More Poems*, No. V).[92] John Holmes, writing in the *Boston Evening Transcript*, took a much broader view, acknowledging that it was 'a shock to see that poor poems by [Housman] can be very ordinary', yet in the last analysis feeling only gratitude that Housman 'gave the last reluctant permission for publication', since it had liberated a number of poems which were indeed 'as good as anything we have',[93] despite the fact that everything in the volume – as Holmes thought – had at some point failed to meet Housman's own high standards for publication in his lifetime. (Among the poems which had should be mentioned Nos. XVIII, XXVI, XXXIII and XLVI, which Housman had removed from *Last Poems* at the proof stage.)

Whatever valuation different reviewers placed on the collection as a whole, by comparison with its two predecessors, and however they differed, often extremely, in their assessment of individual poems in it, most of them were able to recognize that *More Poems*, put together by Housman's brother from his literary remains, gave a more revealing picture of Housman the man than he himself had allowed to appear in his lifetime: thus the volume was, as the *Cambridge Review* put it, 'a welcome gift'.[94] John Holmes made this point succinctly and perceptively: 'In this new book we see Housman himself a little more clearly than ever before, and we may believe that it was this very note that he excluded from the first two books'. The other side of the Atlantic, a similar view had already been proposed in the *Times Literary Supplement*: if some of the poems in *More Poems* were 'echoes', excluded by Housman from his earlier collections because they were 'too like', others – as, for instance, 'Easter Hymn' and No. XLIV (Housman's poem of farewell to Venice and his gondolier friend Andrea, last seen in 1926) – had been left unpublished presumably because they were 'too unlike', and revealed 'Housman's undisguised emotions'.

Of all the reviewers of *More Poems*, E.M. Forster (No. 72) was perhaps best placed to understand the nature of those emotions, and to sympathize most with them. A homosexual and agnostic who had first read *A Shropshire Lad* with deep admiration in 1900 and had been quick to recognize the homosexual strain in the author, Forster had approached the task of reviewing *More Poems* hesitantly, having found Housman the man less congenial than his poems.[95] His doubts had to do, perhaps, with the uneasy mixture in him of personal identification, strong critical approval, and injured *amour propre*; but a sense of duty overcame them, aided by a feeling, as he expressed it to Bloomsbury friends later, that he could 'write about Housman ... so much better than anyone else'.[96] That claim was not, I think, pitched too high: Forster's review, welcoming Laurence Housman's inclusiveness of choice as 'the proper way to edit a person who wrote living stuff', combines empathy and detached literary judgment to a rare degree, and is felicitous in finding the metaphor which will suddenly illuminate its object, as in this description of the forceful combination, in *More Poems* and elsewhere, of Housman's 'matter' and 'manner': 'It is as if [the reader] took up a sampler to estimate its period-value and then observed, embroidered in it, some bitter and explosive truth'.

Not all found Housman's truths explosive, or even truths. The Canadian poet Earle Birney (who referred to Housman as 'a Cambridge professor of Greek') felt that if *More Poems* were still read in fifty years' time, it would not be for their ' "criticism of life" ', which he found limited and self-contradictory, but for the charm of 'casual lines', such as the first stanza of No. IX beginning 'When green buds hang in the elm like dust' (No. 77). Guy Boas, headmaster and founder of the magazine *English*, in a 'review' too long and too general to reprint here, gave high praise to Housman's technique and language but had no use for his one-sided pessimistic view of life: 'As a message it will not do'.[97] And if Housman's message could provoke irritation, together with its apparent internal confusions (set forth with fiercely reductive logic by Jacob Bronowski in No. 78, from the *Criterion*), so too could that 'sentimentality' of which Cyril Connolly had accused his work in the *New Statesman* in May (No. 64), and which Raymond Mortimer charged him with in the same paper in October (No. 67), repeating also, with a barbed suavity, Connolly's view that Housman was 'a poet who appeals especially to adolescence'.[98]

'One likes them, or one does not; there is no more to say', said John Sparrow (No. 70) of *More Poems*; though he did not like all of them, and went on to make some more reasoned discriminations. Most British reviewers of the volume liked it, including the highly intellectual poet William Empson, whose review (No. 76) had an invigorating large-mindedness to it. Unlike his former Cambridge contemporary Jacob Bronowski, with whom he had co-edited the avant-garde magazine *Experiment*, he found Housman's new poems both 'haunting' and solidly convincing, despite what he had found to be the earlier ones' 'pernicious effect on the young' in Japan, where he had taught from 1931 to 1934. Also favourably disposed where one might not have expected it was the editor of *New Verse*, Geoffrey Grigson (No. 74), whose revelation that Housman had been a subscriber to that Auden-centred magazine and a buyer of the work of younger poets is a salutary corrective to any simplistic notion of Housman as a poet who, if not forgotten by the modern world, himself preferred to forget it.

It would have been strange, though, in 1936, when the Spanish Civil War had started and a larger war seemed not far off, if Housman's vision of life, essentially formed at the end of the previous century, had seemed to all commentators totally adequate to the present. So much is apparent from a review (No. 75) by the American poet Robert Hillyer: 'This suspiratory mood, so attractive to me "when I was one and twenty" ' (which meant, literally, in 1916, a year before America entered the Great War), 'seems to me now, when actual despair looms on the horizons of the world, as rather a romantic luxury.' But if Conrad Aiken, an old friend of T.S. Eliot, pronounced Housman's poetry 'thin', and inferior to that of Emily Dickinson (a point also made by Robert Fitzgerald in the *Living Age*[99]), he was still able to concede that Housman, though not 'great', was 'a very fine poet' (No. 71). Peter Monro Jack (No. 69) was less grudging: Housman held 'his generally unassailable position' 'narrowly', but he held it, and had produced a poetry of 'relaxed perfection' which (even in 1936) 'speaks for all of us'. And Eugene Davidson, writing in *Yale Review* (No. 79) was in no doubt at all, choosing for the title of his review a phrase which alluded to the epigraph of *More Poems* and turned Housman's self-styled 'narrow measure' into 'The Span of Housman's Poetry'.

That 'span' referred (as René Elvin had done) to the unusual breath of Housman's audience, and that broad audience had been earned at once by Housman's themes, 'important to our common humanity', and by the purity and sharpness of his tone and technique. Though for Davidson, as for so many other reviewers, *More Poems* was not so good a volume as its predecessors, it was 'a worthy addition' to them; and Davidson's final verdict, making nothing of the 'limited range' adversely recorded by Aiken, simply pronounced Housman 'a great poet', 'very nearly perfect' within that range, whose importance had 'little to do with anyone's world view and still less with how one [felt] about social forces'. Such posthumous praise was not Housman's concern; had it been, he might have been amused, and pleased, to find a critic in 1937 sending out an echo, amplified, of what Hubert Bland, in 'the best review of my poems',[100] had said over forty years before.

IX *COLLECTED POEMS* (1939) AND AFTER

Housman was strongly opposed to the printing of *A Shropshire Lad* and *Last Poems* together in one volume. When, in 1925, he formed the impression (incorrect, as it turned out) that the American publishers of *Last Poems*, Henry Holt & Co., had done this, he sought advice as to whether he could both suppress the joint volume and transfer the American rights for *Last Poems* to another publisher.[101] That feeling had not changed a decade later: in September 1934 he informed his young American admirer, Houston Martin, that the two volumes 'will never be joined together while I am here to prevent it'. It was, he said, 'a silly notion'.[102]

It seems, therefore, hardly likely that Housman would have approved of the publication of his *Collected Poems*. But such a tribute, prevented in Housman's lifetime, became inevitable after his death, if only because the publication by Laurence Housman, in his memoir *A.E.H.* (1937), of eighteen poems additional to *More Poems* must have made a comprehensive single presentation seem the final logical step in establishing the *corpus* of Housman's poetry. The work for this was carried out with Laurence Housman's consent and the editorial co-operation of John Carter – though not, unfortunately, to the approbation of all Housman scholars[103] – and *Collected Poems* appeared in England late in 1939, and in the United States early in 1940. The volume brought together the two volumes, intended to stay separate, published in

Housman's lifetime, the contents of *More Poems*, and the eighteen poems in Laurence Housman's memoir (which appear as 'Additional Poems' I–XVIII). To this already available material were added three translations from Greek tragedy first published in 1890, and five further original poems ('Additional Poems' XIX–XXIII), of which Nos. XIX and XX were published for the first time (though the former, entitled 'The Defeated', also appeared in 1939 in the *Listener*), and the last three were reprinted from magazines in which they had appeared, respectively, in 1881, 1894 and 1902. Though there have been disagreements, not always amiable, about the textual correctness of various poems in the collected volume, their number has not altered: what readers have accepted as the canon of Housman's poetry for the last five decades was what the reviewers confronted in 1939 – a total (excluding the translations) of 177 poems.

Housman's reviewers were not interested in textual matters; nor, in the main, were they concerned with the additional poems published in 1939 or reprinted from 1937. Of the few who commented on the latter, E. Curt Peters felt that, with the exception of 'Additional Poems' I ('Atys'), XII and XXII ('R.L.S'.) they were 'pale echoes of other and better poems in the book';[104] Lawrence Lee, who seemed under the impression that the additional poems were also late poems, found them a non-significant appendix which only proved how little Housman's work had developed: 'It is a satisfying experience to hear a young man sing in clear tones the small tragedy of becoming two-and-twenty. It is not so satisfying to hear a note not much greater, a note hardly varied, from a man at the end of a sheltered, full, informed career which had its opportunities for spiritual growth.'[105]

For the large majority of critics, the publication of *Collected Poems* was, as Cleanth Brooks put it, 'an occasion for making some tentative generalizations on the total value of Housman and his work' (No. 91). Some generalized assessments, already commented on, had been made when *More Poems* appeared, and others (Nos. 80–3) filled the interval between 1936 and the end of 1939. What is noticeable in this latter group is an almost even balance between deprecation and dismissal (on the grounds of *fin de siècle* datedness) on the one hand, and continued sturdy admiration on the other. If Lawrence Leighton, writing for the essentially highbrow audience of *Poetry* (No. 82), could describe

Housman's poetry as a clutch of adolescent 'banalities' dependent 'for its popularity on mere fashion', the poet-brothers Carl and Mark Van Doren, in a textbook 'intended for the use of schools' but also aimed at 'those general readers who are neither proficient in the subject [literary history] nor unconcerned with it',[106] could happily present Housman as a 'classic', whose work combined to a degree unique among 'modern' poets a high average of accomplishment in terms of style with spontaneity of utterance (No. 83). That the response of readers to its spontaneity should be 'immediate' was a reproach neither to Housman nor to them.

The reception of *Collected Poems* was more uniformly favourable, though not completely so. The word 'great' no longer figured among the epithets used to describe Housman, unless one counts its occurrence in a review by Alfred Kreymborg published in the *Living Age*. Like Lawrence Lee, Kreymborg was also reviewing *Last Poems* by Yeats, and for neither critic was Housman his equal. For Lee, Yeats's last poems were a final 'amazing upward turn', a last gathering together of all the phases of Yeats's constantly developing genius into 'the firmest of farewells'; whereas Housman had too often repeated himself in a career that was 'but one small unrising circle perfectly turned'. Kreymborg, too, preferred 'the richer concerns and deeper vitality of Yeats'; nevertheless, though Housman had sung 'pretty much the same song through half a century', he was pronounced to be 'a great little man, a great minor poet'.[107] From the generosity, albeit a touch patronizing, of this American critic one descends by way of Morton Dauwen Zabel (No. 89), who felt that Housman possessed a 'true, if minor, genius' quite incomparable with the 'protest, intensity and courage' of Baudelaire, Hopkins, Yeats and Rilke, to the dry reductions of Cleanth Brooks, who admitted Housman's 'real poetic power' — a power flawed, in his view, by Housman's distrust of wit, irony and metaphor — but could not, finally, feel him to be 'the perfect minor poet' (No. 91).

Not all the American reviewers were so grudging. As if to redress the negative attitudes expressed by Lawrence Leighton in 1938, *Poetry* published in 1940 a notably perceptive and sympathetic article by the poet John Peale Bishop (No. 88), who found in Housman's posthumously published poems the necessary key to the lifelong indirection through which he had expressed himself. If Housman's range was resultantly small, the cause lay not only in his own nature but in that of his age; but the poignancy and value of what he had produced was for Bishop undeniable. Looking at Housman's poetry in terms not of any personal secret but of its public statement, Peter Monro Jack found it totally persuasive, perfect not only in its art but as a description of a recognizably real world, not a 'fancy' one. That it was a traditional poetry, and a musical poetry, was true; but for younger poets, and critics, to dismiss it because it took no account of 'the economic causes and cures of the moment' would be for them to throw away, wilfully and pathetically, 'this living and shining heritage and earnest of their art' (No. 85). Clearly, even in 1940, with America on the verge of war and a sense of Housman's outmodedness in the air, the shock of admiring recognition first registered by Louise Imogen Guiney was still being felt.

Confident in its opening ('No literary reputation of our time is more certain than Housman's'), Jack's review sounds a little, towards its end, like a rearguard action. That note of indignant defence had already been sounded, in an England already at war, by the anonymous reviewer of the *Times Literary Supplement*, who felt that if Housman was 'a minor poet', his minority was of the order of Thomas Gray and Edward Fitzgerald, names which were still assumed to carry some considerable weight even in 1939. For this reviewer, the clarity and melodiousness of Housman's poetry set a standard not easy for later poets to reach; but for them (and for publishers and literary editors) to neglect what was 'still the public requisite' was to risk 'bringing poetry as a whole into contempt'. The battle provoked by *The Name and Nature of Poetry* was still being fought, and it was obvious from this reviewer's reference to 'metre and memorability' on the one hand, and 'exercises in the hispid and raucous' on the other, that he/she was on the side of the traditionalists. Without naming names (except Housman's), the review concluded with an oblique yet magisterial dismissal of more recent poetic styles: 'There may be "art-forms" which wear out, or wear thin after genius has perfected them; but for Housman established metres and a familiar vocabulary were sufficient. The moral seems to be that if these are not serviceable and cannot be made the ground work for further advance and experiment, it is not they which are to blame but those to whom they are useless'.[108] H.W. Garrod, in a long, characteristically feline, yet appreciative retrospective piece published in *Essays and Studies*, wound up in somewhat similar vein. He had not been convinced by Housman's assertion, made in *The Name and Nature of Poetry*, that Collins, Cowper, Smart and Blake were 'the only poets of the eighteenth century': they were simply Housman's favourites. But he had 'the fancy to play Housman at his own game' with respect to the period from 1850 to 1939, and his own choices, asserted first as 'our four best poets', were Arnold, R.L. Stevenson, Rupert Brooke and Housman. This assertion is weakened (as Garrod had weakened Housman's) at the end; yet it is not, quite, given up, and Garrod emerges from his devious style of argument to suggest, clearly enough, the superiority of Housman's poetry to anything currently on offer: 'Matthew Arnold, Stevenson, Brooke, Housman – I do not say that these are, since Wordsworth died, our four best poets; and if I did, nobody would believe me, unless it were Housman. But there would be something in it, beyond the expression of favouritism. With Matthew Arnold died the grand manner in poetry. Stevenson – though to remember him as a poet at all makes a man sixty, or over – Stevenson leads in the modern manner. With this Lost Leader are Brooke and Housman. The march of the modern manner becomes, thereafter, confused; till it is a question whether it would not be better, instead of going on, to go back'.[109]

It was not, however, Housman's fate in 1939 to be valued only by English critics possibly open to the charge of being 'old buffers'. Just as young poets like Sorley and Brooke had spoken up for Housman before and during World War I, so too did proponents of 'the modern manner' at the end of the 1930s, though their approval was less wholehearted: they had, after all, T.S. Eliot to admire, and each other. W.H. Auden's famous poem 'A.E. Housman', first published in 1939 in *New Writing*, was not just a clinical analysis but conveyed some sympathy for Housman's repressed and divided nature as scholar and poet, and we know from Stephen Spender's autobiography that Auden, at Oxford in the late 1920s, thought Housman one of the older generation whom it was worthwhile for a young poet to read.[110] Spender himself, writing in *Horizon* in 1940 (No. 86), wished that

Housman had found the courage to express more of his personality publicly during his lifetime, and reduced the 'essential Housman' to 'perhaps less than fifty poems, in which Housman really says all he has to say'. But since, in Spender's view, Housman at his best had 'great force and passion', and had written 'great poetry if not great poems', fifty poems was hardly an insignificant number for him to be remembered by. And Louis MacNeice, though his review in the *New Republic* (No. 87) tailed off without giving a verdict, did not find Housman's poetry dismissable, however ill it accorded with the renunciation of 'meaning' promulgated in *The Name and Nature of Poetry*. Nor did MacNeice find Housman's poetry repetitious; or if so, not disablingly so. Rather, the *Collected Poems* displayed an 'extraordinary identity of mood' whose 'cumulative effect' was 'exciting'. Even George Orwell, subjecting Housman's poetry to a characteristic exercise in 'plain man' deconstruction (No. 92), not only admitted how strongly *A Shropshire Lad* had struck him in 1920 – for reasons similar to some of those advanced by Benjamin Gilbert Brooks (No. 90) – but ended by expressing his faith in the survival of at least some of them. Fair-minded as he nearly always was, Orwell saw no reason 'to under-rate [Housman] now because he was over-rated a few years ago'.

Whether Housman was, as Orwell seemed to feel, overrated during his lifetime and underrated in the years after his death is not so much for the editor of this volume, as for its readers, to conclude; and their conclusions are likely to be based as much on their own diverse opinions of Housman's poetry as on the critical record assembled here – a record whose individual items are variously ranged on a spectrum stretching from delighted gratitude to a sceptical refusal to be impressed. 'One likes them, or one does not', said John Sparrow of *More Poems* in 1936; ten years later, considering the Jubilee Edition of *A Shropshire Lad*, the anonymous reviewer in the *Times Literary Supplement* (No. 93) may be felt to have been saying much the same thing of Housman's poetry as a whole: 'Many of the arguments about Housman's claim to the title of a poet, and about the merits of his work, when they are not quarrels about the definition of terms, are really but statements of the predilections of the participants, cast in disputatious form'.

It seems to me that, by and large, the articles, reviews and comments collected here bear out this view. Housman's 'philosophy of life' has been varyingly seen as profound and as superficial, as a poignantly true and brave record of human experience and as a cowardly, or curmudgeonly, refusal to face up to all of life's possibilities; Housman's language has been pronounced spontaneous, or stilted, his metrical technique the product of a superb and masterly ear or a mere mechanical jogtrot. Housman's popularity over many decades with the general reader has for some critics provided the final proof of his importance; for others it has proved the opposite. To different critics, and for different reasons (or with no reasons stated), the same individual poems have seemed good or bad. For Orwell in 1940, 'With rue my heart is laden' (*A Shropshire Lad*, No. LIV) 'just tinkled' – though 'it did not seem to tinkle in 1920'. For an American critic of Orwell's generation, Stuart Gerry Brown, the very same poem, in the same year, was evidence that Housman could, on occasion, move out of the place inhabited by 'the minor poets of the world', among whom his place was high, and 'rise up into another realm'.[111]

It would be untrue, however, to suggest that the record of Housman criticism, between 1896 and 1951, inspires nothing more than a despairing 'Quot homines, tot sententiae'. There is much variation of opinion during that period – as indeed there has been in the last four decades, since Housman has continued to remain unignorable and his poetry has continued to be reprinted – but the greater part of that variation is a matter of nuances clustered towards the positive end of the spectrum. The case for Housman can be truthfully described by amending a line from 'Terence, this is stupid stuff' (*A Shropshire Lad*, No. LXII): the 'critical heritage' recorded, and unrecorded, in this collection contains 'much good, and much more good than ill'. On what precise rung of a hierarchical ladder this consensus sets Housman, or where some future consensus may set him, it is hard to be sure; nor may it greatly matter. Housman was a poet valued highly throughout his lifetime, who continued to be valued after it; the prognosis for his survival, and as far more than a period piece, seems healthy. What he would have thought of the company in which John Crowe Ransom placed him in 1951 (No. 94) is impossible to tell, especially as one member of it was only getting started in the year that Housman died; but for anyone of a later generation, to see Housman listed alongside Wallace Stevens, Dylan Thomas and W.H. Auden is not to absorb insult, and it seems probable that Housman himself would have been satisfied enough to be placed somewhere between the 'minor' poets likely to last 'for a few half-centuries' and the 'major' poets who 'need no recommendation' by critics.

NOTES

1 Virginia Woolf, letter to Julian Bell, 2 May 1936; printed in *Leave the Letters Till We're Dead: The Letters of Virginia Woolf*, Vol. VI: 1936–1941, ed. Nigel Nicolson (London: Hogarth Press, 1980), 32–33.
2 See A.E. Housman, letter to Laurence Housman, 20 May 1933; printed in *The Letters of A.E. Housman*, ed. Henry Maas (London: Rupert Hart-Davis, 1971), 335. (Hereafter cited as *Letters*.) Housman says twelve years; estimates from various sources vary from one year upwards.
3 'The Waste Land' had, of course, already been printed by Eliot himself, in the first issue of the *Criterion*, in the autumn of 1922.
4 *The Diary of Virginia Woolf*, ed. Anne Olivier Bell, i (New York: Harcourt Brace Jovanovich, 1977), 34. (Entry for Saturday 13 February 1915).
5 See John Carter and John Sparrow, 'A.E. Housman: An Annotated Check-List', *The Library: A Quarterly Review of Bibliography*, Fourth Series, xxi, no. 2 (September 1940), 172.
6 A.E. Housman, letter to Grant Richards, 5 December 1916; printed in *Letters*, ed. Maas, 149.
7 A.E. Housman, letter to Grant Richards, 12 September 1915; printed in ibid., 140.
8 Grant Richards, *Housman 1897–1936* (Oxford University Press, 1941), 200.
9 See *Letters*, ed. Maas, 295, n. 5. Housman had already, in 1929, declined the offer of the Order of Merit.
10 A.E. Housman, letter to Grant Richards, 9 October 1928; printed in ibid., 271.
11 R.K.R. Thornton (ed.), *Poetry of the 'Nineties* (Harmondsworth: Penguin Books, 1970), 15.
12 W.B. Yeats (ed.), *The Oxford Book of Modern Verse 1892–1935* (1936), xiii.
13 Richard Le Gallienne, 'Wanderings in Bookland', *Idler*, ix (June 1896), 727.

14 A.E. Housman gave this information to his French admirer, Maurice Pollet, in 1933 (*Letters*, ed. Maas, 328). He himself had been told of Morley's involvement by Charles Whibley (see Grant Richards, *Housman 1897–1936*, 13).
15 A.E. Housman, letter to Maurice Pollet, 5 February 1933; printed in *Letters*, ed. Maas, 328.
16 The cartoon, by Bert Thomas, is reproduced in Richards, *Housman 1897–1936*, 203. Two weeks before the cartoon appeared Housman had refused, through Grant Richards, to send Thomas a photograph of himself (see *Letters*, ed. Maas, 203).
17 Hardy had by this time published his last novel, *Jude the Obscure* (1895), and his first volume of poems, *Wessex Poems*, did not appear until 1898.
18 A.E. Housman, letter to Maurice Pollet, 5 February 1933; printed in *Letters*, ed. Maas, 328.
19 Richard Le Gallienne, 'Wanderings in Bookland', *Idler*, ix (June 1896), 727.
20 Richard Le Gallienne, 'A Ballad of London', from *Robert Louis Stevenson: An Elegy, and Other Poems* (1895). Quoted from R.K.R. Thornton (ed.), *Poetry of the 'Nineties*, 60.
21 See *Letters*, ed. Maas, 37 and 390.
22 Kate Freiligrath Kroeker, *Poems Selected from Heinrich Heine* (London: Walter Scott, undated). A number of reviewers spoke of Heine as an influence on Housman's poetry, and he spoke of this himself in 1928 and 1933 (see *Letters*, ed. Maas, 265 and 329). I have not been able to establish the extent of Housman's knowledge of German; but throughout his life he retained a strong affection for Sophie Becker, a German governess in the household of his family friends the Wises of Woodchester in Gloucestershire, and in 1890 he sent her, via the Wises, 'a poem which I have written in her own beautiful language: please tell her this, because otherwise perhaps she may not know it' (*Letters*, ed. Maas, 27). Another letter, p. 260, stated: 'French is the only tongue of which I know enough to keep my translators in order'. Heine's temperament, though not his life-style, bears some resemblance to Housman's, but what may have influenced Housman was not so much Heine's poems in German as some of the turns of phrase found in various English translations printed in Kate Kroeker's book, which have, in advance, a distinctly 'Housmanian' ring. (See especially pp. 15, 57, 59, 80, 100, 152, 193.) For an extended comparison of Housman and Heine, see Tom Burns Haber, *A.E. Housman* (New York: Twayne, 1967), 146–55.
23 A.E. Housman, letter to Laurence Housman, probably April 1896 (printed in *Letters*, ed. Maas, 36).

24 William Morton Payne, *Dial,* xxiii (1 October 1897), 188–9 ('Recent Poetry' section).
25 *Review of Reviews,* xiv (August 1886), 187. The review is anonymous, but is attributed to Richards by Theodore G. Ehrsam in his *A Bibliography of Alfred Edward Housman* (Boston: F.W. Faxon Company, 1941), 17.
26 These figures are given by John Carter and John Sparrow in 'A.E. Housman: An Annotated Check-List' (1940), 173.
27 'New Writers: Mr. A.E. Housman', *Bookman* (London), x (August 1896), 134.
28 A.E. Housman, letter to Grant Richards, 22 July 1898; printed in *Letters,* ed. Maas, 48. Housman's letter preceded Archer's review by ten days.
29 William Archer, *Poets of the Younger Generation* (London: John Lane, The Bodley Head, 1902), 193.
30 *Academy Supplement,* liv (20 August 1898), 170.
31 A.E. Housman, letter to Seymour Adelman, 21 June 1928; printed in *Letters,* ed. Maas, 267.
32 Housman's poem 'Oh who is that young sinner' ('Additional Poems' xviii, first published, after Housman's death, in *John O'London's Weekly,* 23 October 1936) is usually taken as relating to Wilde's imprisonment.
33 Quoted by Laurence Housman in a letter to Allan Wade, 12 November 1954. (See *The Letters of Oscar Wilde,* ed. Rupert Hart-Davis (London: Rupert Hart-Davis, 1962), 713 n. 1).
34 Laurence Housman, *A.E.H.* (London: Jonathan Cape, 1937), 84.
35 See Richard Perceval Graves, *A.E. Housman: The Scholar Poet* (Routledge & Kegan Paul, 1979). Reprinted by Oxford University Press (1981), 135.
36 See *The Letters of George Meredith,* ed. C.L. Cline, iii (Oxford: Clarendon Press, 1970), 1481.
37 Letters from A.E. Housman to Houston Martin, 27 September 1935 and 28 March 1933; printed in *Letters,* ed. Maas, 377 and 331.
38 Letter from Thomas Hardy to Sydney Cockerell, 30 May 1913; printed in *The Collected Letters of Thomas Hardy,* ed. Richard Little Purdy and Michael Millgate, iv (Oxford: Clarendon Press, 1984), 275.
39 Wilfrid Scawen Blunt, *My Diaries,* Part Two (London: Martin Secker, 1920), 372.
40 See Christopher Hassall, *Rupert Brooke* (London: Faber, 1964), 94–5.
41 Rupert Brooke, postcard to Geoffrey Fry, July 1907; printed in *The Letters of Rupert Brooke,* ed. Geoffrey Keynes (London: Faber, 1968), 90.

42 Quoted in Hassall, *Rupert Brooke*, 250-1. The poem was published in the *Saturday Westminster*, 13 May 1911.
43 I am indebted to Christopher Morris, Fellow of King's College, Cambridge, for passing on this remark, which was made in company after Housman's 1933 lecture on 'The Name and Nature of Poetry'.
44 Jon Stallworthy, *Wilfred Owen* (Oxford University Press, 1974), 38.
45 Ivor Gurney, *War Letters*, ed. R.K.R. Thornton (London: Hogarth Press, 1984), 234. 'Harvey' was F.W. Harvey (1888–1957), author of *A Gloucestershire Lad at Home and Abroad* (1916).
46 St John Adcock, *The Glory that was Grub Street: Impressions of Contemporary Authors* (London: Sampson Low, 1928), 120.
47 Ernest Newman, 'Concerning "A Shropshire Lad" and Other Matters', *Musical Times*, 1 September 1918, 393–8.
48 A.E. Housman, letter to Messrs Alexander Moring, 17 August 1906; printed in *Letters*, ed. Maas, 87.
49 John Freeman, 'A.E. Housman', *Bookman* (London), lix (November 1920), 72.
50 Howard Mumford Jones, 'A.E. Housman, Last of the Romans', *Double Dealer* (New Orleans), iii, no. 15 (March 1922), 136–41.
51 See *Letters*, ed. Maas, 189.
52 A.E. Housman, letter to Grant Richards, 9 April 1922; printed in *Letters*, ed. Maas, 192. A letter of Housman's to Sydney Cockerell (3 April 1922) ends with an understated sentence whose terseness is surely expressive of Housman's poetic excitement: 'At this time I am rather full of my own affairs'. On 28 October 1922 Housman supplied Cockerell with the dates of most of the poems in *Last Poems*; these were published by Cockerell in a letter to the *Times Literary Supplement*, 9 November 1936, 908. Norman Page (*A.E. Housman: A Critical Biography* (London: Macmillan, 1983), 129–31) has very plausibly linked the timing of the publication of *Last Poems* with Housman's awareness that his greatest friend, Moses Jackson, was ill with stomach cancer in Vancouver. Jackson died on 14 January 1923, and many of the poems written or finished by Housman in 1922 are appropriately valedictory.
53 See note 16 above.
54 Richard Le Gallienne, 'A.E. Housman's Valedictory', *New York Times Book Review*, 3 December 1922, 2.
55 'Recorder', notice in *Chapbook*, no. 33 (January 1923), 14–15. These comments on Housman were part of a survey entitled 'Literature in 1922', which was almost uniformly caustic and *de haut en bas* in tone towards the various books considered.

56 A.E. Housman, letter to Houston Martin, 26 September 1934, printed in *Letters*, ed. Maas, 361. See also ibid., 223, 225, 227.
57 A.E. Housman, letter to J.B. Priestley, 18 September 1924; printed in ibid., 222. I infer from Housman's letter that he had also read Priestley's piece when it appeared in the *London Mercury*.
58 *Nation and Athenaeum*, xxxii (28 October 1922), 151–3.
59 R.W. Postgate, 'A Defeated Poet', *Freeman*, vi (13 December 1922), 331–3.
60 T.S. Eliot, 'The Metaphysical Poets' (1921), first published in T.S. Eliot, *Homage to John Dryden* (London: The Hogarth Press, 1924).
61 Stephen Gwynn, 'The Poetry of A.E. Housman', *Dalhousie Review*, iii, no. 4 (January 1924), 437.
62 T.S. Eliot, letter to Henry Eliot, 31 December 1922; printed in Valerie Eliot (ed.), *The Letters of T.S. Eliot*, i (1898–1922), (London: Faber & Faber, 1988), 617. It should be said, however, that the publication of *Last Poems* coincided with that of the first issue of the *Criterion*, with which Eliot was preoccupied.
63 H.E.G. Rope, 'On the Poetry of A.E. Housman', *Blackfriars*, xii (November 1931), 674–8. (*Blackfriars* was incorporated with the *Catholic Review*, and published in Oxford by Basil Blackwell.)
64 A.E. Housman, letter to Maurice Pollet, 5 February 1933; printed in *Letters*, ed. Maas, 329.
65 George McLean Harper, 'Hardy, Hudson, Housman', *Scribner's Magazine*, lxxviii (August 1925), 151–7; reprinted in Harper, *Spirit of Delight* (London: Ernest Benn, 1928), 89–99.
66 A.E. Housman, letter to Houston Martin, 22 March 1936; printed in *Letters*, ed. Maas, 390.
67 Reprinted in A.E. Housman, *Selected Prose*, ed. John Carter (Cambridge University Press, 1961), 47.
68 A.E. Housman, letter to J.J. Thomson, 22 February 1925; printed in *Letters*, ed. Maas, 227.
69 See A.E. Housman, letter to Grant Richards, 28 March 1933; letter to H.E. Butler, 15 May 1933; letter to Laurence Housman, 20 May 1933; all printed in ibid., 331–3.
70 I owe this information to Christopher Morris, Fellow of King's College, Cambridge. The other 'impressive lecture' was given at Bletchley Park during World War II by an admiral, on the topic 'How I sank the *Scharnhorst*'.
71 Gerald Bullett, *Week-end Review*, vii, no. 169 (3 June 1933), 637.
72 James Southall Wilson, *Virginia Quarterly Review* (July 1934), 476.
73 Chauncy Brewster Tinker, 'Mr. Housman on Poetry', *Yale Review*, xxiii (Autumn 1933), 167–9.

74 This remark was overheard by Christopher Morris, who kindly passed it on to me.
75 F.R. Leavis, *New Bearings in English Poetry* (London: Chatto & Windus, 1932), 21.
76 T.S. Eliot, letter to Ezra Pound, 30 May 1920; printed in *The Letters of T.S. Eliot*, 384.
77 T.S. Eliot, 'The Boston Evening Transcript', ll. 3–5.
78 It is worth noting that, early in 1926, Eliot appears to have asked Housman to write a piece on Wilkie Collins. Housman politely declined, but wrote that he had been 'much flattered' by the request. (See A.E. Housman, letter to T.S. Eliot, 2 April 1926; printed in *Letters*, ed. Maas, 235). The relation between Housman's lecture and Eliot's views on poetry is explored in persuasive detail in ch. 6 ('Housman and Eliot: A Note on Critical Fashion in the Thirties') of B.J. Leggett, *The Poetic Art of A.E. Housman: Theory and Practice* (Lincoln: University of Nebraska Press, 1978).
79 A.E. Housman, letter to R.A. Scott-James, 21 April 1936; printed in *Letters*, ed. Maas, 392.
80 'Episode of the Month', *National Review*, cvi (June 1936), 712–14.
81 René Elvin, 'Un Grand Poète Pessimiste: A.E. Housman', *Le Mois*, no. 79 (10 August 1937), 155–66. The other French responses were: Louis Bonnerot, *Revue Anglo-Américaine*, xiii (June 1936), 477; Louis Gillet, 'A.E. Housman', *Revue des Deux Mondes*, xxxix (1 May 1937), 208–21; Maurice Pollet, 'A.E. Housman', *Etudes Anglaises*, i (September 1937), 385–401.
82 John Sparrow, letter to the *New Statesman*, May/June 1936; reprinted in Cyril Connolly, *The Condemned Playground* (1945; Hogarth Press reprint, 1985, 57).
83 See *Poetry Review*, xxvii (July–August 1936), 277–83.
84 A.E. Housman, letter to Robert Bridges, 2 July 1923; printed in *Letters*, ed. Maas, 213.
85 A.E. Housman, postcard to Virginia Rice, 15 October 1932; printed in ibid., 324.
86 Laurence Housman, preface to *More Poems* (London: Jonathan Cape, 1936), 7.
87 See Laurence Housman, quoted in A.E. Housman, *Collected Poems and Selected Prose*, ed. Christopher Ricks (London: Allen Lane, 1988), 498.
88 It was discovered, by John Carter, that the final stanza printed in *More Poems* did not belong to this poem. (See *Collected Poems and Selected Prose*, ed. Ricks, 494.) The result, since printed, has been a poem which, to my mind, ends abruptly where it once ended perfectly.

89 Figures from Carter and Sparrow, 'A.E. Housman: An Annotated Check-List', 186.
90 Figures from Ehrsam, *A Bibliography of Alfred Edward Housman*, 14.
91 *Times Literary Supplement*, 24 October 1936, 845–6. Carter and Sparrow give the publication date of *More Poems* as 26 October 1936; thus this review, and a number of others, including one in America, preceded the volume's official appearance.
92 John Gawsworth (1912–1970), 'Housman Posthumous', *New English Weekly*, x, no. 1 (19 November 1936), 117.
93 John Holmes, 'Another Message from the Elder Housman', *Boston Evening Transcript* (Book Section), 7 November 1936, 4.
94 H.F.S., *Cambridge Review*, lviii, no. 1416 (13 November 1936), 104.
95 The relationship between Forster and Housman is described in Philip Gardner, 'One Fraction of a Summer Field: Forster and A.E. Housman', *Twentieth Century Literature*, xxxi nos. 2–(Summer–Fall 1985), 161–9.
96 This statement occurs in a long piece on himself and Housman read by Forster probably to the Bloomsbury 'Memoir Club' in 1937. Its text is in the collection of Forster MSS at King's College, Cambridge.
97 Guy Boas (1896–1966), 'The Poetry of A.E. Housman', *English*, i (1936), 210–22.
98 This view was expressed by Connolly in a letter to the *New Statesman* (6 June 1936) in which he replied to the hostility he had drawn on himself by his original article there. He reprinted it in *The Condemned Playground*, p. 62.
99 Robert Fitzgerald, review of *More Poems*, *Living Age*, February 1937, 550–1.
100 A.E Housman, letter to Houston Martin, 22 March 1936; printed in *Letters*, ed. Maas, 390.
101 A.E. Housman, letters to Grant Richards (4 January 1925) and Herbert Thring, Secretary to the Society of Authors (12 January 1925); printed in *Letters*, ed. Maas, 225.
102 A.E. Housman, letter to Houston Martin, 26 September 1934; printed in ibid., 361.
103 See Haber, *A.E. Housman*, 104–6. Haber's own Centennial Edition of Housman's collected poetry was published in 1959. There has, to say the least of it, been much cross-Atlantic disagreement as to a correct and final version of Housman's text.
104 E. Curt Peters, *Poetry Review*, xxxi, no. 2 (March–April 1940), 155–6.
105 Lawrence Lee, 'The Extension of Poetry in Time', *Virginia Quarterly Review*, xvi (Summer 1940), 481–4.

106 Carl and Mark Van Doren, introduction to *American and British Literature since 1890* (1925; revised and enlarged, 1939).
107 Alfred Kreymborg, 'Poets and Poetry: Hands Across the Sea', *Living Age* (June 1940), 394–6.
108 Review of *Collected Poems*, *Times Literary Supplement*, 9 December 1939, 717.
109 H.W. Garrod, 'Housman: 1939', *Essays and Studies*, xxv (1939), 7–21.
110 Stephen Spender, *World Within World* (London: Hamish Hamilton, 1951), pp 50-1.
111 Stuart Gerry Brown, 'The Poetry of A.E. Housman', *Sewanee Review*, xlviii (July–September 1940), 408.

Note on the Text

I have tried to interfere as little as possible with the text of the material that follows. Where I have felt sure that some oddity of spelling or style was caused by a printer's error, I have made a silent correction. Where, however, it could have resulted from authorial choice, I have made no change, but have added a [sic] to indicate that the word or phrase occurs in the original, and is not a mis-transcription. Earlier commentators on Housman frequently referred to his first volume of verse as *The Shropshire Lad*; I have indicated this and similar inaccuracies of reference by [sic] also.

Any titles attached to the items printed here are those used by their authors, or by the periodicals in which they first appeared.

I have been unable, for reasons of space, to reprint with every item the full range of quotation from Housman's poems which illustrated or amplified it. Many items I have printed with their quotations unabridged; with others I have retained short quotations, especially those bearing on the detail of a writer's argument, while replacing longer quotations by a bracketed reference to the passage and poem quoted. Since the corpus of Housman's poems is not large, I have felt it reasonable to assume that a reader of this book will wish to have close at hand a copy of the creative work on which its material comments.

Original notes are indicated with asterisks; editorial notes are numbered 1, 2, etc.

A SHROPSHIRE LAD
1896

1. Unsigned notice, *The Times*

'Books of the Week', 27 March 1896, 13

The author was Thomas Humphry Ward (1845–1926), Fellow and Tutor of Brasenose College, Oxford, from 1869. In 1872 he married Matthew Arnold's niece, Mary Augusta Arnold (1851–1920), who wrote many widely read novels under the name Mrs Humphry Ward. Ward himself wrote for *The Times*; in 1888 he published *English Art in the Public Galleries of London*, and later edited *The English Poets* 1881–1918.

A newer writer of verse, Mr. A.E. Housman, strikes a decidedly original note in *A Shropshire Lad* (Kegan Paul). The mere mention, here and there, of Ludlow, Wenlock, and Shrewsbury, of Wrekin and Severn, gives a pleasant element of local colour; but this would be nothing if the essentials of thought and music were absent. Happily they are there in no niggardly measure. Mr. Housman has a true sense of the sweetness of country life and of its tragedies too, and his gift of melodious expression is genuine.

2. 'A New Poet', unsigned review, *New Age*

iv, No. 81, 16 April 1896, 37 ('Looks into Books' section)

The author was Hubert Bland (1855–1914), journalist, co-founder and first treasurer of the Fabian Society, friend of

George Bernard Shaw and many other leading figures of the day. He was described by the *Dictionary of National Biography*, in its entry on his wife, the writer Edith Nesbit, as 'a poseur by nature' and 'something more than a philanderer by habit'.

On 27 April 1896 Housman wrote to his brother Laurence: 'I thought the *New Age* review very nice, except the first paragraph disparaging the other chaps.' On 22 March 1936 he wrote to his American admirer Houston Martin: 'The best review I ever saw of my poems was by Hubert Bland the Socialist in a weekly paper called *The New Age* (1896).'

Here at last is a note that has for long been lacking in English poetry – simplicity, to wit. This our time is rife with poets and poetasters, and the most carping critic is compelled to confess that very much of their work is on a very fair level of excellence. But there is so much of it, and it is all so much alike, that although one may have one's preferences, one has the greatest possible difficulty in giving comprehensible reasons for them. A shelf of modern poets resembles a case of trinkets in the window of a jeweller's shop. Examine each brooch or locket carefully in your hand, and doubtless you will find that one differs from another in small details, but the total effect is one of dead and even dismal sameness. In short, the work of the minor poet of the day is a pretty and a pleasing thing, but 'pretty' and 'pleasing' are the strongest adjectives that a sane critic should permit himself to use of it. The workmanship is deft and skilful, the thought marked mainly by a sort of dainty commonplaceness, the metre generally correct, and even musical, in a young-lady-pianoforte-playing kind of way. But the curse of unconscious imitation is over it all. It is all 'derivative', to use the critical slang of the moment. A.B. suggests Rossetti, C.D. recalls Browning, E.F. has evidently soaked himself in Keats, G.H. soars after Shelley (on a broken pinion), I.J. draws his inspiration from Verlaine; and so on through the list. One catches echoes everywhere, and the echoes of Tennyson are thunderous. Thus about once a week we may count on the appearance of a new poet, but not once a lustre upon new poetry.

The little volume before us contains, on well-nigh every page, essentially and distinctively new poetry. The individual voice rings out true and clear. It is not an inspiring voice, perhaps; it speaks not to us of hope in the future, of glory in the past, or of joy in the present. But it says and sings things that have not been sung or said before, and this with a power and directness, and with a heart-penetrating quality for which one may seek in vain through the work of any contemporary lyrist, Mr. Henley perhaps excepted. Let us take an instance, culled almost at random: –

[quotes No. II]

Here is a thought, perhaps nothing so definite as a thought, a poignant emotion rather, that we have most of us experienced at one time or another when alone with the vision of beauty that each recurrent springtime evokes. To have expressed that emotion in laboured phrasing, even though every phrase were of itself a piece of the most exquisite jewelled work, had been – well, not to have expressed it at all – to have lost it altogether in the expression. What was wanted was perfect simplicity, and that perhaps [sic] simplicity Mr. Housman has given it with the swift, unfaltering touch of a master's hand.

This direct expression of elemental emotions, of heart-thoughts, if we may be permitted the phrase, is the dominant note of all Mr. Housman's work as it was of Heine's alone among modern singers. So direct, so inevitable is it that we doubt not some few readers accustomed to the tricky involutions and verbal contortions of contemporary verse will be inclined to think it bald, and to imagine that they discern in it an absence of art. In point of fact, of course, it is not art, but artifice, that is missing. Mr. Housman's artistic range is limited – it lies within narrow limits, even – but within those limits it is little short of consummate. In this small volume there are many flawless stanzas and not a few flawless poems. We will end this brief and quite inadequate review by quoting at length a poem which, if not the best, is the one most characteristic of Mr. Housman's genius.

It is a lonely watcher outside a jail in which next morning his friend is to be hanged who speaks. A footnote tells us that hanging in chains was called 'keeping sheep by moonlight'.

[quotes No. IX]

As we have said, Mr. Housman's poetry is wanting in the note of gladness; that is to say, it is not the highest poetry. But it comes astonishingly near the highest.

3. O.O., review, *Sketch*

xiii, 22 April 1896, 574 ('The Literary Lounger' column)

The author was perhaps Oliver Onions (1873–1961), a very prolific writer, particularly of ghost stories, which appeared in a collected volume in 1935.

When you open Mr. A.E. Housman's 'A Shropshire Lad', you are landed suddenly in the midst of fresh, spontaneous, vigorous poetry; and that is a rare enough thing today, though there are scores of writers who bring you a faint perfume and a pleasant memory of the real thing. The imagination in it is the real, forcible imagination that works in folk-tales, and the form has much of the picturesque conciseness of the old ballads. A chronicle of the heart adventures of a young man, the verses are not all sane and calm. Mixed with the fresh country pictures, the frank loves and hates, there is the world-weariness, and there are the morbid fancies, too, which were never absent from the soul of a youth of sensibility. But even in these moods the singer's admirable talent of brevity does not desert him and lose for him our interest. Here is a comedy and a tragedy in a nutshell –

[quotes No. XVIII]

The verses of Mr. Housman, for all their simple form, are as far removed as may be from insipidity. They have stings in them; they have much frankness, sudden outbursts of affection and of bitterness, and, in their suggested tale of three not very lucky Shropshire lads, real tragic force. The fresh memories of country places make a peaceful setting for the stormy human passions, and Shropshire may be proud that its fields and streams have been sung by this genuine and individual poet, who loves so fervently the

[quotes stanza 1 of No. L]

and who has such home-sickness away from their beauties –

[quotes stanzas 2 and 3 of No. XXXIX]

The keen artistic instinct which has prevented the over-polishing of these interpretations of a crude young man's emotions and experiences is not the least promising thing in this noticeable book of poems.

4. 'Claudius Clear', *British Weekly*
xx, No. 495, 23 April 1896, 9

'Claudius Clear' was the journalist and man of letters William Robertson Nicoll (1851–1923). Originally a minister in the Free Church of Scotland, Nicoll resigned due to ill-health, came to London, and from 1885 until his death edited the monthly theological magazine the *Expositor*. From 1886 he was also editor of the newly established and very influential *British Weekly: A Journal of Social and Christian Progress*, to which he regularly contributed under his pseudonym. (This 'letter to the editor' is thus a letter to himself.) A prominent Liberal and supporter of the social legislation of David Lloyd George, Nicoll was knighted for his political services in 1909.

Sir, – we hear nowadays comparatively little about new poets. I question whether one was 'discovered' all last year. Once upon a time, the poet was regarded as the great man of letters; his place was superior to that of the novelist. Now everything is changed. The popular form of literature is fiction; of praise, and honour, and glory, the story-teller has practically the monopoly. Literary men never feast a poet or a critic; their honours are reserved for novelists. The public was never a greedy purchaser of poetry, though in a few cases the sales of poets have almost attained the figures of recent fiction. Nowadays, while the poet is poorer than ever, he finds his consideration gone, and I saw it plausibly suggested the other day that the office of Poet Laureate would by-and-bye [sic] be abolished in favour of a court novelist. Mr. Alfred Austin may be succeeded by Miss Marie Corelli.

When you think of it, the case of a poet is indeed hard. It is certain that his contribution to literature, if he deserves the name, is of the highest sort. Yet it meets with next to no pecuniary acknowledgement. I doubt whether any living poet earns by his poetry as much as £200 a year. Whereas for a single book, novelists like Mrs. Humphry Ward, Mr. Conan Doyle, and Mr. Hall Caine, would not be willing to take less than £10, 000. As a consequence, the poet is compelled to devote himself to journalism, and even to attempt the novel. Poets make very good journalists sometimes, but as a rule they dislike the business. As writers of fiction, they very seldom achieve success. It is very hard to see what can be done to help them. As a rule, the popular magazines do not nowadays care for poetry. A man like Mr. Kipling can get a good price for a set of verses, but that is mainly for the sake of having his name on the cover; and even Mr. Kipling has found that to bring out a new volume of poems that will bear criticism is a very difficult matter. I am inclined to think that in future for poetry we must look not to literary men by profession, but to those engaged in the ordinary work of the world. The little book which I propose to introduce to your readers today is *A Shropshire Lad* by A.E. Housman (Kegan Paul). I believe, though I am not certain, that Mr. Housman was at one time engaged in the Civil Service, and is now a Professor in University College, London. He is in any case a writer of true refinement and originality. He is not a great poet, but there is an indefinable something about his work which plainly does not belong to prose.

The reader of *A Shropshire Lad* must not expect any effects like those of Barnes in his Dorset poems. Mr. Housman gives us no dialect, neither is there much local colour, although here and there we come on the names of Shropshire towns and hills. The scenery of the country is not effectively rendered. With his adjectives and nouns, and especially the former, Barnes conveyed to his loving students a perfect impression of Dorset in all seasons. Save for the names I have mentioned, Mr. Housman's book might have borne the name of any other English county. Neither does he profess to render the sentiments of the normal Shropshire rustic. It will be doubted by the readers of Mr. Hardy whether Barnes did as much for his own folks. There is, at all events, a conflict of authorities. Here we have given us the thoughts of a lad who goes from the country to fight, who bears about with him continually all that comes in the track of war. There is exile in the poems, and it is so bitter that death beside it is sweet.

> Luckier may you find the night
> Than ever you found the day.

I think I shall best render the impression of this little book by selective typical poems. The first, 'Bredon Hill', is a song of love turned to death and dust.

[quotes No. XXI]

The next is a song of sick exile.

[quotes No. XLI]

The last is a song of death made sweet by the misery of return.

[quotes No. LXI]

I have quoted enough to show that Mr. Housman has an individuality of his own, and that lovers of poetry will do well to watch his work.

5. A.M., review, *Bookman* (London)
x, No. 57, June 1896, 83

The author was probably Annie Macdonnell, the sub-editor of the London *Bookman* (founded in 1891 by William Robertson Nicoll). Housman wrote to his brother Laurence (4 December 1896): 'I feel sure you are wrong in thinking that A.M. stands for Mrs. Meynell [Alice Meynell, 1847–1922]; partly because of the style, which is neither sufficiently correct nor sufficiently pretentious, and partly because the sub-editor's name is A. Macdonnell.'

This review was reprinted (verbatim, except that 'we' replaced 'I' at the beginning of the last paragraph) in the *Bookman* (New York), v (July 1897), 434–5.

Here is a writer who stands outside all the poetical vogues of today. He is neither a mystic, nor a symbolist, nor a devotee of ancient forms, nor an interpreter of the ideal significance of the music-halls. But he is a poet. I have seen no book of verses for years that breathes at least more spontaneity, and very few with as much individuality. Mr. Housman's technical merits might easily be surpassed, but his rhythms and forms call for no criticism. They are simple, sometimes rough, never subtle, save with the subtlety that catches and reflects the mood, and sets the matter to the right tune. His book of lyrics has continuity. You can pick out a story from it, several linked dramas of the lives of Shropshire lads, the one that used his knife in anger, and stood under the shadow of the gallows, and lay long in jail; the one that went for a soldier; the one that, after his struggle for love, lay early in the churchyard. But there is no continuous narrative. The poems are essentially lyrics, outbursts of feelings, often elliptical, cries and sighs from which one may catch a name and the hint of a story. Original as Mr. Housman undoubtedly is, now and then you hear familiar voices in his verse. If he had been more given to making moral reflections than pictures he might have been named a kinsman of Clough. The swing of some of his verses, as if born of the body's motion in the open road with the wind playing round, puts one in mind of the Canadian poet, Bliss Carman, at his best. But I will dare a loftier comparison, and say that there are lyrics here that might have come out of Heine's Song Book. The exquisiteness of Heine and his poisonous sting are both absent. But his methods, though unperfected, are Heine's in the main; and his matter very much the same. The love of fresh hearts in the spring-time, the strife of young passions, the struggle of man with the soil, the homesickness for the West country felt in the dusty streets, imagined as crying from below the sod, for the old life of comrades – out of such things has Mr. Housman woven his verse. Sturdy vigour and pervading melancholy are always there, and one hardly seems to give way for the other. The poet's old friend twits him with his poor consolation when 'pints and quarts of Ludlow beer' bring more sterling comfort. And the poet does not contradict him.

> 'Tis true, the stuff I bring for sale
> Is not so brisk a brew as ale:
> Out of a stem that scored the hand
> I wrung it in a weary land.
> But take it: if the smack is sour,
> The better for the embittered hour.

I have no space to quote as I should like from Mr. Housman's lyric tales of lads that loved and suffered

> By Ony and Teme and Clun,
> The country for easy livers,
> The quietest under the sun.

But here are some verses out of 'Is my team ploughing', the eager questions of a dead man, and the answers from overhead.

[quotes stanzas 5–8 of No. XXVII]

6. Unsigned review, *Guardian*

li, 3 June 1896, 872

The *Guardian* was a Church of England newspaper containing much ecclesiastical news and opinion.

It is pleasant, after all the books of art-poetry that are now the fashion, to come upon a poet who sings with a natural note, and is not too concerned to be clever. Mr. Housman's muse may not be a nightingale, but neither is it a garden-warbler setting up to be a nightingale. It must now be fifteen years or more since we first and last saw Mr. Housman's name to a piece of verse. It was a ballad called, if we remember right, 'New Year's Eve', and was a somewhat Swinburnian twilight of the gods. In this long interval of silence Mr. Housman's style, while retaining its love for ballad-metres, has precipitated its Swinburnism, except for an occasional piece of alliteration, like 'Ah, past the plunge of plummet', and has simplified itself into something which is not unfrequently very beautiful indeed. Out of some sixty-three short poems it is difficult to make a representative choice; but here is a little poem in Blake's manner that seems to us singularly successful.

[quotes No. VI]

A pretty village idyll precedes this, of which we must quote the first verse:—

[quotes stanza 1 of No. V]

As the girl proves worth her salt the idyll ends happily, but that is not the fault of the 'young man'. We wish all of Mr. Housman's poems were as delightful as these; but his vein is, as a rule, more sombre. He sings by preference of 'graves and worms' (not 'epitaphs', for he disdains them), and, of course, these topics are fit matter for poetry. In the ballad beginning 'Is my team ploughing', he touches a very plangent sorrow with a masterly hand. But he is not content to sing the facts of life; he is a philosopher, a disciple of Democritus, and he holds that we are not spirits as the best men have thought, but bodies impatient to be delivered of their skeleton, which he grimly calls 'the immortal part'. 'After all, we shall soon be dead', is not a cheerful faith, as Mr. Housman allows, and happily it is by no means so certainly a true one, as he assumes. It is fair to add that the poet bases upon his principles a philosophy of endurance (though he has two poems advocating suicide), and when he preaches endurance without giving his reasons he can be very stirring, as in the fine opening verses on the Queen's Jubilee, and some of the Soldier poems.

7. Norman Gale, review, *Academy*

1, 11 July 1896, 30–1

Norman Gale (d. 1942) described himself as 'poet, storyteller and reviewer'. His first book was *A Country Muse* (2 vols, 1892); it was followed by *Orchard Songs* (1893), and many other volumes. His *Collected Poems* appeared in 1914.

Because new bicycles and new poets are matters of daily occurrence, it frequently happens that a jaded public allows excellence to make its appeal unheard. If only it were necessary for every fresh singer to provide himself with a material lyre, the dividends paid to their shareholders by companies devoted to the manufacture of these instruments would indeed be beyond the dreams of avarice. Since the stream of song is so copious, it is obviously easy for a thing of poetic beauty to escape its deserved amount of observation; and it would be no hard task to draw up a list of books of verse which have failed in the last three or four years to attract the recognition due to their merits. It is much to be hoped that such a fate will not befall *A Shropshire Lad*, a book that has a hundred claims upon the love of all who are the sincere servants of poetry. In these poems there is a voice with a beautiful sound. It calls, and we are obliged to listen; it continues to speak, and we fear the moment when it will be silent. Mr. Housman has no more ambition to make his way into the cloud of mysticism than he has to waste his time and his tune in the music-halls. It is his desire to keep close to flowers and the soil of their parentage. Life, love and death make for him a trinity to be sung sweetly, purely and reverently; and while employing his heart upon such themes, uttering with bird-like unconsciousness strains that are the founders of our smiles and tears, he lets fall for our keeping exquisite fragments of unsullied song. In an extraordinary volume, not the least extraordinary feature is the abounding presence of verbal felicity. Arresting phrases are as numerous as sparrows in ivy at night; but not one of them convinces us it has been manufactured, so easily does each fall into its place, so simple are the means by which the novel effect is procured. It may be asked whether Mr. Housman is largely in the debt of any past or present king of rhyme. To such a question a sturdy negative must be returned. We suspect that Mr. Housman has read *Underwoods* and *A Child's Garden of Verse* [sic] with especial attention, though this perusal has not caused a Stevensonian sediment of more than a fractional thickness to lie at the bottom of his song. When such a feast of good things has been spread for us, it is somewhat difficult to make a selection for quotation. The two verses which we choose are not as beautiful as many in *A Shropshire Lad*, but they will serve to show our readers how good Mr. Housman's second best is:

[quotes No. XXVI]

In the last verse of 'Reveille' the poet exclaims:

>Breath's a ware that will not keep.

He is a wise father who knows his own children; but Shakespeare might claim the paternity of this line with never a show of hesitation.

8. Louise Imogen Guiney, review
Chap-Book (Chicago)
vi, 1 February 1897, 245–6

Louise Imogen Guiney (1861–1920), the daughter of a general in the Union Army, was born near Boston, but spent the last twenty years of her life in England. She published various collections of poetry, including *A Roadside Harp* (Houghton Mifflin, 1893) and *England and Yesterday* (Grant Richards, 1898). She wrote a book on Edmund Campion (1908), edited the work of various English Recusant poets, and in 1912 co-edited the essays and critical papers of Lionel Johnson.

Some of us, in these days of make-believe greatness, having given up the search for continents, are yet glad to cruise about painfully, on the chance of reaching one Happy Isle. Such an isle, rough rock below and flowered orchards above, is Mr. A.E. Housman's first book: a sort of careless, indignant jewel, bedded in the sea, asking for no mariner's eye. Surely, one of the finest distinctions left to the laity is such a lonely discovery, the identification of a bit of literature. And *A Shropshire Lad* is literature, although it plays at being several other things. For instance, it is not merely rural, but country-bumpkinish, to a degree. Herrick's dear old May poles and wassail-cakes are fantastic as a Versailles masque beside these ugly villageous ingredients: spites, jealousies and slit throats ('demd moist', too, in one ballad); the barracks, the jail, and the hangman's rope. Around these is a frieze of English April, enchanting as Correggio's at Parma, with wet vines, blossoms and fresh young faces. But the beautiful little book, on the whole, is keyed low, so low as approval of suicide, and allowance of blasphemy. At almost every subject it strikes twice or thrice; the best lyrics can all be paired off with their shadows. This nice unrest betrays the artist. Whoever Mr. Housman may be, he is not the Ettrick Shepherd come again. Though he stand frocked, on the Brown Clee with his Muse, alone (in a classic and forgotten phrase),

> – Alone, with earth and sky,
> And her, the third Simplicity, –

he has a certificate about him; he is suppressing ripe knowledge of cities, book and men. He may write autobiographically, concerning a London crowd's unkindness to the alien, a plaint which has a quaint hobble as of the *Child's Garden*:

> Till they drop, they needs must still
> Look at you, and wish you ill.

He may revive, with an innocent-seeming magic, some spoiled or disused phrase, like

> May I squire you round the mead?

or,

> Morns abed, and daylight slumber
> Were not meant for man alive.

In vain: at some turning of the page we catch a princely look, the cried kinship with the *Anthologia* or *England's Helicon*.

> When Severn down to Buildwas ran
> Coloured with the death of man,

has a grandeur and muffled music which Milton might have owned; and the whole of

> On Wenlock Edge the wood's in trouble,

with its sympathetic sense of things bygone, of the tingling human past which lies about no yokel's dreams, could only have come from a hand subdued, and manners and a mind long mellowed. The same may be said of the bitter but magnificent stanzas, 'Be still, my Soul.' Instead of another Skipsey or Gerald Massey, have we not here some one of as exquisite culture as the author of *Ionica*? and with more of native freedom and power. Let Mr. Housman drop the jewsharp, and come from behind the haystack. Though he assure us that he is as jolly a boy as, in the ancient catch,

> – ever did swing in a hempen string
> Under the gallows tree,

yet a moan as of Thessalian seas is under all the concretion and the localism of his lines. Not that Salop, with her romantic manors and dark, stream-belted towns, Salop, a 'coloured county' of rose-red fields, lacks any charm, or that she is not a fit theme for any wise enough to adore her. But the art in this small blue book is 'meant for mankind'. A very little Salop, somehow, is all that we ask of it: next to nothing of Shrewsbury jailbirds, and only so much rosemary and thyme as may serve for universal comfort, wherever there are homesick hearts indoors. For it can afford us larger endowments; moments not only of poignant pathos and honeyed humor, but of the genuine uplift which nothing but original, pungent genius can give. The best in *A Shropshire Lad* is altogether memorable; you cannot shake it off or quote it away. Keen readers will find a masculine moral in the delicious postlude:

> Mithridates, he died old.

Like his poison-proof King, Mr. Housman has tasted a good many dishes, and risen above the commonplaces of criticism, before he rode into print. We know naught of his processes; he does not address his ambitions in public: for which we love him. In short, he is not an author on trial. He does not always, as yet, quite as we would have him do; but, at least, he has nothing to learn concerning what he has chosen to do, or the manner of doing it. One does not dare predict a career for him; much will depend on what he cares to achieve. Again, *A Shropshire Lad* has in it a spirit of ample scorn and of little worship; yet by worship a poet must live. Mr. Housman shows himself a thinker and a fine red-flag pessimist. It is a pity that he should be, in general, so shy of passing for the philosopher he is.

Poetry (as Mr. Arnold insisted, and with fruit), is its own demonstration. Here are two fragments from Mr. Housman's book, the first *On An Athlete Dying Young*. 'Smart lad to slip betimes away.'

[quotes stanzas 5–7 of No. XIX]

And of a crowd at Ludlow Fair, and some there to be envied:

[quotes stanzas 4 and 5 of No. XXIII]

And here are three complete lyrics which lack titles:

[quotes Nos. XV, XI and XXXIX]

O sancta simplicitas! Lovely verbal austerity, heroic, quiet, better than dramatic feeling! As old Basse, in his elegy, sweetly invited Spenser and Beaumont, in their Abbey graves, to lie nearer and make room for a greater third, so may our minor bards stand back a little for a young stranger who, in quality, has hardly a rival among them, and touch their rusty lances to the rim of his shining shield.

9. Unsigned notice, *Literary World* (Boston)

xxviii, No. 8, 17 April 1897, 128

We cannot express our opinion of A.E. Housman's volume of poetry, *A Shropshire Lad*, better than by quoting a few lines from a poem in which he attempts to explain why he writes such gloomy verse:

> Pretty friendship 'tis to rhyme
> Your friends to death before their time,
> Moping melancholy mad:
> Come pipe a tune to dance to, lad.

Mr. Housman answers that, since in this world trouble is sure and happiness a chance, it is wiser 'to train for ill and not for good'; and as for his verse that

> If the smack is sour
> The better for the embittered hour,

most of the heroes of Mr. Housman's verse are either lying in their graves and making from their 'tombs a doleful sound', or else on the verge of suicide or on the gallows. One of the military poems, 'The Recruit', is good.

10. Unsigned notice, *Citizen* (Philadelphia)
iii, No. 9, November 1897, 215–16

It is not only in France apparently that young gentleman [*sic*] can be as sad as night only for wantonness. *A Shropshire Lad*, in this beautifully printed book of lyrics, moves our compassion by his many woes. His sweetheart disapproves of him, and he goes to be a soldier. He is overcome by the extraordinary discovery that people must die sooner or later. Various homicidal and suicidal episodes darken his life. Like a true Englishman he takes his pleasure sadly, –

[quotes stanzas 1 and 2 of No. XVII]

In one of the most tragical lyrics, the crowning thought of desolation is delightfully English:

> And long will stand the empty plate
> And dinner will be cold.

This is the remark of a fratricide apparently after the murder.

Only in the very end of the book does Mr. Housman drop the mask and let us into the joke. Poor little Alice, it will be remembered, was deeply affected by the woes of the Mock-Turtle until the Gryphon said rudely: 'Bless you, he haint got no sorrows. It's only his imagination.' And our author supplies not only the poetry but in another form the criticism of the bluff-mannered gryphon:

[quotes ll. 1–10 of No. LXII]

With the first, fifth and sixth lines of this quotation ['Terence, this is stupid stuff' and 'But oh, good Lord, the verse you make, / It gives a chap the belly-ache'] the reviewer agrees thoroughly, but he would not think, of course, of putting the facts quite so bluntly.

A SHROPSHIRE LAD
1898

11. William Archer, review, *Fortnightly Review*
lxiv, 1 August 1898, 263–8

William Archer (1856–1924) was born in Perth and came to London in 1878. By the time he wrote this review he had become very influential as a drama critic, having performed this function for the *London Figaro* (1879–81), *Tribune, Nation, Star*, and the *World* (from 1884 to 1905). He did much to raise English theatrical standards in the 1890s, and wrote many books on drama and theatre, including *A National Theatre Scheme and Estimates* (1907, with Harley Granville-Barker). Between 1906 and 1908 he published his translation of the *Collected Works* of Ibsen.

Shropshire has not hitherto been distinguished as a country haunted by the Muses. On the spur of the moment, and without reference to books, I can think of only one great poem definitely associated with Shropshire – 'Comus', to wit, written for performance at Ludlow Castle. It is true that on Shropshire soil the doughty Sir John Falstaff slew the Hotspur of the North, after fighting a long hour by Shrewsbury clock. But this is scarcely an inherent association, native to the glebe. Falstaff could have performed the exploit by any other clock. It was mere fortune of war that gave Shrewsbury the honour of keeping time to that immortal combat. Take it all in all, Shropshire is not one of the great literary counties of England.

But Shropshire no longer lacks its poet. Shrewsbury clock has found another place in literature, in a less delightful but still a memorable context:–

[quotes stanzas 4–8 of No. IX]

These are the concluding verses of the ninth poem in Mr. A.E. Housman's book, *A Shropshire Lad*. They are not his best, nor even among his best, but I place them here because they give a sharp foretaste of his quality. His book (his only book, so far as I know) is a very small one. It contains some sixty brief lyrics, occupying less than one hundred pages in all. You may read it in half-an-hour – but there are things in it you will scarce forget in a lifetime. It tingles with an original, fascinating, melancholy vitality.

Mr. Housman writes, for the most part, under the guise of 'A Shropshire Lad' – the rustic namefather of his book. But this is evidently a mere mask.* Mr. Housman is no Shropshire Burns singing at his plough. He is a man of culture. He moves in his rustic garb with no clodhopper's gait, but with the ease of an athlete; and I think he has an Elzevir classic in the pocket of his smock frock. But it is not Theocritus, not the Georgics or the Eclogues; I rather take it to be Lucretius. Never was there less of a 'pastoral' poet, in the artificial, Italian-Elizabethan sense of the word. The Shropshire of Mr. Housman is no Arcadia, no Sicily, still less a courtly pleasaunce peopled with beribboned nymphs and swains. It is as real, and as tragic, as the Wessex of Mr. Hardy. The genius, or rather the spirit, of the two writers is not dissimilar. Both have the same rapturous realisation, the same bitter resentment, of life. To both Nature is an exquisitely seductive, inexorably malign enchantress. 'Life's Ironies' might be the common title of Mr. Hardy's long series of novels and Mr. Housman's little book of verse. And both have the same taste for clothing life's ironies in the bucolic attire of an English county.

Mr. Housman's strong and stern temperament finds expression in curiously simple, original, and expressive verse. In deference to his rustic mask, and probably to something fundamental in his talent as well, he attempts no metrical arabesques, no verbal enamelling. With scarcely an exception, his metres are of the homeliest; yet, in their little variations, their suspensions, their tremulous cadences, we recognise the touch of the born metrist. Mr. Housman's chief technical strength, however, lies in the directness and terseness of his style. There is nerve and fibre in every line he writes, and of superfluous tissue not a trace. He says what he wants to say, not what his measure dictates, or his rhyme; and his words seem to fall into their places with a predestinate fitness which (inconsistent as it may seem) gives us in every second stanza a little shock of pleasurable surprise. His diction and his methods are absolutely his own. He echoes no one, borrows no one's technical devices. If he reminds us of any other poet, it is (now and then) of Heine; yet he is English of the English. We divine his culture in the very simplicity of his style; but (beyond a single allusion to Milton, to be quoted presently) we find no direct evidence of his ever having read another English poet. His verse might quite well be the glorified offspring of the most unsophisticated popular poetry – the chap-book ballad or the rustic stave.

Mr. Housman has three main topics: a stoical pessimism; a dogged rather than an exultant patriotism; and what I may perhaps call a wistful cynicism. His pessimism he formulates again and again:

> The world has still
> Much good, but much less good than ill,
> And while the sun and moon endure
> Luck's a chance, but trouble's sure

This is from a poem in which he excuses himself to certain friends who have complained that he plays only 'such tunes as killed the cow', and have begged him to 'pipe a tune to dance to, lad'. He answers: –

[quotes ll. 15–26 of No. LXII]

In a remarkable poem called 'The Welsh Marches' he seems to give an ethnological reason for this sombre strain in his temperament. At Shrewsbury, he says (in a splendid stanza): –

[quotes stanzas 2, 4 and 6 of No. XXVIII]

Whatever its origin, whether it proceed from the subjection of the Celt to the Teuton, or from some more modern source, Mr. Housman's melancholy is inveterate and not to be shaken off. But there is nothing whining about it. Rather, it is bracing, invigorating. The poet communes with a statue in the Grecian gallery, who reminds him that: –

[quotes ll. 17–26 of No. LI]

Following a curious habit, of which this book offers several examples, Mr. Housman, in another poem, presents a variation of the same thought. This poem is so noble that I must quote it entire. Metrically, it is perhaps the best thing in the book – note the masterly handling of the caesura: –

[quotes No. XLVIII]

Germane to this theme are the two poems on suicide, the one a pocket edition, so to speak, of the other. The longer is by far the finer of the two, but I quote the briefer version for the sake of its brevity.

[quotes No. XLV]

To show how Mr. Housman can touch his world-weariness to absolute beauty, I quote, before leaving this subject, a poem so delicate that even the tenderest breath of praise would only shake off some of its bloom. It has for its motto what I take to be an old local rhyme – if it be not a new one: –

[quotes No. L]

The English language is appreciably the richer for such work as this.

Mr. Housman's patriotism, as it appears in *A Shropshire Lad*, is local rather than national or imperial. His soldiers fight, not so much for the glory of England, as for the credit of Shropshire. Of the joys of battle he tells us little enough. He accepts war as the destiny of a stubborn fighting race, and as a safety-valve for energies that might find a still more noxious outlet in peace. He sings of the sacred bond of comradeship, and, like Mr. Kipling, he has a good deal to say of the price we pay for Empire in blood and tears. He tells in the opening poem of his book how –

> the Nile spills his overflow
> Beside the Severn's dead.

And in a spirited 'Reveille' he sings: –

[quotes stanzas 3 and 6 of No. IV]

Perhaps the most characteristic, however, of all his military pieces, is the following.

[quotes No. LVI]

The third element in Mr. Housman's inspiration is what I have roughly called a wistful cynicism. He dwells, not harshly, but rather with compassion, upon the mutability of human feeling, the ease with which the dead are forgot, the anguish of love unrequited, and the danger that long life may mean slow degradation. Among the crowd at Ludlow Fair, he wishes that those who are destined to die young, 'to carry back bright to the coiner the mintage of man', could bear some mark about them so that they might be honoured and envied. For: –

[quotes stanza 2 of No. XXIII]

One of his most notable little groups of poems turns on the idea that

>A lad that lives and has his will
>Is worth a dozen dead.

By far the best of the group is a dialogue between a dead man and his living friend, the gist of which lies in the friend's last answer: –

[quotes No. XXVII]

As for the pains of love misplaced, have they ever been more poignantly or more briefly expressed than in the two stanzas of this perfect song: –

[quotes ll. 16–23 of No. XIII]

There is a whole heart history in this ingenious and exquisite little work of art.

In a few of Mr. Housman's poems, however, there is no touch of that bitterness of feeling which I have named, or misnamed, cynicism. 'Bredon Hill' (pronounced *Breedon*), seems to me almost unrivalled in its delicate, unemphatic pathos: —

[quotes No. XXI]

This exemplifies one of Mr. Housman's strongest and rarest qualities — his unerring dramatic instinct. In the way of pure contemplation, apart from drama, these four stanzas are almost as good.

[quotes No. XII]

It is long since we have caught just this note in English verse — the note of intense feeling offering itself in language of unadorned precision, uncontorted truth. Mr. Housman is a vernacular poet, if ever there was one. He employs scarcely a word that is not understood of the people, and current on their lips. For this very reason, some readers who have come to regard decoration, and even contortion, as of the essence of poetry, may need time to acquire the taste for Mr. Housman's simplicity. But if he is vernacular, he is also classical in the best sense of the word. His simplicity is not that of weakness, but of strength and skill. He eschews extrinsic and factitious ornament because he knows how to attain beauty without it. It is good to mirror a thing in figures, but it is at least as good to express the thing itself in its essence, always provided, of course, that the method be that of poetic synthesis, not of scientific analysis. Mr. Housman has this talent in a very high degree; and cognate and complementary to it is his remarkable gift of reticence — of aposiopesis, if I may wrest the term from its rhetorical sense and apply it to poetry. He will often say more by a cunning silence than many another poet by pages of speech. That is how he has contrived to get into this tiny volume so much of the very essence and savour of life.

NOTE

* At the time when this paragraph was written, I knew nothing of Mr. Housman save his name. I have since learnt that he is an eminent scholar. I leave the paragraph in its original form, as my guesses seem to have come tolerably near the mark.

12. Unsigned notice, *Outlook*

ii, No. 33, 17 September 1898, 213–14

Mr. A.E. Housman should now come into his own. Very few critics, comparatively speaking, took notice of his lyrics, *A Shropshire Lad*, when the book was first issued in 1896. It has steadily gathered friends, however, and now, when it is republished by Mr. Grant Richards, there are signs that a welcoming little world awaits it. It is rather disturbing to think that a little work of such pensive charm, of feeling now wistful and now manly, and of simple yet rare artistry, should obtain recognition by such slow stages. It is a sign, perhaps, of how spoiled and disturbed the taste of the generation has grown in the main. Mr. Housman's work is reminiscent of a day when poetry was a much more artless and spontaneous art than we know it. That *A Shropshire Lad* came into being so simply and naturally as its smooth and tender flow suggests is, of course, a doubtful matter: it may have taken laborious art, indeed, to achieve this ease and grace. Or it may not. Genius, we have eminent authority for believing, always retains more or less of the spirit of the child.

13. Unsigned review, *Academy*

lv, 8 October 1898, 23–5

This is virtually the second edition of Mr. A.E. Housman's poems, which, first given to the public two years ago, are now re-issued by another publisher, Mr. Grant Richards. This new edition comes timely, when attention has been called to the book by Mr. William Archer's article in the *Fortnightly* [see No. 11 above]. The *Fortnightly*, which under its former editor was felicitous in the 'discovery' of new writers, has certainly sustained its tradition by the proclamation of Mr. A.E. Housman (to be distinguished from Mr. Laurence Housman, also a true poet, though of a more recluse and unpopular kind). Because we have very earnest praise to give Mr. Housman, we shall begin by certain protests, not against him, but against his critics, or rather some excesses of his critics. He comes upon reviewers with a surprise of novelty; and under such circumstances the reviewer is all too apt in extremes of reaction, as though the new thing were not only a right thing, but *the* right thing. Directness is not the note of most modern poetry. It is emphatically a note of Mr. Housman; and accordingly critics write as though directness *à la Housman* were your only wear in song, and his predecessors like sheep had gone astray. We can see in Mr. Housman's directness an excellent thing for Mr. Housman's aims, without repudiating all other modes of excellence. We can applaud in him a new, true, and individual note, without bidding all his fellow-singers give place to him, like a critic cited in the advertisement pages at the end of the book. There has been too much of this during late years. First Mr. Robert Bridges was our one authentic voice; then Mr. William Watson was the *jeune premier* among English poets; then Mr. John Davidson was the sole true minstrel of modernity; and but the other day Mr. Stephen Phillips was discovered to be the real Arabian bird. Meanwhile, we do not cry down Joachim, because we cry up Sarasate; we admit a pantheon in music – why not in poetry? Let us be only too thankful if we have many poets with diverse gifts. We, at any rate, shall not join in the parrot-cry that the last-found poet is in the major key, and all the rest in the minor. One reviewer is so grateful for Mr. Housman's directness that he tries to make him out what emphatically he is not – the simple, wholesome, manly, rural singer, who loves football and cricket, and can drink beer and break a rival's head as well as make rustic love. One would suppose a new Norman Gale [see No. 7 above] (where is he, that mere directness should be thought such a new note?) Strangely surprised would the reader be who adventured upon *A Shropshire Lad* with such a preconception. He sings of cricket, it is true, but in this fashion:

[quotes stanzas 2 and 3 of No. XVII]

God-a'-mercy! Does Mr. Stoddart, that 'Son of Grief', lead his men into the field, 'trying to be glad?' And what price on his captainship, if he did? We are temped to address Mr. Housman, after Browning:

> O my Housman, A.E. Housman, this is very, very sad!
> I cannot mistake your meaning, that would prove me blind or mad
> What! they think so at the wicket, those young batsmen lithe & firm,
> Think on what a little mirth will keep them from the curling worm?
> Nay, but rather thinketh Jackson facing Albert Trott, I know,
> Thinketh upon how much art will keep him from the curling slow!

Clearly, nothing can be more misleading than to regard this poet as a specimen of the healthy, life-enjoying, country bard.

Mr. Housman, as a matter of fact, is a peculiar combination, and the originality which has attracted reviewers arises from that peculiarity. On the one hand is the sweet breath of the fields, on the other the stern and sombre endurance of the dweller in cities. It is the note of the caged thrush, the scent of the unforgotten copse and hedgerows still haunting with wildness its enslaved voice. No more iron philosophy has been sung in this day than that which some reviewers acclaim as rustic and homely. Just so men listen delighted to the rustic note of the caged bird, missing its inward tragedy. Or rather, the combination is piquant to them in poet as in bird, and they do not stop to analyse the source of a delight. Mr. Housman is (in no disparaging sense) a monotonous singer, 'a poet of one note in all his lays.' In all his poems is present the contrast between his happy country youth and the grim reality of his adult city life. This chord is struck in one quiet, pathetic, almost Wordsworthian lyric, entirely representative of this aspect in Mr. Housman:

[quotes No. XL]

That is one aspect of Mr. Housman. The other is the philosophy with which he encounters his 'lost content'. It is a grim and pessimistic philosophy. Your pessimist, according to temperament, either whines or 'grins and bears it'. In the latter there are variations. Mr. Housman mourns and bears it. Man is thrown together from pre-existent elements, and dislimns like a summer cloud, again to be brought together in fresh combinations. We are swayed by ancestral passions, and our ancestors live in us again. As what has been, so what shall be; and each must take his portion while it lasts – having drunk the little sweet, he must drink also the much sour. And for consolation – a living ass is better than a dead lion. It is a familiar position: the philosophy of Ecclesiastes (as Ecclesiastes is usually read) *plus* the doctrine of heredity. It is made impressive by the downright sincerity of the poet and his power of expression. Expression – that is what it all comes back to. This union of remembered country sights and scents and sounds with most urban pessimistic philosophy, is dignified by virility, and brought home to us through a fulness of feeling which creates art. On the whole, it more creates art than is guided by it. Like all modern poets of the truly direct kind (apart from the eloquent Byronic school, which is not really direct), Mr. Housman is unequal. He is unequal as Wordsworth was unequal, and from the same cause. Where his feeling is not strong enough to inspire him, he lapses into mere rhymed prose. Where his feeling is acute, he pierces to the quick. And he seems quite ignorant when he is inspired or uninspired.

At the same time, as will have been gathered, nothing could be less Wordsworthian than this poet's general style. It seems rather founded on the old ballads. In some of the characteristic pieces quoted by Mr. Archer (who, we need hardly say, is not among the critics to whose rashness we took exception) the effect reminds us of Heine. The verses proceed at a respectable but not striking level, until in the final stanza some unexpected turn takes us by surprise, and casts a reflex glory on all which has gone before. In this gift or art Mr. Housman seems to us alone among English poets. Such a poem in which the dead man asks a string of questions about the living, ending with the query whether his friend has found a better bed than his:

[quotes stanza 8 of No. XXVII]

It is cynical, poignant, arresting; quite a piece with Mr. Housman's treatment of love, in which love appears always as a tragic misfortune.

In the other class of poems the pregnant compression is carried right through. One can only say the verse is *quick* — there are no means of describing or conveying it, save itself. Take this as a brief sample:

[quotes No. XXXII]

The brevity of life, the piercing compassion for one's fellow-Mayfly, have never been more keenly conveyed. They could only be so put by a very sensitive poet with a vital unbelief in the future life. And the poem contains Mr. Housman's philosophy and attitude towards life in a nutshell. This one insistent note, like the cry of a bittern, sounds lonelily through the book. Sometimes he frankly repeats a *motif* in several poems. Thus two successive poems sing the folly of giving 'the heart out of the bosom'. The second is superfluous, for the first has said the thing once for all, and the repetition is distinctly weaker. More often the iteration is disguised by the varying form of utterance. The haunting cry of fate, heredity, and passing away is presented over and over again with striking skill in variation. There is the wild sadness and mystery of the Celt in this poem.

[quotes No. XXXI]

That is better than direct, it is subtle, it is suggestive: not idly does the poet claim for himself, in another poem, a strain of Cymric blood. In that other poem (the fine and striking 'Welsh Marches') the Celtic note of immemorial regret is heard in such a stanza as this:

[quotes stanza 5 of No. XXVIII]

That has magic in it.

We like Mr. Housman least in the few poems where he attempts a lilting metre, which he does not seem to us to handle skilfully. But allowing this, allowing a proportion of poems where simplicity becomes insipidity, this is yet the annunciation of a new and valuable voice in present poetry. Sometimes grim, strong, close-knit, commanding attention by its virile pessimism; sometimes haunting and melancholy; sometimes taking us by a piercing and Heinesque surprise at the poem's close; monotonous, but not wearying; grave, sad, sincere, unsuperfluous, with a latter-day simplicity, less simple than it seems; it is individual work, to which the reader will return with deepening interest and admiration. For it is rarely that simplicity is combined (as it is here combined) with the self-consciousness of the modern poet, yet a simplicity without affectation.

14. Unsigned notice, *Bookman* (London)

xv, No. 85, October 1898, 27

When these poems appeared nearly three years ago we gave them a hearty welcome; and we feel now that their republication must be one of the chief events of the present season, be the others what they may. Of all our younger poets is there one so spontaneous, so genuine, so directly human as Mr. Housman? The others have their own qualities, but he has that of immediate appeal to the heart. He has imitated no one, though Heine may have inspired him. Unambitious in manner, his technique, judged by his purpose and plan, is yet almost faultless. He has the lyric gift, and he has used it for the honour of the West Country, for the revelation of country hearts, of rustic passion and tragedy.

15. Unsigned notice, *Athenaeum*

No. 3702, 8 October 1898, 488

A Shropshire Lad, by Mr. A.E. Housman, is not, of course, new, but Mr. Grant Richards is to be congratulated on securing such excellent verse to reprint. Mr. Housman has attained to an effective simplicity ('attained' – for simplicity nowadays seems unnatural), which, with his brave outlook on life, the frank loves and hates of his lads and lasses, makes a book distinguished above the ruck. It is that sort of easy reading which is hard writing. 'The New Mistress' (poem 34), where the rejected lover decides to serve his queen as a soldier, would make an excellent popular song; and lest this should seem a depreciatory remark, we may quote two poignant lines which suggest classical models: –

> Others, I am not the first,
> Have willed more mischief than they durst.

We hope to hear more of Mr. Housman as poet.

16. 'The Funereal Muse', *Literature*
iii, 29 October 1898, 387–9

Literature was published by *The Times*. The first few sentences of paragraph one are omitted. The review is unsigned. The 'forty-fifth number' of *A Shropshire Lad* is actually No. XLIV.

The heart of Wordsworth could dance with the waving daffodils; and even the painfully sensitive imagination of Shelley – on the whole, perhaps, a source of more pain to him than pleasure – could yet soar heavenward with the skylark. But the most modern of our modern poets are subject to the perpetual obsession of one intolerable thought. They simply cannot feel for thinking: or at any rate they cannot for thinking continue to feel for a longer period than suffices for the production of the briefest possible 'spurts' of song. If they chance to begin a poem in some happy mood of surrender to their 'simple, sensuous, passionate' impressions of nature or man, the odds are that the 'native hue' of their emotions will be sicklied o'er with the pale cast of thought before they have penned half a dozen stanzas.

Here for instance is Mr. A.E. Housman in the re-issue of his one volume of poems *A Shropshire Lad* – a re-issue which we are glad to welcome in these pages (the original edition having appeared before the birth of *Literature*) because Mr. Housman's admirers hitherto, if fit, have been undoubtedly few, and he deserves beyond all question that his remarkable poetic gift, and in particular his singular and striking individuality both of genius and expression, should be much more widely appreciated than they are. There are lyrics in this volume which for simplicity, force, directness are worthy of Burns at the moments when he was most himself and least what Edinburgh lionizing occasionally made him. When Mr. Housman is content – or, perhaps, we should say when his essential 'modernity' will allow him – to give us a simple emotion simply felt, whether pleasurable or painful matters not, we know of few, if any, living poets who are capable of stirring us so deeply, yet with so austere a parcimony [*sic*] in the employment of their means. There is not a note of rhetoric, not a touch of literary artifice in his work from end to end. Nor would we reproach him for preferring – within reason – the tragic side of life as a subject of poetry to its happier aspects. The short but very striking piece of eight quatrains [No. IX], which perhaps attracted most attention in the original issue of *A Shropshire Lad* – the musings of a friend of the condemned criminal's on the fate of a youth left for execution the next morning in Shrewsbury gaol – was, of course, a perfectly fitting subject for the poet. Even so vaguely passionate a protest against life as this that follows – a thoroughly 'modern' exercise on the Sophoclean text that 'not to be born is best' – may pass as legitimate in theme, apart from the strange and startling intensity with which it is treated: –

[quotes No. XLVIII]

This is a note which has not been struck in English poetry with anything like equal power since the death of the author of 'The City of Dreadful Night'; and the poet, who has to find a voice for everything, does well to give utterance when the mood is on him even to such a *De profundis* of pessimism as this.

But the mood is only a mood like another, and it is one, moreover, in which no man could really long abide without providing a subject for a coroner's inquest. Indeed, the very reason why the poem satisfies one is that it is so obviously the utterance of intense feeling untempered by thought, which would at once, of course, confront the poet with the metaphysical contradiction of an unborn 'I'. And it is thought – the ever-recurring thought of mortality, of death and the grave – which obtrudes itself upon Mr. Housman's poetry with an incessancy which at last becomes monotonous. Judged, in fact, by the contents of this little volume, his is a positively funereal muse. *A Shropshire Lad* contains sixty-three numbers, and upon a careful examination of them – giving the benefit of the doubt, deciding *in favorem vitae*, in fact, in every instance which is only lugubrious without being unmistakably sepulchral – we reckon that in nearly half of them the poem, however cheerful in its commencement, drifts away at its close to the image or the thought of death. Three short poems following one after another turn on the succession of a lad to a dead friend's sweetheart, or of a girl to a dead friend's lover, while the third of the three neatly hits off both combinations in the person of a supplanting youth, who himself dies, and is in his turn supplanted by a comrade. Mr. Housman cannot see 'the lads in their hundreds to Ludlow come in to the fair' without wishing that he were able to distinguish those 'that will die in their glory and never be old'. In his forty-fifth number he congratulates a friend, quite in the manner of Hedda Gabler, on having had the pluck to commit suicide – of course for good and sufficient reason. In the next he recommends the same course to a friend: –

[quotes No. XLV]

The next but one, entitled 'The Carpenter's Son', is a sort of versified 'last dying speech and confession' delivered from the hangman's cart. A little further on we find a poem of six stanzas ending with the enquiry: –

[quotes stanzas 5 and 6 of No. L]

We turn a couple more pages and come upon the poem of 'The True Lover', in which a girl lying on her lover's breast inquires 'What is it falling on my lips, my lad, that tastes of brine', and discovers that he has cut his throat.

And so on *usque ad* – we had almost said *nauseam*, and may certainly say *taedium*. Occasionally, but very occasionally, Mr.

Housman allows us the relief of a patriotic and martial note, though it is characteristic of him even then that he seems to value soldiering much less for the opportunities which it offers to a young man for serving his country than for the unique facilities which it affords him for winning a speedy and honourable death. And yet, when the humour takes him, he can write like this in 'The Merry Guide': –

[quotes stanzas 1, 2, 4, 6–9, 11–15 of No. XLII]

This is certainly very charming, though even here the symbolism suggested by the dead leaves and Hermes the Shepherd of departed souls does certainly look in the direction of Orcus. In this case, however, Mr. Housman has wisdom and good spirits enough to stop before reaching the Styx. We strongly advise him to do so more frequently. His passion for the society and conversation of Charon will not improve his admirable poetry; and, indeed, if he does not break himself of it betimes, he will be in danger of becoming what no poet has a right to be – a bore.

17. Unsigned review, *Saturday Review* (London)

lxxxvi, No. 2245, 5 November 1898, 613

When this volume was originally published, nearly three years ago, it attracted little attention, and to the majority of readers it is now presented for the first time. *A Shropshire Lad* is a collection of between sixty and seventy short lyrical poems, forming what the Germans call a 'cyklus'. Their most salient characteristic is an extreme naiveté, and it might for a moment be supposed that the author belonged to the category of John Clare and Stephen Duck, and was really a stalwart and melancholy yeoman. A very slight study, however, shows that the Shropshire Lad has not marched upon London with a wallet and a blackthorn, but that his songs reveal at every turn the most refined mental cultivation. Moreover, the simplicity, the apparent artlessness of his address, is presently discovered to be the very finest art, and what we took for naiveté is really a careful and remarkably successful dramatic experiment. We cannot understand Mr. Housman in the least unless we dismiss from our minds the fallacy that his verse is like the music of the linnet, that only sings because he must.

Accepting the fact that Mr. Housman is a deliberate artist, and not a rustic improvisatore, we are left indifferent as to the amount of personal experience which may or may not have gone into the making of his book of lyrics. We are left regarding them as a dramatic product. The Shropshire Lad, then, is a citizen of the south-western corner of Salop; he has been brought up by the banks of the Ony and the Teme. His home is close to Knighton, over the border in Wales; his market town is Ludlow; sometimes, striding along Wenlock Edge, that interminable downy foreland, he reaches Much Wenlock, and pushes on to Shrewsbury itself. Most of all, he knows the sequestered delicate country between Bishop's Castle and Bucknell, and can assure us, better than any other poet living, that 'Clunton and Clunbury, Clungunford and Clun, are the quietest places under the sun'. It is no part of his business to tell a story; but we gather details as we listen to him. He has lived for friendship mainly in his fresh, outdoor youth, and of his two greatest friends one is dead and the other is in gaol for murder. He has had sorrow with his people, sorrow with the land, sorrow with his girl. Quite young, and in these easy sleepy places, he has learned what disenchantment means. Even at Knighton 'lads knew trouble when he was a Knighton lad'. He has seen young fellows kill themselves, or take to drink, or enlist as soldiers; there have been moments when he thought of one or other of these releases for himself. But the impulse passed, and here he is in London, the ugly, ill-built city, dreaming of the football and the cricket, the jingling of the harness and the smell of the ploughed earth, patient, but longing all the time for rest: –

[quotes stanza 6 of No. L]

This is the theme of these quiet lyrics, which possess in a very unusual degree the fatalistic love of the home life, the nostalgia of the acres, which is so pathetic in transplanted country-folk, and so seldom finds adequate literary expression. But even here it does not find expression in descriptive passages, nor in apostrophes to the elements of natural beauty, such as the poetry of the last hundred years in England has made familiar to us. With something of the Wordsworth tone in his verse, Mr. Housman has no touch of Wordsworth's attitude to nature. His landscape lives only when animated by human figures, and these are almost exclusively muscular young men and cold maidens of the yeoman class. His confessions, sighs and ejaculations take forms which have reminded some of his critics of Heine, but in this we are not in accord with them. The Shropshire Lad has none of the Heinesque bitterness, and little of the Heinesque vigour and agility of mind. Rather we are reminded by him of the rural votive epigrammatists of later Greece, of the sweet and pensive poets who sang in the choir of Meleager.

We are apt to forget that what seems faded and conventional to us in these last Greek lyrists was once fresh enough. No doubt the critics of the second century commended Antipater of Sidon for his 'unadorned precision and uncontorted truth'. Hence, while we confess that Mr. Housman's lyrics have given us remarkable pleasure, we are forewarned against being the dupes of his simplicity. He is not really naive; this delicate poetry is one of the last refinements of civilisation, one of the dying cries, perhaps, of imagination strangled in the coil of excessive education and general juvenile knowingness. It expresses, with a delicious moan in the voice, the disease of youth that finds nothing left to live for when the stir of the pulse begins to slacken. It expresses, too, something less morbid than this, namely, the intense and mechanical sadness of the young man thwarted by circumstances in the instant conquest of life. It is inspired by a curious and poignant sympathy with others in these troubles, so that the habitual egotism of the lyrist is replaced by a note of anxious or dejected sympathy, which, if infinitely sad, is infinitely amiable also. What would, if egotistical merely, prove tiresome and morbid, is lifted into pathos by the gallantry and tender regard of the singer.

Among recent writers Mr. Housman bears likeness to but few. He offers us occasionally a touch of thought or a turn of the vernacular which recalls R.L. Stevenson. He obtains, occasionally, the same sort of magic thrill by dint of extreme simplicity. With this somewhat remote exception, Mr. Housman is not of the breed of our most recent poets, and he may be congratulated on having contrived, without any sacrifice to nature or good sense, to produce in this jaded age a little volume of perfectly original verses. The Shropshire Lad is not well judged by brief citations, but we cannot help giving one specimen of his art: –

[quotes No. XVII]

This seems to us to be curiously perfect in its way, and to own absolutely nothing to recognised contemporary models. If Mr. Housman should write nothing more, this little book of his is yet likely to keep his name fresh in the history of poetry.

18. Charles Sorley on *A Shropshire Lad*

15 May 1913

Charles Sorley (1895–1915), poet, educated at King's College School, Cambridge, and Marlborough College. He studied in Germany from January to early August 1914, when he returned to England and enlisted in the Suffolk Regiment. He was killed at the Battle of Loos, 13 October 1915. His collection, *Marlborough, and Other Poems*, was published in 1916.

This was a paper read to members of the Marlborough College Literary Society and was printed in *The Letters of Charles Sorley* (Cambridge University Press, 1919), 48–53. Sorley had already given a paper on John Masefield, of twice this length, at Marlborough on 3 November 1912.

I am writing this paper under the impression that to the majority of my hearers A.E. Housman, as a poet, is not familiar. It must have been some German who first remarked that the best critic of Shakespeare is Shakespeare; from which we may deduce that the most competent critic of the Shropshire Lad is probably the Shropshire Lad himself. Consequently I do not feel many misgivings in making this paper little more than an annotated edition of selections from his works. And further, since I am presenting him tonight, as a dealer accustomed to puffing objects and possessions of real price might once in a way exhibit a curio without much comment, since the value of that curio depends very much on its defects: I shall avoid the role of either champion or iconoclast; nor burden you with any very startling exaggeration of his talents.

Mr. Lascelles Abercrombie, in a very brilliant book on Thomas Hardy which I have not read, has tried to define the poet as one who, having searched and reached a final idea or philosophy of the universe without him: having looked also, and found the essential distinctive kernel of the personality within him: can express the results of his successful search in words most suitable and most fair. The inadequacy of this definition may be measured by the fact that, according to it, the perfect poet would be Mr. A.E. Housman. He has come to a conclusion about the universe: he has found the essence of his own personality: and of these his expression is (to use purely two misused words) compleat and perfect. Let us see.

First, to show that as a language-maker alone, apart from what he expresses, he is second to none of his contemporaries and can sit beside almost any other English poet, except Shakespeare: I would read the following extracts.

>   IV ('Reveille'), stanzas 1, 2;
>   XXVIII ('Welsh Marches'), stanzas 1,2.

Now for his expression of his idea of the universe – the first postulate of Mr. Abercrombie – not only is it plain; it could not possibly be more plainly presented.

>   VII ('When smoke stood up from Ludlow');
>   XXVI ('Along the field as we came by');
>   XLVIII ('Be still, my soul').

And here I would add a note. The fact that rest is to be the end of Housman's existence prevents him, once for all, from being a great poet. None the less he stands high among the ungreat. He does not therefore advise sensuality as long as life lasts, like that dewy rhetorician Fitzgerald. And he looks forward and would welcome rest: but not the smooth accessible unearned rest that the average hymnast likes to point: not the charming semi-conscious post-prandial rest of Mr. W.B. Yeats: not even the more ideal but somewhat stagnant-smelling rest, Rossetti's 'Sunk stream, long unmet' – but a cold hard deathy [sic] rest, welcomed not for itself, because it has no pleasure to offer at all, but welcomed as less than the other evil, the evil of existence in an ailing earth.

But this somewhat self-satisfied dislike of life breeds no dislike of his fellow-partners in it. Indeed, one of the qualities in his nature that he brings into strong relief is a strong almost defiant love of man *quâ* man: of his fellow-creatures, for being creatures. He has given it a perfect expression; as in these:

IX ('On moonlit heath');
XXII ('The street sounds to the soldier's tread').

The quotations I have given you thus far may have produced a somewhat false impression to the effect that Housman is not much more than a peevish and perverse dyspeptic. This is not so at all. His idea of the universe and himself, and his impression of it, without any modification or inconsistency, can, if turned upon other sides of life, come very near nobility indeed. These following are as fine as anything I know.

I ('1887');
XXXV ('On the idle hill of summer')

I do not know much about the Greeks: perhaps something less than I ought to: but is has struck me that Housman would have pleased them very much. His perfect restraint and refinement of obloquy or irony: no less than his limited and reasonable conclusions about the universe: would have charmed many lesser Greek philosophers with the charm that is produced by reflecting 'That's exactly what I think too: and if I had had to express it, I should have expressed it in precisely the same way.'

XII ('When I watch the living meet').

Not only the perfect dual grammatical antitheses of the first two stanzas: but the root idea and thought of the poem culminating in a restrained regret that sensual pleasures are not practised after death, which makes the philosopher superior to their indulgence on earth – Greek, typically Greek. This side of his nature is startlingly stoical: as also is his cold refusal to take any pleasure in life except the grim but, I should think, fairly satisfying pleasure of knowing that 'high heaven and earth ail from their prime foundation' and pitying the ignorance of others on this subject. For this is the only thing he allows to give him pleasure, this, and Shropshire.

Shropshire. For Shropshire is the root of the inspiration of the man. And let us turn aside for a moment to consider a remarkable feature of his poetry – its earthiness. Every century or so poets have been returning to the earth, and with their return poetry becomes alive and true once more. Such a return was made at the end of the eighteenth century. And, as is inevitable with any noble movement in this country, it became before long vulgarized. Tennyson vulgarized it. A paltry poet in general, Tennyson is most pre-eminently paltry and superficial when he sings about nature and earth. He was not long in hedging her in with the shapely corsets of alliterative verbiage. Meredith was the first to break through this barrier and discover her again in her truth. England, however, was so busy reading Tennyson that they thought Meredith a clever novelist but too smart for them; and no poet at all. In our own days another poet has returned in truth to the earth – of course I am talking of Masefield. His return was purely emotional, and probably less interesting than the purely intellectual return of Meredith. Both men set out in exactly the opposite direction, but, being true poets, are making for exactly the same end. But what I wish to make clear here is that, in a much more limited and local way, Housman expresses the same root ideas, limited and localized, as they. All through the closing years of last century there has been a grand but silent revolution against the essential falseness and shallowness of the mid-Victorian court-poets. But all true poets (that is, poets who insist on truth) have been consciously or unconsciously in revolt: and Housman, whose fine hall-mark is his cold bare truth, is not the least of those (in the words of Earth's greatest seer) 'who read aright Her meaning and devoutly serve.'* This is how he read her:

XXXI ('On Wenlock Edge');
LV ('Westward on the high-hilled plains').

Such is the man. And if I were asked to put in one sentence his essential features, I should say they were primitive impulses and emotions, purged and civilized, as it were, but never essentially altered or improved, by a restrained and balanced intellect. And I should add that it was wonderful how restrained and balanced that intellect was, so that it is content with nothing but cold truth: that truth of his with its obstinate magnificent rejection of ideals, that so consistently chooses the evil and refuses the good as to make the evil something grand as well (so that we might well call him 'the hero that the grand refusal made'): and his fine artistic truth, which makes his portrait of himself so unflattering and admirable. And though his rejection of ideals bars the road to the stars and there is nothing noble, no onward motion in his poetry, there is much in it that is good to read. This compound of civilized instinct with primitive emotions has made him at his best reach the highest point of primitive virtue ('Woman bore me, I will rise'); and at his worst he never sinks below the demands of civilized morality. And if there is nothing ennobling in him, there is nothing that can lower man: if he has rejected ideals, he has purged and corrected reality. He lacks the attractive virtues of high striving and endeavour, but he keeps the somewhat duller virtues of temperance, patience and truth. He has no faith: but he has certainly no fear. And whatever else he is or is not, he is always himself. Perhaps no other English poet has been less influenced by the thoughts and words of the speakers of his or indeed of any other time. One thing and one only mated with his personality has produced his poetry, and that one thing is Shropshire. For Shropshire is the only true begetter of his poems. It has been the fitting flame to set alight his impotent irascible independent egotism. It is not certain whether anyone is the better from the *Shropshire Lad* ever having been written. But it is certain that it never would have been written, had the writer not been unavoidably controlled [*sic*] to write it ... But why do we go on admiring him thus? He does not want our admiration!

XXI ('Bredon Hill'.)

NOTE

* G. Meredith, *Poetical Works*, p. 321 ('Hard Weather').

19. James Elroy Flecker, conclusion (unfinished) of 'The New Poetry and Mr. Housman's "Shropshire Lad"'
Undated, pre-1915

James Elroy Flecker (1884–1915), poet, dramatist and diplomat. Educated at Uppingham School and Trinity College, Oxford, Flecker published the first of his five books of verse, *The Bridge of Fire*, in 1907. He entered the consular service in 1908, serving first at Constantinople and then, from 1911 to March 1913, in Beirut as Vice-Consul. He spent his last two years, in ill-health, in Switzerland, dying at Davos in January 1915. His *Collected Poems*, edited by J.C. Squire, were published in 1916; his most celebrated work, the poetic play *Hassan*, appeared in 1922.

This early, unpublished and unfinished essay (printed in Flecker's *Collected Prose* (Heinemann, 1922, 222–8)) was concerned 'to show that the significance and trend of modern poetry is the creation of a new poetical language to supersede the Victorian convention'. After referring, *inter alia*, to Stephen Phillips, William Watson, Swinburne, late Tennyson and Oscar Wilde's 'The Sphinx', it concludes with the following pages on Housman.

... But of all volumes of modern verse the 'Shropshire Lad' is the most complete vindication of this new and simple style, and is therefore a fit example to be given here.

Mr. A.E. Housman is famous as a classical scholar. This fact, and the fact that among these loving descriptions of country life and manners we find a classical manner and view of life, or even a classical theme, make it all the more surprising that he should have so entirely broken away from the tradition that gave us Tennyson's 'Ulysses', Swinburne's 'Erechtheus', or Mr. Murray's Swinburnian translations of Euripides. It is curious and pleasant to find interspersed among these village songs stray memories of the distant past of a distant land:

[quotes stanza 2 of No. XV]

This poem is marked by no difference of style from the others; and no one can fail to recognize here as elsewhere a happy exactness, a delight in making the point that, apart from any reference to the subject, mark the scholar. We are reminded of Landor at his briefest and best. Another poem, called 'The Merry Guide', describes how a youth with mien to match the morning, a youth with friendly brows, led the poet across glittering pastures, and by hanging woods, and by silver waters to the music of the great gale. The guide is some mysterious stranger, we know not who; the secret, previously hidden for so long, is in the last verse wonderfully revealed:

[quotes stanzas 14 and 15 of No. XLII]

We have begun by dwelling on an aspect of this work which, though fascinating, is not of paramount importance. At all events, the extracts serve as an introduction to anything there may be to say on the metres of the 'Shropshire Lad'. Except by Mr. Davidson in his powerful tales in verse, the simple stanzas of the ballads have not been often successfully used in the nineteenth century. In this book there are no complicated or involved measures, and no blank verse. There is one metre, however, the structure of which calls for especial notice.

[quotes stanza 2 of No. XXI]

It is a charming metre: the scazonic effect of the last line is wistfully harmonious. I would not rashly call it new. Who can lightly glance over all English Poetry with its manifold wealth of form to resolve such a question? But doubtless the author invented it for himself, and it is a fine invention, or, at events, a fine resuscitation.

There is also a simple metre rhyming in couplets, which the poet uses to obtain a majestic grace rather foreign to the quiet compassion, or compassionate horror, of the rest of the book:

[quotes stanza 2 of No. XXVIII]

We may compare with these powerful lines the elaborate and

sumptuous metaphor in the first verse of 'Reveille', which is in the older style:

[quotes stanza 1 of No. IV]

Within metres almost as limited and simple as those employed with ascetic choice by the author of 'Émaux et Camées' [Théophile Gautier], Mr. Housman exhibits a great subtlety of workmanship. It would not only be dreadfully prosaic, but also rather unfair to expose at any length his wizard tricks. The infinite joys that all true lovers of poetry find in the deft manipulation of verbal sounds are almost too sacred for explanation. Let a short poem be quoted almost at random:

[quotes No. LX]

The quiet and forcible alliterations of the first and last lines, the surprising vigour of the third, the impressive slowness of the fifth line is remarkable. There is, moreover, an art in the juxtaposition of sounds about which it is rather sacrilegious to talk, not because of any superhuman merit in this particular poem, but because the art of melody is one of suggestion, and not of code. For we must not over-praise Mr. Housman. As an inventive author we neither need nor dare compare him with the great names of the past. The verse of Mr. Bridges shows only too well by its combination of impeccable technique and extreme dullness and dearth of ideas, that it is all too easy to make lines sound pleasant in English by using simple language and simple metres. Spoken English is so intrinsically beautiful that a phrase like

> Look not left nor right

goes straight into poetry. Thus the very medium employed saves writers who employ the simpler style from those lapses into weakness or ugliness that beset the Victorians. It is far easier to preserve the virtues of terseness and strength in short and simple lines than in long and involved metres. A quiet style could never perpetrate such a line as that

> Who prop, thou ask'st, in these bad days, my mind?

which Matthew Arnold permitted to remain through edition

after edition of his works at the head of a fine sonnet. It is of course true that verse which is technically easy to construct is liable to lapse into carelessness of substance and idea; and the 'Shropshire Lad' is not free from weak and sentimental poems, from poems where the military subject is left to itself, as it were, to create an impression of strength, and others that express a mood and a thought so fleeting as to be without value. But, and this could be said of few books of vigorous poetry, there are no cacophonous lines.

Mr. Housman has achieved this fine result mainly because he has used pure spoken English with hardly any admixture of poetic verbiage. Indeed, some may blame him for putting such pleasant phrases into the mouths of peasants. If Browning was to be blamed for making his nobles talk slang, shall we not blame the poet who makes his peasants talk English?

While Mr. Housman's real justification for this is the great superiority of artistic effect, it is nevertheless a serious mistake to imagine that all peasants talk a coarse and corrupt tongue. Certainly in some parts of England a dialect is spoken which is fit only for caricature. But in other parts, such as the Welsh Borderlands, the natives speak in marvellously pure English. Similarly, Mr. Hardy's peasants talk at times the most excellent English, and a similar charge of unreality has been brought against them. Mr. Hardy seems to attempt some defence for this, when, at the beginning of 'Tess', he explains the refined speech of his heroine by a reference to the fourth standard of the Board School. It is a prosaic, but probable explanation. At all events Mr. Housman can by no means be said always to transcribe the peasant speech. It is his to invent, not to copy, and he makes subtle alterations which affect the poetry without changing the general impression of simplicity. The poem on Bredon Hill, of which a verse has just been quoted above, is put into the mouth of a peasant lover. He might possibly have talked of 'coloured counties', or used some very similar phrase. But no lover would have said the lark was 'about' him in the sky. He would have said 'above' undoubtedly. The change gives strength to the metre, and vigour to the phrase; but it is thoroughly artificial.

But it is not the subtlety of its language but its unity of subject, and its charm of feeling that has made the 'Shropshire Lad' almost a famous book, and enabled it to weather indifference. There is something even Homeric in his treatment of the old theme, Love, War, and Death, in a simple and young community. His lovers affect no higher idealism, no trappings of middle-class sentiment. The sense of the bloom fading from the rose, of the close following of death upon Love is the note of the Greek Anthology:

[quotes stanza 4 of No. XII]

Moreover, lest we get any idea of some foolish Arcadia where pine the lovesick swains, there are poems on suicide, murder, and 'men that tread on air'. For better or for worse fierce sins and a ghastly retribution are features of all English village life:

[quotes stanzas 5 and 7 of No. IX]

The whole poem is very terrible; and then in the next we are back again [Flecker's essay breaks off here.]

20. Holbrook Jackson, 'The Poetry of A.E. Housman', *To-day*

v, August 1919, 203–10

Holbrook Jackson (1874–1948), author, editor, editorial director of National Trade Press, Ltd. Jackson was the editor of *T.P.'s Weekly* (1914–16) and of *To-day* (1917–23). He published various books on literary subjects and literary figures, including *The Eighteen Nineties* (1913).

I have always held that a poet need not be a poet, that, in fact, he may even be something quite other than a poet, and yet contribute to our great heritage of song. I shall not quote instances, although there are many, but one of the most remarkable in our time is that of Mr. A.E. Housman, about whom we know very little, save that he is a professor of Latin at Cambridge University, a philologist of distinction, and, most important of all, author of 'A Shropshire Lad.' It is a book whose title forms very little indication of the contents. It might be a novel, or a play, or a dissertation on the youth of Salopia. But it is none of these. It is also a very little volume, but big with poetic importance. During the last thirty years or so much fine poetry has been added to English literature, but few if any poets satisfy so completely both the demands of literary opinion and the human heart.

Alfred Edward Housman was born on March 26, 1859, and was educated first at Bromsgrove School, and afterwards at St. John's College, Oxford, where he took his M.A. degree. From 1882 to 1892 he followed the humdrum pursuits of a Higher Division Clerk in the Patent Office. In the latter year scholarly predilection took him from the Civil Service, and he became Professor of Latin at the University of London, a position held by him until 1911, when he was appointed to the Chair he still occupies at Cambridge. He has also attained the distinction of honorary membership of his college at Oxford. His poems were published in 1896, but his literary work since that date has been devoted entirely to classical and philological studies. In 1903 he edited 'Manilius,' Book I, and Book II in 1912; in 1905 the performed a like service for 'Juvenal'; for the rest the printed results of his scholarship may be found in the files of the *Journal of Philology*, the *Classical Review*, and the *Classical Quarterly*. Such facts are all that Mr. Housman will permit to be published. He has no sympathy with the modern craving for personalia, and the fact of his having written a volume of poems, which is treasured wherever there is love of good poetry, does not, in his opinion, form a sufficient excuse for the toleration of a nearer public approach. Naturally we should like to know more of the man who wrote such perfect poems during a limited period of his life, and then, for some unknown reason, laid down the lyre, apparently for ever. There is this, however, to be said: the poems of A.E. Housman have won to the hearts of poetry-lovers without any exterior aid. They have been advertised very little, remarkably few articles have been devoted to them, and, as we have seen, their author has consistently avoided anything which could be construed as personal propaganda. Housman has put himself into his work and kept himself out of the shop window. Let us, therefore, turn to the man as revealed in his work.

If I were a poet I would crave no higher acceptance (I do not think there is any higher acceptance) than that of those who are living the strenuous life of the hour in whatever walk it has pleased fate to call them. If, in addition, I received the appreciation of those who were cultured and scholarly, I should be doubly pleased. Now I think the poetry of A.E. Housman has qualities which compel both forms of acceptance. Let me give an instance of the sort of thing I mean. I met an acquaintance who had returned to England from one of the wildest parts of Central America. The war, he told me, had so affected his affairs out there that he had no recourse but to return home. 'And what are you doing with yourself?' I asked; and I want you to mark well his reply. He did not say 'Nothing in particular', or 'Oh, just loafing around,' although he was doing nothing in particular from the average point of view. He said: 'I am staying down at — (mentioning a military encampment near London) reading "A Shropshire Lad" to the soldiers – and, by gad! don't they love it!'

Incidentally, and surprisingly, taking into account Housman's scholarly life, many of the poems in 'A Shropshire Lad' move to the sound of bugles, and all of them are robust as a man of action rather than a scholar might understand robustness. Yet they have none of the staccato boisterousness which distinguishes the soldier-poems of Rudyard Kipling, or the traditional romanticism of the sailor-poems of Sir Henry Newbolt. I use the comparison not in disparagement of either Kipling or Newbolt, but by way of distinguishing one type of poetry from another. Housman is equally robust, or manly, if you like, but he brings deeper reflection to his theme, less apparent effort, and he is passionate where they are emotional. He does not depend for effect upon the heroics of splendid activity, but upon the meditative reactions of soldiering. For instance, let us take his moving lyric called 'The Recruit':

> Leave your home behind, lad,
>   And reach your friends your hand,
> And go, and luck go with you
>   While Ludlow Tower shall stand.

> Oh, come you home of Sunday
> When Ludlow streets are still
> And Ludlow bells are calling
> To farm and lane and mill.

There, in brief lines and simple words, you have concentrated the feelings of those who lose a lad to soldiering, and they imply the feelings also of the recruit himself in association with home sights and sounds. But there is no mawkish regret. The pensive note is natural and universal. You find it also in the popular music-hall ballad, 'We don't want to lose you, but we think you ought to go,' put, of course, less poetically and less profoundly, but none the less truly. Nor does Housman reject the martial and patriotic appeal of soldiering:

> And you will list the bugle
> That blows in lands of morn,
> And makes the foes of England
> Be sorry you were born.

The patriot element of the poems does not depend for effect upon flags and trumpets. Cheers and tears companion one another, and such tumult as they have is inward, the beating of a humble and a contrite heart at the tragedy of patriotic heroism and sacrifice.

The two themes, tragedy and heroism, go hand in hand; not apart, as in false romance. Housman's soldier is brave in the great spirit. He does not go to war convinced that he will escape with his life; he goes to war convinced that he may lose his life, and, because it is necessary, he goes willingly, cheerfully, hoping for nothing but the good luck of good fortune.

Nor does the poet forget the more human accessories of soldiering. He does not separate his Shropshire lad from love and good cheer. You feel always that there is a girl lurking in the back-ground with warm heart for the soldier lad, and, at the end of the day's march, a tankard of ale:

The lads in their hundreds to Ludlow come in for the fair,
  There's men from the barn and the forge and the mill and the fold;
The lads for the girls and the lads for the liquor are there,
  And there with the rest are the lads that will never be old.

And somewhere the soldier's thoughts go back to the girl he left behind him:

A.E. HOUSMAN

> Is my girl happy
>   That I thought hard to leave,
> And has she tired of weeping
>   As she lies down at eve?

You get glimpses of soldiers marching away, and of mothers' eyes and hearts following them, and you are given to understand that such things are hard to bear on both sides, as you always did understand, although you never tire of being reminded of it; and also that there are valiant hearts capable of facing and bearing such trials. In a beautiful lyric the quintessence of regret is revealed with a master's touch:

> With rue my heart is laden
>   For golden friends I had,
> For many a rose-lipt maiden
>   And many a lightfoot lad.

Some of Housman's lyrics have all the grace of the little songs of the Shakespearean era.

The philosophy of the poems may be described as a cheerful pessimism. You are reminded somewhat of Omar Khayyám – with the mysticism left out. But the fatalism is all there, although it is never the reconciled, and, on the whole, hopeless fatalism of the East. I cannot find any marked trace in Housman's point of view of hopefulness for to-morrow. There is sufficient of pain and joy in to-day, and the net result of the whole business of life is somehow good. Life is a buffeting, but there is joy in the battle:

> Clay lies still, but blood's a rover;
>   Breath's a ware that will not keep.
> Up, lad; when the journey's over
>   There'll be time enough to sleep.

One would imagine that the author of 'A Shropshire Lad' took the same view of death as Walt Whitman. Not so much that death is a benignant mother, welcoming all at length with open arms; although equally benignant, death for him is more in the nature of an impersonal fact steeped in the infinite wisdom of quietness. Since we needs must die some day, and since it is our nature to stave off that day as long as possible, it is on the whole wise to die. He is reconciled as the philosopher is reconciled:

> Yet down at last he lies
> And then the man is wise.

There is one poem in the little book in which the Housman point of view seems to have crystallized. The poet is upbraided by 'A Shropshire Lad' for his melancholy lay, and he is bidden to 'Pipe a tune to dance to,' and the implication is that beer is more exalting than such verse:

> Why, if 'tis dancing you would be
> There's brisker pipes than poetry
> Say, for what were hopyards meant,
> Or why was Burton built on Trent?
> Oh many a peer of England brews
> Livelier liquor than the Muse,
> And malt does more than Milton can
> To justify God's ways to man.
> Ale, man, ale's the stuff to drink
> For fellows whom it hurts to think:
> Look into the pewter pot
> To see the world as the world's not.

But actually the poet refuses to do so, for the reason that he is aware of the mischief following such proceedings. I do not know whether we are to take literally the poet's confession that he has often been to Ludlow Fair and left his necktie God knows where! I should say not. But I think we are justified in taking literally the following explanation of his own attitude to his own Muse:

> Therefore, since the world has still
> Much good, but much less good than ill,
> And while the sun and moon endure
> Luck's a chance, but trouble's sure,
> I'd face it as a wise man would,
> And train for ill and not for good.
> 'Tis true, the stuff I bring for sale
> Is not so brisk a brew as ale:
> Out of the stem that scored the hand
> I wrung it in a weary land.
> But take it; if the smack is sour,
> The better for the embittered hour;
> It should do good to heart and head
> When your soul is in my soul's stead;

A.E. HOUSMAN

And I will friend you, if I may,
In the dark and cloudy day.

People are frightened of the word pessimism, and the word optimism has become a folly and a weariness of the flesh. Nowadays it is tripped about the market-place like a vain thing, so that wise folk shun it. But one should beware of labels whatever they are. Actually there is no pessimism and less optimism. Those of us who are blessed with health of body and mind, and even those who have only health of mind, are impelled by instinct to be as happy as possible, so long as they are not thinking about their little or their great woes. Perhaps, after all, happiness that comes naturally is the only form of health, and the healthy person resents a spurious happiness whether in verse or laughter. Housman must be ranked amongst the happy poets because he is strong enough to look sorrow in the face.

Despite the eternal regret which Housman shares with the Book of Ecclesiastes, with Lucretius, with Omar, with Keats, his most restless lines burn with the bright stillness of Pater's gem-like flame. It is the stillness of depth and intensity; an English calm of manner reflecting balance and control of feeling. A.E. Housman is very English, and his sense of love reaches nearest to passion at thought of the English scene. Shropshire in all her pastoral loveliness lives in his verses and there is no shire more English despite its proximity to Wales. Whether he sings of noble Shrewsbury herself where

> The flag of morn in conqueror's state
> Enters at the English gate:
> The vanquished eve, as night prevails,
> Bleeds upon the road to Wales;

or Ludlow; or Teme or Borne or Severn, or 'the wild green hills of Wyre,' the Wrekin, or 'the high-reared head of Clee,' he catches and enchains in his art the colour and character of place and the love thereof. Generally he achieves his effects by the difficult way of simplicity. He has no tricks either of metre or manner. He sings in the great tradition. Sometimes he surprises by the fine excess of well-conceived imagery, but more often by excessive fineness of thought and feeling in fastidiously chosen and inevitably placed words of the simplest class. He is a poet apart from 'movements.' The decadence which saw the birth of 'A Shropshire Lad' passed it by. Housman was in it, but not of it. Whilst every young poet of the nineties was dipping his bucket into foreign and often not very clean wells, he was quaffing the undefiled waters of English song. Something of the spirit of folk-song, something of Elizabethan lyricism, something of peasant dialect song, but in normal language, and something of all that is sweet and strong and simple of the English poetry, which does not depend for attraction upon conceits or tricks, or need to experiment, because it is allied with a tradition which cannot die.

21. Harold Monro on Housman
1920

Harold Monro (1879–1932), poet, editor and entrepreneur of letters. He started to publish his own poetry, and that of others, from the Samurai Press, Cranleigh, Surrey, which he founded in about 1906. In 1911 he founded the *Poetry Review*, in 1913 the Poetry Bookshop in London (which continued to operate until Monro's death), and in 1919 the *Chapbook*, a monthly magazine that ran until 1925.

In *Some Contemporary Poets* (pp. 17–18), Munro attributes the 'new movement' in poetry preponderantly to *A Shropshire Lad*, 'the influence of which can be heard ringing through the verse of more than half the younger living poets of the strictly *English* school'. For Monro, *A Shropshire Lad* was 'the antithesis of that bulky pomposity of late Victorianism'.

Section I of Part III ('Poets and Poetasters of Our Time'), *Some Contemporary Poets* (Leonard Parsons, 1920), 47–50.

The style of A.E. Housman is built of a combination of all the principal elements of popular poetry. His subjects are those most common to human existence; friendship, love, character, heroism, homesickness, crime, death, the last figuring in excessive proportion to the others; at least a quarter of his book is solely about Death. He uses the traditional ballad-forms and song-forms; his rhythms are of the simplest kind; many of his poems tell a story; all contain at least the elements of a story, and all 'sing'. He very frequently rouses feelings of pity; he stimulates love of home and of the native-land; he excites admiration for heroic action; he touches constantly and ironically on the disappointments of young love. All the most ordinary things that people do, see or think in the course of their little lives are mentioned in his poems. Two salient characteristics mark them as different from the rest of their kind: his philosophy of life and death, and some peculiar personal method in his use of vocabulary and form.

Some one has called *A Shropshire Lad* the 'English Rubaiyat' – a suggestive comparison. These English lyrics present a western version of that philosophy of life contained in Fitzgerald's beautiful fragment from the Eastern poet. Neither work is pessimistic: each offers a compensation for the certainty that death is a final end to personal existence. The western compensation is Friendship, a word the true meaning of which clergymen and social workers try to confuse by spelling it 'Brotherhood'.

Mr. Housman's style can be analysed with as much ease and more success than it can be imitated. It is coloured by the very frequent use of local names: Shropshire; Severn; Ludlow; Shrewsbury; Bredon; Corve; Teme; Hughley. It is characterised by the persistent recurrence of a certain type of word or phrase, chiefly rustic: boys; lovers; lads; wedding; fair; sweetheart; chap; friend; comrade; youth; one-and-twenty; good people; my love and I; the lads and the girls; fortunate fellows; country lover; girls go maying; golden friends; Dick and Ned; rose-lipped maiden and lightfoot lad.

It shows the greatest forbearance, containing not a word too many and revealing a complete resistance to the common temptation to add ornament, the yielding to which has ruined the style of many a lesser poet. It conveys the appearance of ease, and the feeling of vigour. It is truly a style: not a *manner*. Lastly, where it includes poetical devices or the use of inversion, these are so discriminatingly managed as to render them either unobtrusive, or else noticeably and characteristically proper to their context.

The compilation of *A Shropshire Lad* evidently covered a period of several years. Its poems appear to represent successive phases of a disciplined literary development: they are suggestive individually of a series of recreative holidays, of spasmodic escapes from the atmosphere of a scholarly routine. Their most inventive metrical innovation is best represented in that well-known lyric, 'Bredon Hill'. Here we have an ordinary half-rhymed, three-stressed quatrain; the unrhymed lines with a feminine termination. The structure and rhythm of the stanza is such, according to the traditions of English verse, as to make the reader expect the certainty of a halt at the end of each fourth line. The device, therefore, of adding a fifth line, with a plaintive echoing cadence, to each quatrain is one which never fails to produce a pleasurable surprise both in the case of each stanza and on every new reading of the whole poem.

Our complaint against A.E. Housman must be that he is not a genius. In the steady light of such talent, we others are able to sit down comfortably, and examine, joint by joint, the artificial structure that we suspect, while no flash interferes with the routine of our analytical speculations. Thus it has happened that his followers have developed a kind of school of designed pseudo-perfectitude, based vicariously upon, but uninformed by the native impulses that flow through the stanzas of that new intellectual folk-poetry he has so deftly invented.

LAST POEMS
1922

22. 'The "Shropshire Lad" again', *Times Literary Supplement*
19 October 1922, 622

The review is unsigned.

It is long since the music of *A Shropshire Lad* first enchanted men's ears, and since that wonderful outburst of song it has been mute through so many springs and autumns that we had nearly given up the hope of hearing it again. But here is the voice once more, in an accent as identical as one book may have with another. So swift, indeed, is the renewal that, if the older verses had not pretty well committed themselves to heart, we should imagine ourselves to be reading *A Shropshire Lad* again: –

> The plum broke forth in green,
>   The pear stood high and snowed,
> My friends and I between
>   Would take the Ludlow road.

Again that road beckons us into a land of radiance and sorrow, loveliness and briefness. But as we take it, feeling it the same, and feeling also the same outlook in the poet, we become aware of a certain difference, after all, in what seemed an identity. It is not a change of scene or temper, but lies in the pitch and quality of the writer's feeling. A phrase in Mr. Housman's terse and interesting foreword is enlightening as to what the change may be. Speaking of the unlikeliness of his writing much more poetry, he says that he 'can no longer expect to be revisited by the continuous excitement' under which he wrote the greater part of his earlier book. These words are significant, not as regards his own poetry only, but all lyrical poetry. It is not always, or ever perhaps – whatever one writer of great lyrics might have said – 'emotion recollected in tranquillity'. The poet's labour may be cool enough, but his sensibility must be in the vividest excitement if its elements are to fuse. The rareness of *A Shropshire Lad* was that under what its writer avows to have been a stress of great emotion his feelings poured themselves unstintingly into a faultless mould.

The mould is the same here, and, speaking humanly, faultless; but the degree of fusion is not quite the same. Is it sheer fidelity to an old love that makes one think there are few poems in this new book, even when its shortness has been allowed for, which, like so many in the other, steal the heart with golden dreams, stab it as with a knife, or give a passionate sense of beauty and comradeship? We hardly think so. Perhaps the singular feat of transferring a very subtle consciousness to impersonate the country lad, in a way that was by turns simple, exquisite and brutal, could only be achieved at a very high tension. In this little book we are more aware of a process; it does not give the sharp thrill of immediacy so often, or ring so deep. It has lost a little of the vividness; there is less, for instance, of that enchanting nearness to the hills and trees. Yet the power of vision is there, if not the impulse, and the music is there, too; notice Mr. Housman's slight but beautiful variation in these verses on his own melody and that of others: –

[quotes stanzas 1 and 2 of No. XL]

And so through two other stanzas to the end, where he resigns his joys: –

[quotes stanza 5 of No. XL]

In his 'Epitaph on an Army of Mercenaries', which was published in the war, Mr. Housman has obeyed an impulse, and condensed it in a superbly tense epigram. But his longest poem, 'Hell Gate', is perhaps the most interesting in the book, since here he leaves his usual scene for a wholly imaginative one, handling the sinister idea so well as to make us wish he would roam more often. Why, if he can do that, should these be his 'Last Poems'?

But this book itself may supply the answer. The vein that he chose first, and keeps, must have been the truest expression of his feeling. It seems, in essence, a romantic feeling, though his classic, definite form and the starkness of his mood may appear to deny that. But there is the romantic note in its defiance, in the regrets, the sense of homelessness; and when one of his characters says,

> I, a stranger and afraid
> In a world I never made,

we seem to catch the apprehensiveness which has called for resolution. Romance and the real are queerly blended in the friendships and violence of his country lads. Under the keen sense of mortal, lovely things there is a youthful melancholy, which may explain why the incitement to write more poetry has dwindled. But a sensibility with very marked limits will live, if it is deep enough, as we can see in a case like Poe's; and Mr. Housman's verse, unmistakably individual in accent, should live because it has expressed some passionate moments with the last felicity.

23. Edmund Gosse, 'The Shropshire Lad', *Sunday Times*
22 October 1922

Edmund Gosse (1849–1928) was privately educated, then worked as an assistant librarian at the British Museum, as a translator for the Board of Trade, and (1904–14) as librarian of the House of Lords. He combined these various duties with a prolific career as poet and man of letters, publishing books on such figures as Donne, Jeremy Taylor, Coventry Patmore and Swinburne, as well as *Father and Son* (1907). His *Collected Poems* appeared in 1911, his *Collected Essays* (in five volumes) in 1913. He was knighted in 1925.

Housman responded to Gosse's review in a letter of 25 October 1922 saying, 'I thought you were very nice about me in the Sunday Times', and copying out for him the poem 'Tarry, delight' (later published as No. XV in *More Poems*), which he had omitted from *Last Poems*.

Reprinted from Edmund Gosse, *More Books on the Table* (1923), 21-6.

Twenty-six years ago a slender volume of poems by an unknown hand was cast upon the world. Christians were being murdered in Crete and the Kaiser was congratulating Mr. Kruger on his repulse of the Jameson Raid; so universal was the stagnation of the world that the noise of these events went echoing from pole to pole. The English poetry of the moment was in keeping with the luxury and somnolence of life; it sang of Fléet Street and the music-halls, it was delicately gregarious. The new poet of 1896 wrote in a tone which clashed abruptly with this artificial and ornamented elegance. The little thrilling songs of the Shropshire Lad were severe and bare, not acquainted at all with the gaiety of towns, but concerned exclusively with the meditations of a lonely life, haunted by memories of an extreme instinctive simplicity.

The verse of Mr. A.E. Housman, therefore, belonging to no recognised school, and disdaining every species of extrinsic attraction, was very little noticed at first, was even dismissed by hasty reviewers as creditable 'minor verse' of small significance. But clearer-sighted or sharper-eared readers found themselves arrested and then bewitched by its secret beauty, which enslaved the ear as some subterranean music of goblins might do, heard at twilight in a sequestered glade. Its charm, once detected, remained indestructible, and since 1896 all catholic lovers of poetry have known that though new bards in myriads arise and push the old bards into obscurity, there is one pure, small sound that can never be silenced – the flute of the Shropshire Lad piping where

> Clunton and Clunbury,
> Clungunford and Clun,
> Are the quietest places
> Under the sun.

But the little volume had no successor, and when a quarter of a century had passed over it, leaving it as fresh but as disconcertingly isolated as ever, it might well seem that Mr. A.E. Housman would live among our notable poets on the score of an 'output' as scanty as that of Gray or Collins. Suddenly, without any preliminary flourish, there comes to us a second volume, of the same slender dimensions as the first, in which the familiar voice speaks to us again out of the cloud. It is the same voice; it is a continuation of the old theme, for the tone, which was so clear and personal in 1896, is as individual as ever in 1922.

If there is any change at all, it is in the direction of a completer technical excellence. In the original volume there were, as we may prove by returning to it, one or two pieces in which the metrical skill was a little dubious, where the tune wavered on the instrument. In the new volume I cannot discover any fault of this kind, the mastery of technique having become complete, the music impeccable. But there is no essential difference, and for this my thanks are offered to the Muses. Essentially we wanted an expansion, not a change, in this sensitive, unique, and unrelated thing. We wanted, not another *Shropshire Lad*, but more of the old one, and that is what we have got.

It is well that we hold exactly what we wished for, since we are to receive no more. A sad little foreword says that those pieces are now published because it is not likely that the poet will 'ever be impelled to write much more.' The word 'much' just keeps the door of hope ajar, but we must take it that these poems, most of which were written before 1910, represent the final harvest: –

> We'll to the woods no more,
> The laurels all are cut,
> The bowers are bare of bay
> That once the Muses wore;
> The year draws in the day
> And soon will evening shut:
> The laurels all are cut,
> We'll to the woods no more.
> Oh, we'll no more, no more
> To the leafy woods away,
> To the high wild woods of laurel
> And the bowers of bay no more.

There were sixty-three pieces in the original collection, and there are forty-one in the present, so that we may take it that one hundred short lyrics will be Mr. Housman's bequest to posterity. There are many writers of profuse and successful production who might well wish that they could cut down their publications to a century of as much excellence as this.

Mr. Housman is not one of those poets for whom the choice of a subject is needless, and for whom all subjects are equally good, Coleridge, in a whimsical utterance, seems to hold that diversity of theme is the essential characteristic of free poetical genius. There is something to be said for a formula that explains such wide expanses as the work of Browning and Victor Hugo, but intensity may be gained at the expense of breadth. Mr. Housman, at all events, has, as it seems to me, only one subject, which he treats in a hundred ways. He is the poet of *desiderium*, of the unconquerable longing for what is gone for ever, for youth which has vanished, for friends that are dead, for beauty that was a mirage.

This hopeless desire is concentrated on one scene of English landscape, silent and vague hills and solitary fields which certain proper names identify with a particular district – namely, with that part of the pastoral county of Salop which borders westward on the hills of Wales. Mr. Housman never describes this country, but he indicates its character in a way which exceeds the impression made by any topographical survey, however accurate. I have wandered on 'the high-hilled plains,' needing no guide but one little olive-coloured book of verses: –

> And I would climb the beacon
> That looked to Wales away.

For a collection of lyrics at all analogous to *A Shropshire Lad* (as now concluded) I do not know where we can turn save to the *Buch der Lieder*. The form of Mr. Housman often closely resembles Heine's: –

> In the morning, in the morning,
>   In the happy field of hay,
> Oh, they looked at one another
>   By the light of da
>
> In the blue and silver morning,
>   On the haycock as they lay,
> Oh, they looked at one another –
>   And they looked away.

There the outward resemblance to Heine is complete, more so than is usual with Mr. Housman, but the essential character of the work even here is not really Heinesque. The reflective melancholy, what I have called the *desiderium* of the Shropshire Lad, is something radically distinct from the cynicism of the great German lyrist, and is not occupied, as his was, with anger and repulsion, with irony and humour. It is a thing much more simple and primitive; it is almost passive in its brooding sweetness. Moreover — and this is perhaps the source of Mr. Housman's intimate charm — it is always mysterious. Nothing is told right out; the emotion is veiled and discreet; we are left to conjecture what is the exact nature of it. The language which this poet employs is not merely severe and chaste, it is often colloquial; it seems to tell the most natural things in the simplest speech. But below this quiet surface there is a ceaseless mystification, an obvious sense that the half is not told us: —

> The night is freezing fast,
>   To-morrow comes December;
>   And winterfalls of old
> Are with me from the past;
>   And chiefly remember
>   How Dick would hate the cold.
>
> Fall, winter, fall; for he
>   Prompt hand and headpiece clever,
>   Has woven a winter robe,
> And made of earth and sea
>   His overcoat for ever,
>   And wears the turning globe.

That is all, and it seems enough, told in this austere and lucid language; yet how little it explains of all that it is needless for us to know! This is the very essence of perfect lyrical writing, to be a polished pebble flung into dark waters, awaking one circle after another of wonder and reverie and vague emotion, 'infinite longing, and the pain of finite hearts that yearn,' as another poet says.

In the new volume there is perhaps nothing so violent as *The True Lover* or *On Moonlit Heath and Lonesome Bank*, in which Mr. Housman was emphatic in extending his sympathy even to murderers and suicides if they were the desperate victims of an unselfish passion. The indulgence of unupbraiding affection covered, as with a mantle, sin and even crime. These are sentiments which may be dangerous in prose, but to verse all things are permitted. In the new book we have similar tragedies, but expressed, or hinted at, with less intensity. The poet plucks the blue blossom that springs at the four cross-ways: —

> It seemed a herb of healing,
>   A balsam and a sign,
> Flower of a heart whose trouble
>   Must have been worse than mine.
>
> Dead clay that did me kindness,
>   I can do none for you,
> But only wear for breastknot
>   The flower of sinner's rue.

The longest piece in the collection — *Hell Gate* — is certainly the most powerful which Mr. Housman has published, yet can be ruined by partial quotation. It is a dream of punishment and eternal pain, mitigated only by the enduring love of those for whom error and disgrace veil not a whit the inner beauty of a soul whose sins are misfortunes and whose shame is accidental. The whole philosophy of *A Shropshire Lad* is involved in the tenderness and the horror of this vision, to my mind one of the most extraordinary which the present age has produced. *Hell Gate* gives me a suspicion that if Mr. Housman had chosen to cultivate this sulphurous fury he might have written a new *Inferno*. The vision of the accoutred soldier, all on fire, pacing as a sentinel before the gate of hell, and shining from far off as a spark against the darkness,

> Trim and burning, to and fro,
> One for women to admire
> In his finery of fire,

who, as the poet approached,

> turned his head,
> Looked, and knew me, and was Ned,

is overwhelming. Throughout this little volume regretful pity and shadowy passion pass and repass like the flaming sentry at the gate of hell, and the poet stands and gazes in a trace of melancholy pain. And hopeless longing is the end of it all: —

> So here's an end of roaming
>   On eves when autumn nighs;

A.E. HOUSMAN

> The ear too fondly listens
> For summer's parting sighs,
> And then the heart replies.

24. D.C.T., 'Professor Housman's Last Poems', *Cambridge Review*

xliv, No. 1077, 27 October 1922, 46

The first sentence is partially in error; the first edition of *A Shropshire Lad* had been published twenty-six years before, but not by Grant Richards.

It is twenty-six years since Mr. Grant Richards published the first edition of *A Shropshire Lad*; some of us have been asking for more ever since. And now Professor Housman gives us forty-one final lyrics, which all true lovers of the best and purest art in modern English verse will sit down and taste, slowly and critically, a little at a time, and one may safely add, with no sense of anticlimax. For a great feat has been accomplished, and a true poet and consummate craftsman has repeated a triumph.

Not that the new book can be described as a mere sequel to the old, for the almost uncanny similarity in so much of it only emphasizes the subtle difference in the remainder. *Last Poems* is the inevitable complement, more thoughtful, more hopeless, more mature. We do not find the happy lyrical cry of some of the pieces of 1896 – of 'From Clee to Heaven the Beacon Burns', or 'High the Vanes of Shrewsbury Gleam', with little of that 'poetry of names' which has made the former book ring so peculiarly true to that still too rare bird, the genuine Salopian who knows at first hand his Clee and his Ludlow and his Wenlock Edge. This is rather a book of farewell:

> We'll to the woods no more,
> The laurels all are cut,

sings the minstrel on the first page, and ends no less exquisitely with a little masterpiece, 'Fancy's Knell', so fragile that one dare not quote.

Only half the length of its predecessor, this final book of poems succeeds in avoiding its occasional lapses in technique, if not its proverbial fatalism, and the change is for the good every time. Two only, as far as we know, have been printed before: the 'Epitaph on an Army of Mercenaries' from the *Times*, of the early August of 1914, already secure of fame, and a delightfully characteristic piece – the second in the book – which we noticed in *The Trinity Magazine* some two years ago. The rest is new, and our Housman is our Housman still, a lyrist who stands alone today with the Poet Laureate and Mr. de la Mare and Mr. Yeats, not unworthy of such high company.

For above all he has not lost his greatest asset – a priceless gift of phrase which flashes out again and again

[quotes ll. 3–4 of No. XXI]

or

[quotes ll. 5–6 of No. XIX]

or

[quotes ll. 1–4 of No. XXXIII]

One thinks of *The Ancient Mariner*, sometimes of *Hamlet*.

It will be interesting as time goes on to see what particular niche in the temple of fame this worthy upholder of Cambridge classical learning and sweet song is destined to occupy. The reader closes the book with the same feelings as he closes the Book of Job and the *Rubaiyat*, feelings of the hopelessness of things mingled with admiration of their beauty so skilfully captured and set down for all who have ears to hear. It would perhaps be ungracious to expect more of any poet.

The Shropshire Lad has grown old, and this last bequest shows it: we admire no less, but we hope no more. It will be best to leave the last word to Mr. Housman himself, and his book to the verdict of posterity, in quiet confidence of the result. So let us take two passages almost at random.

[quotes stanzas 2 and 3 of No. XL]

and lastly, one entire poem:

[quotes No. XXVII]

25. B.S., review, *Manchester Guardian Weekly*

vii, No. 18, 3 November 1922, 352

It is a little unkind of Professor Housman to accompany his gift of charming verses with a resolution to give the world no more. Here are forty poems, of which ten were written last April. What reason is there why other Aprils should not produce at least their five? Intrinsically, none; but Professor Housman loves conclusions; nine out of ten of his poems turn on death. He does not believe in survival; and death presents to him, in consequence, the sinister appeal of an object which having two sides can never be seen except from one. In the case of his own muse he would evade the dilemma by himself pronouncing the sentence and presiding at the obsequies. The magic of his art has been a household word in the land for nearly twenty years, during which he has been silent; not, however, because he has lost it.

[quotes stanza 1 of No. XV]

Such is his marvellous description of the clock striking for the noosed criminal whose hour is come; and it is not very far from his thought that we are all more or less such criminals, some luckier than others in that their date is rather longer postponed, or unluckier in that they have longer to contemplate the approach of it; while, as for our guilt, it belongs in its various degrees to the world that made us what we are. How beautiful that world is:

[quotes stanza 1 of No. XL]

and how unrelenting:

[quotes stanza 3 of No. XXXV]

Seldom is it that a poet, at odds with life, has the candour to reduce his difference to terms as quintessential as these! But the mainspring of Professor Housman's muse is, after all, dissatisfaction, dissatisfaction with all but beauty, nor is the exception so important as it seems; for those who regard it as the only value beauty is but a shadow of itself.

[quotes stanza 2 of No. XXVII]

How delicately lovely the expression here, how radically sentimental the thought, offering consolation in one line merely to have the pleasure of brushing it away in another! The classic purity of Professor Housman's outlines and the assurance of his subtle craft must not blind the reader to his sentimentalism. If death is the end of all things life loses many values which are a source of high inspiration to believers in a life beyond; and one of the values which it loses is, surely, its interest in death. Death becomes merely the dark background in front of which the values that remain stand out more vividly. The function of art in that case is not to keep on reinforcing the black, but to enhance our enjoyment of the lights and colours while we have them.

[quotes stanza 8 of No. I]

Professor Housman himself endorses the point, but he does not act up to his recommendation; the thought of parting is so much with him that, in his beautiful Epithalamium itself, he reminds us that a man cannot so much as marry a wife without abandoning a best man! That, certainly, is a case of $2 + 2 = 4$, with a vengeance.

26. J.C. Squire, review, *London Mercury*
vii, November 1922, 94–5

John Collings Squire (1884–1958), noted 'Georgian' poet, literary editor of the *New Statesman* from 1913, founder of the *London Mercury* and its editor from 1919 to 1934. He was knighted in 1933.

Twenty-six years have passed since *A Shropshire Lad* was published. It had been written, as the author now parenthetically tells us, under the influence of a 'continuous excitement' in the early months of 1895. He became Professor of Latin at Cambridge; he edited *Manilius*; he and everybody else grew older. For twenty years it has been a common question in the Press and elsewhere whether he was writing any more, and, if so, when he would publish. No answer ever came from Mr. Housman; except once, and then only with eight lines on a great national emergency, he preserved as a poet an obstinate silence; the papers got from him neither poems nor news of poems. This year a sudden revisitation of the muse brought his secret hoard to the number of forty-one poems; he has now unlocked them, as he says, lest too much time should pass and the turning of the key be left to other hands.

Many of the 'new' poems are old; the more recent are not easily distinguishable from the others. 'Comrade, look not on the west', he says; but he looks always at the west. His paganism, modern paganism, with a Christian heart, unreconciled, remains unchanged; the world is an evil and beautiful place, and death ends both the evil and the beauty. We must endure the one and enjoy the other while we may; then we shall go the way of better fellows. There are new forms of stanza in the book, but they are natural modifications of the old; the book is an extension of the first book, and it is as good. That is the surprising thing; though the author's heart and mind, thought and speech are unmodified, though the ageing man is what the youth was, no slackening of effort is perceptible in their reiterations of the old things. Every genuine moment of impulse should produce good work from a real poet; Mr. Housman, keeping long silent in its absence, has never written except from a genuine impulse; and his gift of concentrated labour is unimpaired. A few new images; that is all. These are 'extra numbers' to the *Shropshire Lad*, as good as the old, and no different – except for the strange imaginative outbreak *Hell's Gate* [sic], and a few poems which look far backward.

The book closes with three perfect poems of farewell, all full of an autumnal beauty. He takes leave successively of life and the hopes of life, of the landscapes he has loved, and of his art. In youth there was always a prospect of summers beyond the snow:

[quotes stanza 6 of No. XXXIX]

The hills and valleys, the shining roads, and the forests which 'would murmur and be mine' are now haunted by others. 'Possess', he says to them:

> as I possessed a season
> The countries I resign

for Nature cares nothing as to what strangers find her meadows and 'trespass there and go.' And the young days are gone when at evening after labour he would play for the dancers; the song will fade with the singer:

[quotes stanza 5 of No. XLI]

'It is not likely', says Mr. Housman, 'that I shall ever be impelled to write much more'. The 'Last' in the title sounds determined; there is a faint hope in that 'much'. Ten more poems, five more, one more poem, would be worth waiting for; one could say of him what could be said of few other artists, living or dead, that any addition to his works would enhance his position. Not one poem in the new volume is weak; a single overcrowded line is all the fault I can find with it; and anything more he might publish would assuredly be one more cut jewel on the string. He is the perfect artist who perfectly conceals his art, never writing except sincerely, working and working until his verses, after the utmost elaboration, produce the effect of complete, and spontaneously musical, colloquialism. But stop at any epithet and admire its adequacy; investigate the rhythms; look at the arrangement of the vowels, the open vowels, the end-lines with their open a's and i's, the assonances, the concealed, gently constraining alliterations, and you will find what must be at once the example and the despair of other poets. With a hundred poems, wearing the air of one who does not over-estimate the importance of the feat or of any mortal achievement, Mr. Housman has quietly taken his place among the most illustrious of English poets.

27. Amabel Williams-Ellis, review, *Spectator*

cxxix, 4 November 1922, 641–2

Amabel Williams-Ellis (1894–1984), a prolific author and journalist, was the daughter of John St Loe Strachey (an editor of the *Spectator*) and, from 1915, the wife of Clough Williams-Ellis, the architect who, *inter alia*, designed and built the village of Portmeirion in North Wales. From 1922 to 1923 she was literary editor of the *Spectator*.

I suppose that we have all of us – as we handled at last some long-expected volume – wondered about all the different impacts that this very book will be causing in a dozen dissimilar situations. If it is a book of poetry, the end of such a train of speculation is often the thought that these impacts will, alas! be undeservedly few and languid. But when the author of *A Shropshire Lad* breaks his silence of twenty years the case is altered. Mr. A.E. Housman is that rare being, a poet with a public. Indeed, his one chance of being misjudged may be that he is too popular. I think not a few people who did not come under the influence of *A Shropshire Lad* when it appeared have been put off by hearing *Bredon Hill* set to music and sung in drawing-rooms in an orgy of sentimentality. Every rhythm is altered, every meaning falsified. But a single glance at the book itself or at *Last Poems* will put right that misconception in any mind which had perceived and resented the tame version.

What was the peculiar quality in Mr. Housman's first collection which gained it popularity and exposed it to distortion? *A Shropshire Lad* was a small volume of poems ostensibly about the country, about country things and country people. The poems were short – 'terse' is the word obviously applicable; they displayed some annoying mannerisms. An almost ecstatic love of beauty was to be found in them, a peculiar musical quality, also a definite and conscious limitation of form and theme. But these qualities were only adjuncts. The whole point of the book was its poignant tone of realistic stoicism. Here was the quality that gave it flavour, a taste as strange and as individual as that of a quince. The character of the book was such that its great popularity implied in a large number of people assent to its attitude towards life.

Whatever is the particular quality or opinion in the reader which responds to Mr. Housman's touch, it would seem to be present – indeed to make itself very actively felt – in a great number of his countrymen. There is somewhere in us a string that he can make sound him back his own note. Take the following poem, No. IX in the present book:

[quotes No. IX]

That would be a poem perhaps not impossible of comprehension for a Frenchman, a Chinaman, or an Italian of taste, but we do not get the full flavour of that poem unless we read with it the next – No. X – which concerns the various anaesthetics in whose clouds man hides himself – love, combativeness, drink, and good fellowship. Still more necessary is No. XI, whose homely note completes and correlates its predecessors: –

[quotes No. XI]

We read it aloud. Do you not feel the polite silence with which the Frenchman, the Chinaman and the Italian await our explanation? It will not do! English weather, English ale, and an English trouble! We shut the book up and hurry away with it clutched the closer for their incomprehension, avoid the quotation from Marcus Aurelius, with which the civil Italian endeavours to meet us halfway, and only cheered a little by the Frenchman's quotation from Benjamin Constant: 'La poésie n'existe jamais en France que comme véhicule ou comme moyen. Il n'y a pas ce vague, cet abandon à des sensations non refléchies, ces descriptions si naturelles, tellement commandées par l'impression que l'auteur ne paraît pas s'apercevoir qu'il décrit.'[1]

'These descriptions – so natural that the author no longer seems aware that he describes.' Hardly perhaps that he writes – that is the impression that Mr. A.E. Housman's work probably gives to an unsophisticated reader. In almost each of the forty-one poems in this book he has achieved that complete fusion of rhythm, sound and sense which characterize a perfect work of art.

Has the significance of *A Shropshire Lad*'s popularity ever struck the governors and critics of the English, I wonder? Will they notice – or, if they notice, understand – the sale figures of *Last Poems* (they are sure to be extraordinary for a book of lyrics)? Will any of the new candidates for Parliament who are even now polishing up their knowledge of human nature remember the spirit of certain trench songs and hymn-tune verses – 'I want to go home' and 'Raining, raining, raining', for instance? They were Mr. A.E. Housman with more humour and less art in the irony. *Disenchantment*, one of the most popular of war books, tells the same story, though here the mood is a little different. Mr. A.E. Housman and the 'P.B.I.' [poor bloody infantry], the ultimate private soldier, had far less original enchantment than Mr. Montague. He arraigns the sergeant-major, or at most the 'red-hats' or the Cabinet. Mr. Housman questions and condemns a whole world that he did not make, a world to which he is bound by no implicit bargain, a world whose framer he does not fear to reproach – 'Oh, Thou who didst with pitfall and with gin...' 'The book is then,' the reader may ask, 'a cross between Omar Khayyam and Mr. Montague's study of the war with Germany?' It is nothing of the sort. The book is a collection of lyrics.

[quotes No. XXVII]

NOTE

1 'Poetry in France never exists except as a vehicle or as a means. There is not that vagueness, that giving way to unconsidered sensations, those descriptions which are so natural, so governed by the impression, that the author seems unaware that he is describing.'

28. Unsigned notice, *English Review*

xxxv, December 1922, 579

The editor of the *English Review* was Austin Harrison; but I am unable to establish whether he wrote this notice.

Twenty-five years is modern immortality, but *The Shropshire Lad* [sic] will claim a longer day than this. A generation after we meet him again with enthusiasm rather damped by the threat of the title, but then 'last' means 'latest' as well. The same elusive magic, perhaps a bit greyer, but still with the great note of old folk-songs, telling of the tragic comedy of living, being young, being old, being dead and forgotten. The same simple chime packed [sic] with a broken, jolly heart. The men who fought the French and the men who fought the Germans meet in their English love of cakes and ale and the girls at Ludlow Fair; they are all Shropshire lads, full men if disillusioned. Only a little does the Don get through in 'Epithalamium', in 'Hell Gate', and in 'The Oracles', which bewray [sic] him in their stately, scholarly measure; but for the rest the Shropshire Lad is still amongst his hills and moors – a brave philosopher of the soil which made him, unspoiled by Anno Domino [sic]. No! not last poems! not yet!

29. John Freeman, 'Hail and Farewell', *Bookman* (London)

lxiii, No. 375, December 1922, 153–4

John Freeman (1880–1929), poet and critic, self-taught in Greek, and in English literature. He left school at thirteen and entered an insurance company, of which in 1927 he became secretary and director. Like his American contemporary Wallace Stevens, he kept the 'literary' and 'insurance' sides of his life in separate compartments. He published the first of many books of poems, *Twenty Poems*, in 1908. In 1920 he won the Hawthornden Prize; his *Collected Poems* appeared in 1928.

Like a tree blooming strangely and serenely for a second time under a stormy late sky, Mr. A.E. Housman follows his *A Shropshire Lad* of 1896 with *Last Poems* of 1922. So securely is the earlier volume lodged in the affections of readers that it is wonderful to think that its recognition was not instant and ample. More than one publisher, it is said, forfeited the privilege of presenting *A Shropshire Lad* to the public, by mere blindness or apathy; more than one reviewer passed its excellence by; and thus it was but slowly that Mr. Housman gained his readers – never, it is safe to assert, to lose them but continually to add to their number. Was it not Coventry Patmore who said of his own collected poems, 'I have written little, but it is all my best'. So might Mr. Housman write, and what he has candidly said by way of preface is:

[quotes Preface in full]

He follows this with a lovely refrain – at once induction and farewell:

[quotes Prefatory Poem]

The farewell note is repeated in the last (the forty-first) of the new poems, 'Fancy's Knell':

> When lads were home from labour
> At Abdon under Clee ...

Between the induction and the last poem there is a collection of lyrics so singular and exquisite that almost the only adequate way to recommend them to readers would be to quote shamelessly from every page. Failing that attractive method, it must be said that the new poems do not fall short of the perfection of the old, and that some have a melody which might not be found in the first collection. For melody the stanzas just cited may serve as example, and for suggestive power the strange verses entitled 'Hell Gate' (from which quotation would be impossibly brutal) are a supreme instance in modern lyrical poetry.

Having said this, all has been said, from one point of view; but much might still be said of the attitude of the author, as declared in *Last Poems*. Conversation, which flared up exuberantly on the instant of the book's publication, brought forth the suggestion that there is a somewhat marked parallel between Edward Fitzgerald and Mr. A.E. Housman. In the poetry of each there is an attitude of agnostic endurance; in each the endurance is the successor to waste, to:

> The expense of spirit in a waste of shame;

in each there is defiance as well as endurance; and in each a superb technique to express the sombre philosophy. True that Fitzgerald did not invent the substance of his 'Omar Khayyám'; but adapted it and fused it with his peculiar fire. And true too that Mr. Housman speaks dramatically, using a nameless soldier for the purpose of his expression; but his soldier is typical rather than personal, and has no independent life. And there is at least one instance of likeness between the two poets, which is so conspicuous as to be curious; for Fitzgerald writes:

> Oh Thou, who man of baser Earth did make,
> And who with Eden did'st devise the Snake;
> For all the Sin wherewith the Face of Man
> Is blacken'd, Man's Forgiveness give – and take –

and Mr. Housman:

> We for a certainty are not the first
>   Have sat in taverns while the tempest hurled
> Their hopeful plans to emptiness, and cursed
>   Whatever brute and blackguard made the world.

Indeed the whole of this poem (the ninth in the volume) is harmonious with the cry of the earlier agnostic with whom Fitzgerald has made us familiar, and

> The troubles of our proud and angry dust

are the troubles of both poets alike. More explicit yet in its unconscious echo is Mr. Housman's twelfth piece:

[quotes ll. 15–24 of No. XII]

There is a desperate irony in this acquiescence beyond the touch of any proud or foolish defiance. The attitude is more rigorous than that of 'Omar Khayyám', but it is dictated by the same disillusioned or never-illusioned confrontation of the 'sorry scheme of things'. Fitzgerald's technique, his amazing flowering in a new measure, made even this desperate attitude acceptable; and Mr. Housman's command of his medium – so consummate, so accustomed, so tranquil – acts in the same way. Not that there is any chance of the latter writer's position being challenged for a disabling pessimism; *all things to all men* is the common clamour, in a day when one view is hardly preferred to another. Happily Mr. Housman is neither denounced for his philosophy nor ignored for his pure, disengaged poetry; and if there should come a time, within the experience of men now living, when this philosophy itself (like that of our other sombre apostle, Mr. Hardy) is a thing of the dusty past, the pure disengaged poetry of *A Shropshire Lad* and *Last Poems* will yet endure the corruption of time.

30. Unsigned review, *Outlook*

1, No. 1297, 9 December 1922, 500

With such a poet as Mr. Housman it would be sheerly insulting to feel any doubt of the uncompromising statement made in the title of his book. We have his first poems and now his *Last Poems*; and we are left face to face with a mystery which, since it can hardly be cleared up during the author's life, if ever, is not very profitable to discuss. He does but add to it by his reference to 'the continuous excitement under which in the early months of 1895 I wrote my other book'; and, as is only natural, he shows no desire to dispel it. We must wait for an answer that, very likely, we shall never receive. Who (for it was not Mr. Housman) 'listed for a soldier? And why?

These themes are too strong and too persistent in the *Shropshire Lad* to be entirely disregarded or to be taken as part of the ordinary poetic material. They recur in the present collection; and it may be taken that 'continuous excitement' continued for at least a little while after its predecessor went to press.

[quotes stanza 1 of No. XIII]

Who will swear, without exact and careful reference, that was not first published nearly twenty years ago? We proceed; and lads go to market, go sweethearting, are hanged or 'list for soldiers. There is, perhaps, nothing in this part of the book to equal the best of the *Shropshire Lad*, but also hardly anything which might not have taken its place in that sequence. At one point the cynicism grows thin and conventional:

[quotes No. XXI]

The first verse is characteristic Housman on the lower level: the poet not inspired but immensely competent to carry on through his want of inspiration. The second is merely cheap, and, were it in the *Shropshire Lad*, would scream its failure at the reader. But this is the only real lapse. And as we go further we come on a small handful of poems that are very good without precisely demanding inclusion in the *Shropshire Lad*.

One of these is the remarkable *Hell's Gate* [sic] – remarkable it would be for this, if for no more, that it runs to over one hundred lines and is therefore the longest piece Mr. Housman has written. The poet treads the road to Hell, finds the sentinel in mutiny at the gate, recognises in him a friend; and they turn home together:

[quotes ll. 87–94 of No. XXXI]

It is not easy to believe that this piece was written within several years of 1895. The graceful *Epithalamium* belongs to another category with its most happy of all attempts to reproduce a certain passage from Sappho:

[quotes ll. 15–22 of No. XXIV]

The best of all are the two or three poems of farewell and backward-looking which close the book. Among them the *Epitaph on an Army of Mercenaries* is a magnificent and marmoreal exception, too well known to quote. But the others have a gentleness and mellowness not to be demonstrated in any other way.

[quotes stanzas 1 and 2 of No. XL]

Or there is the exquisite metrical invention of:

[quotes stanza 2 of No. XLI]

It would be absurd to pretend that this new volume balances the old; it would be absurder still to pretend that we value it only, or even chiefly, on account of the old. It is difficult indeed to weigh with even scales anything now done by Mr. Housman. He, as a poet, has become a legend. His earlier book has had so great an influence on so many developing minds, so great, if indirect, an influence on the development of modern poetry. Others, we are not the first, have owed him a loyalty beyond criticism and beyond reason. But that very loyalty leads one back to reason and criticism, however painfully, and to the declaration that here is the completion of a poetry, however meagre in extent, which is solid and consistent and lovely.

31. Lee Wilson Dodd, 'The Stoic Muse', *Literary Review*

23 December 1922, 335

Lee Wilson Dodd (1879–1933), poet, novelist and playwright, author of *The Great Enlightenment* (poems, 1928). He graduated from New York Law School in 1901, and practised law until 1907, when he became a full-time writer. He taught at various American colleges, including Smith, Sarah Lawrence, and (1932–3) the Yale School of Drama.

The *Literary Review* was published by the *New York Evening Post*.

Since the appearance of A Shropshire Lad twenty or more years ago, Housman (it is high time to stop calling him Mr. A.E. Housman, for he belongs with the immortals) has been silent. And now comes a sheaf of forty-one lyrics, most of them brief. Meanwhile, during those years of silence the presses of the world have groaned with production. Mr. Wells, for example, has written a library, while Housman has composed a few lines of verse. Yet it is probable that a hundred or so words by Housman will be remembered, treasured (though never by many), long after the million or so words by Mr. Wells have been forgotten.

Why? But I leave that question to ponderers over the eternal paradoxes of art.

Housman has not, it seems to me, a bountiful nature. He loves the passions of life, his fellow men, the beauty that is in the world (how strangely!); he is bitter with anguish because life is brief and hard, death certain and final, beauty a breath that passes. The universe is indifferent to its chance creations, and therefore cruel. Nature – 'heartless, witless nature' – must be faced open-eyed, without romantic illusions, with a brave but despairing resignation. This is the white-hot yet stoically-endured burden of his soul. The range of his deeply felt ideas is restricted. He strikes the same grave, ominous notes again and again. His rhythms are restricted, too, and repeat themselves, as do his images. When you have read one of his lyrics you might almost say that you have read them all. Indeed, a sensitive reader might well receive the final, deep clear edged impression of the man from a single line:

> My sword that will not save.

Is it merely fantastic to suggest that the whole man is there?

No; for there – just there – is this poet's secret: every line is a quintessence; he can pour his full passions, the molten metal of himself, into a quiet, restraining phrase and fix it forever:

[quotes No. X]

Well, when a thing is perfect in its kind it is – perfect. There is nothing further to be said.

32. J.B. Priestley, 'The Poetry of A.E. Housman', *London Mercury*
vii, December 1922, 171–84

John Boynton Priestley (1894–1984), novelist, dramatist, essayist, critic, social historian. At the time of this review he had just settled in London (after army service in World War I and three years at Cambridge), and was just beginning the long and prolific literary career which culminated in his appointment, in 1977, to the Order of Merit (which Housman had declined in 1929).

The review was reprinted without change in J.B. Priestley, *Figures in Modern Literature* (London: John Lane, The Bodley Head, 1924), 77–102.

Mr. A.E. Housman is easily our most surprising poet. His first surprise was *A Shropshire Lad* itself, one of the most astonishing volumes in a very astonishing literature. It came to us practically a full-grown masterpiece, and the production of what used to be regarded as a lyric poet's maturity. He gave us no interesting juvenilia to examine; we have never seen the beginning, when he was working under half-a-dozen conflicting influences, when his own manner was only half developed. His next surprise was to maintain an almost unbroken silence for over a quarter of a century – to be exact, from 1896 to this present year. As time went on it seemed to us that he had said what he had had to say in a clear, unfaltering voice, and then, having eased his heart, had passed on in silence. It was as if a man in a noisy crowded company had suddenly broken his silence with a few golden words, and had then closed his lips for ever. But no, in this present publishing season there has come, out of the blue, his third surprise, a new volume of lyrics bearing the characteristic title – *Last Poems*. About a quarter of it was written last spring, but the remainder of the poems belong to a period between 1895 and 1910. It is not what most people, who do not know their man, would expect it to be; it is not a scrapbook, nor does it show us the spectacle of a writer trying to parody himself; it is as little senile as the earlier volume was juvenile; it is the *Shropshire Lad* over again, neither better nor worse, but naturally somewhat different, a little lacking in the lyrical freshness of the earlier poems, but often freer and bolder, and here and there (particularly in the nightmarish *Hell Gate*) breaking new ground. There is no reason why these two volumes, with the poems kept in their present order, should not be bound up together to form the two sections of one complete volume, which certainly should be given the covering title of *A Shropshire Lad*. This last point can hardly be disputed, and it seems to me important, mainly because Mr. Housman has carried over the peculiar method of the earlier book (which, as we shall see, may be called 'dramatisation') into the later one, which therefore cannot be fully appreciated unless it is understood to be the *Last Poems of A Shropshire Lad*. For this reason I need make no apology for treating these two volumes, only containing one hundred odd short lyrics in all, as one, and for occasionally referring to them collectively as *A Shropshire Lad*.

In a certain volume that professes to review the poetry of the last thirty years, a volume that deals at some length with all manner of poets, from Lord de Tabley to Professor Robert Nichols, there are but two references to *A Shropshire Lad*, and each time it is called the work of Mr. Laurence Housman. The mistake in the name we can afford to ignore, as it does at least keep the poems in the family, but surely it is very curious that such a book should be only referred to in passing and not discussed. *A Shropshire Lad* has been reprinted a dozen times, so that in such a detailed survey it could at least have been given some little notice, if only as popular verse – 'the sort of thing the public likes.' But the fact is, Mr. A.E. Housman's little volume has always been left to speak for itself, for critics have always tended to ignore it. Yet it is reprinted time after time; it has been widely read and, I fancy, widely discussed; its influence upon younger poets has been immense; and it has by this time passed lightly, easily, unopposed, into our great tradition of lyrical verse. Why, then, this silence? Has its merit always been taken for granted as something beyond dispute? Is an acquaintance with its fine, perhaps unique, qualities and great influence assumed to be part of our general knowledge? Or are there other, very different, reasons why it is so often passed over? I think there are, and that they are too numerous to be tabulated here; but a few of them are worth noticing. In the first place, there are a great many critics who are only impressed by a sheer bulk of writing; they must be continually reminded of a writer's existence by new work, or they forget him. Those who deal largely in essay-reviews like nothing better than the appearance of book after book by names that have gradually gathered about them a safe cluster of attributes, the use of which renders the task of criticising a contemporary as easy as that of appreciating Shakespeare and, of course, much more entertaining. Unfortunately, Mr. Housman, probably knowing nothing of this preference, comes along with an almost full-grown masterpiece, resets it once or twice, and then, only after twenty-five years have passed, produces another volume, thereby giving little opportunity for that easy talk of 'still the same note, but a little more of this and a little less of the other,' which carries one so comfortably to the bottom of a column. Another and more important reason for this critical neglect is concerned with the charge of 'pessimism' that has been urged against these poems. There are a great many people in this country who seem to circle about literature in order that they may occasionally swoop down and carry off some morsel of comforting doctrine: they look for an inspiring message and go through a volume of verse with one eye open for tags to round off their half-hour talks to plain men; they are generally in search of what they are pleased to call 'vision,' and they are apt to find it in some very strange places. Such an attitude of mind towards literature is unfortunate, but it is not, I think, quite so hopelessly wrong as the prevailing mode of criticism would have us believe; it has at least some health in it, and that is more than can be said of some more fashionable methods of approaching letters; but it has, of course, the serious disadvantage of encouraging cheap thought, and a shallow optimism, and of estranging those who hold it from a very fine company of writers. It has certainly made many refuse the clear but bitter draught held out to them by Mr. Housman, and so, for better or worse, we have been spared the endless comment and quotation that has fastened upon some other kinds of verse. As for the charge itself, it is too general, too vague, to be worth detailed discussion in such a brief essay as this. The whole question of the 'pessimistic' poet is sufficiently tangled to be meat and drink to Mr. Chesterton himself. To say that a man is at once a poet and a pessimist is to be guilty of a contradiction in terms. Every work of art is an affirmation; your true, thorough-going pessimist would never think it worth while to create anything; a man without hope would never accept the labour of writing, for he could only write in the hope of being read, and surely that is almost the height of sanguine expectation. I, for one, am quite ready to lay my hand on my heart and declare that any person who is willing to take the trouble and risk of writing and publishing a volume of poems is optimistic enough for me. If – to return to *A Shropshire Lad* – it could be proved in some way that, acting under its influence, a number of young men had – let us say – committed suicide, as the over-enthusiastic disciples of Hegesias, the 'orator of death,' are said to have done at Alexandria, most of us would be disturbed, probably horrified, and rightly so. But even then, writing as one who sees magnificent poetry in the volume, I must confess that I should be also somewhat mystified, for the more fine poetry there is in the world the less reason there is for quitting it so hurriedly and needlessly.

There are, of course, more reasons than these why *A Shropshire Lad* has been, as it were, courted in private and shunned in public; but it is very doubtful if they are worth finding. We, in this place, can certainly turn with more profit to the poetry itself. An analysis of the content of these hundred or so short poems is not to my present purpose, but, on the other hand, for reasons that will appear below, some notice of the poet's attitude – or, if you will, of the mood that inspired these things – seems to me absolutely essential. The poems are not, as it were, threaded on a string in either volume; they have not that sort of unity, that dependence upon one another, which we usually find in – say – a sonnet-squence; but nevertheless one spirit breathes through them; they flow out of one central mood. We cannot explain this dominating mood in terms of something outside poetry, such as a system of ethics or a definitely formulated philosophy. Judged by such alien standards, the poet is contradictory and downright perverse in his determination to make the worst of things; thus his running grievance, on examination, can be resolved into two separate complaints that are not at all consistent; in the first, life is lovely enough, but all too short, and death is the enemy of happiness; in the second, existence itself is a misery only to be endured until the welcome arrival of death the deliverer. Yet when we are actually reading the poems we never feel that the poet is thus cancelling out his complaints. No, because such a contradiction (which would be very awkward if poetry were what some people think it is, philosophy in fancy dress) is not really there – indeed, has nothing to do with the actual poetry at all. In order to find it, we have to make a gigantic falsification; we have to translate that strangely beautiful logic of the whole being of Man which we call poetry into that smaller drier logic which is simply a part of Man's intellectual apparatus. If, when engaged in the hopeless task of disentangling the myriad threads of a poem's fabric, we make references to systems of belief, schools of philosophy, and the like, we do so for the sake of mere convenience, and such references are purposely loose and vague, a mere wave of the hand towards a supposed point of the compass for a fellow-traveller's guidance.

In that fine poem *On Wenlock Edge*, we hear of the old city of Uricon and are told:

> Then, 'twas before my time, the Roman
> At yonder heaving hill would stare:
> The blood that warms an English yeoman,
> The thoughts that hurt him, they were there.

I seem to see that Roman lurking behind all these poems. He was, I imagine, of the early Empire, saturated in all the nobler ideas of his time, and deeply versed in its great literature – a Stoic, but one not disdainful, in some moods, of the opposite camp. He it is who has given these lyrics, for all their English softness, that touch of iron, that suggestion of the chisel; who has brought in the soldier, and made the lads leave their scythes rusting in the deep grass; who has made the volume seem one long meditation upon death. He had bided his time until the creeds were crashing down and the world was gazing blankly at the towering bleak formulas (then so hard and clear in outline, now grown so shadowy), that science had erected; this was his moment, and he took it; so that in this pretended speech of West Country lads and lasses, these songs of an English countryside with the 'hedgerows heaped with may,' we hear his many promptings, and they become clearer as the tale is told. He was not always near at hand, this Roman of ours, when the poet was writing; I fancy he knew little or nothing of such things as –

> There pass the careless people
>   That call their souls their own:
> Here by the road I loiter,
>   How idle and alone.

or better still —

> That is the land of lost content,
>   I see it shining plain,
> The happy highways where I went
>   And cannot come again.

or again, this verse, one out of many in the new volume —

> I sought them far and found them
>   The sure, the straight, the brave,
> The hearts I lost my own to,
>   The souls I could not save.
> They braced their belts about them,
>   They crossed in ships the sea,
> They sought and found six feet of ground,
>   And there they died for me.

But, on the other hand, sometimes he does more than prompt; here and there he seems to have taken up the chisel himself in the high Roman fashion: —

> Be still, my soul, be still; the arms you bear are brittle,
>   Earth and high heaven are fixt of old and founded strong.
> Think rather, call to thought, if now you grieve a little,
>   The days when we had rest, O soul, for they were long.

Meditations upon death are nothing new to those who know their English literature. If a man of these islands has any command of style, it will not be long before he is brooding over the grave. The subject of death must be a real boon to our anthologists. But *A Shropshire Lad* wears its cypress with a difference. Not one of our poets — not even Webster, Blair, or Beddoes — has been more concerned with death than this one, who cannot write even a little song in praise of Spring without the sharp shadow falling across the sunlit blossom: —

> And since to look at things in bloom
> Fifty Springs are little room,

A.E. HOUSMAN

> About the woodlands I will go
> To see the cherry hung with snow.

But most of our poets, and indeed rhetoricians, have very naturally taken the medieval or romantic, as opposed to the classical, the Christian as opposed to the pagan, view of the matter. Seeking an image or symbol, the English imagination, essentially romantic, has always turned eagerly to the worms, skeletons, skulls, coffins, and what not of the Christian pageantry of death. A casual reader would probably declare that *A Shropshire Lad* too is full of such things. In reality it is not – as anyone may see for himself. The poet has at once turned to a newer, and gone back to an older, fashion of regarding death. Practically all the old fantastic and frightful imagery has disappeared. In one of the poet's moods, and particularly in the earlier poems, we see death as the great dark curtain against which the lovely things of life stand out pathetically small and bright. All the lovers in *A Shropshire Lad* cry out upon the piteous brevity of life: they see only a little way before them that house of dust where –

> Lovers lying two and two
> Ask not whom they sleep beside,
> And the bridegroom all night through
> Never turns him to the bride.

Our existence is but a little halt on the immeasurable frontiers of this great country of the dead, a land that knows nothing of either the pains of hell or the delights of heaven; and we have so little time to breathe and move and feel:

> Speak now, and I will answer.
> How shall I help you, say,
> Ere to the wind's twelve quarters
> I take my endless way?

And so, more recently, as he reviews the enchanted Autumns of the earth he falls into the same mood, tempered by more resignation and losing some of its former urgency, and tells us to

> Possess, as I possessed a season,
> The countries I resign...

But when his mood hardens into Senecan despair of 'the embittered hour,' the life of this world takes on darker hues, and death is no longer a menace, for it promises rest and sleep and forgetfulness: —

> Now, and I muse for why and never find the reason,
> I pace the earth, and drink the air, and feel the sun.
> Be still, be still, my soul; it is but for a season:
> Let us endure an hour and see injustice done.

And at times, as in a very characteristic poem in the later volume, he will but steel himself to endure, making no truce with either this world or the next, the laws of God or Man; but only making a gesture of almost Oriental resignation:

> And how am I to face the odds
> Of Man's bedevilment and God's?
> I, a stranger and afraid
> In a world I never made.

We have seen enough now of the mood that lies behind these poems to know that not only is it not the common fit of depression that it first appears, but that it is distinctly uncommon — indeed, an entirely individual state of mind. But the form in which it is expressed does even more to give the poems their unmistakable, personal note. Most of the chief characteristics of that form will be noticed in their turn, but before we come to speak of them it is well that we should remark the general scheme or design of *A Shropshire Lad* — the particular mould, as it were, into which this molten mass of thoughts and emotions has been poured. The book, be it noted, is not called *Dust and Tears, Poems in Exile, The Iron Days,* or anything of that kind: it is called *A Shropshire Lad*. Now Mr. Housman is, I take it, a native of the place, but I do not suppose for one moment that at the time he was composing these lyrics he always referred to himself as a Shropshire lad or asked new acquaintances to address him as such. In short, what he did in this volume was to depart from the usual practice of our modern lyric poets: instead of directly expressing his various moods he partly dramatised them in a more or less definite atmosphere, on a more or less consistent plan. By doing this he dowered his work with a certain concrete and particular effect, the success of which is one reason for its power. It might easily have proved a source of weakness, as it has done since to some poets; it is the sureness of his touch, that mark of the artist, that has made his experiment so successful. He has been singled out and applauded as the originator of the 'topographical' or 'praise-the-place-where-I-was-born' manner in verse, which has become so fashionable. But the modern craze, as a mere craze, for eulogising one's native place probably owes more to those two gentlemen who have sung of Sussex with such geniality and gusto. And we have only to think of Barnes, T.E. Brown, and Tennyson himself, to name only a few, and what they had been doing not long before, to see that setting poems in a certain definite locality and atmosphere (even to writing them in dialect, which was, I think, wisely avoided in *A Shropshire Lad*) was neither a new device nor even an old one newly restored. It is, I repeat, his sureness of touch that calls for our praise. For the purposes of a lyric poet, the partial dramatisation has been done to perfection. If the poet wishes to drop the slight mask and speak out directly in his own person, as he does here and there, the continuity of the poems is not broken, and we are not irritated by a demand to jump out of one atmosphere into another. Indeed, there are all degrees of dramatisation, shading off one into another, in these two small volumes, and in any long study it would certainly be worth while examining them and trying to decide what the poet has gained by adopting so unusual a plan, gained, that is, not in this poem or that, but in the whole mass regarded as a complete and distinct work. What is certain to my mind is that of all our lyric poets who have deliberately gone to the countryside and assumed the smock-frock, which leaves out of count poets like Burns and Clare who had no need to go, not one has grappled with the resulting problems more successfully than this poet of Shropshire. With extraordinary skill and tact, he has contrived to avoid the two pitfalls into one or other of which most of his fellows have fallen. Firstly, he has kept out that suggestion of the pastoral with its Corydon and Phyllis, its perfumed sheep and beribboned stage crooks, which we find so often in the poetry of earlier men. Secondly, he has avoided a mistake common to poets who have written since *A Shropshire Lad* appeared – the mistake of leaving one's artistic judgment to the mercy of certain theories and so insisting upon one's readers admiring the muck-heap and smelling the manure. There was Wordsworth, of course, who managed to avoid both these extremes, but then he contrived to dig a special pitfall for himself, and as everyone knows what that was, there is no need to enlarge upon it. One would like to hear Wordsworth on *A Shropshire Lad*! I fancy he would strongly disapprove of it, and yet it comes nearer to one part of his famous theory than his own work ever did. Perhaps he would be astonished to learn that many of us who confess to being Wordsworthians in and out of season yet recognise in this later and lesser poet of ours an artist, in the narrower sense, more tactful, delicate and scrupulous than he, the great W.W., could ever claim to be.

Our English tongue has always favoured two particular kinds of short poem, the single cry and the dancing narrative, the Lyric and the Ballad. For them it has ever been an instrument nothing short of marvellous in its subtlety and range. It is a language that is always ready to lilt and fall into strange and beautiful cadences; it would be for ever on the wing. For this very reason it has always proved itself a difficult medium for a third kind of short poem, which we may call the Epigram. Here is a form that demands no flight of wings, but a chisel and the graven stone; that asks for clearness, brevity, weight, words frozen into miraculous phrases and not words grown riotous, fluttering, and piping their way into immortality. Strive as we may to create the Epigram, the language is always against us; it will leap and dance and sing instead of falling into beautiful attitudes. So-called epigrams, witty-pointed couplets and quatrains, we have, of course, in plenty; but the real epigrammatic note is rarely heard in our poetry, and when we do hear it we may be sure that something like a miracle has been wrought in the craft of verse. So far, perhaps, we deal in commonplaces; but no matter, for what follows is no commonplace. In the poetry we are considering there can be discovered all three forms. Through the familiar supple warp and weft of Lyric and Ballad there runs the stiff and shining thread of epigram. But the metaphor is ill-chosen, for even your brocade can be unravelled, its threads disentangled and laid apart; whereas here, in this poetic form, we have not a woven thing, but a blend, never quite the same in any two poems, yet always there, personal and unmistakable.

The influence of the ballad upon *A Shropshire Lad* is obvious, and need not detain us long. At first sight many of these poems might seem to be dreadful parodies of folk-songs. They have the same simplicity of form, the same apparently artless manner, but with a very different spirit informing them. They have the same rare qualities; high imagination and dramatic intensity governed by a fine sense of artistic reticence; throughout there is the same strict economy of means. Such verses as these:

> My mother thinks us long away;
>   'Tis time the field were mown.
> She had two sons at rising day,
>   To-night she'll be alone.

and

> Oh, lad, what is it, lad, that drips
>   Wet from your neck on mine?
> What is it falling on my lips,
>   My lad, that tastes of brine?

have the ring of the fine old ballads. Although every situation is strongly conceived, and all the resulting emotions strongly felt by the poet, yet it is mainly by the exercise of his power of compression, his artistic thrift, that he achieves such dramatic force and intensity of feeling. He does not allow an emotion to be entirely diffused by expending too many words upon it. The reader's imagination must take wing to follow the narrative in this poetry, as it must do to appreciate the old ballad literature. Thus, in that poignant lyric *Is My Team Ploughing*? all we hear are the two voices, one questioning and the other answering – the reedy cry from the grave, and the full-blooded tones of the living man. Again, in *The True Lover* there is nothing but a vague dreadful whispering in the darkness: it has the piteous appeal of such a thing as *Clerk Saunders*. But that other form, the Lyric, is naturally the basis of the whole volume. Indeed, many of its readers may be surprised that it should be necessary to go outside the Lyric to explain the peculiar charm of these poems. But such doubters have only to compare them with the work of men who were strictly singers and not gravers at all, let us say Shelley and Swinburne (but not Milton and Keats), to understand the necessity of referring to other forms. As we have seen, the expression is a curious blend, easy to recognise anywhere, but still never quite the same in any two poems. Therefore we shall not be surprised to find here and there in *A Shropshire Lad* an almost purely lyrical note:

> Loveliest of trees, the cherry now
> Is hung with bloom along the bough.
> And stands about the woodland ride
> Wearing white for Eastertide.

and

> Oh, see how thick the goldcup flowers
> Are lying in field and lane,
> With dandelions to tell the hours
> That never are told again.

and

> With rue my heart is laden
> For golden friends I had,
> For many a rose-lipt maiden
> And many a lightfoot lad.

or from the last poem of all –

> Ours were idle pleasures,
>   Yet, oh, content we were,
> The young to wind the measures,
>   The old to heed the air;
> And I to lift with playing
>   From tree and tower and steep
> The light delaying,
>   And flute the sun to sleep.

– verses that are lovely in the old way that we know so well. But one cannot go very far without coming across that third thing, the touch of the epigram. Even some of the quotations I had selected as examples of lyrical flow began to show traces of it, and I had to set them aside. As an instance, even in this verse:

> Oh, tarnish late on Wenlock Edge,
>   Gold that I never see;
> Lie long, high snowdrifts in the hedge
>   That will not shower on me.

My ear at least begins to catch a ring slightly different from that of the verses I have already given. But the epigrammatic note is everywhere in these octosyllabic verses, from which everything but the bare essentials has been cut away. Even if you are still thinking of the epigram as some pointed witty quatrain, four lines taken almost at random from that curious apologia which is the last poem but one in *A Shropshire Lad* will serve your turn very well:

> Oh many a peer of England brews
> Livelier liquor than the Muse,
> And malt does more than Milton can
> To justify God's ways to Man.

As it stands, that is a capital epigram of the ordinary kind. But when I talk of the epigrammatic note I am rather thinking of a certain felicity of phrase, not, as in our great romantics, a felicity in the power of suggestion, when a single word can open out wonderful vistas, but one of roundness and completeness, yet with an appeal transcending that of mere wit. It is, of course, the glory of such familiar things as Landor's *Proud word you never spoke* or *I strove with none*, or, not to disdain propaganda, his much less familiar epigram *On seeing a hair of Lucretia Borgia*:

> Borgia, thou once were almost too august
> And high for adoration; now thou'rt dust.
> All that remains of thee these plaits unfold,
> Calm hair, meandering in pellucid gold.

These are epigrams proper, but the note of them can be heard in very different forms; the great sonneteers all have it; and it is here, the gift of our Roman, quietly working miracles in *A Shropshire Lad*. Take the last verse of that magnificent poem *To an Athlete Dying Young*, and you cannot fail to catch it:

> And round that early-laurelled head
> Will flock to gaze the strengthless dead,
> And find unwithered on its curls
> The garland briefer than a girl's.

But it is everywhere in the work of this poet, whose power of control, whose strong feeling for artistic reticence and thrift, notwithstanding his other rare gifts, constitute his greatest virtue as an artist. It has enabled him to take time and distil his thoughts and emotions into a fine essence. It has enabled him to cut away all wordy excrescences and, as it were, shape his expression like a spear-head. Some people, even some not unintelligent critics, have declared that anyone can write this kind of poetry if he will only take enough trouble. But such persons are suffering from a delusion, which would quickly vanish if they once sat down in earnest to prove they were right. The difficulty is not in merely taking trouble but in knowing what kind of trouble to take: in other words, any fool can keep on altering and altering, but to bring a piece of work nearer and nearer to perfection with every added stroke needs an artist. I fancy such mistaken notions largely come from the application of the term 'polished' to literary style, for it makes people think of polishing shoes and silver, a process at once entirely dissimilar and much less difficult.

That preference for the concrete and that distrust of the abstract, which are commonly supposed to be the mark of a good poet, are very noticeable in *A Shropshire Lad*. Indeed, sometimes its author seems to keep too close to the ground, which is an error, but pardonable because it is on the right side. There is a solid earthiness in his style that can be too suggestive, at times, of a lyrical Caliban. It is this earthiness, along with his characteristic directness of style, that makes him appear positively brutal to some of his readers. He is essentially a masculine stylist, going straight to the active voice of the verb and the concrete thing, and ruthlessly divesting his style of unnecessary adjectives and woolly abstract terms. Such a line as 'Clay lies still but blood's a rover' is typical of his manner. He has, indeed, made war upon the ubiquitous adjective, and concentrated upon the bare noun and verb until they have done most of the work. He has replaced the usual wearisome host of similes by a few apparently simple but astonishingly apt metaphors, and in this way he has given his style directness, force, and a certain 'tang.' The shortest examination of such passages as these, chosen with no particular care because there are so many to be found –

> His folly has not fellow,
> Beneath the blue of day.

or

> The blood that warms an English yeoman,
> The thoughts that hurt him, they were there...

or again

> Before this fire of sense decay,
> This smoke of thought blow clean away ...

will do more than I can, beating in the air, to show his method and exactly what it has achieved for him. Notwithstanding his notable restraint in the use of metaphor, simile, and figurative language generally, his imagery, when it does come, is usually startling, original. He loves to flash a sudden tremendous image across one's imagination:

> 'Tis a long way further than Knighton,
> A quieter place than Clun,
> Where doomsday may thunder and lighten,
> And little 'twill matter to one.

Or, again, take that audacious image in one of the later poems on a dead friend who —

> Has woven a winter robe,
> And made of earth and sea
> His overcoat for ever,
> And wears the turning globe.

So, too, his adjectives, when they come, are not the least of his minor felicities. Having once known them, who could forget 'the *labouring* highway,' 'the *glancing* showers,' 'the *coloured* counties,' and 'the *springing* thyme,' and 'yonder *heaving* hill,' and similar unforeseen but happy marriages of word to word. Crowded together like this and ruthlessly torn out of their context, they may seem to point to some rather tiresome devotee of *le mot juste*; but set in their proper places they are indeed sparkling little gems of fine writing.

There are no intricate measures in *A Shropshire Lad*, and it is clear that its author relies very little upon the charm of metre. The new volume repeats the favourite measures of the old one, and shows that the poet has no taste for metrical experiments. He is fond of the octosyllabic line and ballad measure in its simplest form. Here and there he makes clever use of a five-line stanza, which is a striking variation on the old Short Measure, the first and third lines being unrhymed and having each a redundant syllable, the second, fourth, and fifth lines rhyming together. This peculiar metrical structure gives to the fifth line of the stanza the air of being an afterthought, which is made to add considerably to the poignant force of the verses in which it is used:

> They tolled the one bell only,
> Groom there was none to see,
> The mourners followed after,
> And so to church went she,
> And would not wait for me.

But throughout *A Shropshire Lad* the poet's appeal does not depend upon a highly elaborate and cunning arrangement of vowel sounds and so forth. I am writing of a poet and not a mere dauber in words, and I do not mean for one instant to imply that he has no skill in the manipulation of vowel sounds and in other technical devices. In the verse quoted above – to take the nearest example – the two 'o' sounds echoing down the verse from the first line, like the chime of the bell, show us that he knows what he is about. But he is not one of our masters of verbal music. Those rapturous, infinitely beguiling phrases that linger about the ear for ever are not for him. But, nevertheless, even here he has accomplished something that not only increases our admiration but makes his work a fruitful study for other poets. In his moments of passionate stress he has given us, within that terse and finely tempered style of his, the true ring and cadence of ordinary natural speech. A comparison – not of the odious kind – will perhaps throw light on a matter that is difficult to explain in a few words. Another poet of our time, Mr. W.B. Yeats, has always laboured, and on the whole successfully, to give his style a similar directness and naturalness, but at the same time he has always pursued a delicate research of his own into the endless possibilities of stressed language, so that all his best poems move to lovely little tunes of his own, which must be caught before the peculiar beauty of his work can be appreciated. So, too, all Mr. Walter de la Mare's finest things have their own music, come out in that exquisite stammer of his, and this too must be caught on the very threshold of appreciation. One would not, of course, have these two fine poets any different: they express themselves to our admiration. But this lovely personal music is not to be found in *A Shropshire Lad*; in its place, within the simple metrical framework, is that cadence of our common human speech which no ear can help recognising and no heart can reject. Take it at its very simplest:

A.E. HOUSMAN

> We still had sorrows to lighten –
> One could not always be glad; [sic]
> And lads knew trouble at Knighton
> When I was a Knighton lad...

Now, that is apparently as plain and straightforward as prose, but, print it as you like, you cannot make it into prose; if you simply say the lines you must sing them, and if, on the other hand, you begin by singing them your voice must inevitably fall into their natural affecting cadence. It is this that makes his mournful folk seem to cry from the heart, as few others do in the poetry of our time. And though *A Shropshire Lad* has had such a great influence, though traces of that influence can be discovered in all manner of unlikely places in contemporary verse, I know only one or two of our younger poets who have been able to reproduce this curious characteristic. But perhaps too many of them are now more concerned with the look of a poem on the printed page than with their reader's ear.

Affirmative statements are the necessities of criticism, negative statements only its luxuries. It may be entertaining to be told the hundred-and-one things that a work of art is *not*, but it is not strictly necessary. But if one declares that So-and-so's poetry has such and such fine qualities, and contents oneself with doing that, there are some people who are always ready to think that one has dowered So-and-so with every virtue known to letters, who are quick to protest that So-and-so is not a Homer or a Shakespeare. Solely, then, for the benefit of such persons, who are to be found even in the best company, let me cross to the other, the negative, side and declare what, in my opinion, is not to be found in Mr. Housman's poetry. It knows nothing of those supreme moments that are only to be met with in some half-dozen of our poets; it has not those brief spells when poetry suddenly becomes sheer magic, and the poet himself nothing less than a wizard; and it is never possessed by that consuming rapture that is perhaps the innermost secret of Shelley; nor has it any great range and scope, or that power of transmuting all life into poetry which is the majestic glory of the greatest poets. Compared with their wide domains, it is nothing but a little estate. But it is a little estate that is exquisitely ordered. And, to turn once more to words that I have been compelled to use again and again in this brief discussion, there is in it something distinct, individual, personal. It is easy to write verse that is highly novel but not worth reading, as so many people do; it is not very difficult to write verse that is quite readable but not original, as many others do; but to create lyrics that have certain rare literary qualities and, further, have their creator's personality clearly stamped on them, is to have some kinship with the great masters. A line from A.E. Housman is as unmistakable as a line from Milton, Shelley or Wordsworth, and bears the same impress of the poet's individuality; and to me the difference between the modern poet and these three Titans, on this count of original force, is one of degree alone, for I hold him to be of the same imperishable kind.

33. H.J. Davis, 'An English Poet', *Canadian Forum*
iii, January 1923, 118

An extract from this review's last paragraph. Elsewhere in his review Davis makes the point that Housman's bitterness and pessimism, which might have been unpopular in the 1890s, fitted in well with the post-World War I atmosphere.

He has written lyrical ballads in the actual language of simple men. He has overcome the difficulty which Wordsworth found so hard to deal with. For he has managed to preserve not merely the words, but the order and rhythm of ordinary simple speech. No. XI and No. XIV of the *Last Poems* are almost perfect examples of this, and elsewhere we constantly meet lines such as these:

> The young man feels his pockets
> And wonders what's to pay.

or these:

> And if they think, they fasten
> Their hands upon their hearts.

and perhaps even more frequently in *A Shropshire Lad* he was content to use unchanged the music of ordinary speech. It is this which gives his work its fine flavour. Such forms of speech are timeless – neither new nor old – and common, with the mark of no dialect or cult upon them. They are the bones of language, and are not subject to the accidents and mortality which quickly destroy the beauty of flesh and brain. They give to his works that shape which by its firm solidity is endowed with the quality of permanence.

34. Stewart Marsh Ellis, review, *Fortnightly Review*

cxiii, New Series, 1 January 1923, 164–8

Stewart Marsh Ellis, (d. 1933) came of a military family and was a cousin of George Meredith. He was educated at Hermosa School, Ealing, then by a private tutor. He published a number of books on Victorian writers, including Meredith, his earliest being *William Harrison Ainsworth and his friends* (2 vols, 1910).

This review was reprinted in Stewart Marsh Ellis, *Mainly Victorian* (London: Hutchinson, 1925), 263–8.

In all the annals of English literature there is no analogy to the case of Mr. A.E. Housman's intermittent spring of poetry. Other poets, such as Keats and Chatterton, have left but a small volume as evidence of their genius, but the reason is generally to be found in the fact that they died young, before consummating (or exhausting) their powers –

Cut is the branch that might have grown full straight,
And burnèd is Apollo's laurel bough.

But, on the other hand, these have escaped the fate of their choicest poems being engulfed and lost in the dreary wastes of 'Collected Editions', compact of superfine binding and unreadably small print.

Mr. A.E. Housman's bequest to posterity and fame is two small books. Over a quarter of a century ago – in 1896 – he offered without any preliminary flourishes of trumpets or press puffings, a slim little book of verse entitled *A Shropshire Lad*. Beyond its title, which was, perhaps, unusual for a work emanating from a Professor of Latin at University College, London, there was no hint before perusal that this was a unique book – one that was to strike a new note of music in English poesy, to be a literary influence for all time, to have numerous imitators. It appeared, and critics and general readers (at once, for a marvel, in agreement) instantly realised that here was something fresh, a song that sang what had never been heard so poignantly before – 'the long, long thoughts' of a boy, and more, the intense sadness of regret for lost youth, friends long dead, and all the beauty and brave days that are no more: –

[quotes *A Shropshire Lad*, No. XL]

There was something about the haunting cadences of these little songs that touched the very spring of tears – like the sad, wan notes of the shepherd's fluting pipe heard by the dying Tristan, left with only memories of life and love; something far and remote and elusive like 'the horns of Elfland faintly blowing'. They expressed the Soul of Memory: –

[quotes stanzas 1 and 4 of *A Shropshire Lad*, No. LII]

Now, after 27 years, and again unheralded, Mr. Housman has provided a little pendant to *A Shropshire Lad*. It is described as Last Poems, and the author states 'it is not likely that I shall ever be impelled to write much more'. There is hope, in that reservation, for his readers that some or a few 'more' poems may yet be written, despite the melancholy song which ushers in the present collection: –

A.E. HOUSMAN

[quotes ll. 1–6 of Prefatory Poem]

The new book is smaller than its predecessor, and, therefore, does not contain quite so many exquisite things. The theme and the setting are, happily, the same as found expression in *A Shropshire Lad*: it is the continuation of a familiar song, not a new melody. Once more the poems voice the memories of youth and sad regret for the beauty of the past that is dead – youth that was spent and beauty that was realised amid the vales and hills of Shropshire: –

[quotes stanzas 1–3 of No. XXXIX]

But the summers come and the years go by, and the winter of life draws in with the dreams of youth unfulfilled: –

[quotes stanza 7 of No. XXXIX, followed by stanza 9 of No. I]

A new generation arises and dreams the old visions of love and beauty like those that went before, and like an eternal treadmill the tragedy is repeated. The facts of life kill romance, and loveliness fades in the glare of sordid disillusion. Mr. Housman again expresses his brooding melancholy for the frequent untimely fate of youth cut off in some act of passion: –

[quotes stanza 2 of No. II]

Three consecutive poems, *The Deserter*, *The Culprit*, *Eight O'Clock*, picture lads on the eve of execution, and are touched with a note of understandable pessimism:

[quotes stanza 4 of No. XIV]

The poet voices bravely the lawless claims of youth and hot blood: –

[quotes ll. 1–14 of No. XII]

In a previous article I endeavoured to demonstrate that the work of Mr. Thomas Hardy was not, to an excessive degree, pessimistic in the ordinary and accepted sense of the word. It would be more difficult to establish the same contention in the case of Mr. Housman, for he is frankly pessimistic in many of his poems, though, perhaps, fatalistic would be the more correct word to use. One of the most melancholy of his songs, by the graveside of a friend, faces the painful truth that memory and love of the dead will fade: –

[quotes stanzas 1, 3 and 5 of No. XVIII]

Truly, it is the saddest thought in the world – that the passing years will inevitably bring forgetfulness of the lonely dead, however dearly they once were loved and however poignant was the grief that broke over their grave. Surely, some echo of that intense sorrow and emotion should linger there for ever; but no, the years pass, the flowers wither, the weeds are triumphant, and the headstone sinks down. Who can forget Swinburne's wonderful but terrible lines: –

> Love deep as the sea as a rose must wither,
>   As the rose-red seaweed that mocks the rose.
> Shall the dead take thought for the dead to love them?
>   What love was ever as deep as a grave?
> They are loveless now as the grass above them
>   Or the wave.

All sincere poetry is the conscious or unconscious expression of momentous personal experience, even though it may appear sometimes as but the reflection of a passing mood. Mr. Housman has never revealed or hinted how far his poems may reflect his own experiences. He states that *A Shropshire Lad* was mainly written when the author was in a state of 'continuous excitement', and presumably the same words apply to his later work. But, inevitably, in years to come, the world will want to know more. Poets, like Byron, Shelley, and Keats, who wrote of great passions and emotions, cannot escape this posthumous curiosity which asks to what extent they lived their poems and if they found 'the lover's crown of myrtle', if not better, at least equal to 'the poet's crown of bays'.

In the same way it will be matter for future speculation whether the author of *A Shropshire Lad* once worked on a farm and went ploughing

A.E. HOUSMAN

When smoke stood up from Ludlow
And mist blew off from Teme

and it will be matter for wonder how a college don knew so much about the call of the drum and the life of a recruit. Whatever the facts may be, we are not concerned to elucidate them. Mr. Housman is a poet, and, as in his first book, he continues to be the pre-eminent poet of the young soldier — a sad one, it is true, for his vision looks to after the battle. *Illic Jacet, Grenadier, I 'listed at Home for a Lancer, Wake Not, Soldier from the Wars Returning* are in the category. Finest of all is this:

[quotes No. VII]

Twenty lines, and what a train of imagery and thought they kindle with strange subtlety of suggestion — every line a picture for the imagination. This new book contains an even more powerful imaginative poem, *Hell Gate* — a vision of a soldier in the Inferno which must be read in its longer completeness. It is different from any other poem of Mr. Housman's in its bizarre detail, for generally he only suggests. But it resembles the others in that it concerns friendship — in this case, friendship triumphant. Mr. Housman is the poet of infinite sympathy for the fallen; no sinner is beyond his understanding and compassion. Even a flower plucked at the grave of a suicide by the crossways moves him to exquisite comprehension: —

[quotes stanza 4 of No. XXX]

Beautiful Shropshire has won its own distinctive poet; and Ludlow, Wenlock, Bredon Hill, Clun, and Teme are now as strong a [sic] literary significance as Grasmere, Ayr, Olney, and Newstead.

35. G.H.C., review, *Sewanee Review*
xxxi, January 1923, 123–4

The author was George Herbert Clarke, editor of *Sewanee Review*.

The author of *A Shropshire Lad* (1896) has not disappointed us in his *Last Poems*, despite the lapse of twenty-six years. Both volumes contain unimpeachable poetry, sensitively conceived and exquisitely phrased. The appearance of *Last Poems* is an event of real importance.

The author is well known to students of the classics as a Latinist of high order, professor at Cambridge, editor and critic; but above and beyond these things, he is a veritable poet. He prefaces his new book with this explanation: –

[quotes Preface in full]

The note of the earlier and later volumes is one: it is that of a companionably courageous melancholy in the face of 'life's mere minute', as the poet contemplates the unescapable vicissitudes of all human experience, the inexorable changefulness (even the heartlessness and witlessness) of nature, and the ache of the soul in its effort to find the way to an authentic freedom. The poems are memorably wistful, indeed hauntingly so, with a pity-fibred irony that makes for fortitude, and a diction so novel in its melodies and connotations that fortitude becomes akin to happiness. To borrow Mr. Housman's own phrase, used in another connection, his poems are 'full of joy and woe'.

Of the forty-one poems twelve impress the reviewer as of outstanding merit, and of these again two seem to reach the acme of this poet's peculiar excellence of mode and meaning, – namely, *The West*, symbolic sunset verses that will 'have the heart out of your breast'; and *Hell Gate*, an imaginative adventure of extraordinary fascination, told with the severe and sombre beauty that its theme requires, yet with that brooding rebel-wonder that is in so much of Mr. Housman's work. The stanza quoted below is taken from *The West* and the few lines that follow conclude *Hell Gate*.

[quotes stanza 4 of No. I followed by the last ten lines of No. XXXI]

It is superfluous to say of such writing that it searches the heart. Why it does so with such insistent power is still the unknown quantity in the work of our first lyrists, who are not many.

36. Wallace B. Nichols, 'Mr. A.E. Housman's Return', *Poetry Review*

xiv, No. 1, January–February 1923, 27–9

Of all types of poets the lyrist is least expected to be gifted with a wide range, whether thematic or intellectual: let him but sing, and what else matters? No one, for instance, blames Herrick for not possessing either the variety of Shakespeare or the depth and height of Milton. In considering the dramatic or epic poet the critic must look for many more qualities than in considering the lyric poet; it is therefore easier to assess – perhaps, also, because easier to assimilate quickly – the work that is but song, song, song. The same reasons, it may be presumed, are behind the greater appeal of the lyrist to the poetry-reading public. The writer of an epic or of a poetic drama requires more sustained attention, to say nothing of a more comprehensive knowledge of poetic equipment and technique. But to understand or appreciate a lyric needs no essential previous knowledge of poetic form, still less of philosophic terms and eternal arguments. It is just a question of momentary feeling and nothing more, and, if the feelings are fired, then the lyric has done its work and, like good wine, needs no bush.

It is easy, then, to understand why Mr. Housman's lyrics have so great a popularity, combining, as they do, the appeal that properly belongs to their *genre* and the appeal that belongs individually to their power of firing the feelings. Also, in the particular case of *Last Poems* there is added the intriguing fact of the poet's long silence after an initial great success – a silence, in the circumstances, surely unique. It is debatable whether the publisher would be selling so many copies of this book if it were its author's sixth or seventh volume.

Last Poems is a book of the same character as *A Shropshire Lad*; that is to say, it treats of similar themes in a similar manner, and it can be said at once ungrudgingly that the manner has suffered, in the interval, no diminution in felicity. The book, as also its single predecessor, has its limitations, but limitations in lyrical work – which was the thesis of my opening paragraph – do not necessarily form a damning fault. If they did, Heine, Burns, Lovelace, even Catullus himself, were damned beyond salvation as lyrists, a contention only perversely to be proven.

So much for limitations in theme. But when it comes to limitations in form, can the same be said? He would be a rash critic who attempted to convict Heine or Catullus of poverty in metrical invention. But the case of Mr. Housman is not as theirs; the charge can be brought home to him of writing in very few metres and stanza-forms. Taking *A Shropshire Lad* and *Last Poems* as one book – which virtually they are – this becomes especially noticeable and entails a certain effect of monotony to the ear. Singly each poem is fresh; in bulk, they become – metrically that is to say – after a time, stale. But the same could be said, and with no definite disparagement, of a musical programme devoted entirely to the works of Chopin.

Chopin, however, is Chopin, and Mr. Housman is Mr. Housman, and to point out what is *not* in a book is an unjust method of approaching what *is* in it. A book which contains such perfect lyrics as 'The night is freezing fast', 'Epitaph on an Army of Mercenaries','Tell me not here, it needs not saying', and 'Fancy's Knell' is one upon which the critic, more especially if he happens to be a poet himself, can expatiate appreciatively – and enviously. Such moments of inspiration come rarely to any lyrist; they seem to have come – happily for us, happily, too, for posterity – to Mr. Housman less grudgingly than to many.

It is not necessary to give a taste of his quality to any abundant extent; his work is already too well appreciated to need being served in minute portions in the form of appetizers, but the following stanza from'Tell me not here, it needs not saying'

(No. XL) is such that I cannot refrain from endeavouring to share my own personal delight in it with as many others as possible:

[quotes stanza 3 of No. XL]

This has, it seems to me, that royal magic which is so rare and, when achieved, is so delicate a possession. This is a book to buy and not to borrow, a book to buy again if the copy is lost.

37. Clement Wood, 'The Shropshire Corydon: Opus II', *Nation* (New York)
cxvi, No. 3007, 21 February 1923, 222–3.

Clement Wood (1888–1950) was educated at the University of Alabama, then at Yale. A lawyer and schoolteacher, he was also an extremely prolific poet, publishing his first volume in 1917, and the author of books on many topics, including the lives of Warren Harding and Herbert Hoover.

It is to be doubted if any poet of the worth of A.E. Housman will go into the dark, leaving behind as light a pack of verse as he will have done. Fivescore and four slight lyrics, in two slight books – he has done much of the winnowing which time is used to doing. His worth is no less in the gold of his lines than in the spread of his influence. Heine before him thrice distilled vinegar with nectar; but Heine had much of the doubt of maturity, where Housman is all the wisdom of youth. Heine at times too used a long note, a wide gesture; Housman graves heaven and hell on the head of a pin. This is what he has taught the hovering flock that cannot top the clouds beside him. What O. Henry harvested from Poe in the short story, brief span and stabbing end, this man brought to the lyric. Nothing of his published since *A Shropshire Lad*? Never was idea so errant. His yearly output o'erleaps itself. Look in the volumes signed by other singers, to see how the heart of Housman has set the pitch, and the tongue of Housman uttered the music. He has never – he will never be dumb, for a long space. His wind-blown seeds bud and bloom in land and far island and up chill peaks. His cherry is hung with new snow with every spring.

Last Poems is but first poems published last. There is less of the crashing chord as the knife stabs home, by a trifle; there is a bleaker gust from a chiller land whining without the door; but almost any two poems from the two groups could be undetected changelings. There is the wide hollow wisdom of nineteen in the opening lines:

[quotes Prefatory Poem]

It is hard to pass a page without quotation. 'The West' is rich with his restrained loveliness:

[quotes ll. 3–4 and stanzas 2 and 11 of No. I]

The next poem flushes us with one choking new rhythm:

> Her limbecks dried of poisons
> And the knife at her neck.

But this is not heard again. The draining close of 'Grenadier', the subtle alteration of the theme of 'Lancer', the old majesty of 'Soldier from the Wars Returning', the trumpet note in:

[quotes stanzas 3 and 7 of No. IX]

This is the Housman that the lesser seedlings miss. The appalling vigor breaks in little lines like:

[quotes ll. 17–18 of No. XL and stanza 1 of No. XXXIII]

Over and over again the strain is of futility:

[quotes ll. 8–10 of No. XXXVIII, ll. 17–22 of No. XXIX, and stanza 2 of No. XIX]

There will be a startling break into a music as marching and triumphant as the peak of Lepanto:

The King with half the East at heel is marched from lands of morning;
Their fighters drink the rivers up, their shafts benight the air.

But the bitter brave moral is never far absent, as in this glittering Epitaph on an Army of Mercenaries:

[quotes No. XXXVII]

In place of the bitter trilogy of love dramas in the earlier book, we have here a group around the lad upon the scaffold. The charming whimsy 'Terence, this is stupid stuff' has briefer, sharper rebirth here:

[quotes No. XXI]

Only once do we detect a mood stronger and deeper than in the older singing:

[quotes ll. 1–8 of No. XII]

It were too much to expect this defiance to hold to the end:

[quotes ll. 9–16 of No. XII]

Shall we say that here was – that here is forever – a great minor poet, and let it slide at that? The lines say that no Pope or Dryden won each precious word more thoughtfully or felicitously; the tunes say that Campion's self spoke no more magic than this living Elizabethan youth. Why, then, is he not more than a great minor poet? What have others that he lacks? It is of course in part that he did not find nor seek the surge and thunder of 'Dauber', of 'Saul', of 'Tamerlane', of 'Lear '; nor the supreme ecstasy of the odes to the west wind and to Philomel, nor the star song of Kubla Khan. Deeper than this is a pervading craft that is at the end a fatal lack. Let us see what he does, to know thereby what is undone.

To this singer life is a plain thing. There are love, war, death noble and ignoble, spring and winter ... They are all young, as he knows them. Life never deepens for him beyond the vision of his Shropshire lad – a youth who has never seen twenty, as we span it, and never can. This is at once his crown and his crime. Here are all the conventions of pastoral poetry, worn, it is true, as a Joseph's coat. How would he be as Godiva? To word it otherwise, life is ever an affair of lad and lass, with him. To all of us it is this, with more, with much more. This is the eldest, spring-sweetest part; but there are deeper hells than Romeo knew or Juliet guessed. He must talk of the naked belly of a vast beautiful steam boiler, the wild-duck flight of airplanes raining death upon a countryside, in terms of Corydon and Thyrsis ... his crime and his crown. Why did he never grow up and out of the morbid wisdom of nineteen? The verses have all the beauty – pardon, dear master, for what the limbeck shows – of brainlessness. Perhaps after all this is all beauty: perhaps beauty stops at the threshold of one score. Was Socrates cross-eyed when he wept with joy at the beauty of a dotard's glimpse of the majesty of sky and taller man? We hold that he was not: to all of us this wider, maturer vision comes. This singer is a voice out of an impossible youth of the race; passed, and now impossible. We must have a man's singing from a major poet. Thus he is as he is: we are richer for the gap he has filled with melody; but we must turn to the stern, horrid crumbling of young dreams, and the wider dreams he could not know, and we must know and be.

38. William A. Norris, review, *New Republic*

xxxiv, No. 430, 28 February 1923, 26

Norris was an instructor in English at Harvard University.

No one, I think, could expect anything new in a new book by A.E. Housman. An exquisite and self-conscious pessimism, such as his, is the last refinement of poetry. Once achieved, it is changeless. It sees the finger at the lips of joy, and looks beyond the flower to the fruit, and beyond that to dissolution. It has stripped the world of all the illusions that support life; but is poignant and healthy in proportion to its love for those illusions.

After Mr. Housman had written *A Shropshire Lad* there was nothing left in the world for him to do. In its blundering way, the world seemed to know it; he became a minor classic. To the critic the Shropshire Lad was soon a closed book, as much as any book in a spoken tongue is ever closed to criticism. Now Mr. Housman has himself opened the book and slipped between its covers, quietly and with a deprecatory gesture, half a hundred more poems. But it is the same book, unchanged in any way, for such poetry is not measured by bulk. It is irrelevant to say that this latter half of his book contains no poem so nearly perfect as To an Athlete Dying Young [*A Shropshire Lad*, No. XIX], and few lines like

> And overhead the aspen heaves
> His rainy-sounding silver leaves.
> [*A Shropshire Lad*, No. XXVI, ll. 13–14]

It would be irrelevant to do anything at all but read the book, were it not for those apostles of progress in literature who are already calling *Last Poems* an echo of the Shropshire Lad, and accusing the author of weeping through forty-one poems over the mortality of mortals.

Let us admit that the addition of forty-one poems to the original fifty-three [*sic*] accentuates Mr. Housman's narrowness of subject matter as well as his singleness of purpose. There are many poems in the new volume that might be called alternate versions of poems in the Shropshire Lad. Moreover, his technique, being an amazingly delicate instrument with few strings, is less novel in a hundred poems than in half that number.

It may not be strictly true that the single poem is the unit by which a poet should be judged, but certainly the adventurous facility of our younger poets has led us to pay more attention to an author's work as a whole than to the few best examples of his work. Mr. Housman suffers by such scrutiny.

Apparently it requires many platitudes to defend Mr. Housman. All his poems are based on one formula: life is as short as it is vivid; its end is as inevitable as its beauty. This platitude is written large on the face of Shropshire, where the lass is wooed on the grave of her dead lover, where the young man dares not look too long at the sunset over Wales, and where the better of two lads is hanged and the other turns gladly to friends who still face the daylight. Life goes on like this, not only by Bredon Hill and Wenlock Edge, but the world over. Stated thus, it is a platitude to smile at, but it is the formula on which much of the finest poetry has been written, and it is as compelling a theme today as when it ran dark and insistent under the eager tissue of Elizabethan literature.

Only he, of course, who has a great zest for life can be a great pessimist. If we ask for only a little, we are apt to get it and be satisfied; and then we rail at those who find life less than their dreams of life. The measure of Mr. Housman's avidity is to be found as much in his technique as in his subject. His reverence for beauty leads as surely to a delicate and consistent economy of phrase and cadence, as it does to an occasionally brutal statement of the inadequacy of existence. In this respect he differs widely from Swinburne, with his monotonous prodigality, under which his lamentations become a mood and then a disease. It is significant that Mr. Housman's metrical range is very limited, while within his few conventional patterns he is so discriminating of values as to achieve surprising variations of effect. Neither Marvell nor Herrick, nor any other seventeenth century poet, was more exquisite in his use of the tetrameter couplet and quatrain.

I have digressed from pessimism, an attitude toward life, to the handling of syllables and lines. The connection is not obvious, but it is sound. Mr. Housman's desire for perfection is balked in all directions but one. It recoils upon itself from all corners of normal human activity, giving us his frankly unconstructive pessimism. But in the ordering of words to express this pessimism, there is no barrier to his desire, and he gives us such lines as these:

[quotes stanzas 6 and 7 of *A Shropshire Lad*, No. XIX]

I take these lines from the Shropshire Lad, because I think they excel, in delicacy of tracing, any eight lines in the later book. And as I have already said, the books are one.

I hope that little will be said about *Last Poems*. It is not food for the multitude, and the less attention there is drawn to it now, the less irrelevant foolishness will be uttered. Mr. Housman is already the priceless possession of a relatively small body of readers. He can never be anything more, or anything less than that.

39. William Rose Benét, 'The Book of the Month: A.E. Housman's "Last Poems"', *Bookman* (New York)

lvii, No. 1, March 1923, 83–5

William Rose Benét (1886–1950) was the elder brother of the poet Stephen Vincent Benét. He was himself a poet (his verse autobiography, *The Dust Which is God*, won a Pulitzer Prize in 1941) and a journalist, associated particularly with the *Saturday Review of Literature*.

Our after-the-war days have been, profoundly, days of disillusionment. This feeling has been reflected in our literature. The late nineties of the last century were days of disillusionment no less. But it was disillusionment of a different description. We hope to build. For *fin de siècle* Yellow Bookery there was no hope in achievement on this earth. There was only the hope of escape – the hope to die. This statement may be overemphatic, but I think the general distinction holds true.

A.E. Housman published in the late nineties some sixty poems which reflected the spirit of the close of the century, though they were of a grain that set them immediately apart from the characteristic work of that period. Now, in our own time, after long silence, he issues his 'Last Poems', and strangely enough they fall in very well with the spirit of our own time. At least they are 'good medicine' for our time; even though it is not too brash of us to assert beyond their general conclusion that it is still worth while building, worth while enjoying and striving while we live.

Yet Housman also says that. We shall see this presently.

Few realize that Housman was thirty-seven years old when *A Shropshire Lad* was published, and that now he is about sixty-four years old. When he remarked in his tiny foreword: 'It is not likely that I shall ever be impelled to write much more. I can no longer expect to be revisited by the continuous excitement under which in the early months of 1895 I wrote the greater part of my other book, nor indeed could I well sustain it if it came', there is a mild irony in the statement. Housman has, indeed, completed his 'century' – if we take the word in the sense that cricketers use it when any cricketer amasses one hundred runs. Housman has written a few over one hundred poems, and on these hundred or so poems, many of them most brief, his whole reputation rests.

Now if I were to add one letter to the word 'century', making it 'centaury', from the Greek *kentaureion*, in that word you would have the essence of his gift to our age; for centaury is the name of a herb said to have been used medicinally by the centaur Chiron, the instructor of the young heroes. And as Chiron was to the youth of his day, in his stoicism, sad wisdom, and the virtues of his magic herb, so is Housman to the younger poets of our own.

We find in him knowledge of the flesh, and through the flesh, knowledge of the spirit. Each leaf of his books astringently medicines. The words of a poem in *A Shropshire Lad* revealed his purpose:

[quotes ll. 43–58 of *A Shropshire Lad*, No. LXII]

That is what I meant by 'good medicine'. I said I would explain why I thought Housman's counsels brave. Well, when he takes his questioning to 'the heart within that tells the truth', his conclusion is, after all other reflection:

The Spartans on the sea-wet rock sat down and combed their hair.
[l. 16 of *Last Poems*, No. XXV]

It is a courageous conclusion. The conclusions of most of his poems are courageous; they are certainly stoic.

Deep disillusionment and deep rebelliousness are in him also; but he has mixed us a 'bracer' from the hemlock of Socrates.

Examining *Last Poems* more closely we find, quite naturally, less about young love in it, as much again, about battle. There is also Housman's obsession with the idea of the gallows. Oftener, it seems to me, in the songs of the first book 'the feather pate of folly' bore 'the falling sky'. Once indeed, out of more sombre pages, flashed the talaria of Hermes, flickering the presence of the god of eternal youth.

[quotes stanza 15 of *A Shropshire Lad*, No. XLII ('The Merry Guide')]

'Fancy's Knell', which ends *Last Poems*, is a far, faint echo from that time, when

[quotes ll. 21–4 of No. XLI]

In execution I find *Last Poems* little, if at all, inferior to *A Shropshire Lad*. There is, perhaps, nothing quite so perfect in its poignancy as was that first cry of youth, 'When I was one-and-twenty'. Yet the work in *Last Poems* is again admirably compact, admirably reticent, often admirably melodious. Again many lines, many verses, deeply imprint the memory. It had seemed, when one first read in the first book 'Farewell to barn and stack and tree', that never again could a man render so perfectly the atmosphere of mortal tragedy. But, in *Last Poems*, we have 'Eight o'Clock', stark fatality, perfectly presented in eight lines. We have also the bitterly moving poem just before it, 'The Culprit', which could not possibly be bettered in expression. And in 'The rain, it streams on stone and hillock' is what seems, to me at least, about the truest transcript of a man's grief for a fellow man that has ever been versified. It is intolerably searching in its recognition of the casuistry of human sorrow, in its setting of the lips and lifting of the chin – till the last verse leaps out with sudden terrible eloquence.

In 'West and away the wheels of darkness roll' is a most original image, springing from a more scientifically accurate view of the world in space than most poets have taken:

[quotes stanza 2 of No. XXXVI]

Such is the deftness of Housman's technique. The depth of his thinking can be illustrated by these eight lines:

[quotes No. X]

In the above we get some idea of Housman's intensity of feeling as well as the range of his powers of visualization. His poem 'The laws of God, the laws of man' is like to become a testament for free thinkers. 'Hell Gate', the longest poem in *Last Poems*, reveals fiery dramatic imagination. 'Lancer' may be excerpted from to illustrate the power of his irony. It epitomizes by inference both the glamour and the waste of war:

[quotes stanzas 3 and 4 of No. VI]

One triumph of technique impresses as it has always impressed. A.E. Housman is one of the few living poets who knows how and just where to end a poem. His terminations are remarkably effective. His gifts of condensation, elimination, and intimation contribute to this.

[quotes stanza 5 of No. XIV]

Technique accomplishes it, but the effectiveness of the poem springs more deeply from the power of the emotion behind it. All the poet's gifts would prove void were it not for the intensity of a point of view to which all his poems are but footnotes.

Several people have commented recently upon his debt to Heine's 'Buch der Lieder' in 'Sinner's Rue.' This poem seems indeed an unacknowledged translation of

> Am Kreuzweg wird begraben
> Wer selber sich bracht um:
> Dort wächst eine blaue Blume
> Die Armesünderblum, etc.[1]

Housman has evidently been long enthralled by the poems of Heinrich Heine. But even in this case he assimilates the poem in such a way as to make both phrase and cadence chiefly his own.

Of the influences and circumstances that sharpened Housman's point of view we know but little. We know that the same shire that fostered Hazlitt is Housman's shire. We know that after leaving Oxford he clerked for ten years in the Patent Office and for nineteen years was professor of Latin at University College, London – that in 1911 he went to Cambridge where he is still professor of Latin, that he has written for philological journals and edited Manilius and Juvenal. We have read of him as an odd and 'cranky' personality – we can weigh the obsessions of his mind, calculate from the form and tone of his work its peculiar strains and stresses. But the intimate man remains a mystery.

If the permanence of poetry be in proportion to the intelligent emotion it evokes, Housman's poetry should certainly endure. His style is wholly his own. He is master of a certain kind of strict expression. And he is still, in many ways, the noblest Roman of them all.

NOTE

1 Kate Freiligrath Kroeker, *Poems Selected from Heinrich Heine* (London: Walter Scott, undated), translates these lines as follows:

> At the cross-roads he lies buried
> Who ended his life in shame,
> And there grows a pale blue flower,
> The felon's flower by name.

The literal translation of the second line is 'Who killed himself'.

40. O.W. Firkins, 'Living Verse', *Yale Review*
xii, July 1923, 850–2

Oscar W. Firkins taught at the University of Minnesota.

In reading Mr. Housman's 'Last Poems' one is moved to say that the imagination has been re-discovered. One does not finally quite say this; one thinks with pleasure and regard of other writers; but the heart refuses to disown its first reckless hyperbole. Poetry still lives in spite of versifiers. The work is singularly free from all those fripperies of innovation under which the lack of true originality is more or less ingeniously dissembled. There is hardly a word, a metre, that would have halted the readers of 'Locksley Hall' or 'A Blot on the Scutcheon'; the freshness in these poems is internal. Be it said at the start that they are far from amiable and winsome; they are narrow in range and dark in colouring, taking their theme or text from the darkest and narrowest of all the objects of human contemplation – the grave. It is strange and sad enough that the living voice, that rare and tardy visitor, should be heard from a coffin; but life, from any source, is precious. The childbed and the bridebed and the deathbed – things which we remember to have seen associated in places so oddly distant as a paragraph of Hawthorne's 'Seven Gables' and the beginning of a fetid tale by Maupassant – are brought together constantly by Housman. The last two are combined in the ensuing stanzas in which the Deserter, lying in the arms of the woman, hears the drum (the 'Man' and 'Woman' are supplied by us):

[quotes stanzas 1–5 of No. XIII]

The woman first holds him with endearments, then looses him with gibes; she scoffs at Death, her rival:

> 'Sail away the ocean over,
>   Oh sail away,
> And lie there with your leaden lover
>   For ever and a day.'

This deserter, after all, rises and goes, though it is not God or country that inspires him. The cross does not shine above these graves, nor the flag wave over them; there is no resurrection for perishing man, nor redemption for an earth whose travail is imperishable. But the man goes; his friends die, and he dies with them. His fidelity is bitter, even blasphemous; he will curse readily enough 'whatever brute or blackguard made the world'. If these forty-one short lyrics have sometimes the plaintiveness of a wail, they have more often, and more characteristically, the curt trenchancy of an imprecation. There are no formal oaths, but, like oaths, the speeches are projectiles.

Even in pure beauty Mr. Housman's hand is sure. He can seize – we had almost said 'snare' – a landscape in a phrase. Take bits like the following: 'The silver sail of dawn' (simple but lovely image), 'the golden deluge of the morn', 'night welled through lane and hollow'. He can even write an 'Epithalamium' which recalls Milton by its classicism and Spenser by its warmth. The words are few. His verse reminds us of a hound, spare and sinewy and swift, and unswerving in its pressure on the quarry. The speech of the reticent is powerful; decades of silence add their drastic emphasis to Mr. Housman's sombre valedictory. The man seems half averse to speech; it is as if each thought had wrested leave to speak from the poet's reluctant taciturnity. Despair for once is masculine, for its words are robust and few, and it acts with all the energy of hope.

41. Edward Sapir, 'Mr. Housman's Last Poems', *Dial*

lxxv, August 1923, 188–91

Edward Sapir (1884–1939), anthropologist and linguist; also a poet. Born in Germany, he came to America as a child and graduated from Columbia University in 1904. From 1910 to 1925 he was chief of the Anthropology Division at the Canadian National Museum. He was an early student of American Indian languages and cultures and a pioneer in the phonemic method of linguistic analysis. He published *Language* in 1921, and was Sterling Professor of Anthropology and Linguistics at Yale from 1931 to his death.

Laying down this little volume, as bitter as it is wistful and as gentle and strong to break futile things as a man's strength on a twig, one muses back to its predecessor of nearly thirty years ago. How *A Shropshire Lad* sang out honestly from gallows' heights, how it gave sadness and the beauty of the countryside a new hardness, and how, beside its clear, silver, inexorable voice all the organ music of the aesthetes quickly hushed into dead velvet – all this we remember. *Last Poems* speaks with a slightly new accent, while telling of the same spiritual country. The former volume drew exact lines on the land and noted carefully the passionate steps of puppets, each on his given line, each to his useless point. In *Last Poems* there is less drama, less interested amusement in the process, a more explicit concern with the journey's end. Where *A Shropshire Lad* was athletically grim and waved its pessimistic formula with a blitheness that was not all mockery, the later poems reflect and mutter and sigh. 'Tis the same tale, but there's a different telling on't. And so, while our memory of the more significant book is as of a clear view in the cool, green morning, we come out of its successor's pages with eyes half-closed and with a dreaminess of sunset.

The contrast finds illustration within the covers of the book itself, for some of it is pure Shropshire Lad, notably Eight o'Clock:

[quotes No. XV]

This is as tart and unwinking as you will, with all of its philosophy carefully held down in the implications. There are no remarks, there is no squeal. Its futility is not a meditated thing, rather fate's impertinence thrust into the impatience and the lust of life, for of the hours we are told that he 'counted them and cursed his luck'. They are still worth the counting. Futility has not yet sunk into the heart of man. Elsewhere we are told:

[quotes No. X]

Explicit futility, a nicely cherished disgust that the poet has made over into a pessimism too sweet to smart. Such poems as this make of *A Shropshire Lad* a sort of protesting hillock on the smooth, verdant plain of Victorian-Georgian poesy. The 'continuous excitement' of 1895 that Mr. Housman speaks of in his preface had lifted him safely above the plain. He walks the plain now, not in the dead-earnest fashion of a real Victorian-Georgian, to be sure, rather with a foreign grace, with a reserve which somehow fails to realize the company he is in. We even find stratified poems, poems in which an honest workmanship of any perfectly honest squire ('Oh, to the bed of ocean, to Africk and to Ind') [ll. 14–15 of No. XIX] supports (or undermines) another layer ('And the dead call the dying/And finger at the doors') [ll. 9–10 of No. XIX].

A Shropshire Lad had in much of its imagery something cold, sharp, precipitated, something of the momentaneous power that we attribute to an unexpected rustle in dead leaves. There is less of this quality in *Last Poems*, but it is present. The first poem is full of it:

> The sun is down and drinks away
> From air and land the lees of day
>
> The long cloud and the single pine
> Sentinel the ending line
>
> Oh lad, I fear that yon's the sea
> Where they fished for you and me

These strangenesses are not awkward, not sought. They have more suddenness than ingenuity; they suggest omens, possibly, rather than pictures. Even the slightly euphuistic passages ring true, such as:

> And let not yet the swimmer leave
> His clothes upon the sands of eve.

It is ungracious and pedagogical to contrast, to mark off epochs. Yet a brief glance at our current exasperation, the better to fix Mr. Housman for our envy, a cordial good-bye to what is no longer strictly ours, and a vain question will not be thought too heavy a load of analysis. For, having laid down the *Last Poems* and mused of the lad, we find ourselves automatically closing the little book – and the manner of its closing is a symbol – not curtly, with a businesslike indifference, nor too lingeringly, with many browsings back and forth between the reluctantly closing covers, but slowly and decisively. We should like to feel ourselves more excitedly in the midst of Mr. Housman's work, but it will not go. A truth that we nearly hate whispers to us that there is no use pretending, that these lines lilt too doggedly and too sweetly to fall in quite with our more exigent, half-discovered harmonies, that many of the magic turns catch us cruelly absent-minded. And, most disappointing of all, for we are a little disappointed, and vexed at being so, we cannot seem to pool Mr. Housman's pessimism with our own. We seem to feel that our zero does not equate with his, that each has a different mathematical 'sense' or tendency.

We discover, as we probe into our puzzling disaccord, that we already love the Shropshire Lad as we love our Coleridge and our Blake and begin to divine that we were a little hasty in dating our modern drift from Mr. Housman's first volume. Its flare and its protest were a psychological, a temperamental, phenomenon, not a strictly cultural one. Its disillusionment was rooted in personality, not largely in a sensing of the proximate age. Hence while Mr. Housman seems to anticipate and now to join with us in our despair, he is serene and bitter where we are bitter and distraught. His cultural world was an accepted one, though he chose to deny its conscious values; our own perturbations, could they penetrate into the marrow of his bone, would not find him a sympathetic sufferer. In the larger perspective his best work is seen to be a highly personal culmination point in a poetic tradition that is thoroughly alien to us of today, and nothing demonstrates this more forcibly than the apparent backwash in some of the *Last Poems*. There is no backwash in spirit or in style, there is simply the lessened intensity that allows general, underlying cultural traits to emerge. His zero and our zero do not square for the reason that his is personal where ours is cultural.

Finally, the vain question. Such work as Mr. Housman's, admirably simple and clear, classical, as it is, once more raises the doubt as to whether we can truly be said to be expressing ourselves until our moods become less frenetic, our ideas less palpable and self-conscious, and, above all, our forms less hesitant. Our eccentricities have much interest and diagnostic value to ourselves, but should it not be possible to cabin their power in forms that are at once more gracious and less discussible? One wonders whether there is not in store for English poetry some tremendous simplification. One prays for a Heine who may give us all our mordancies, all our harmonies, and our stirrings of new life with simpler and subtler apparatus. There is room for a new Shropshire Lad.

42. F.L. Lucas, 'Few, but Roses', *New Statesman and Nation*
xxiii, 20 October 1923, 45–7

Frank Laurence Lucas (1894–1967), poet, novelist and scholar; Fellow of King's College, Cambridge, from 1920 onwards; Lecturer, and later Reader, in English at the University of Cambridge. He edited the works of John Webster, and published some thirty other books. Among the last was *The Greatest Problem, and Other Essays* (London: Cassell, 1960), which includes his long late essay ' "Fool's Errand to the Grave": The Personality and Poetry of Housman.'

'Few, but Roses' was reprinted without change in the *Dial*, lxxi (September 1924), 201–8.

A recent writer on Tennyson has suggested as an explanation of the hero-worship of the Victorians that 'the more the scientists shook their faith in God, the more did they invest their contemporaries with divine attributes.' One may suspect that the cause lay rather in the seriousness with which that age took things generally. But, at all events, the motive has ceased to work with us, and in a Cambridge teeming with savants who split, not the traditional hair, but the atom itself, no devout hand lays wreaths of bay on the steps of Whewell's Court. And whereas enthusiasts swarmed stealthily up the very elms of Farringford to watch a short-sighted laureate disport himself at battledore and shuttlecock, not a head turns now as down King's Parade passes the author of the Shropshire Lad. Not that, in this particular case, one would recommend the most undaunted American 'big game' hunter to attempt closer approaches; or that in general any one need sigh for Victorian *Schwärmerei* here again; but there are other extremes. We have learnt to take Professor Housman for granted as a poet; perhaps we have learnt the lesson a little too thoroughly. Must we wait to bury Caesar before we praise him to the full, for the earth to cover it before we realize how much has meant to us this shadow of a great rock in the weary land of modern verse, so boundless and so bare? Professor Housman has given us his 'last' poems; so that we can see his work, it is to be feared, already as a whole, if not so steadily as posterity. For that posterity will read him, seems to me as (humanly) certain, as it is dubious if there are more than two other living English poets of whom the same can be said. When Last Poems appeared, the reviews paid, indeed, their tributes to his verse and style and beauty – such tributes as adorn the wrappers of half a hundred other poets, in the inflated currency of to-day; but when it came to certain other characteristics, there appeared in their criticisms a tone ludicrously like the reluctant testimony of conjured devils. The view of life that breathes through these poems, the essence of their being, was passed gingerly over, with a mild deprecation, perhaps, of some particularly defiant utterance, or a pious wish that Professor Housman were less pessimistic – much as one might sigh what an agreeable play Hamlet might be without that depressing prince. Indeed, it recalls the advertisement I received the other day of a selected edition of Voltaire: '*Tout en reproduisant la physiognomie du poète philosophe, l'auteur s'est appliqué avec le plus grand soin à ne rien laisser passer qui pût choquer les susceptibilités de qui que ce soit,*'[1] — a recommendation calculated to make the dead chuckle in his grave.

But one cannot believe that posterity, if statesmen allow us that luxury, will fall into this half-hearted, impertinent folly. Wondering what the Georgians really thought and felt about existence – turning wearily from piles of little poets who busied themselves scrabbling [*sic*] illuminated miniatures in the margin of the book of life, and with slight disgust from such typical Georgianisms as Sir Oliver Lodge and Canon Barnes exchanging bouquets of pious nothings before edified audiences at the British Association – they will find here one answer to their question, one personality among so many echoing masks, one reading of life, wrong maybe, but blurred and corrupted at least with no optimistic emendations, and rendered into English of a purity that English literature has not surpassed. Some, rejecting his interpretation, will yet recognize, if they are human, that in moods, at least, they too have felt the same, and will hope, if they are wise, that though differing they enjoy him none the less; and some, sharing his view of life, will know that they enjoy him yet the more. And nobody will deprecate.

In pre-war Cambridge, which seemed so much more exciting than it does now (though this is doubtless mere middle-age) one of the greatest of excitements was the newcomer's discovery everywhere, in its little red binding, of the Shropshire Lad – the expression, so long inarticulately wanted, here found at last, of the resentment, the defiance, the luxuriant sadness (sentiment, I suppose, some will call it) of youth. With what expectation one waited in the Lecture Theatre of the Arts School amid an audience that seemed unworthily sparse, for the first sight of the poet – and in what perplexity one went away! Could this quiet, immaculate figure, setting straight, with even-voiced, passionless, unresting minuteness the jots and tittles of a fifth-rate ancient whose whole epic was not worth one stanza of his own – could this be the same? Only the lines about the mouth with their look of quiet, unutterable distaste, only the calm, relentless, bitter logic, as of destiny itself, with which some sprawling German commentator was broken into little pieces and dropped into the void, seemed in the least recognizable features. One came away feeling as if one had been watching a disguised Apollo picking the oakum of Admetus – divinely – but oakum! Had I known them then, I should surely have thought of those lines of Matthew Arnold to (of all things in this connexion) a Gipsy Child:

> Is the calm thine of stoic souls, who weigh
> Life well, and find it wanting, nor deplore:
> But in disdainful silence, turn away,
> Stand mute, self-centred, stern, and dream no more?

And had I been a prophet, I should have thought too of the verse that follows:

> Once ere the day decline, thou shalt discern,
> Oh once, ere night, in thy success thy chain.
> Ere the long evening close, thou shalt return,
> And wear thy majesty of grief again.

But in those days Last Poems were beyond our hopes, and none dreamed of a second sunrise that should make the Sphinx of the desert once more a Memnon of the dawn. It was cause for gratefulness enough that the Shropshire Lad was there – that and the poetry of Morris – to bear one through the war.

Arnold, indeed, the poet-professor of the sister University with his classicism and his Virgilian majesty of sorrow, is Professor Housman's nearest kin in English literature; and for a third to join with these, we must look to the disdainful yet tender brevity of Landor. In no other three of our poets have the spirits of Greece, Rome, and England found that happy mixture of their elements which lives in them – the grace and lucid sadness of the flutes of Hellas, the proud glitter and the stab of the short Roman sword, the sweetness and strength of the English countryside. Arnold doubted more, and wailed because he doubted, till harder men lost patience with his 'nibbling and quibbling' about belief; he was sometimes prim; and, unsurpassed as his best work is, and far wider in its range, he had not, technically, the sureness of the later poet's touch. Landor was less subtle and, likewise, less sure. It is a curiosity of literature that so late in the development of English poetry it should have been possible to bring harmonies so new, so invariably perfect out of some of its most hackneyed metres. Swinburne produced many of his miracles by brilliant modifications of old metrical forms. Beddoes recaptured, as no one since has done, the secret magic of Elizabethan blank verse. But Professor Housman modifies little and recaptures nothing; though the Carolines used some of his verse-forms to perfection, they are not like him. And when one sits down and puzzles where one has seen anything really akin to this Melchizedek, there comes only the unexpected half-answer: 'In Heine.' The belief that there is here more than coincidence is strengthened when one recognizes in the flower of Sinner's Rue no other than the German's *Armesünderblum* – the blue floweret that grows at cross-roads on the mounds of the slayers of themselves. But this does not go far towards explaining how his effects are produced; it is easy to docket the artifices he so boldly and openly uses, such as the assonance and alliteration of:

> Ah, past the plunge of plummet,
>   In seas I cannot sound,
> My heart and soul and senses,
>   World without end, are drowned.

A.E. HOUSMAN

> His *fo*lly has not *fe*llow
> Beneath the blue of day
> That gives to man or woman
> His heart and soul away.

> There flowers no balm to sain him
> From east of earth to west
> That's *lost* for ever*last*ing
> The heart out of his breast;

or the haunting

> From all the woods that autumn
> Bereaves in all the world.

It is simple to note the repetition carried even beyond Roman bounds till, once, it becomes a little self-caricaturish:

> The goal stands up, the keeper
> Stands up to keep the goal.

But the charm endures where these devices are not; there are so many strings to this bow with its sweet swallow-song – pause and shift of stress, fingering and vowel-play, and, above all, the skill which keeps the diction of these lyrics so simple and close to the directness of prose, without ever transgressing that fatal boundary, by its perfect intermingling of the unexpected word with the speech of everyday, of the unexpected thought with the looked-for conclusion. Indeed, his Shropshire lads talk with just that 'wild civility' for which Herrick praised his love:

> There flowers no balm to *sain* him ...

> From far, from eve and morning
> And yon *twelve-winded sky*...

> But men at whiles are sober
> And think by fits and starts,
> And if they think, *they fasten*
> *Their hands upon their hearts.*

But perhaps the supreme example of the sudden sting the verse leaves in the hearer's heart, as with all the wonder of a serpent's suppleness it glides away, is in the last but one of all the poems:

> On russet floors, by waters idle,
>   The pine lets fall its cone;
> The cuckoo shouts all day at nothing
>   In leafy dells alone;
> And traveller's joy beguiles in autumn
>   Hearts that have lost their own.

In the second volume, as a whole, indeed, if there is any development, it is an extension of this device of sudden check and unexpected pleasure to the rhythm also:

> 'What sound awakened me, I wonder,
>   *For now 'tis dumb.*'
> 'Wheels on the road, most like, or thunder:
>   Lie down; 'twas not the drum.'

or, best of all:

> Wenlock Edge was umbered,
>   And bright was Abdon Burf,
> And warm between them slumbered
>   The smooth green miles of turf;
> Until from grass and clover
>   The upshot beam would fade,
> *And England over*
>   Advanced the lofty shade.

And, with this, there goes a growing boldness in the surprises of the thought, a use of metaphors quite 'metaphysical,' such as that ironic 'foolscap' wherewith night's cone-shaped shadow crowns the earth eternally, or that last mantle which cured Dick's lifelong hatred of the cold:

> Fall, winter, fall: for he,
>   Prompt hand and headpiece clever,
>   Has woven a winter robe,
> And made of earth and sea
>   An overcoat for ever,
>   And wears the turning globe.

These things produce their complete effect just because the power to contrive them is controlled with a rigid economy; so that the general impression these lyrics leave is of a strength that never needs to strive or cry, a beauty whose quality is never strained. 'Schiller,' observed Coleridge, 'sets you a whole town afire. But Shakespeare drops you a handkerchief.' And, as there is no strain, so there are no collapses; if we could spare anything, it would be some of the poems on soldiers and on gallows. But such exceptions are few, and the most serious challenge to Housman's position will be his want of bulk. I do not think that need trouble us greatly; these poems, as Meleager said of Sappho's, are 'few, but roses.' The poems of Catullus are likewise few.

But the spell of this poetry does not live merely in its technical perfections, in its pure beauty, in the happy way it has won a province of its own, like Hardy's Wessex, in the heart of England, in the flowery grace with which it wears its ancient learning, so that the reader recognizes on Shropshire lips, with a stab of spiritual homesickness, the well-known accents of Sarpedon and Achilles or some echo of the laconic fortitude of Rome; and the water, not of 'Nile' only, but of Simois and Scamander, Ilissus and Tiber,

> spills its overflow
> Beside the Severn's dead.

It is, as Milton demanded, not only 'simple' and 'sensuous,' but 'passionate' also, as the perfect in style often fails to be; and it is 'criticism of life' after Arnold's heart. Not popular criticism, indeed; pessimism so unflinching and inflexible is to be found in few English poets apart from Hardy and James Thomson. And even Mr Hardy has sometimes wavered and of late grown mysteriously to resent the name; there is nothing in Professor Housman's work that could lend itself to such irony as the recent spectacle of babes and sucklings chanting a judiciously selected chorus of The Dynasts in honour of the Prince's visit to Dorchester.

This attitude to life many good people find bewildering and indecent:

> 'Terence, this is stupid stuff;
> You eat your victuals fast enough.'

Browning, at the rare moments when the voice of a groaning creation pierced his complacent ears, took refuge in the plea that one could really only speak for oneself and that he found life very tolerable. To others, life seems like the cave, not of Plato, but of Polyphemus; to a favoured few the ogre grants the boon of being last devoured; are they expected gratefully to rejoice in the commodiousness of the cavern and the courtesy of the Cyclops? The injuries of existence are deep enough without that insult; and from the conventional consolations tossed like straws to the drowning, they turn to the last shreds of certainty, their own feelings before the shadow-pageant of phenomena, their power to appreciate the irony of the comedy, the beauty of the tragedy of things. A Swift, frenzied by the spectacle of the 'oppression that makes a wise man mad', cries '*Vive la bagatelle*':

> And the feather-pate of folly
> Bears the falling sky.

A Thomson, again, finds in the defiance of despair despair's one palliative, as the old king of Pontus in poison poison's antidote.

> Mithridates, he died old;

and it is not the open eyes of disillusion that stumble worst,

> as you and I
> Fare on our long fool's-errand to the grave.

Pessimism is not depressing to those who have faced it, and pride may be one of the deadly sins, but it gives not the ignoblest human answer to the menace of eternity. The oracles are dumb, the odds impossible; but –

The Spartans on the sea-wet rock sat down and combed their hair.

It is of poetry like this that Cardinal Newman's words are true: 'Poetry is the refuge of those who have not the Catholic Church to flee to and repose upon.' Those who deprecate its pessimism do not realize that they are asking for the building without the foundation, the body without the life. If there were not the despair, there could not be the passion; if there were not the tragedy, there could not be the majesty of grief.

> The troubles of our proud and angry dust
> Are from eternity and shall not fail.

NOTE

1 'While reproducing the countenance of the poet-philosopher, the author has taken the greatest care to let nothing pass that might offend anyone's sensibilities.'

43. J.C. Squire, 'Mr. A.E. Housman'
1923

From *Essays On Poetry* (London: Hodder & Stoughton, 1923), 152–9.

'A Shropshire Lad' appeared in 1896. It attracted little attention when it first came out, but it soon began to percolate underground, and after a few years it had become, what it still remains, a powerful influence over artists and the treasured companion of thousands of readers. It was a little book, and a masterpiece. Its author, when he published it, was a young man. But he relapsed into silence. He became professor of Latin at Cambridge, he edited one of the obscurest classics he could find – expending enormous labour on it and great wit – and only once or twice in twenty-six years did he publish a poem which proved that his impulses and his powers were undiminished. Now, all new (I think) except the epigram on the Expeditionary Force, forty more poems appear in a valedictory volume. Mr. Housman condescends to a short preface. It may, since it is the first statement he has ever made about his own writing, be quoted in full:

> I publish these poems, few though they are, because it is not likely that I shall ever be impelled to write much more. I can no longer expect to be revisited by the continuous excitement under which, in the early months of 1895, I wrote the greater part of my other book: nor, indeed, could I well sustain it if it came; and it is best that what I have written

should be printed while I am here to see it through the press and control its spelling and punctuation. About a quarter of this matter belongs to the April of the present year, but most of it to dates between 1895 and 1910.

He has waited a quarter of a century, and the spirit which prompted the delay is very evident in the preface. At all events, he has made no mistake now. If there were some who thought that any successor to the 'Shropshire lad' must be an anti-climax, they may change their minds. At first shock the reader who has cherished 'A Shropshire Lad' may think, as he comes upon the familiar rhythms and thoughts, that the second book is an overflow from the first, a weaker repetition. But it will not take him long to discover that it is, in fact, a continuation and a continuation at the old level. He will discover 'The West,' then 'The Epithalamium,' and one by one these new poems will creep into his heart and become part of him, as did the old ones. In a day he will not know from which of the two books many of these poems came.

Mr. Housman has not printed his new poems in the order of their composition, and he has given no hint as to their respective dates. It would be possible to speculate as to which were the latest written. In one or two there is a tinge of retrospect which is convincing; and it may be that a tendency to look at things astronomically has grown on him. There are in these lyrics several audacious and magnificently successful images suggested by the contemplation of the earth as a planet – in contrast with a particular beloved spot of earth or human being. Such a phrase as:

> And up from India glances
> The silver sail of dawn

might have occurred in the earlier book; but there seems a new largeness in the picture of the dead man who has put on his winter overcoat of land and sea, of that other dead man (buried in South Africa) who has the Pole Star beneath him, and of the earth's 'towering foolscap of eternal shade,' circling as the sun circles. Speculation, however, is dangerous; and even were full information given, 'results' would be very slight. In manner, since we know that a quarter of these poems are new, there has been only a slight change, if any. I should say that 'Hell Gate' – a powerful thing, which looks like the record of a dream – was recent, but I am not sure. It is possible that where there is a direct reminiscence of an early poem – as, for instance, in the line, 'The rain, it streams on stone and hillock,' which is twin of the old poem, 'The wind it blows through holt and hanger' – we are in contact with a poem of the Shropshire Lad period. But the whole of the new verses are so obviously by the old hand that nothing in this way can be determined with certainty. And the mood, whatever may be true of the manner, has not changed at all.

It may be that, when these poems are arranged in chronological order, those who study them will be able to trace some slight development in Mr. Housman's style; but they will record no change in his themes, none in his attitude towards the world. All that could be said of the poet of 'A Shropshire Lad' can be said of the author of 'Last Poems': nothing less and nothing more. He has an unquenchable desire and no hope. He is acutely sensitive both to the cruelty and the beauty of life, but even when most intensely aware of them he sees both under the shadow of obliterating death and against the background of a blind featureless eternity about which he has no theories and with which he feels not even the slightest and most occasional mystical contact. It is a consolation that the cruelty will pass, and a torture that all human love and all natural loveliness must go with the blossoms into nothingness; he must endure the one when he can and enjoy the other while he may. Endurance is difficult and calls for perpetual self-reminders, and enjoyment when keenest brings the strongest return of the knowledge that it is transient. He is never visited by any glimmering of comfort regarding the ultimate meaning and destiny of things; 'somehow good' has no reflection in his vocabulary; on the whole, should he qualify his agnosticism in terms he would incline to the view that the universe is under an evil government, if any. All the old characteristic broodings recur in the new collection. His soldiers who go doomed to the fight are types of all mankind, battling briefly against an invulnerable fate; whether they are kicking against the pricks, or stoically resigned, their preoccupation is the same, and their end the same. He puts it now with an ironic humuor, which half conceals pain, now simply and directly out of the bared heart. One soldier ends his song with:

> For in the grave, they say,
>   Is neither knowledge nor device
> Nor thirteen pence a day.

And another:

> So here are things to think on
>   That ought to make me brave,
> As I strap on for fighting
>   My sword that will not save.

He thinks as he watches another:

> Too full already is the grave
> Of fellows that were good and brave
> And died because they were.

All his doctrine about the race is summarised in two analogous passages in this book:

> Our only portion is the estate of man:
> We want the moon, but we shall get no more.

> To think that two and two are four,
>   And neither five nor three,
> The heart of man has long been sore
>   And long 'tis like to be.

Beyond question he states his own position in these sentences, a position put even more briefly in a couplet elsewhere:

> I, a stranger, and afraid,
> In a world I never made.

In his old book he put his conclusions in two of the finest of all his verses: the noble and massive stanzas in which he addressed his soul with 'Let us endure an hour and see injustice done,' and those others in which he exhorted himself, since springs must be so few, to go and look at the cherry-trees in bloom. We have them here again: 'The Spartans on the sea-wet rock sat down and combed their hair' is the last line of one poem. There is another which 'hath a most dying fall' and begins exquisitely, sighingly, with:

> Tell me not here, it needs not saying
>   What tune the enchantress plays
> In aftermaths of soft September

> Or under blanching mays,
> For she and I were long acquainted
> And I knew all her ways.

It is spoken to all who wander with delight about the woods and fields he knew, listening as he listened to the shouts of the cuckoo, watching as he watched the falling of pine-cones and sheaves standing in moonlight, comforted as he was comforted by the Traveller's Joy that 'beguiles hearts that have lost their own,' and it tells them, before it is too late, to:

> Possess, as I possessed a season
> The countries I resign.

That resignation will not be completed yet; Mr. Housman, while he is alive, will not escape himself; he is not of those who are calloused by age. But the other resignation, after the example we have seen of his astonishing self-control as an artist, we may unhappily take to be final. He abandons his art with as beautiful a farewell as any poet ever wrote:

> When lads were home from labour
>   At Abdon under Clee,
> A man would call his neighbour
>   And both would send for me.
> And where the light in lances
>   Across the mead was laid,
> There to the dances
>   I fetched my flute and played.
>
> The lofty shade advances,
>   I fetched my flute and play:
> Come, lads, and learn the dances
>   And praise the tune to-day.
> To-morrow, more's the pity,
>   Away we both must hie,
> To air the ditty
>   And to earth I.

So there he leaves us: with a hundred lyrics. It is a peculiar phenomenon in the history of poetry: a hundred lyrics, of which the majority are, humanly speaking, perfect; no failures, no padding, none of the crude attempts of youth, none of the merely habitual versifyings of senility, no effort to conquer any form but the one, none to write a 'major work.' No English poet has been so ruthless with himself as an artist; that alone would make him unique. He is equally singular in manner and in attitude: a sort of blend of Baudelaire and Heine who is nevertheless as English as he could be. Posterity, which always amuses itself with this game, may 'place' him. What is certain is that he is bound to be a considerable figure in our poetical history, and that his poems, unlike many great works, will continue to be widely read. It is a strange quality in him that his very pessimism attracts those who like pessimism nowhere else. He is honest and courageous; he incites in the end, to honesty and courage; he stimulates enjoyment even while he laments; and his music is so beautiful that whatever he says must delight. Young men and lovers will find all their secret thoughts in him, and finding them will be comforted; and to poets he will be a standard. Whatever his limitations may be, he has written scarcely a line which is not perfectly musical, scarcely a word which is not accurate and necessary. He has disciplined himself to such a point that there is at least one poem in his new volume which does not contain a single adjective; he is always lucid, always truthful, and when he uses an epithet he uses it to some purpose. This is a matter apart from philosophy. Even hymn-writers could study him to advantage.

44. J.F. Macdonald, from 'The Poetry of A.E. Housman', *Queen's Quarterly*

xxxi, Fall 1923, 122–37

Rather to Housman's own surprise, I think, the world has accepted *A Shropshire Lad*. It has not, of course, had the amazing vogue of Omar Khayam [sic] but it has steadily grown in favor and influence until it has quietly taken its place as one of the minor classics of our literature. Its sale must have been very considerable. There were seven new editions or reprints in the decade after it was first published and I don't know how many since in England

and America. There is something curious in this growth of Housman's reputation. He himself kept out of the public eye and the professional critics practically ignored him. Indeed there are only two articles on him listed in the guides to periodical literature up to November of last year, one by William Archer in 1898, the other by Holbrook Jackson in 1919 [see Nos. 11 and 20 above]. And yet one had only to mention *A Shropshire Lad* in any group of poetry lovers to see eyes light up and hear favorite bits lovingly quoted.

After more than a quarter of a century Housman last October published another little volume which he resolutely calls *Last Poems*. It has been received with favor in every quarter from a friendly cartoon in *Punch* to a laudatory review in *The Times*. The reviewers, of course, are not agreed about the exact points in which *Last Poems* fall short of or surpass *A Shropshire Lad*. Most of them, however, declare that, so far as metre and rhythm are concerned, the later book merely repeats the few simple measures of the earlier one. The anonymous reviewer in *The Times*, Mr. Priestley in *The London Mercury*, and S.M. Ellis in *The Fortnightly Review* [see Nos. 32 and 34 above], are in substantial agreement. Let Mr. Priestley speak for all: 'There are no intricate measures in *A Shropshire Lad*, and it is clear that its author relies very little upon the charm of metre. The new volume repeats the favourite measures of the old one, and shows that the poet has no taste for metrical experiments. He is fond of the octosyllabic line and ballad measure in its simplest form. Here and there he makes clever use of a five-line stanza, which is a striking variation on the old Short Measure, the first and third lines being unrhymed and having each a redundant syllable, the second, fourth, and fifth lines rhyming together.'

My head goes round. Is this generation of reviewers deaf, or do they never read poetry aloud? Housman once protested in reviewing a new edition of Ovid: 'It is hard to write without bitterness of the loss of time inflicted on an intelligent student by editors who cannot even be trusted to hand down the discoveries which their betters have made.' Change 'editors' to 'reviewers' and the protest holds. For William Archer writing in *The Fortnightly Review* of August, 1898, before he knew anything of Mr. Housman save his name, made this discovery:

'Mr. Housman is no Shropshire Burns singing at his plough.

He is a man of culture. He moves in his rustic garb with no clodhopper's gait, but with the ease of an athlete; and I think he has an Elzevir classic in the pocket of his smock frock.... In deference to his rustic mask, and probably to something fundamental in his talent as well, he attempts no metrical arabesques, no verbal enamelling. With scarcely an exception, his metres are of the homeliest; yet in their little variations, their suspensions, their tremulous cadences, we recognize the touch of the born metrist.'

Precisely; but it requires an ear to recognize it, and, unfortunately for himself, Mr. Priestley has demonstrated on page 183 of last December's *London Mercury* that he lacks that useful organ. He quotes, evidently from memory, this stanza out of one of the most haunting little poems in *A Shropshire Lad* – 'a poem', says Archer, 'so delicate that even the tenderest breath of praise would only shake off some of its bloom.'

> We still had sorrows to lighten,
> One could not be always glad,
> And lads knew trouble at Knighton
> When I was a Knighton lad.

Mr. Priestley interchanges 'be' and 'always' in the second line, apparently without any warning from his ear that 'One could not always be glad' is unmetrical and discordant.

'The new volume repeats the favourite measures of the old one, and shows that the poet has no taste for metrical experiments,' says Mr. Priestley. Here are the facts. Housman uses 21 different measures in the 63 poems in *A Shropshire Lad*. Only 9 of these measures recur once or oftener in the 41 lyrics that make up the *Last Poems*. Two of these are used in 5 poems, one in 3, one in 2, and five in 1 each. No less than 18 new measures are introduced. Let me put this another way. In the 63 poems there are 21 different measures; in the 41 there are 27. In the 104 poems that form the two little volumes, there are 39 different measures, 28 of which are used only once. It is true that two measures used 22 times in *A Shropshire Lad* occur 10 times between them in *Last Poems*, but it is an amazing deduction from this fact that 'the poet has no taste for metrical experiments.' Where else in English poetry, except possibly in Thomas Campion's *Books of Airs*, can one find so great a variety of measures in 104 consecutive poems?

It is quite true that Housman is fond of the octosyllabic; about one-third of all the lines in the two volumes are octosyllabic. But he has few poems wholly in octosyllabic verse. To be exact there are 13 in *A Shropshire Lad* and only 2 in *Last Poems*. All but one of these are written in couplets, or in quatrains of two couplets. Moreover, the octosyllabic lines in *Last Poems* are outnumbered by both six syllable and seven syllable lines. It is interesting to note that he has only one poem in decasyllabics, and only two others in which there are any lines of ten syllables. All three of these are in the new volume.

The range of his metre is very great, the lines varying from four to fifteen syllables in length. Still more remarkable is the amount and the subtlety of variation within a single stanza, and the almost uncanny felicity with which the stresses of the metrical pattern coincide with the normal accents of the sentence. Let anyone who has an ear for poetry read even this one stanza and judge of Housman's control of metre and of the reliance he places on its charm:

> The chestnut casts his flambeaux, and the flowers
> Stream from the hawthorn on the wind away,
> The doors clap to, the pane is blind with showers.
> Pass me the can, lad; there's an end of May.

How perfectly that 'clap to' echoes the bang of the door slamming shut; how admirably the young man's disgust at his spoilt walking trip is voiced in the closing line. And then the magic of

> Stream from the hawthorn on the wind away

– why one can see the blossoms grow dim in the distance with the dying cadence of that unbroken line. But enough of metre for a moment – those who have ears need no persuasion and those who have none are deaf to it.

The most interesting review of *Last Poems* that has come to my notice is that by Mr. Clement Wood in the New York *Nation* of February 21 this year [see No. 37 above]. As no summary could do justice to his conclusions or preciosities of style, one is forced to quote at some length:

'Shall we say that here was – that here is forever – a great minor poet, and let it slide at that?... Let us see what he does, to know thereby what is undone.

'To this singer life is a plain thing. There are love, war, death noble and ignoble, spring and winter. They are all young as he knows them. Life never deepens for him beyond the vision of his Shropshire lad – a youth who has never seen twenty, as we span it, and never can. This is at once his crown and his crime. Here are all the conventions of pastoral poetry, worn it is true, as a Joseph's coat. How would he be as Godiva? ... He must talk of the naked belly of a vast beautiful steam boiler, the wild-duck flight of airplanes raining death upon a countryside, in terms of Corydon and Thyrsis ... his crime and his crown. Why did he never grow up and out of the morbid wisdom of nineteen? The verses have all the beauty – pardon, dear master, for what the limbec [sic] shows – of brainlessness... This singer is a voice out of an impossible youth of the race; passed, and now impossible. We must have man's singing from a major poet. Thus he is as he is; we are richer for the gap he has filled with melody; but we must turn to the stern, horrid crumbling of young dreams, and the wider dreams he could not know, and we must know, and be.'

After the first shock of surprise at finding such stuff in a reputable weekly like *The Nation*, one is inclined to shrug his shoulders at this posturing of a minor critic, and, to use his own elegant phrase, let it slide at that. But his pronouncement that Housman is only a minor poet deserves consideration. First, however, one may correct some misstatements. Corydon and Thyrsis, those age-old Sicilians, are nowhere to be found in Housman. But we have Tom and Dick and Ned and Fan and Nancy – English all. Nor does one know how Mr. Housman would have talked about 'the wild-duck flight of airplanes raining death upon a countryside.' He doesn't anywhere mention them. Nor does he talk at all about 'the naked belly of a vast beautiful steam-boiler,' apparently to the disappointment of Mr. Wood who, like many other people nowadays, seems to think the machinery of life more important than life itself. Housman, evidently, is too quiet, his passion is too restrained to suit the taste of Mr. Wood. And yet, surely, a critic of discernment may be stirred by the trumpet blare of Mr. Sandburg's praise of Chicago,

> Hog-Butcher for the World,
> Tool-maker, Stacker of Wheat,
> Player with Railroads and the Nation's Freight-handler,

A.E. HOUSMAN

> Stormy, husky, brawling,
> City of the Big Shoulders:

without letting it wholly deafen him for the still music of Housman's,

> Clunton and Clunbury,
> Clungunford and Clun,
> Are the quietest places
> Under the sun.

A great minor poet – is that to be the judgement finally passed on Housman by our classifying age? Even if it is he may be in good company. Some time ago a casual statement in a manual on Greek literature almost took my breath away. 'Among the Greek minor poets', it began, 'Pindar and Sappho' — . Pindar and Sappho – who wouldn't covet their companionship on the slopes of Mount Parnassus? Is Burns a minor poet? Is Gray or Blake? What is the test? No one imagines Housman with his two slender volumes of lyrics should take rank with Shakespeare and Homer, with Dante and Vergil. No, nor with Browning and Wordsworth, or Shelley and Keats. These men in sheer bulk, in range and breadth are altogether beyond him. A minor poet – yes, if you like, but one who writes genuine poetry.

Few critics would agree on just what is meant by 'minor poet', but most critics are in substantial agreement about the term 'minor poetry'. It is graceful verse, conceived in man's wit and ingeniously constructed to suit the prevailing taste. A couple of specimens will enable us to see the characteristics of the type.

> The night has a thousand eyes,
> And the day but one;
> Yet the light of the bright world dies
> With the dying sun.
>
> The mind has a thousand eyes,
> And the heart but one;
> Yet the light of a whole life dies
> When love is done.

This graceful well constructed little lyric has so obvious and appealing sentimentality that it is now a hackneyed concert piece, a favorite encore number. Put beside it Housman's

> Into my heart an air that kills
> From yon far country blows:
> What are those blue remembered hills,
> What spires, what farms are those?
>
> That is the land of lost content,
> I see it shining plain,
> The happy highways where I went
> And cannot come again.

The breath of passion that trembles through these exquistie lines comes from a depth of feeling below anything Mr. Bourdillon ever communicates to the readers of his verse. We, too, can see through our tears that lost land 'shining plain'. Take this other selection of Bourdillon's from the *Oxford Book of Victorian Verse*:

> The lark above our heads doth know
> A heaven we see not here below;
> She sees it, and for joy she sings;
> Then falls with ineffectual wings.
>
> Ah, soaring soul! faint not nor tire!
> Each heaven attain'd reveals a higher.
> Thy thought is of thy failure; we
> List raptured, and thank God for thee.

This poem is sure, sooner or later, to get into the school readers. It has all the qualities that attract educationists who regard poetry as the handmaid of morality – a pretty little sentiment, a bit of the pathetic fallacy, and a nice little moral which can be rubbed into the sullen souls of shamefaced boys for at least a full half hour. There is no chance of Housman's farewell to a soldier suffering this fate. But its virile drum beat somehow comes thumping at a man's heart:

> Now hollow fires burn out to black,
> And lights are guttering low:
> Square your shoulders, lift your pack,
> And leave your friends and go.
>
> Oh never fear, man, nought's to dread,
> Look not left nor right:
> In all the endless road you tread
> There's nothing but the night.

Verse like that comes only from men who, as Emerson says, 'live from a great depth of being.'

It is the passion of Housman's verse that lifts it far above the conventional gracefulness of minor poetry — its passion and at times its breadth and humor. The very spirit of the countryside with its slow, endless gossip is in these eight lines:

> Oh, when I was in love with you,
> Then I was clean and brave,
> And miles around the wonder grew
> How well did I behave.
>
> And now the fancy passes by,
> And nothing will remain,
> And miles around they'll say that I
> Am quite myself again.

Perhaps these three little lyrics of two quatrains each are enough to prove my point but if anyone prefer a greater sweep and a deeper-throated music let him read number XLVIII in *A Shropshire Lad*, the noblest poem in the volume both in metre and language, a poem in which Housman rises into what Arnold himself could hardly deny is the 'grand manner.' To talk of it as minor poetry, with the suggestion that term conveys of mere prettiness and conventionality, is so obviously absurd that we may dismiss the topic.

In the little preface to *Last Poems* Housman says, 'I can no longer expect to be revisited by the continuous excitement under which in the early months of 1895 I wrote the greater part of my other book, nor indeed could I well sustain it if it came ... About a quarter of this matter belongs to the April of the present year, but most of it dates between 1895 and 1910.' If the inspiration has been fitful since that wonderful spring, it has been none the less genuine. *Last Poems* fully sustains the high reputation won by *A Shropshire Lad*. It has almost everywhere the note of intense feeling expressed in language of absolute precision, and of such great simplicity that it is almost vernacular. It is doubtful if any other English writer uses so high a percentage of words of one syllable, slightly over 84 per cent. in *A Shropshire Lad* and a little over $85\frac{1}{2}$ in *Last Poems*. Further, only 1 per cent. of the words are three syllables, about $\frac{1}{7}$ of 1 per cent. four syllables. The disyllables are about $14\frac{1}{2}$ per cent. in the earlier volume and less than

13 per cent. in *Last Poems*. There are no words of more than four syllables and most of these are compound adjectives as in the 'valley-guarded granges' of 'The Merry Guide.' Indeed the words are not merely short but simple homely words chosen, as Wordsworth advised, from 'the real language of men.' It is noteworthy too that the language is everywhere concrete. The famous adjectives that Milton used in stating the essential qualities of poetry are peculiarly fitted to describe these poems of Housman – 'simple, sensuous, passionate.'

The old figures of *A Shropshire Lad* reappear, with the exception of the rival lovers, but spring has changed to autumn, or rather the thought of autumn colours the poet's vision of spring. The earlier lyrics are remarkable for the vivid colors Housman delights in – gold, silver, scarlet, red, azure, and the white of snow, and the cherry and hawthorn bloom. In *Last Poems* the dark, the grey of mists, black and russets and tans predominate. Instead of the spring sun we have the rains of autumn. The whole landscape is darker. Moreover, the twenty odd flowers, white and gold and blue, are replaced by a bare half-dozen, most of them of duller shade. The difference in color between the two volumes is very marked. *A Shropshire Lad*, too, has almost everywhere the air of morning in its descriptive passages; *Last Poems* have the shades of evening or the gloom of night. Further, there is something almost sinister in these later mornings. Instead of the drum-beat of 'Reveille'

> Up, lad, up, 'tis late for lying:
> Hear the drums of morning play;
> Hark, the empty highways crying
> 'Who'll beyond the hills away?'

we have the half humorous protest

> Yonder see the morning blink:
> The sun is up and up must I,
> To wash and dress and eat and drink
> And look at things and talk and think
> And work, and God knows why.

One poem expresses in brief the whole atmosphere of *Last Poems*. Moreover, it is an amazingly vivid bit of astronomy as well as a sombre piece of symbolism.

A.E. HOUSMAN

West and away the wheels of darkness roll,
Day's beamy banner up the east is borne,
Spectres and fears, the nightmare and her foal,
Drown in the golden deluge of the morn.

But over sea and continent from sight
Safe to the Indies has the earth conveyed
The vast and moon-eclipsing cone of night,
Her towering foolscap of eternal shade.

See, in mid heaven the sun is mounted; hark,
The belfries tingle to the noonday chime.
'Tis silent, and the subterranean dark
Has crossed the nadir, and begins to climb.

One sometimes feels in reading the poems of Thomas Hardy that their diction is that of scientific prose. It conveys nothing beyond the regular and precise dictionary meaning of the words. But Housman even in his barest and most realistic poems uses words that suggest more than they state. The two brief poems, 'The Culprit' and 'Eight O'Clock' could hardly be less decorated than they are. There are just two adjectives in the seven stanzas and the words are of the simplest. Yet note the effect.

THE CULPRIT

. . . .
My mother and my father
Out of the light they lie;
The warrant would not find them,
And here 'tis only I
Shall hang so high.

. . . .
For so the game is ended
That should not have begun.
My father and my mother
They had a likely son,
And I have none.

EIGHT O'CLOCK

He stood, and heard the steeple
Sprinkle the quarters on the morning town.
One, two, three, four, to market-place and people
It tossed them down.

> Strapped, noosed, nighing his hour,
> He stood and counted them and cursed his luck;
> And then the clock collected in the tower
> Its strength, and struck.

What it is that grips our heart-strings here? No doubt there is something that defies analysis, but this thought of a family with 'a likely son' dying out in failure and disgrace brings a lump in the throat. The pity of his end! And how bitter it is to die on this bright and bustling morning as the chimes toss down the quarters to the busy market-place. The premonitory whirr before the first stroke of the hour falls and with it the trap-door under the doomed man, seemed to the tense nerves of the poet a conscious effort of the old clock to brace itself for the moment of horror when it struck. For sheer artistry in making metre enforce the thought these two stanzas would be hard to match. Yet this is the author that Mr. Priestley says 'relies very little upon the charm of metre.'

A good deal has been said in recent reviews of *Last Poems* about Housman's pessimism. On this side of the Atlantic, at least, pessimist is just one degree below bolshevist as a term of abuse. We dislike the fact, indeed we shut our eyes to the fact, that in this world every religion, every culture, that stood the test of long years had in it a core of stoicism by which it endured even if it couldn't rejoice and triumph. And we are prone to confuse stoicism with pessimism. Galsworthy has a sketch in *A Commentary* of an old deep sea fisherman lamed by accident and reduced to a precarious livelihood won by selling pennyworths of groundsel for canaries. 'In the crowded highway, beside his basket, he stood, leaning on his twisted stick, with his tired, steadfast face – a ragged statue to the great, unconscious human virtue, the most hopeful and inspiring of all things on earth, Courage without Hope.' In Housman the virtue is a conscious one – he has no illusions about what the future holds for him. In 'The Oracles' he tells us how the ancient voices are dumb but the heart of man still answers and how from that oracle he heard the priestess shrieking

> That she and I should surely die and never live again.

He answers doggedly

> Oh priestess, what you cry is clear, and sound good sense I think it;
> But let the screaming echoes rest, and froth your mouth no more.
> 'Tis true there's better booze than brine, but he that drowns must drink it;
> And oh, my lass, the news is news that men have heard before.

And then with only italics to indicate that the next lines are quoted he gives the substance of the message brought to Leonidas at Thermopylae by an excited messenger:

> *The King with half the East at heel is marched from lands of morning;*
> *Their fighters drink the rivers up, their shafts benight the air,*
> *And he that stands will die for nought, and home there's no returning.*
> The Spartans on the sea-wet rock sat down and combed their hair.

One need hardly point out the inference; what the Spartans did we also can do.

But the doing is not easy and Housman makes no attempt to delude either us or himself about the inevitable end. This is what gives the profound pathos to number XXXIX in *Last Poems*. The youth who delighted to climb the highest hill and watch the glow fade out of the western sky, now turns in middle age to the shelter of his room and the glow of his lamp to shut out the night and the thought of night. When he was younger, as he puts it:

> The year might age, and cloudy
> The lessening day might close,
> But air of other summers
> Breathed from beyond the snows,
> And I had hope of those.
>
> They came and went and are not
> And come no more anew;
> And all the years and seasons
> That ever can ensue
> Must now be worse and few.
>
> So here's an end of roaming
> On eves when autumn nighs:
> The ear too fondly listens
> For summer's parting sighs,
> And then the heart replies.

Moreover, nature has ceased to comfort as she did in the days of *A Shropshire Lad*. Then he felt her sympathetic comradeship:

> In my own shire if I was sad,
> Homely comforters I had:
> The earth, because my heart was sore,
> Sorrowed for the son she bore.

But now he realizes that his old faith in nature was only a spell cast over him by that enchantress,

> For nature, heartless, witless nature,
> Will neither care nor know
> What stranger's feet may find the meadow
> And trespass there and go,
> Nor ask amid the dews of morning
> If they are mine or no.

The one faith that burns clear in his poems from first to last is trust in friendship. Over and over this is voiced. The country lad going up by train to London with his hand aching because that morning

> So many an honest fellow's fist
> Had well nigh wrung it from the wrist,

feels he must keep from shame in the great city because his friends have faith in him. The lad in number XXXII of *Last Poems* had a passion for friendship. When he mused in boyhood

> It was not foes to conquer,
> Nor sweethearts to be kind,
> But it was friends to die for
> That I would seek and find.

But the friends died for him. That is the tragedy of the war.

> They braced their belts about them,
> They crossed in ships the sea,
> They sought and found six feet of ground,
> And there they died for me.

Friendship is the theme of 'Hell Gate', the most remarkable and most original poem in the new volume. A lad pacing sadly across the 'uncoloured plain' with his dark conductor sees in the shadow beneath the towering wall in the distance a spark stir to and fro. Though he says not a word the sombre guide answers his unspoken question,

A.E. HOUSMAN

> At hell gate the damned in turn
> Pace for sentinel and burn,

As they approach, the sentry vaguely reminds him of a sentry in an earthly corps. When Sin and Death, warders of the gate, rose to give entrance to their lord and father, then

> The portress foul to see
> Lifted up her eyes on me
> Smiling, and I made reply:
> 'Met again, my lass,' said I.
> Then the sentry turned his head,
> Looked, and knew me, and was Ned.

Even at the gate of hell, friendship triumphs. Ned straddles in revolt across the entry and with his musket from hell's arsenal shoots down his king.

> And the hollowness of hell
> Sounded as its master fell.

The two friends take the backward track in silence:

> Once we listened and looked back;
> But the city, dusk and mute,
> Slept, and there was no pursuit.

This brief summary gives no conception of the cumulative effect of the incidents in the poem or of its weird Dantesque power of description. I do not know anything just like it in English. But through it all the passion of friendship is the shaping force.

It is the pity of having to leave one's friends that makes the poem he chooses to close his *Last Poems* so wistful and pathetic. He tells how he used to play the flute for country dances and how

> The youth toward his fancy
> Would turn his brow of tan,
> And Tom would pair with Nancy
> And Dick step off with Fan;
> The girl would lift her glances
> To his, and both be mute:
> Well went the dances
> At evening to the flute.

But now

> The lofty shade advances
> I fetch my flute and play:
> Come, lads, and learn the dances
> And praise the tune to-day.
> To-morrow, more's the pity
> Away we both must hie,
> To air the ditty,
> And to earth I.

It is superfluous, almost impertinent, to call attention to the sigh of regret and resignation in those closing lines. It is the very spirit of Gray's *Elegy* in twentieth century form.

Whether Housman plays the flute I do not know, but his choice of it seems peculiarly appropriate. For his verse has the very tones of that instrument, clear, mellow, piercing, with something added of the undertones one catches in old folk songs. It appeals to lovers of poetry whether they be unread or as cultured as Housman himself. His poems in their restraint, their simplicity, their clear outlines are essentially Greek; in their pathos, their poignancy, their tremulous sensibility, they are Celtic and Romantic.

Housman, indeed, is the poet of a temperament. It narrows his range while it deepens his intensity. To an increasing number he makes a peculiar appeal. Nature has not proved the consoler that Wordsworth found her and that Arnold expected she would more and more become. Most of our poets of to-day – that is those of them who think at all – have fallen back on a dogged stoicism and an intense joy in whatever glimpse of beauty may be caught as we journey on what Housman in one of his rare moments of bitterness calls our 'long fool's errand to the grave.' And so Housman's thought is to-day in what Arnold calls 'the main stream of ideas.' Whether this explains his influence I am not sure – it may in part – but I am sure that with the exception of Thomas Hardy, no living English poet has had such an effect on the work of his fellow-craftsmen. Echoes of *A Shropshire Lad* are everywhere from Masefield to Edna St. Vincent Millay. His work is bound to bulk large in the anthologies of twentieth century poetry. Indeed his place in English literature seems to me as secure as that of his spiritual kinsman, Thomas Gray.

45. Osbert Burdett on Housman
1925

Osbert Burdett (1885–1936), educated at Marlborough College and King's College, Cambridge. He edited the series *Makers of the Modern Age*, and among his many books about literary figures was one on Blake (*English Men of Letters* series, 1926).

Reprinted from Burdett, *The Beardsley Period* (London: Lane, 1925), 167–72.

We now come to a writer, who must be included here because he developed as a genuine modern poet one of the themes out of which the artistic sympathies of the period was [sic] woven. He was alone, I think, in the fullness and sincerity of his apprehension of it, and this places him outside the circle of men who were mainly abortive seekers in all but the technics of writing; but this solitary eminence emphasizes the vitality of the Pagan ideal for which he stood, an ideal that absorbed his soul while it attracted the senses of men who were not scholars. I refer, of course, to Mr. A.E. Housman. It is significant of the reverence with which he regarded the Pagan ideal, that though cradled, as it were, in London, he discerned it where it still survives, not in the appetites that haunt our city streets, but in the English countryside where the old life has been least altered. He studies it there, because the life there reminds him most of the humanity that he admires in Pagan times and classic authors. Like them, he is wistful before death, which he will not seek to explain away by entertaining any hope of immortality. Like them, he admires excellence of body and brain, especially the noblest of the virtues, courage. Like them, to him life is tragic, and most moving for the opportunity it gives to display the heroic qualities in man. Again like them, he believes that suicide may be a noble act; and his heroes are not famous or eccentric people, but local athletes at some moving moment of their lives, country-folk, indeed humanity itself as it lives under ancient rural traditions:

> The lads in their hundreds to Ludlow come in for the fair,
>   There's men from the barn and the forge and the mill and the fold,
> The lads for the girls and the lads for the liquor are there,
>   And there with the rest are the lads that will never be old.

We are fated to lose our battle, he seems to say, but that does not matter so long as we live and die bravely, remembering that where we stand the Greeks and Romans stood, and could do no less and succeed no more.

Unlike other writers who have found their most congenial influence in classic literature, Mr. Housman revives the substance rather than the accidents of Paganism. He is grave, noble, austere, and writes of the body with a dignified simplicity as if it had always been to him the foundation, and not the disturbance, of human life. There is a simple strength, a grave sweetness in his utterance, which is very moving. Such lines as

> Lovers lying two and two
>   Ask not whom they sleep beside,
> And the bridegroom all night through
>   Never turns him to the bride

fall on the ear with an antique beauty, a sense of vanished splendour, such as is given by the sight of a piece of Greek sculpture unexpectedly found in some uncrowded corner of a country house. There is a rebuke in this poetry, as there is in Greek sculpture, for all that is not simple, restrained, and strong. Only in its reverence for what has perished from the world is there anything romantic in its wistfulness. No writer is more original. He has no modern models or imitators, and did all other modern verse perish, Mr. Housman's poems would be like the Greek Anthology of our tongue. Life, to him, has much good but more ill for humanity, and it is this note of disillusion, in a scholarly sense very unlike that characteristic of the decade, which, with his classic sympathies, binds him to, but places him above, it. His work is small in quantity, but he is perhaps the only poet, technically a minor, who seems too great for such a term. The most manful sight in the world to him is that of a Greek statue, and we feel that he has assimilated the living secret of its nobility as few connoisseurs or æsthetic admirers have ever done. Every true author is the writer of some one book, but Mr. A.E. Housman is the author of none other. He reached his aim at a single, deliberate stride, for the *Last Poems* admittedly date, for the most part, from the period of *A Shropshire Lad*, and contain nothing, even the War poems, that are not akin to it. The earlier patriotic poems would have seemed an excrescence if patriotism were not a Hellenic virtue, and I mention them here to make one criticism on the 'Epitaph on an Army of Mercenaries,' which has been called the best poem produced by the War. It certainly shows Mr. Housman's technical resources at their most splendid; the rhythm is so superb that people seem to overlook the meaning, which is outrageous in its patronage of God. But the display of metrical mastery reminds us how much skill was spent on the apparent simplicity of the earlier volume, which has earned for him the reputation of a dozen of its size. Compared with his, the Paganism of Swinburne, Symonds, Pater, seems a literary and scholastic affectation. Indeed his 'home-sickness' was not inverted, but real. The result was a book that was original and enduring, and by comparison with it the other work of the decade is seen to be not the new creation that it believed, but the final exhaustion of an impulse.

46. Iolo Williams on Housman

1927

Iolo Williams (1890–1962), educated at Rugby and King's College, Cambridge. Bibliographical correspondent of the *London Mercury*, 1920–39, journalist on *The Times* from 1936 onwards. He published his first volume of poems in 1915, an edition of Sheridan's plays in 1926, and also wrote books on aspects of natural history.

Reprinted from Iolo Williams, *Poetry Today* (London: Herbert Jenkins, 1927), 60–7.

In the year 1896, a certain distinguished Latin scholar published his first – and until comparatively recently his last – book of verse. The scholar's name was A.E. Housman, his book was called *A Shropshire Lad*, and it contained sixty-three short lyrics. A constant stream of editions had succeeded that first edition, and I should imagine that a larger number of copies has been sold of this book than of any other book of verse by a living writer. It is impossible to read *A Shropshire Lad* without realising that here is a collection of poems that is almost pure gold throughout; and for multitudes of readers, who never set foot in Shropshire, these poems have made familiar – almost to holiness – the county where

> The vane on Hughley Steeple
> Veers bright, a far-known sign,

and

> Clunton and Clunbury,
>   Clungunford and Clun,
> Are the quietest places
>   Under the sun.

I commented earlier in this essay on melancholy as a prevailing cast of mind among a very large number of English poets and – I might have added – of lovers of English poetry. Never has this been more forcibly illustrated than by the popularity of *A Shropshire Lad*, for Mr. Housman's philosophy is one of gloom almost savagely emphasised, from which no escape, in the ordinary sense of that word, is allowed to the reader. No concessions are made. The poet cannot sing a *Reveille* without concluding with the thought that

> Clay lies still, but blood's a rover;
>   Breath's a ware that will not keep.
> Up, lad: when the journey's over
>   There'll be time enough to sleep.

He cannot see the cherry-tree in bloom without thinking of the time when he will no longer be there to see it. He cannot sing *God Save the Queen* at a jubilee without reflecting that

> Now, when the flame they watch not towers
>   Above the soil they trod,

A.E. HOUSMAN

> Lads, we'll remember friends of ours
> Who shared the work with God.

Death for him is an ever-present companion, the fate of all things lovely, and the desert of all things foul. It is a state of mind which only the strong could bear, and it is no wonder that he counsels suicide to the weak: –

> And if your hand or foot offend you,
> Cut it off, lad, and be whole;
> But play the man, stand up and end you,
> When your sickness is your soul.

Yet, if there is no escape from the oppression of death, there are alleviations. There is everywhere physical beauty to be seen and adored, and there is the feeling that the glory of life lies in the struggle with circumstance, not in the victory, and that the soul of man is, indeed, all the nobler in that defeat is the inevitable end. The attitude is one of pessimism without surrender, of despair without weakness.

How great is the love of, the exultation in, beauty which manages, in *A Shropshire Lad*, to survive the fatalism of the poet's attitude, is shown by a score of stanzas which are known to almost every lover of poetry. The loveliness of the English spring has perhaps never been put more feelingly, more exquisitely, than in the poem which begins

> Loveliest of trees, the cherry now
> Is hung with bloom along the bough,
> And stands about the woodland ride
> Wearing white for Eastertide.

Or, again, in that other one,

> 'Tis time, I think, by Wenlock town
> The golden broom should blow;
> The hawthorn sprinkled up and down
> Should charge the land with snow.

Throughout the work there is instant recognition of those things which are good and lovely in the world, the flowers, the wood tossing under the storm, the poplars sighing 'about the glimmering weirs', the young men racing, or playing games, or coming in to the fair. These things do not cease to be beautiful, to the poet, because all the time he feels the presence of their doom; rather are they the more beautiful for that, and the more to be admired while the 'seventy springs' yet endure.

The feeling of strength, which is in these poems, comes from their diction and versification, as much as from their thought. Victorian poetry, it may be said – so far as it is possible to generalise on such a subject – laid the emphasis of poetry very largely on a heightening of language, and in the exclusion of plain words and images. The poet was expected to feel, and speak, differently from other men, and to hold himself aloof from the ordinary commerce of the world. The result was, inevitably, that many poets thereby made themselves appear not greater, but weaker, than their fellow men, and seemed to isolate themselves because they were too frail to sustain the buffets of ordinary life. Mr. Housman broke right away from this tradition. He chose, habitually, the plainest words and metres, wherein to express his thoughts; he aimed rather at exactitude than at grandiloquence. That this was deliberate on his part is, I think, clear, for he is capable of the purely verbal effect when it suits his purpose, as witness such a stanza as

> Wake: the vaulted shadow shatters,
>   Trampled to the floor it spanned,
> And the tent of night in tatters
>   Straws the sky-pavilioned land.

But as a rule he makes his effects by the sparest means. He delights in the octosyllabic, in preference to the more resounding decasyllabic, or heroic, couplet. He never puts in a word just because it sounds fine, and he is not afraid of the most homely images, such as

> And long will stand the empty plate,
>   And dinner will be cold,

or

> Where shall one halt to deliver
>   This luggage I'd lief set down?

Moreover, if his sense demands it, he is quite prepared to write a passage in a completely colloquial, almost slangy, style, which must have sounded strangely, to the ears of 1896, in a book of verse which there was no taking anything but seriously:

> 'Terence, this is stupid stuff:
> You eat your victuals fast enough;
> There can't be much amiss, 'tis clear,
> To see the rate you drink your beer.
> But oh, good Lord, the verse you make,
> It gives a chap the belly-ache.
> The cow, the old cow, she is dead;
> It sleeps well, the hornéd head:
> We poor lads, 'tis our turn now
> To hear such tunes as killed the cow.'

Is there any other poet, I wonder, who has dared so to parody his own style in his own first book?

It was *A Shropshire Lad*, I believe, that more than anything else set the minds of the young poets of the twentieth century working in new ways, exploring new subjects and new methods of treatment. In particular this book taught them to appreciate economy of means, to see through the sham of mere lavishness of phrase and sound, and to try to cultivate what one may call an *honest* technique of poetry. Chiefly through the influence of Mr. Housman the sharper, brisker, lyric measures came back into popularity, and it began to be realised that it was possible to express a solemn emotion in forms other than the sonnet. At the same time there was nothing outrageous about Mr. Housman's influence, nothing wantonly iconoclastic. There was no seeking after the merely strange, no attempt to please the gutter by reproducing its stench. There was only a fervent, yet simply-expressed, realisation of the loveliness of the English countryside, of the beauty of life, and of the sadness of death – which things are, after all, the material of most of the greatest English poetry. It was not an influence to which fools took kindly, for it left them very little with which to clothe their folly. But it was one of the healthiest influences – in spite of the pessimism of *A Shropshire Lad* itself – for it was in the direct descent from the best of our own poetry, and from that of Greece and Rome before it.

Naturally, Mr. Housman's influence took time to work its effect, and, as I have tried to point out, there were other sane influences at work, among them that of Dr. Bridges. But there was in *A*

Shropshire Lad the flash of something sharp, and bright, and rich, which was the very thing which, as one century passed into another, was needed to set England off on a new era of poesy.

47. H.W. Garrod, 'Mr. A.E. Housman'
1929

Heathcote William Garrod (1878–1960), classical scholar, Fellow and Tutor of Merton College, Oxford, from 1901, Professor of Poetry at Oxford, 1923–8. He also published books on Wordsworth (1923), Coleridge, and other non-classical authors. His commentary on Manilius II was published in 1911, the same year as Housman's edition. Housman wrote politely to him about it (24 October 1911), but severely criticized it later, in the preface to his edition of Manilius V (1930).

This essay is the printed form of one of Garrod's lectures as Oxford Professor of Poetry and is reprinted from H.W. Garrod, *The Profession of Poetry and Other Lectures* (Oxford: Clarendon Press, 1929), 211–24.

I have confessed before to a fondness for the poetry of Fellows of colleges. I have not observed that the world in general shares it with me; but I have not allowed that to worry me. I like Matthew Arnold; and, as he did, I like Gray: Gray not too much, but I like him. I even like old Tom Warton, who was contemporary with Gray, and has some of Gray's merits. Warton, I suppose, unlike Matthew Arnold, will be remembered, not as a poet, but as a professor of poetry, and as the first historian of our poetry. He belongs, in any case, to an order of Fellows of colleges which has gone beyond recall. He loved the tavern better than the lecture-room. He was the last of the 'jolly' dons. But coming to a period nearer my own, and, I suppose, a more respectable one, I like the poetry of Rupert Brooke, who was a Fellow of a Cambridge college. I like the poetry of J.S. Phillimore, of Gerald Gould, of Godfrey Elton, all of them Fellows of Oxford colleges. And yet again, I like the poetry of Mr. A.E. Housman. Mr. Housman is a Fellow of Trinity College, Cambridge. Even so, the Latin that he teaches there he learned in Oxford. Two terms ago, speaking of Mr. Humbert Wolfe, I put it to his account that he was the only poet I knew who had taken a first in Greats. I believe I was one out; and though that should teach me caution, yet Mr. Housman, I verily believe, is the only great poet who, taking the same school, has ever been ploughed outright. I do not say that from malice; though, if I wanted to be quietly malicious, I do not see why I should not. But I record it as a material circumstance. I put it in as evidence – if we knew what it was evidence of, we should know all about poetry; of which at present we may sum all our knowledge by saying that the spirit bloweth where it listeth. However, here is a poet, the most considerable of his generation, who refused learning in his youth, and has since dedicated himself to it with deadly austerity. He stands to-day the first scholar in Europe; if this country has had a greater scholar, it will be only Bentley. The sum of his achievement in poetry is two small volumes of verse, separated from one another by an interval of near thirty years; and the title and Preface to the second of them intimating to us that we must expect no more. It is not often that a man may sit and choose which of two immortalities he will. Mr. Housman, I truly think, has had this singular privilege; and to a good many people, perhaps to most, he will seem to have used it perversely. As plainly as what a man does can tell us what he thinks, he has told us that he thinks more highly of scholarship than of poetry, that he prefers to be immortal along that line. For the perpetuity of his fame as a scholar, he has laid the foundations deep and broad; and has done all his work as though only that mattered. What he has done for, and in, poetry, he has done with a savage insouciance, as though he could say all that he had to say in verse by biting his lip. I suppose that there will always be scholarship in the world; and the hard and narrow immortality that comes by it Mr. Housman can count on. But I am not sure that, biting his lip at poetry, he has not been caught in the act: arrested and frozen into a second immortality.

Meanwhile, one of the facts of his poetry is his contempt for it. He is the only poet I know whose primary interest is exact knowledge. That he is a scholar most persons are aware who read his poetry; but they are aware of it in a rather dim and careless fashion: as though it were an accident and an irrelevance. Of no man's life can nine-tenths be irrelevant; least of all of a poet's life. I cannot think it a matter of indifference that Mr. Housman is a scholar, nor that he is the kind of scholar that he is. He is the kind of scholar that bad scholars call a 'mere' scholar; that is to say, he mixes with his scholarship nothing that appeals to any other instinct than the instinct for knowledge. The drier the knowledge, the better: the less it leads anywhere, the safer. Much of his time has been given to editing Latin poets. But you will search his works in vain for any expression that betrays a sense in him that poetry is what it is, or that the scholarship of poetry is, in any respect, different from, or better than, entomology, palaeontology, or the geometry of hyper-space. His favourite poet is a writer so difficult and obscure that, of persons in this room, perhaps not ten have heard his name, and, of living Englishmen, I vow that Mr. Housman and myself alone have read him from cover to cover, and only Mr. Housman has understood him. I do not mean that Mr. Housman's scholarship is not, often, very lively. Mr. A, an eminent living scholar, had a disciple, Mr. B; and Mr. B was so unwise as to publish a book. 'I suppose', writes Mr. Housman, 'that Mr. A, when he perused Mr. B's book, must have felt somewhat like Sin, when she gave birth to Death.' That is what I call being lively – you will see that it is not very different from being deadly. Mr. Housman's scholarship has these emotional passages. But they are so far proper to his purely scientific temperament that they are provoked only by the unscientific behaviour of other scholars. For him scholarship is a science, as much as any other of the sciences; and the death of it is the intrusion into it of qualities proper to other departments, those qualities, in particular, which belong to *belles lettres* and to poetry. Across the page of Mr. Housman's scholarship there falls never so much as the shadow of literary appreciation. You could no more suspect him of poetry than you could suspect Darwin or Linnaeus.

So much about Mr. Housman's scholarship I have felt obliged to say. For myself, like other people, I am more interested in his poetry. I think he would think us all wrong; though not, I fancy, for the right reasons. In any case, I have no wish to disparage scholarship. Bad poets are at least worse than bad scholars, and they are infinitely more numerous. And touching good poets and good scholars, let me say at any rate this much. We do not, I think, sufficiently reflect how rare, in comparison with genius, is consummate learning. That learning should be less admired than genius is natural enough. Men admire what is grand most of all when it seems to be done easily, and the mark of genius is its divine facility – it may endure agonies, but it does *not* take pains. Learning, on the other hand, must both take pains and give them. Mediocrity, or less, can appreciate genius. But learning can be known only by its like. The effects of genius are easily apprehended. It is sensibly known in the quickening of the blood, the tension of the nerves, the fine thrill of the whole being. It does not merely move us; it drives us before it, as the wind the leaves. It has something stinging and compelling. It accomplishes its end in being felt. We never inquire – or we are foolish if we do inquire – what it would be at. There *is* a sense in which genius, mysterious as it is, is the most intelligible of all things. But learning is at once less direct in its aims and less clear in its effects. One thing only it seems to share with genius – its unhappiness. It rises up early and late takes rest. There is a pallor upon its cheek, and in its eye a latent fever; and over all its attainment there broods the shadow of something missed and desired.

I hope that these reflections, general as they are, will not seem too distant and irrelevant. I cannot think them so. I was brought up in what is called scholarship; and I was familiar – if my memory serves me rightly – I was familiar with Mr. Housman's scholarship before I read his poetry. There is an unhappiness in his scholarship, just as there is in his poetry. He edits poets in the manner of a man hating poetry. He criticizes critics with an inhumanity grounded on the fierce conviction that there is no truth in man. Speaking of the difficulty of arriving at a good text of his favourite Latin poet, 'the faintest of all human passions', he writes, 'is the love of truth'. Take truth in what sense or in what connexion you will, Mr. Housman, I think, really believes that. There is no truth in man or woman. This gloomy persuasion informs his scholarship. This gave birth in him to his poetry, his hate of poetry, his fear of poetry. For really and truly, as I think,

Mr. Housman does hate poetry – poetry and all those parts of life which make up into poetry. He is a scholar because he hates poetry; seeking from scholarship an anodyne for the wounds which poetry has wrought in him; not expecting to find here, any more than in life, truth in other men; but finding, here as elsewhere, a savage satisfaction in detecting, and blazoning, other men's falsehood, the intellectual dishonesty and incompetence of all the world save himself. Of his fellow scholars he is pleased, in one place, to sum the merits by a sentence from Swift: they are 'as little qualified', he says, 'for thinking as for flying'.

To Swift Mr. Housman bears a considerable likeness; save that, firstly, he is a better poet, and secondly, he is more mysterious. Like Swift, he waits for a world 'ubi saeva indignatio cor ulterius lacerare nequit'.[1] Life has done him some injury; the nature of which I am not curious to inquire beyond what his poetry tells us. If we may believe what it tells us, once 'in glory and in joy' he 'followed his plough along the mountain-side'.

> Is my team ploughing
> That I was used to drive?

Once he had loves, who now has only hates. There is no truth in man or woman.

> His folly hath not fellow
> Beneath the blue of day,
> Who gives to man or woman
> His heart and soul away.

But there was truth in himself:

> If Truth in hearts that perish
> Could move the powers on high,
> I think the love I bear you
> Should make you not to die....

But now 'all is idle'. Once he had loves. Once, like other men, he had friends; and drank with them from sheer good-fellowship, who drinks now in no better cause than that of self-forgetfulness. He had friends. But they were even more unlucky than himself. 'Souls undone, undoing others', the more respectable of them were murdered, the less engaging were hanged. Ned, and one or two others, lie long in Shrewsbury gaol. Here and there a lucky one got away, and enlisted for foreign service. 'The enemies of England' saw these and were sick. Of these 'lads' and 'chaps', as their poet calls them, some found a second service, in 1914, in that army of mercenaries who, 'in the day when heaven was falling', 'held the sky suspended', defending 'what God abandoned'. These 'took their wages and are dead'. It is odd that the most striking poem which the war produced should have this sardonic ring. These 'chaps' were the lucky ones: though their girls walk now with other 'chaps'. Next blest were those who took a pistol and put a clean ending to the sickness which was their soul:

> Oh soon, and better so than later
> After long disgrace and scorn,
> You shot dead the household traitor,
> The soul that should not have been born
> . . . .
>
> Now to your grave shall friend and stranger
> With ruth and some with envy come:
> Undishonoured, clear of danger,
> Clean of guilt, pass hence and home.

A fine funeral march. For the morality of it, God knows.

Some few more tender memories, indeed, this poet's youth offers; but the sweet tenderness of them makes only chaplets for headstones:

> With rue my heart is laden
> For golden friends I had,
> For many a rose-lipt maiden
> And many a lightfoot lad.
>
> By brooks too broad for leaping
> The lightfoot boys are laid;
> The rose-lipt girls are sleeping
> In fields where roses fade.

Those golden friends will outlast, I think, the gaol-birds, and suicides, and chaps that were hung; for they have met that immortality which there is in a commonplace when it is handled by a master of the classical manner. Of the golden lads that were swift of foot, there was one who merited an individual elegy; and for him, summoning again his purest classical manner, Mr. Housman has woven this unfading laurel:

> The time you won your town the race
> We chaired you through the market-place;
> Man and boy stood cheering by,
> And home we brought you shoulder high.
>
> To-day, the road all runners come,
> Shoulder-high we bring you home,
> And set you at your threshold down,
> Townsman of a stiller town.
>
> Smart lad, to slip betimes away
> From fields where glory does not stay,
> And early though the laurel blows
> It withers quicker than the rose.
>
> Eyes the shady night has shut
> Cannot see the record cut,
> And silence sounds no worse than cheers
> After earth has stopped the ears:
>
> Now you will not swell the rout
> Of lads that wore their honour out,
> Runners whom renown outran
> And the name died before the man.
>
> So set, before its echoes fade,
> The fleet foot on the still of shade,
> And hold to the low lintel up
> The still-defended challenge-cup.
>
> And round that early-laurelled head
> Shall flock to gaze the strengthless dead,
> And find unwithered on its curls
> The garland briefer than a girl's.

Of this beautiful elegy I am ashamed to qualify the praise. Yet I cannot let it pass without voicing an uneasiness and embarrassment which the first two stanzas of it create in me. The poem as a whole has been so truly felt, and to the verse and the diction so much art has been brought that it would be pedantic to prefer nature; and yet these perfections have been framed, I feel, in a setting not only false but preferred for its falsity.

A.E. HOUSMAN
The time you won your town the race...

Mr. Housman was at an English public school; he was an undergraduate here in Oxford; he speaks of himself somewhere as a 'Son of Sorrow' playing, or playing at, cricket and football, and I dare say he played at running races. But the athlete of his poem is his fellow-townsman; the scene a market-place; the prize a municipal challenge-cup; the victor was 'chaired' shoulder-high. I am even prepared to believe that the victory was celebrated in 'pints and quarts of Ludlow beer', and that the poet and his friends (I draw inferences here from other poems) lay down in the road 'in lovely muck' and went home leaving their neckties God knows where. I say 'I am prepared to believe' that. But no: I am prepared to be told it. But it will not do. And why does Mr. Housman do it? Do you really see him all that degree interested in the Ludlow sports – if in Ludlow they hold sports? This false-pastoral twist is altogether too tiresome. I hate vulgarisms; but I hate 'fakes' still more; and I do not know what to call this false pastoralism if I am not to be allowed to call it a not too clever fake.

The trouble pervades nine-tenths of the *Shropshire Lad*. The very title prepares you for a false world. I do not mean that Mr. Housman is not so far a Shropshire Lad that he has vivified and glorified large tracts of that pleasant country-side – I reckon it with my best luck that I first made acquaintance with these poems in a village not twenty miles from Ludlow. But the rest is fake: the town-and-county patriotism; the lads and chaps with their ploughshares and lost neckties; the girls with their throats cut, and their lovers that were hanged for it. I call it false pastoralism. It is not quite the pastoralism, it is true, of Mantuan or Spenser or Pope. Since those days, there has flowed under the bridges of pastoral a good deal of Villon and water, of Verlaine and absinthe. But I do not know that it has made the pastoralism of Mr. Housman either more intelligible or less false.

Utterly false this world of his, of course, is not. Open his heart, and you will find written there, I do not doubt, not Cambridge, but Clunbury and Clun. Nor do I question that the stuff of his poetry is the stuff of a real experience. I believe it of him more readily than of some other poets; because only so could it have happened that his best work should, in this false setting, yet shine so true – perhaps *glower* so true would be nearer. When Mr. Housman lifts his eyes to the hills whence the strength of his youth came, sure enough (we might wish it otherwise) he sees gaols and gibbets and ditches strown with 'lovely lads and dead and rotten'; and sure enough Ned and Dick and himself are or were, all of them, of all men most miserable. But was it not enough that they should be that, without being dressed, or undressed, into tiresome allegoric personages? If there be no truth in man nor woman, if the heart be so made that every wind which blows through it clanks chains and shakes a gibbet, must we none the less make a charade of it?

I suppose we must leave poets to do things in their own way. Very likely Mr. Housman uses these veils and pretences out of some mercy to himself and others. Yet he rarely writes like a merciful man; and I am inclined to seek a different explanation; and to find it in what I have already said. Mr. Housman hates poetry, and he believes that all men hate truth. His poetry is wrung from him, as from so many poets, by some pain of life:

> Und wenn der Mensch in seiner Qual verstummt,
> Gab mir ein Gott zu sagen was ich leide.[2]

Some god gave it to him to say what he suffers; but he would rather have been given the power to hold his tongue. He hates poetry sufficiently, and he so little credits men in general with any genuine taste for the truth, that he will not be persuaded to take pains enough to deal truly with his material. He will not be more true with it than he thinks good enough for his readers; and he knows what he is doing. His gaol-bird stuff, the cruder of his macabre pieces, the curiously elaborated perversity of such poems as *The Immortal Part* – these nine-tenths of his readers have preferred to his best work; and he knew that they were going to do so. That some of these poems are absurdly false, he knows, without caring. Even so, into all of them he has put – from an instinct for truth which he is never quite able to suppress in himself – enough of truth to make them poems not to be dismissed without consideration. If I call Mr. Housman's poetry an astonishing medley of false and true, in the long run I am praising it; for it is a marvel that it should be so true as it is, under the conditions which he has deliberately imposed upon it.

Lest I should be misunderstood, the best of it — much of it, that is — is wholly true and set beyond cavil.

> When I watch the living meet
>   And the moving pageant file
> Warm and breathing through the street
>   Where I lodge a little while,
>
> If the heats of hate and lust
>   In the house of flesh are strong,
> Let me mind the house of dust
>   Where my sojourn shall be long.
>
> In the nation that is not
>   Nothing stands that stood before;
> There revenges are forgot,
>   And the hater hates no more;
>
> Lovers lying two and two
>   Ask not whom they sleep beside,
> And the bridegroom all night through
>   Never turns him to the bride.

There is no gainsaying perfections of that order; and perhaps I could find near a score of pieces equally adequate in feeling and expression. I suppose none of us were ever very happy about our war poetry, the patriotic verse, I mean, of the Great War. Simonides, Horace, Wordsworth — take any of it to these high tests, and it seems almost sordid. Let me take a poem of an earlier war — which of our wars I know not; but it must have been somewhat earlier than the Boer War. What a great war we thought that, and how little and provincial it looks since! This was a yet littler war. But here are some lines of Mr. Housman's which it provoked, neither little nor provincial, but sufficiently answering high needs:

> On the idle hill of summer,
>   Sleepy with the flow of streams,
> Far I hear the steady drummer
>   Drumming like a noise in dreams.
>
> Far and near and low and louder
>   On the roads of earth go by,
> Dear to friends and food for powder,
>   Soldiers marching, all to die.

> East and west on fields forgotten
>   Bleach the bones of comrades slain,
> Lovely lads and dead and rotten;
>   None that go return again.
>
> Far the calling bugles hollo,
>   High the screaming fife replies,
> Gay the files of scarlet follow:
>   Woman bore me, I will rise.

The *Shropshire Lad* was first printed in 1896. The greater part of it was written early in 1895. Mr. Housman tells us so much himself, in the Preface to *Last Poems*. That Preface contains some few words of self-revelation such as its author is commonly shy of. Most of these early poems, he says, were written in the early months of 1895, under the condition of a 'continuous excitement'. Of the nature of this excitement nothing is said: save that it was such that it is not likely to revisit its poet; 'nor indeed', he says, 'could I well sustain it if it came'. Let us not ask too many questions, therefore. But I had this passage in mind when I said that Mr. Housman, besides hating poetry, feared it. He has a real superstitious fear of it, I believe. The same superstitious fear of his own poetry haunted Byron, as I have noticed elsewhere. And both poets react upon their fear in the same fashion. They meet it with a kind of gloomy insolence; and it deprives both of them of the power of being perfectly sincere; and even of the will to be so. They are only perfectly sincere in their best moments; and in despite of themselves. But I have a further, and not illegitimate, curiosity about the 'continuous excitement' which brought to birth the poems of the *Shropshire Lad*. For I take Mr. Housman to mean that these poems were written in, and from, the passions or emotions which they treat. That is interesting, because it has not been the way of some great poets. It was not the way of Byron, who speaks of his poetry as the language of his *sleeping* passions – when his passions were awake, the poetry in him died, he tells us. It was not the way of Wordsworth. Wordsworth's way was Byron's way; he had to set some interval between his emotion and the expression of it. But we must take poets as we find them; and it is interesting when they reveal anything of the conditions in which they work.

Between Mr. Housman's *Shropshire Lad* and his *Last Poems*

there lies, as I have said, an interval of nearly thirty years. But it is a less real interval than it seems. Three-fourths of the *Last Poems*, he tells us, were written between 1895 and 1910. They are the belated reverberation of the shock, or excitement, of the *Shropshire Lad*. The other fourth part of the *Last Poems* belongs to the April of 1922. About that month and year, again, I would not wish to show an impertinent curiosity; but the mention of it by Mr. Housman may serve to remind us how unpredictable are the comings and goings of poetical inspiration. Most of us, I suppose, who had read the *Shropshire Lad* somewhere near the time at which it first appeared felt some sense of disappointment with *Last Poems*. That was wrong. We looked for some advance in art, some new curiosity of theme, some widening of range. We forgot that we were dealing with a poet who had a strong distaste for poetry – for his own poetry a distaste, if I may say so, almost insolent. Very instructive, in this connexion, is the reason that he gives for printing these *Last Poems*; he thinks that he had better print them while he can himself see to the spelling and punctuation. If you know his scholarship, its savage absorption in the minutiae of pointing and orthography – and, indeed, in all minutiae – you will know that this is not affectation; but that what truly interested him about this last volume was that it should have deadly accuracy. For one or two of the pieces in it I have a liking beyond what I have for a good many of the earlier poems; one or two of them seem to me softer, more tender, more feminine. Too much of the *Shropshire Lad* is marred by what I will call a sham masculinity. The trick of this sham masculinity Mr. Housman learned, I have always fancied, from Stevenson. The pessimism of Mr. Housman, like the optimism of Stevenson, has an exaggerated masculinity which alienates. I cannot but think, I may add, that Mr. Housman owes to Stevenson something of both the verse and the diction of his poetry. And there are other likenesses: such, however, as may perhaps be explained out of the interest both have in some French poets.

About Mr. Housman's verse and diction – both so individual in their melancholy bareness, in their damped-down fire – I had wanted to say something – indeed, a good deal; but I have left myself no time. I am not sure that, fifty years hence, he will not be principally esteemed for the classical finish of his best work; that this will not be the 'immortal part' of him, 'the steadfast and enduring bone' surviving 'the man of flesh and soul' who to-day is so interesting to us. Indeed, I do not know why else he writes. Who despises more than he all that 'fire of sense' and 'smoke of thought', as he calls it, which has made his poetry so interesting to his contemporaries? Why any writer writes, perhaps no one knows. The simplest explanation is that we write because we want to, and there is nobody to stop us. That does not, of course, explain why we do it so badly. But here is a writer, a poet, who does not want to write at all; and indeed he has sworn never to do it again. But Jove laughs at 'last poems'; he scents from afar yet more last poems. From Mr. Housman I do not know whether we shall get them. But he has written, and he may do so again, in his own despite; hating poetry, thinking life a false thing, cursing the flesh and blood in him. But there is no lust of the flesh quite so strong as the craving of art. Among many false obsessions, that, I think, is real with Mr. Housman, the veritable tyrant of his mind.

Of all this I could have wished to say a good deal more. I have lost myself – which of his contemporaries has not? – in the enigma of the man. What matters, and what will outlast curiosity, is the pure and cold art of his good work. But we are human creatures; and this enigmatic figure – one of the most notable of our time – this enigmatic figure, lonely, irresponsive, setting us so many questions and answering none of them, crediting none of us with truth or intelligence, but allowing us to make what we can of the fire and ice that contend in his nature, the Byronic and the donnish – we may be forgiven if we look at him a little like men who have forgotten good manners. It is his fault if we stare.

NOTES

1 'Where savage indignation will no longer tear his heart'. The words are Swift's epitaph for himself, and are inscribed on his tomb in St Patrick's Cathedral, Dublin.
2 'And when man is silent in his agony / A god gave me the power to say what I suffer.' The lines are from Goethe's play *Torquato Tasso* (1789). Many years later when, in his seventies, Goethe fell passionately in love with a girl of 18, he used them as the motto for his 'Marienbad Elegy'.

48. Charles Williams, 'A.E. Housman'
1930

Charles Williams (1886–1945), poet, novelist, reviewer, critic and biographer. After an education at St Albans School and University College, London, Williams joined Oxford University Press in 1908 as a reader, and remained there all his life. Among his volumes of poetry are the long Arthurian poems *Taliessin through Logres* (1938) and *The Region of the Summer Stars* (1944).

Reprinted from Charles Williams, *Poetry at Present* (Oxford: Clarendon Press, 1930), 30–9.

When Mr. Housman wrote the lines

> Therefore, since the world has still
> Much good, but much less good than ill,

he recorded not only his own but also Hardy's vision of this world. But the temper with which his verse has expressed that vision, continuously and epigrammatically, is very different from Hardy's. The revolt and distress which exist in the older poet's work are not to be found either in *A Shropshire Lad* or in *Last Poems*. The two books contain altogether 104 lyrics, with a prefatory paraphrase to the second from Théodore de Banville. No living poet has presented work of such small extent, such unvarying perfection, such renewed intensity, and such catastrophic despair. The illusion, the dream, the desire that things ought to be different, have here no place. Mr. Housman has invented no god to blame; he has, it seems, left behind, so far as man can, even the wish for happiness. Perfect in word, perfect in spirit, these poems arise from a depth of bitter resignation which has not hitherto found expression in English verse. There have been cries of romantic personal despair, but this verse is classic in its restraint and calm balance.

Not that every poem is explicitly concerned with the 'much less good than ill'. A reader who opened *A Shropshire Lad* at the beginning could read the first sixteen poems without finding in it more than an occasional stanza of darkness, and without necessarily holding it to be more than dramatic or semi-dramatic. For those sixteen contain love-songs, a ballad lyric, and one or two as exquisite nature-poems as any in English, especially the famous 'Loveliest of trees, the cherry now' which ends

> And since to look at things in bloom
> Fifty springs are little room,
> About the woodlands I will go
> To see the cherry hung with snow.

This satisfying stanza might have been written by a young romantic poet; the sense of death is used as it is used in Nash's 'Queens have died young and fair'; it seems to be allied to Romeo's great outcry and Keats's 'cease upon the midnight with no pain'. It is only in the seventeenth poem that there certainly enters another style of verse, where the young cricketer mocks at his own occupation –

> See the son of grief at cricket
> Trying to be glad.

> Try I will; no harm in trying.
> Wonder 'tis how little mirth
> Keeps the bones of man from lying
> On the bed of earth.

Grief is here no longer a delicious mood accentuating the contemplation of beauty, but the natural state of man from which he is tempted to escape by death. And as the reader passes on he finds that this state is the one in which Mr. Housman's imagination normally perceives man to be, but that grief is too small a name for it. It has no cause, for any momentary cause to which it might be attributed is less than itself.

> The troubles of our proud and angry dust
> Are from eternity and shall not fail.

Here are poems enough on broken or thwarted love, of man for woman or of man for man; enough on parting, and the life and death of soldiers; enough on those who in the past or present are put to death by their fellows. To explain all these things Mr. Hardy has recourse to a metaphysic, but Mr. Housman will have nothing to do with any such attempt to ease the intellect.

Mr. Hardy has invented or borrowed a god to argue with; Mr. Housman dismisses the First Cause in a line – 'whatever brute or blackguard made the world'. Some laws, it seems, that First Cause has made; some laws, certainly, man. And these laws, if we can, we had better keep.

> How am I to face the odds
> Of man's bedevilment and God's?
> I, a stranger and afraid
> In the world I never made. [sic]

The motive is not really cowardice; it is rather that since we can do no better we had better do that.

It is inevitable that, with such a theme, and with certain poems which are a direct encouragement to suicide, the question of suicide should be raised. The business of a poet, of course, anyhow of a poet of a certain kind, is to express his imagination of the universe. Whether that imagination has any practical effect on our lives, and if so what, is a question for us and not for him, and it is an impertinence for us to inquire what effect it has had on his own. Nor is it to be overlooked that by the varying subjects and varying moods of and in which these poems are written, Mr. Housman has created almost everywhere a semi-dramatic effect. But if a poet has given us an harmonious imagination of life it is all the more satisfactory if a mere intellectual question arising out of it can be shown to be answered by its very nature. If we ask these two small books, 'But why should a man go on living?' an answer is there; there are several answers. The first is that, though life is an enemy, death is also an enemy. The exquisite sense of beauty, expressed in the highest form of traditional poetry, is too dear to be parted with – 'the cherry hung with snow,' 'the silver sail of dawn',

> The Sun at noon to higher air
> Unharnessing the silver Pair
> That late before his chariot swam,

and so on.

> Could man be drunk for ever
> With liquor, love, and fights –

but he can be drunk so long with such love that only in the very last crisis will he give up the indulgence, though he pays for it in his sober moments. Secondly, if those sober moments are too agonizing he will, anyhow, end them. It is the old undeniable answer — nothing is intolerable, for when indeed things are intolerable we die, either by our own will or against it.

The third and fourth answers are so much in the very heart of this verse that it is ridiculous to speak of them as 'answers' at all. They go before the question; they prevent it being asked; they are part of the nature of things which the verse is marvellously expressing. But in so far as they can be spoken of separately, the third answer is that we go on because we have to go on. Call it self-preservation, call it duty, call it what you will when a name for it is demanded, part of man's very burden is that he is so intensely alive that he is reluctant to cease. 'The troubles of our proud and angry dust' are not quite intolerable; 'bear them we can, and if we can we must'. We cannot die until we can, and when we can we do. Man has become conscious of his nature, and this is his nature. He lives, not from self-preservation or from moral duty, but from something more profound which he only knows because it is himself.

The last answer, put crudely and impossibly, is friendship. Friendship has not been praised so highly as it should have been; of this dearest mitigation of human existence the great poets seem to have been careless in their verse. Perhaps the long preoccupation with romantic and sexual love has caused its serener satisfaction to be neglected, even when it accompanies and is part of that other love. But Mr. Housman, who has no concern for romantic love except as a keen and often thwarted delight, has restored the love between friends to something approaching its right place. When the two books have been read this is left in the mind as the chief satisfaction, the most enduring peace of man. That many of the poems are on exile from friends — either by death or absence — makes no difference. The first poem in the *Shropshire Lad* is on the companionship of men of the same regiment; the last poem in *Last Poems* is on the communal dance at evening on the village green 'at Abdon under Clu' [sic]. Between them many of the 104 poems look to the love between friends as their subject or speak of it in their phrases. But perhaps that of all which prints it most clearly on the reader's mind is the poem called *Hell-Gate*. There the poet, with the devil by his side, approaches the gate of hell, where sit Death and Sin, and 'the damned in turn Pace for sentinel and burn'. When they come near

> the sentry turned his head,
> Looked, and knew me, and was Ned.

Recognizing his friend, the sentinel straddles across the way lest he should enter.

> But across the entry barred
> Straddled the revolted guard,
> Weaponed and accoutred well
> From the arsenals of hell;
> And beside him, sick and white,
> Sin to left and Death to right
> Turned a countenance of fear
> On the flaming mutineer.
> Over us the darkness bowed,
> And the anger in the cloud
> Clenched the lightning for the stroke;
> But the traitor musket spoke.
>
> And the hollowness of hell
> Sounded as its master fell,
> And the mourning echo rolled
> Ruin through his kingdom old.
> Tyranny and terror flown
> Left a pair of friends alone,
> And beneath the nether sky
> All that stirred was he and I.
>
> Silent, nothing found to say,
> We began the backward way;
> And the ebbing lustre died
> From the soldier at my side,
> As in all his spruce attire
> Failed the everlasting fire.
> Midmost of the homeward track
> Once we listened and looked back;
> But the city, dusk and mute,
> Slept, and there was no pursuit.

It is the strangest and one of the finest of Mr. Housman's poems: strange because in some ways it is so unlike him – with its old mythology and its entire peace, and in some ways so like him, with its colloquial and convincing phrases. Many things have been said at hell gate since Dante and Milton passed there, but few phrases are so satisfying as that of this newcomer; to Sin's smile

> 'Met again, my lass', said I.

It is as great in its way as Farinata in his burning tomb.

And this leads to the manner of Mr. Housman's verse. Of all our modern poets perhaps he and Mr. Yeats alone can manage so well what may be called 'the traditional-poetic' and the 'colloquial-poetic'. But not even Mr. Yeats has used them in such close connexion, and given us therefore an additional aesthetic delight. It would be easy to spoil a poem in the traditional style by using a phrase of modern slang in it; and easy enough to spoil a poem in modern slang by an injudicious attempt to mingle with it lines or stanzas of traditional beauty. But to mingle the two styles so that neither is out of place and that the whole achieves its poetic effect – this is a rarer thing and a triumph, and this Mr. Housman has done. Take, for example, the following poem:

> The fairies break their dances
> And leave the printed lawn,
> And up from India glances
> The silver sail of dawn.
>
> The candles burn their sockets,
> The blinds let through the day,
> The young man feels his pockets
> And wonders what's to pay.

It might be held that the word 'candles' is the one which permits of the transmutation; for this, both by its own nature and by its associations, is allied to both manners. 'Night's candles are burnt out' and 'a pound of candles' – these are the two worlds of speech which are here united. The poem is an example also of the way in which that whole region of faerie and beauty and romanticism is brought into harmony with the controlling idea. For it does not (and this is the distinction of the poem) lose its own value; it remains part of the loveliness which is the temptation to and strength of life.

But if Mr. Housman can do this, and add to his persuasiveness by it, that persuasiveness is due, partly at any rate, to another characteristic of his style – his extraordinary directness. Few poets are so sparing of their inversions; stanza after stanza will run on almost as if it were written in prose. This directness can be observed in the passages that have been quoted, or in

> These are not in plight to bear,
> If they would, another's care.
> They have enough as 'tis: I see
> In many an eye that measures me
> The mortal sickness of a mind
> Too unhappy to be kind.

How slight are the variations from direct speech there! And where they occur they never suggest themselves as coming merely for the convenience of the verse. Questioned and considered, they may nevertheless admit that such a technical convenience was at least a part of the reason for their existence, but it is normally the emotion alone which seems to control the place of every word. Doubtless this is what should happen with all poets, but doubtless also it does not. Inversion so soon becomes a trick, and the writer adds it to the little store of gadgets which help him to shape a poem – the easy adjective, the convenient rhyme, the superfluous phrase. Mr. Housman keeps his poems as free from superfluity as Landor's. There is a kind of poetic innocence about them, a virginity of behaviour which increases the intensity of the message they bring. Their lack of decoration combines with their lack of metaphysic to leave on the reader the impression of a single hard curve down to death. Blake would have hated Mr. Housman's design, but he would have loved its edge.

> O never fear, man, naught's to dread,
> Look not left nor right:
> In all the endless road you tread
> There's nothing but the night.

So completely does such a stanza persuade the reader that he accepts it in every way as final, though (intelligently) he knows it isn't. Even Mr. Housman perhaps derives a little pleasure from editing Latin poets. But that signifies nothing, any more than the similar fact that if this particular poem is part of that night, then it is – so far – an extremely enjoyable night. But against that objection, as has been said, Mr. Housman has provided. *Something* keeps the man treading that endless road through the night, and, whatever it may be, the satisfaction communicated by these poems is a part of it.

THE NAME AND NATURE OF POETRY
1933

49. Lascelles Abercrombie, 'A.E. Housman on Poetry', *Manchester Guardian Weekly*
xxviii, No. 23, 9 June 1933, 454

Lascelles Abercrombie (1881–1938), poet, educated at Malvern College and Owens College, Manchester. Abercrombie started to publish poetry in 1910; his *Collected Poems* was published by Oxford University Press in 1930. He also published a critical study of Thomas Hardy (1912) and *Principles of English Prosody* (1923). He was, successively, Lecturer in Poetry at Liverpool University (1919–22), Professor of English at Leeds University (from 1922) and at Bedford College, London (1929–35). From 1935 he was a Fellow of Merton College, Oxford, and Goldsmiths' Reader in English.

Those whose business it is to choose annually the Leslie Stephen Lecturer are to be congratulated on having this year secured – it might be said, perhaps, on having at last secured – Professor A.E. Housman for that office. The electors can scarcely have failed all these years to recollect the presence in their University of one of the finest poets, who is also one of the greatest scholars in Europe. It is true that a poet and a scholar is not necessarily a critic of literature; but that such a poet and such a scholar as Mr. Housman has not remarkable powers of literary criticism no one would easily believe. Just that, however, is what he himself does expect us to believe. He begins by reminding us how emphatically, twenty-two years ago, in his inaugural lecture as the Professor of Latin, he repudiated all claim to the faculty of literary criticism; and he goes on: 'In these twenty-two years I have improved in some respects and deteriorated in others; but I have not so much improved as to become a literary critic, nor so much deteriorated as to fancy I have become one.' Hence it is that, while acknowledging the honour done him by the electors, 'I condemn their judgement and deplore their choice'. What this means is simply this: that Mr. Housman's standards of literary criticism are very severe. Even so, the incredible myth that he is not a literary critic is now finished. If he had wished to keep it going he should not have allowed himself to be elected Leslie Stephen Lecturer.

His main argument, indeed, is nothing very new, though it has seldom been put so persuasively and with such force and confidence. 'Poetry is not the thing said but a way of saying it.' That can hardly be denied, but the inference from it will depend on just what is meant by 'a way of saying it.' Apparently, in Mr. Housman's view, this does not involve 'meaning': 'Meaning is of the intellect, poetry is not. If it were, the eighteenth century would have been able to write it better.' But if poetry is not 'meaning', what is it? It is language; it is the diction of a poem that makes it poetical. Mr. Housman quotes 'Take, O take those lips away', and remarks, 'That is nonsense, but is ravishing poetry.' Well, it may be nonsense, but nonsense is something; the poet is not 'saying nothing'. But Mr. Housman offers experimental proof: a verse in the Prayer-book version of the Psalms is poetry, in the Authorised Version it is not. This is a game in experimental criticism as old as Aristotle, and can be played even more strictly than Mr. Housman plays it. Change but a single word in a phrase of poetry: 'Out, out, brief candle'; put 'short' for 'brief' and note the result. But will anyone say that 'short' *means* the same as 'brief'? The argument, in fact, as Mr. Housman promised at the outset, treats its subject 'with some degree of precision', but nevertheless leaves us asking for a little more precision. No doubt we should have had it if humanity did not set limits to the length of a lecture. But what is invaluable in this lecture is not its theory, but the criticism which illustrates the theory. Notably independent of current fashion, and of the very pith of true criticism, are the cursory but masterly comments on seventeenth, eighteenth, and nineteenth century poetry. Withal, the lecture as a whole is a most shapely and beautiful composition. And what it tells us of Mr. Housman's own experience as a poet will be perfect treasure-trove to his critics and to anyone at all interested in the psychology (and physiology) of the art of poetry.

50. G.W. Stonier, 'Professor Housman on Poetry', *New Statesman and Nation*
v (New Series), 24 June 1933, 856/8

G.W. Stonier (1903–85), born in Sydney, educated at Westminster and Christ Church, Oxford. Radio playwright, author and journalist; assistant literary editor, *New Statesman and Nation*, 1928–45.

Professor Housman's lecture on poetry was widely reported in the press when it was delivered at Cambridge in May. It had the news value of a sudden declaration by Mr. Montagu Norman; in addition it was remarkably lively, personal, and quotable. Public utterances are not usually valuable to-day, but this lecture, part criticism and part confession, makes an admirable addition to the two volumes of poetry (why does not Professor Housman relent and publish the third?), and should be read by everyone who still reads poetry.

For Housman is probably the last considerable poet who has appealed to a large audience as well as a small one *for the same reasons*. Yeats, for example, is prized by a minority for quite different achievements from the anthology pieces. But there is only one side to the poems of *The Shropshire Lad* [sic] and *Last Poems*, and whether one likes it or not, it is unmistakable. So far as criticism of Housman goes, there has been agreement on most points, except that some critics stress the element of false pastoralism, while others, going all out, put him with, and above, Heine and Catullus.

The Name and Nature of Poetry is statement rather than definition, and to that extent may disappoint. The definition, implicit in its argument though not quoted, is Milton's 'simple, sensuous and passionate'; and as this is true of a mass of English poetry, good and bad, many readers will take it for granted, as Professor Housman does. What, then, does he add to our traditional conception of poetry? The peculiar interest, first, of the reinforcement coming from this particular poet – a poet's statement usually goes beyond critical analysis. Second, a fresh colouring of old truths (or beliefs, if you prefer), which affect us emotionally rather than intellectually. Taken to pieces, this lecture contains nothing that will be 'new' to readers of poetry, and yet its general effect is so positive and individual that to disparage this effect would be absurd. Criticism, no more than poetry, can be purely intellectual without losing three-quarters of its value, and Professor Housman's lecture is excellent proof of this.

'Poetry is not the thing said but a way of saying it'. 'Even when poetry has a meaning, as it usually has, it may be inadvisable to draw it out.' What Professor Housman values in poetry is the emotional vibration set up by certain combinations of words and not by others; that is, as it were, his test of recognition – he reduces it even to a set of physiological reactions, watering of the eyes, constriction of the throat, and the shiver up the spine. Possibly he overlooks the intelligence here! But no doubt, if pressed, he would admit that poetry may be an enjoyment of the mind.

This particular *virtue* of poetry he finds in whole poems, in a verse and even a single line. His enjoyment works in small units, so that he claims perfection, a *small* perfection, in many places where other critics would go on looking for larger things. Blake and Shakespeare he exalts together: in the end, Blake is the more 'purely poetical'. This is the opposite point of view of those who would point out, for example, that one of Shakespeare's finest lines is Lear's 'Never, never, never, never, never,' and that to detach it from the whole play and acknowledge merely the virtuosity of the trochaic line in a passage of blank verse would be to miss the main point. By poetry, then, Professor Housman means the lyric, and a lyrical quality which can be isolated for its magic in a phrase.

No wonder that he hates the eighteenth century! Much (too much) of his lecture is devoted to proving that the lyricism in Dryden and Pope is usually inferior.

[quotes 'There was a whole age ...' to ... 'is intellectually frivolous.']

Dryden's 'improvements' on Chaucer are cited and some of them are shocking; but it is argument by means of the worst example, which can never cut deep. Surely it is fatal to look for the *same* quality, and expect the same enjoyment, in Dryden and Blake?

And if 'the combination of dissimilar images' is essentially unpoetical, what of Donne (unmentioned) and Gerard Hopkins? The real test of Professor Housman's conception of English poetry comes in the nineteenth century; the first half strengthens his case, the second finally lets it down – the strain, at any rate, must be met there; but he does not even refer to the Victorians.

One can argue about details and even disagree with some of the main points of Professor Housman's book, but *The Name and Nature of Poetry* remains a positive and integral piece of criticism which is particularly valuable at the moment when poetic currents are going the other way.

51. J.C. Squire, editorial note, *London Mercury*

xxviii, No. 164, June 1933, 97–9

Housman's Leslie Stephen Lecture, on which *The Times* reported, was given in the Senate House, Cambridge, on 9 May 1933. Sending a copy of it to his brother Laurence (20 May 1933), Housman wrote: 'I am not proud of this, which I wrote against my will, and am not sending copies outside the family. But its success here has taken me aback. The leader of our doctrinaire teachers of youth is reported to say that it will take more than twelve years to undo the harm I have done in an hour ... '

[...] The title of the lecture was *The Name and Nature of Poetry*; he said the right things and he was the man to say them. [...] He told the straight truth about poetry: and it came best from him as being unchallengeably a very great lyric poet and now, alas, almost the senior of all our poets.

The *Times* summary was, we found, eagerly read and cherished by all sorts and conditions of people whom we had never suspected of an interest in such matters. It was like a bugle-call, or the All-Clear signal after an air-raid: the population stirred again, saying 'Thank Heaven *that's* over!' For, during at least ten years, the field of poetry and of poetical criticism has been invaded by swarms of people who haven't the least conception as to what poetry is, and who have affixed the name to things which have no relation at all to what has been called poetry through all the long past. Dons, who would have been better employed (though actually unscientific minds perhaps ought not to be employed there either) in psychological laboratories, have peeped and botanized over masterpieces, trying to analyse the unanalysable with no reference to emotion or imagination; and a swarm of alleged poets and critics, dull and solemn, have arisen who test poems by their intellectual content – their own intellects not usually being either subtle or profound – though in some circles a lack of humour and feeling seems to be taken as proof of profundity. The few good poets have asked themselves when the nuisance would be abated. The many who respond to poetry have been bewildered, wondering whether the literary world was mad or themselves: particularly as almost the whole of the literary press seemed to have gone over to dyspepsia, formlessness, and the notion that the Muse was meant to be the servant of notions, philosophical or political or ethical. They are all breathing more freely now.

52. D.W. Harding and L.C. Knights, 'Flank-Rubbing and Criticism', *Scrutiny*

ii, No. 2, September 1933

D.W. Harding (b. 1906), psychologist, literary critic and frequent reviewer for *Scrutiny*. From 1933 to 1938 he taught psychology at the London School of Economics, and from 1945 to 1968 was Professor of Psychology at Bedford College, London. With Gordon Bottomley, he edited

A.E. HOUSMAN

(1937) *The Complete Works of Isaac Rosenberg.*

L.C. Knights (b. 1906), author of many scholarly and critical books, was a member of the editorial board of *Scrutiny* from 1932 to 1953. From 1933 to 1947 he was Lecturer in English, University of Manchester; then Professor of English at Sheffield (1947–52), and Bristol (1953–64); and from 1965 to 1973 King Edward VII Professor of English at Cambridge.

This is a response from *Scrutiny* (edited by F.R. Leavis, of whom Housman's lecture was widely held to be a criticism) to J.C. Squire's editorial in the *London Mercury*. 'Knightly sword' is an allusion to the knighthood awarded to Squire in 1933.

There is, of course, room for a good deal of difference of opinion about the merits of contemporary writers and their relative importance for the future. All the same, one could hardly be anything but amused by the trumpetings with which the *London Mercury*, in its June editorial, turned out the Old Guard against the Reactionaries – those who have reacted, that is, against the traditions of late nineteenth-century poetry. Professor Housman's lecture on *The Name and Nature of Poetry* provided the occasion. 'It was like a bugle-call, or the All Clear signal after an air-raid: the population stirred again, saying "Thank Heaven *that's* over!" For during at least ten years, the field of poetry and poetical criticism has been invaded by swarms of people who haven't the least conception as to what poetry is, and who have affixed the name to things which have no relation at all to what has been called poetry through all the long past'. It seems that the invaders are in flight and the editor of the *Mercury* (who has a pretty fair idea 'as to what poetry is' – witness his remark that most of Donne's verse would be better in prose) can now, beer-mug of stout-fellowship [hyphen *sic*] in one hand, knightly sword in the other, flourish defiance behind their backs.

In itself the reappearance of this section of 'the population' after ten years in the cellar is of no particular importance (though one is glad to hear that Sir John is 'breathing more freely now'); it is the tone of the editorial that is significant, – rotarian unction is invariably a sign that there are friendly flanks near by. The *Mercury* mentions no names, rightly assuming that its audience will make a fair guess at 'Dons ... who have tried to analyse the unanalysable ... alleged poets and critics who test poems by their intellectual content' etc., and that it will applaud.

That the *Mercury*'s assumption is justified is proved by reference to the recent files of literary journalism. A representative selection of specimens from various articles and reviews showing a recrudescence of animus against Mr. Eliot has seemed worth making (a) because Mr. Eliot's poetry provides something of a test; (b) because those pronouncements which sound so brave in isolation lose something of their effect when they are recognized as fragments of a group chorus; and (c) because it is interesting to notice the non-literary motives which may influence literary criticism: now that Mr. Eliot has taken the unpopular side in religion and politics those who have never appreciated the quality of his verse find it safe to deny his achievement.

[The last two paragraphs give examples of recent hostility to T.S. Eliot. The second (final) one concludes:] ... The recent outbreak of derogatory articles will not provide that [i.e. 'sensitive and exact literary criticism']. They for the most part reveal nothing beyond their authors' thankfulness at being able safely now to set aside the writer whose work implicitly condemns their own shoddiness of thought and feeling.

53. Gorley Putt, review, *Scrutiny*

ii, No. 2, September 1933, 207–8

Samuel Gorley Putt (b. 1913), educated at Cambridge, worked for the BBC Talks Department (1936–8) and served in the R.N.V.R. in World War II. He has published various books, including *A Reader's Guide to Henry James* (1966). He was awarded an O.B.E. in 1966, and from 1968 was Fellow and Senior Tutor of Christ's College, Cambridge.

This is the middle section of a review entitled 'Go to the

Professors!' It dealt also with B. Ifor Evans, *English Poetry in the Late Nineteenth Century*, and Humbert Wolfe, *Romantic and Unromantic Poetry*.

Many who enjoyed the charm of Professor Housman when he delivered his Leslie Stephen lecture will be sorry to see its appearance in cold print. He elected to pour Johnsonian scorn on the metaphysicals, and with Arnold to dismiss the eighteenth century. But his valuable discrimination between the normal 'solidity of excellence' of Dryden and Pope, and their occasional lapses in mistaking 'impure verbiage for correct and splendid diction', has been overlooked by those who prefer to intone with the professor poetry which 'does but entangle the reader in a net of thoughtless delight'. (And this refers to Blake!)

Far more noteworthy than the lecture itself as a sign of the times has been the concerted yelping of the higher journalist critics to which it gave excuse. It would have been over-sanguine to expect much lively criticism of English poetry from a professor of Latin, but Mr. Housman's qualifications were such that his most jocular utterances have been echoed with solemnity; and conversely among the *Times* leaders, where solemnity is wont to be found, there appeared on the morrow of the lecture a column of skittish triumph:

When the whole lecture is published ... and this very dogmatic, academic age ... learns the full sacrilege of Mr. Housman's remarks upon Donne and the metaphysicals, upon Dryden, and upon Pope, there will be some pretty outcries – or perhaps a dignified and discreet silence.

Cultured people who feel that *The Shropshire Lad* [sic] is (except, perhaps, for Flecker and Rupert Brooke) the last appearance of the real thing in modern poetry have welcomed this pamphlet as making it safe for them to be quite explicit about the state of their taste. There has been a good deal of amusing explicitness.

54. R.R., review, *Adelphi*
vi (New Series), July 1933, 305–7

This review was by Richard Rees (1900–70), editor of the *Adelphi* from 1930 to 1936. Rees, educated at Eton and Trinity College, Cambridge, inherited his father's baronetcy (awarded in 1919) in 1922. Of strong humanitarian and left-wing sympathies, he lectured for the Workers' Educational Association from 1925 to 1927. He was a close friend of George Orwell, and the author and editor of books on him, on John Middleton Murry, and on Simone Weil.

'Poetry is not the thing said but a way of saying it,' says Professor Housman; and in this short, delightful essay (the Leslie Stephen lecture for 1933) he almost persuades us that the value of a literary critic, too, lies not in what he says but in the way he says it. For Housman's views on poetry are neither new nor remarkable and where they are debateable he does not enter into the pros and cons, but by his way of writing about poetry we know that he knows what he is talking about, and he communicates some of his knowledge to the reader – or so we flatter ourselves. His literary opinions are of a kind which is at present, like his unforgettable poetry, very unfashionable and it is a sad commentary on the state of culture that his own university of Cambridge has learnt so little from him that it could become the headquarters of a bastard science of literature by the side of which his own severely restricted achievements appear the very flower of humane culture. This fifty page essay is a better credential to the value of an institution which provides a monastic retreat for gifted minds than any of the bulky volumes of anaemic and almost psychotically ingenious scholarship which are now in vogue. Cambridge, indeed, has enabled Housman to remain too unsympathetically aloof from the contemporary outside world, but he does help to counteract its abuses to the extent that he remains, in his own field, uncontaminated by them.

But it is a problem how a mind so deeply sensitive could remain fixed in the apparently wilful bitterness of *The Shropshire Lad* [sic]. His *Last Poems*, appearing 27 [sic] years later, showed no essential change; and in this little essay we see a mind which has retained its integrity and beauty and perhaps mellowed a little, but scarcely developed.

[two quotations, end-on, from *The Name and Nature of Poetry*]

These meagre extracts do not do justice to the beauty of Housman's style, but they will sufficiently indicate that his opinions are both familiar and tentative. The book, however, is a delight to read and should be procured by everyone who is specially interested in poetry. I hope that some day Housman will be studied at length by one of those rare literary critics – Mr. West or Mr. Fausset, perhaps – who can relate literature to life. With his infrequent inspiration, which lands him sometimes in bathos but sometimes rises to white hot passion and beauty, with his scrupulous intelligence, his sensitive taste, and his apparently confirmed pessimism which looks so mean beside the pessimism of Hardy or beside the generosity of his own emotion, he is a first-class problem in literature and psychology. Professor Housman thinks that classical scholarship is his 'proper job'. Not so. He is a poet and a literary critic and therefore one of the few creative writers of our time who will be remembered.

55. Basil Davenport, 'The Terrier and the Rat', *Saturday Review of Literature* (New York)

1 July 1933, 673–4

Basil Davenport (1905–1966), American author and editor. He translated Rostand's *L'Aiglon* (1927) and wrote the introduction to the Centennial Edition of Housman's *Collected Poems* (New York, 1959), edited by Tom Burns Haber.

There can be no need, for readers of *The Saturday Review*, to enlarge upon the uniqueness of Professor Housman's place in literature, to comment again upon the unexampled phenomenon of those two perfect books of poems, appearing almost a generation apart, or to repeat once more that brief stoic preface to the 'Last Poems', which is to some of us the most thrilling prose ever written by a poet, not even excepting the preface to 'Adonais.' There can be no need to recall these things; but they must be borne in mind, in any consideration of his new book, 'The Name and Nature of Poetry', delivered at Cambridge as the Leslie Stephen Lecture. It is in a sense disappointing, if only because one expects so much from him; but it is in its way his 'One Word More' – the book in which he, who in his writing has expressed the most poignantly personal emotion only under the protection of a half-dramatic assumed personality, and who in his life has become a legend for unapproachability, now speaks, a very little, almost with intimacy. And his lecture shows many of the same qualities that appear in his poetry, especially the peculiar fusion of romantic intensity and classic restraint which is shown in the very form of his verse, with its inheritance both from the ballad and the epigram.

Professor Housman's essential position is the extreme romantic one, in the tradition of Coleridge and De Quincey, that one cannot define poetry, but one can (if one has the proper sense, which is a rare one) know it when one sees it; and he declares further that whatever poetry is, it is entirely non-intellectual, and has nothing to do with the meaning of what it says. To illustrate his first point he gives examples of verse which is poetry, and verse which is not; and to support the second, he cites the same verse of the forty-ninth psalm as it appears in the Prayer Book and in the Bible, giving his testimony that the former, 'But no man may deliver his brother, nor make agreement unto God for him,' 'is to me poetry so moving that I can hardly keep my voice steady in reading it,' while the latter, 'None of them can by any means redeem his brother, nor give to God a ransom for him,' 'I can read without emotion.' And he adds a few tests by which he himself knows that he is in the presence of poetry: 'I replied that I could no more define poetry than a terrier can define a rat, but that I thought we both recognized the object by the symptoms which it provokes in us.' One of these, he says, is a bristling of the hair, accompanied by a shiver down the spine; another is a constriction of the throat and a precipitation of water to the eyes; and a third is a sensation as of a spear going through the pit of the stomach.

This, like all good romantic criticism, is exciting; but it is hard to make useful. The virtue of romantic criticism is that it will meet a masterpiece of a new kind upon its own ground, instead of misjudging it by the standards of other types; its fault is that it precludes all intelligent disagreement or real agreement; it will allow only similarity or difference of taste. I have long regarded Emily Dickinson with respectful envy for the accuracy with which the top of her head appeared to come off, or a chill to sweep over her, in the presence of real poetry and nothing else. I have often enough felt that *frisson*, but what I call my taste tells me that, like Grimm's Lad Who Did Not Know What Shuddering Was, I frequently shudder at trivial poetic stimuli, and fail to do so at important ones. So with these symptoms of Professor Housman's, I have compared experiences with a number of my friends, and we all find that we are more likely to feel them at Field's 'Little Boy Blue,' or at 'common tunes that make you choke and blow your nose,' than at works which we enjoy much more deeply.

There is, of course, more to the question than that; and though Professor Housman will not tell us so, he will let us find it out. Part of the remaining secret he merely hints at in his lecture, telling us at the beginning, as what he calls his only qualification for giving it, 'all my life long the best literature of several languages has been my favorite recreation' – and particularly, one may venture to guess, that of Greece. Certainly one can tell by his writings he has made the poetry of Greece a part of his mind as no other writer now alive has done; so much so that he is able to incorporate in his own 'Epithalamium' the best translation I know of Sappho's '*Espere, panta pheron*';[1] and in his 'Far I hear the bugle blow' he has taken Sarpedon's speech to Glaucus and not translated but transmuted it, producing very Homer in purely English speech.

That is no doubt one part of the purity of his taste; and another part of the secret is that whether he admits it or not he uses his reason to judge verse. For whether or not he can use his mind to determine what is poetry, he unquestionably uses it in this lecture to determine what is not poetry, which goes some way toward doing the same thing.

He does so with brilliant effect, speaking out boldly with the voice of the century in which he was born, and denying the name, in opposition to modern fashion, to the most characteristic verse of the eighteenth century, and to such modern writing as 'does not resemble, in form or content, anything which has heretofore been so called.' It is at first surprising to read his condemnation of the late seventeenth and eighteenth centuries, for it is in them that his rare predecessors are most to be found. Mr. Housman's own cast of feeling and expression are as nearly unique as may be; but it is in that period that one seems to hear them. Marvell, for instance, in the lines

> The grave's a fine and private place,
> But none, I think, do there embrace

has his epigrammatic antithesis, his irony and understatement. And Samuel Johnson, in his 'A Short Song of Congratulation,' everywhere suggests him again:

> Wealth, my lad, was made to wander;
>   Let it wander as it will;
> Call the jockey, call the pander,
>   Bid them come and take their fill.

which has exactly Mr. Housman's manner of throwing all the work on the essential noun and verb that another writer would give to an adjective.

> Wealth, my lad, was made to wander;
>   Let it wander as it will

— it has just the accent of

> Clay lies still, but blood's a rover,
>   Breath's a ware that will not keep.

But these are of course not in the grand manner, not in the 'correct and noble diction,' upon which the eighteenth century particularly prided itself; it is this which Professor Housman attacks, in a manner which it is a joy to watch, with a humor which is no small part of his ability as a critic and even as a poet. For a sense of humor being (I think, in part) a sense of proportion, must be a valuable property of the critic, and if it prevents the poet from some fine excesses, it will save him from some which might be not so fine. Mr. Housman's own sense of the ridiculous, of course, not only inspires his glorious parody 'Fragment of a Greek Tragedy' (which contains such superb lines as 'To this well-nightingaled vicinity'), but appears, though sometimes grimly, all through his work, and has saved him from a Byronism into which his bitter view of the world might otherwise have led him.

There is indeed a certain quality of bitterness, often to be found in the literature of other nations – Catullus's *'Caeli, Lesbia noster, Lesbia illa, illa Lesbia'*[2] is one of the great examples – which is comparatively rare in English. Mr. Housman has it oftener than most English poets: the second stanza of 'The fairies break their dances' –

> The candles burn their sockets,
> The blinds let through the day,
> The young man feels his pockets
> And wonders what's to pay

has the same wry-mouthed disdain as the *Lesbia illa,* and 'The chestnut casts his flambeaux, and the flowers' has the same intensity in its curses on 'Whatever brute and blackguard made the world.' But oftener Mr. Housman will end such a poem in the dry, tight-smiling manner of

> To think that two and two are four
> And neither five nor three,
> That heart of man has long been sore – [sic]
> And long 'tis like to be.

That sardonic perception of the humor of one's own emotions is characteristically modern, one of the numerous ways in which Mr. Housman can be regarded as the first of the post-Victorians; it is the evident ancestor of such a recent stanza as Elinor Wylie's

> As one by one our faiths are shaken,
> Our hatreds fail: so mine for you.
> – Of course, I think you were mistaken,
> But still, I see your point of view.

But though in this explicit form it is one of the properties of our time as an underlying current of thought, it is characteristic of English literature. There is something remarkably British in Carlyle's remark 'Gad, she'd better,' when he was told that Margaret Fuller had decided to accept the universe; for the alternative, of defying the universe, has always appeared a little ludicrous to the Briton, although to the Frenchman or the Roman or the Greek it may well appear sublime.

And 'The Name and Nature of Poetry' is written not only with humor but with good humor. It is written in the great English university tradition, which recognizes two things, one, that Shakespeare did not write textbooks, and two, that even the best of every season's novelists has not written Shakespeare; and that produces an intellectual climate in which it is pleasant to find oneself. Even within that warm tradition, the tone of this lecture is mellow, a surprising thing and a pleasant one to discover in its author. Many of the anecdotes of the thorny wit with which he is said to have scourged erring editors of Juvenal and adoring American pilgrims are no doubt apocryphal, though some are probably true; however, the number of such stories bears witness to their subject's reputation. The modern *poietai apoietai*, the poets whom he thinks are no poets, he does not name, nor even particularize their work; when he says of it that since it is not poetry it may be something better, and so we should not risk blaspheming against it by calling it by the old name, and adds that when the Children of Israel were given the bread of angels to eat in the wilderness, 'they did not call it quails; they rose to the occasion, and called it manna,' we recognize the old sardonic irony, but the sharpness is lost in the fun.

In the main body of his lecture, he maintains that poetry is non-intellectual and cannot be defined, which so far as it goes is true enough, and then goes on to illustrate that what it is not can at any rate be ascertained by the intellect; and in the account of his method of working with which he concludes, he offers the same wilful half-truth, to which any one with sufficient perception may fit the other half.

Having drunk a pint of beer at luncheon [he says] – beer is a sedative to the brain, and my afternoons are the least intellectual portion of my life – I would go out for a walk of two or three hours. As I went along, thinking of nothing in particular, only looking at things around me and following the progress of the seasons, there would flow into my mind, with sudden and unaccountable emotion, sometimes a line or two of verse, sometimes a whole stanza at once, accompanied, not preceded, by a vague notion of the poem which they were destined to form part of

... When I got home I wrote them down, leaving gaps, and hoping that further inspiration might be forthcoming another day. Sometimes it was ... but sometimes the poem had to be taken in hand and completed by the brain, which was apt to be a matter of trouble and anxiety, involving trial and disappointment, and sometimes ending in failure.

This does not sound unlikely in itself, but at first it comes as a shock to any one who cherishes in his memory that sentence from the preface to the 'Last Poems': 'At my age I can no longer expect to be visited by the almost continuous poetic excitement under which ... I wrote the greater part of my previous book, nor could I well sustain it if it came.'

But the two can, of course, and must be, reconciled. What that deceptively simple recipe for writing a perfect poem leaves out of account is the 'continuous state of poetic excitement' of which he does not speak in his lecture, but which must have been there, boiling constantly under the crust of conscious thought, and ready to break out as soon as consciousness was relaxed. It is singularly characteristic of the synthesis of the romantic and the classic which is Mr. Housman's idiosyncrasy, that he would thus give that excitement its way during the afternoons, the least intellectual portion of his life. What he does not tell is what it was like to live in that state of poetic excitement which he could not now well sustain, and what caused it. He does not tell us; and he never will.

I am glad of that. I think that the poetry of the romantic revivalists is more thrilling to a schoolboy who reads and understands it in general terms, than to a college student who is furnished with the all too full details which the poets themselves supplied of the domestic difficulties which inspired them. And though we may presume that excitement implies an exciting cause, I am glad that we shall never know what the cause was which during a certain time filled the poet's mind with thoughts of hanging and suicide, of soldiers untimely shot and girls unfaithful to their dead sweethearts, and one or two more such themes that he was fain to think of, I believe, rather than of the thing itself. In that respect, at least, it may be said, he is with Shakespeare; no one can read the Sonnets or the 'Shropshire Lad' without guessing at the tragedy, and no one will ever know what the tragedy was. It is true that as the poet of 'A Shropshire Lad' grows older, he grows more indifferent to our knowledge or ignorance; in 'A Shropshire Lad' he proudly conceals his wound; in 'Last Poems' he still more proudly lets fall a hint or two, in 'Hell Gate' and 'When the eye of day is shut,' for us to do what we like with.

But beyond that he will not go; he remains himself. And his latest book is, if not all one might have hoped (as a singularly tantalizing footnote on what he is *not* going to tell of his discoveries in metrics shows), it is what we might have expected. The only change is that the smile with which he faces the world is somewhat less tight-bitten. The heart-broken stoic of the poems has become an Epicurean, a figure, like Lucretius, scarcely more unbending, but happier. And if, as we may guess, we may think of him as enjoying now the best literature of several languages, and the noble beer of English universities, then we who owe to him some of the most intense pangs, whether of pleasure or pain it is hard to say, that poetry has given us, must be glad of that.

NOTES

1 The first three words of a two-line poem by Sappho, one of her *Epithalamia*: 'Oh evening star, bringer-back of all [scattered by the bright morning].'
2 Catullus, *Carmina*, LVIII: 'O Caelius, our Lesbia, that Lesbia, that Lesbia, [the only person Catullus loved more than himself and all his own] ...'

56. Karl Schriftgeisser, from a review, *Boston Evening Transcript*

8 July 1933, Book Section, 1

This review bore the title 'On the Need for Emotion in Poetry: A.E. Housman delivers a Lecture in which Modern Verse is Attacked by Magnificent Indirection'.

[...] If Mr. Housman had not been the poet that he is, these pages might escape notice; unless they were by a new and young poet arisen to restore poetry and the criticism of poetry to the level from which the cold intellectuals of our time have driven it. Coming from Mr. Housman, whose silence has been one of the criterions [sic] of his art, the words have attracted a great deal of attention. It is hoped that they may do some good. For after the essays of T.S. Eliot and those who cringe at his feet, the words which Mr. Housman offers so modestly are good to hear. [...] T.S. Eliot has shown the way to sterility, a way willingly followed, and perhaps not unnaturally followed, the times being what they are. But the road has a turning. Without the body, of what use is the mind? What is the virtue of understanding if we have lost the ability to feel? [...]

This lecture is exciting reading. I do not know when I have read a book so brief but so stimulating in all its aspects. Reading it has been a privilege and not a duty, for it seems to me that when the humble and retiring teacher of Latin stood on the platform and talked to the students at Cambridge last May, he gave the answer, long needed, to the question, 'What is wrong with modern poetry?' Without mentioning a modern poet (except himself), without intimating that he is aware of one's existence, he has made it possible to clear the shelf of a half dozen recent volumes of poetic criticism and to substitute this slim, red-covered book of fifty pages of everlasting truth.

57. R.P., 'Exponent of Pure Poetry', *Christian Science Monitor* (Boston)

29 July 1933, 8

Critics long ago discovered that the poetry of Mr. A.E. Housman could not be neatly pigeonholed as 'classic' or 'romantic', and the same thing appears to be true of his literary criticism. The present essay displays all the familiar qualities of his poetry: a style marked by simplicity and purity of diction, ease and economy of movement, austerity of taste and lucidity of expression, with underneath it all an intense romantic nostalgia, the vague, beautiful, desperate ideals of an incorrigible dreamer. Though Mr. Housman has himself expressed in an early poem the opposition in his blood of Celt and Saxon, dreamer and craftsman, his disciplined craftsmanship tends to make one forget how undisciplined are his emotions. The voice is Jacob's voice, but the hands are the hands of Esau.

The thesis of this wholly delightful discussion of poetry is romantic to the core. Briefly, Mr. Housman is an exponent of 'pure poetry': there is a magical essence in poetry, which is not in prose; it has nothing to do with what the poem is saying; it cannot be defined but is recognised by the physical sensation which it causes in the reader. This is the burden of his essay, presented in a cooly [sic] rational manner and supported by exquisitely chosen pieces of poetry. Fundamentally it is the point of view of the Abbé Bremond, though the appearance of mysticism is carefully avoided. Blake, to Mr. Housman, is the supreme lyrist, and is best appreciated when his meaning is least understood.

There is nothing very original in this theme. It embodies what everyone must admit to be at least a half-truth. The magic of words is not susceptible of logical analysis, and a certain small body of poetry derives all its beauty, while all true poetry derives much, from the magic of words. But the denotative and connotative meaning of words is certainly as important as their sound in the evocation of that magic. If Blake's words were deprived of all intellectual content, the result would no more be poetry than Lewis Carroll's 'Jabberwocky'. The question of the relative poetic importance of intellectual content and verbal music is not to be settled by assuming a mystical gulf, on one side of which everything is poetry, on the other side everything prose. The purest 'poetry' (if by that is meant verbal music) has an alloy of 'prose' (intellectual meaning), while, as Mr. Housman admits, a statement packed with profound, imperative meaning may also have the highest degree of verbal music.

Such a recognition does not explain the essence of poetry, but it should make us chary of restricting the term to the particular sort of poetry which most moves us – as Mr. Housman does. One of the most sensitive and piquant parts of his essay is devoted to arguing that Dryden and Pope were not poets. Much that is said on this score is well said and stands as a refreshing contrast to the Sitwellian preciosity which prompts so much contemporary laudation of eighteenth-century poetry, but the fact remains that Mr. Housman has no other grounds for his statement than the fact that these poets do not give him a shiver down his spine when he reads them. Mr. T.S. Eliot might reply that good Pope gives him a shiver when bad Shelley doesn't, or – taking a different view – that a good detective story gives him a greater shiver than either, thus proving the uselessness of the shiver as a gauge of poetic value.

Nevertheless, for distinction of manner and a discreet exercise of the most refined sensibilities, Mr. Housman's criticism ranks with Mr. Eliot's – a high honor, whatever its analytical shortcomings.

58. T.S. Eliot, review, *Criterion*
xiii, No. 1, October 1933, 151–4

Thomas Stearns Eliot (1888–1965), poet, dramatist, literary critic, author of *The Waste Land* (1922) and *Four Quartets* (1944), founder and editor of the *Criterion*; also (as listed in *Who Was Who 1961–70*) honorary Deputy Sheriff of Dallas County.

In return for various press cuttings about the lecture, sent by his sister, Katharine Symons, Housman wrote to her (25 October 1933): 'I enclose another one, which is amusing, because its author, T.S. Eliot, is worshipped as a god by the writers in the paper [*Scrutiny*] which had the only hostile review.'

It has long been known to the majority of those who really care about such matters, that Mr. A.E. Housman is one of the few living masters of English prose; and that on those subjects on which he chooses to exercise his talents, there is no one living who can write better. We hope that he may consent to collect his scattered prose writings: the immortal Preface to Manilius is not as accessible as it ought to be. In the present short essay which was the Leslie Stephen lecture for this year, Mr. Housman is addressing himself to a larger audience, and has adapted himself perfectly to the requirements of such an occasion; and this lecture will serve admirably to introduce his prose to those who are unacquainted with it.

Mr. Housman's prose owes its distinction to the power which separates all first-class prose from the merely efficient: a certain emotional intensity. I say 'a certain' merely as a reminder that you cannot abstract completely an identity recognizable in all great prose. Nor is this intensity to be confounded with explicit emotion arising from or suitably infused into the subject matter, such as indignation, scorn or enthusiasm. It is the intensity of the artist, and is capable of informing any subject-matter, even the most abstract, the most arid, or the most impersonal, narrative, expository, or scientifically descriptive. The present subject, however, gives Mr. Housman a wider range than those with which he is accustomed to deal; for he is both a nineteenth (or twentieth) century romantic poet and an eighteenth-century wit; and here, in his appreciation and his expression, he is able to expose both aspects in happy union.

We must keep in mind that this essay is a lecture; and the exigencies of a popular lecture require the author to select his points very carefully, to aim at form and proportion rather than connected profundity, and to avoid going too deeply into anything which is, for the purposes of the moment, another problem. We must not, in short, judge a lecture on Poetry as if it was a book on Aesthetics. The author may himself walk the straight line, but if he is to say anything at all in the time it is difficult for him, if not impossible, not to make assertions which, if pressed firmly and indefatigably by an unfriendly critic, will not yield a concentrated drop of heresy. I think that such a critic might be able to extract (1) the Essence of Poetry Theory, (2) the Pure Poetry Theory, (3) the Physiological Theory. None of these theories can be flatly denied without equal error; I do not believe that Mr. Housman maintains any of them to a vicious degree; I mention them in the hope of sparing other critics the trouble of denouncing Mr. Housman for what he does not maintain.

Repeated meditations led me first to suspect, that there are surprisingly few things that can be said about Poetry; and of these few, the most turn out either to be false or to say nothing of significance. There are a great many things worth saying about one kind of poetry or another; and a good many might not have been said if their authors had not been under the impression that they were talking about all Poetry, when they were only talking about the kind of poetry they liked. Those who indulge in the Essence of Poetry fantasy are given to using 'touchstones', or test lines, which are almost always true poetry, and usually very great poetry. What none of them gives us, yet what we are apt to delude ourselves into believing they give us, is an absolute dividing line between Poetry and Not-Poetry. Mr. Housman does not actually say that the poetry of the eighteenth century (by which he means primarily Dryden and Pope) is not poetry, or rather he seems to say both that it is and is not; but it seems to me, with all due respect, that he is giving himself unnecessary pains. We know that there has been much greater poetry both before and since, and that is all that we need. You can assert that Pope was a poet, or you can assert that he was not a poet; if you enjoy his poetry it does not matter, and if you do not enjoy it that does not matter either. Whichever assertion you make will depend upon some definition of Poetry, explicit or implicit, which you cannot compel anyone else to accept. I feel a certain sympathy with Mr. Housman's acid comments on the poetry of the seventeenth and eighteenth centuries, because I suspect that both have lately been for some amateurs a fashion rather than a taste. But when he suggests that the 'poetry' and the 'wit' in the metaphysicals can be separated as the sound and rotten parts of an apple or a banana with a knife, I am more than doubtful.

When Mr. Housman asks himself: 'Am I capable of recognizing poetry if I come across it?' I would unhesitatingly answer for him, so far as one can for any human being, in the affirmative. But there is more to it than that. You cannot divide human beings, in this respect, as you might separate compasses which are true from those which have more or less deviation. Mr. Housman's quotations, in this lecture, show about as sensitive and refined a perception as any human being can aspire to. But, in this way, is he quite fair to Dryden? and what is much more important, for here he is concerned with a poet for whom he feels almost unqualified admiration, is he quite fair to Blake? I am sure that Blake would not be happy about it, but we have not here to do with Blake's feelings, but with the Problem of Meaning. There is probably no ground for taking issue with Mr. Housman; and I have no space here to develop the difficulties involved in any theory; but I cannot leave the subject without at least affirming the extraordinary complexity of the problem, and the mazes of intellectual subtlety into which it is bound to lead the conscientious enquirer. 'Meaning is of the intellect, poetry is not.' I should not like to deny this, still less to assert it; I am in the same quandary as Mr. Housman is with Pope. For what do we mean by meaning? and what by intellect? 'Poetry indeed seems to me more physical than intellectual'. Well, here again, is something I should not like to deny; but I am not sure that I know what 'physical' and 'intellectual' mean. But from the bottom of page 47 to the end of the lecture on page 51 Mr. Housman has given us an account of his own experience in writing poetry which is important evidence. Observation leads me to believe that different poets may compose in very different ways; my experience (for what that is worth) leads me to believe that Mr. Housman is recounting the authentic processes of a real poet. 'I have seldom', he says, 'written poetry unless I was rather out of health.' I believe that I understand that sentence. If I do, it is a guarantee – if any guarantee of that nature is wanted – of the quality of Mr. Housman's poetry.

59. Edith Sitwell on Housman

1934

Edith Sitwell (1887–1964), poet, elder sister of Osbert and Sacheverell Sitwell; author of, *inter alia*, *Façade* (1922), *Gold Coast Customs* (1929) and a study of Alexander Pope (1930).

A.E. HOUSMAN

Reprinted from the chapter entitled 'Pastors and Masters' in Edith Sitwell, *Aspects of Modern Poetry* (London: Duckworth, 1934), 13–18.

It may, indeed, be said that with the exception of those great poets, Gerard Manley Hopkins and W.B. Yeats, and with the possible exception of Francis Thompson, the poets writing between the years 1880 and 1900 had little or nothing to recommend them. On the one hand, we had the lifeless if pretty falsities of the unhappy Ernest Dowson, though it cannot be said that these are entirely false, for occasionally a genuine feeling slips through. On the other hand, we have what is claimed to be the perfection of Mr. A.E. Housman's 'Shropshire Lad.' I have the greatest respect for the integrity of Professor Housman, and I am not intending any discourtesy to him when I say that to my feeling, the cramped and rheumatic eight-syllable lines, the threadbare texture in which he finds, as a rule, his expression, are not suitable to his themes. Ploughboys never moved so elegantly, men about to be hanged never expressed their sentiments with such neatness; the broken-hearted groan or they whisper, but they do not confine their outpourings to the brevity of such epigrammatic quatrains as these. In short, life and death are not like that. Yet, strangely enough, in Marvell's great poem 'To His Coy Mistress,' T.S. Eliot's great poem 'Whispers of Immortality,' the vast imagination of these is preserved within the prim eight-syllable line, and this, indeed, even heightens the effect in both these poems, shows us, in its narrow grave, the eternal skeleton. Wherein lies the difference? In the fact that we feel a controlled and terrible passion underlying Marvell's and Eliot's verses, an explosive force heaving beneath the surface of the lines.

'The Shropshire Lad' [sic] is claimed to be great poetry because of the bareness of the line, the absolute lack of decoration. But to my feeling, that bareness is due as much to lack of vitality as to anything else. It is certain that the greatest impressiveness of emotion is gained by an absolute simplicity. But in Professor Housman's poems one reader, at least, feels that this simplicity is not invariably the result of passion finding its expression in one inevitable phrase, inhabiting it as the soul inhabits the body, but is sometimes the result of a thin and threadbare texture. This texture is not strong enough to contain an explosive force, or the possibility of a passionate upheaval under the line. The rigidity of the structure does not seem like the rigidity of grief; it seems to arise from stiffness, from an insufficient fluidity. The verse is for the most part rhythmically dead. This is not always the case, however, as we shall see if we read 'The Immortal Part.'

> When I meet the morning beam,
> Or lay me down at night to dream,
> I hear my bones within me say,
> Another night, another day.
>
> When shall this slough of sense be cast,
> This dust of thoughts be laid at last,
> The man of flesh and soul be slain
> And the man of bone remain?

This is nearly, but not quite, great poetry.

If we read these lines, and the equally admirable poem 'Is My Team Ploughing,' we shall find in both a control that is impressive; and the poems are not understated. In both the rigidity is necessary to the theme, and is the rigidity of grief.

Compare 'The Immortal Part,' however, with these lines from Mr. Eliot's 'Whispers of Immortality,' and we shall see the difference, admirable as is Professor Housman's poem.

> Donne, I suppose, was such another
> Who found no substitute for sense;
> To seize and clutch and penetrate,
> Expert beyond experience,
>
> He knew the anguish of the marrow
> The ague of the skeleton;
> No contact possible to flesh
> Allayed the fever of the bone.

These lines, bare as the immortal skeleton, are, like Professor Housman's, based on the eight-syllabled norm; but Mr. Eliot's have the strength of the bones, that are no longer held together even by the cold. They have the undying passion that has known all experience and has learnt that all is vain.

I think one reason that Mr. Eliot's lines have this appalling impressiveness is that the first and third lines are not rhymed, so that a freezing air creeps through the gap. Another difference between the two fragments quoted is that Professor Housman's lines move faster than Mr. Eliot's, which is always the case with eight-syllabled lines which are rhymed A – A, B – B, unless some strength of consonants, some broadening or deepening or lengthening of the line brought about by the vowel-scheme, alters this otherwise inevitable result.

Professor Housman's understatements are rarely impressive. To my astonishment, I find that Mr. Charles Williams [see No. 48 above], a critic who is usually possessed of great discernment, when speaking of a poem called 'Hell Gate,' in a later volume than 'The Shropshire Lad,' claims that 'Many things have been said at Hell Gate since Dante and Milton passed there, but few phrases are so satisfying as that of this newcomer: "To Sin's Smile," "Met again, my lass, said I." '

'It is as great in its way,' continues the critic, 'as Farinata in his burning tomb.'

How can this cramped and trivial phrase be held to be great? In what way does it increase our experience? What passion does it express? What wisdom does it contain?

But to return to 'The Shropshire Lad'; a spurious pathos, springing, however, from a perfectly genuine feeling, is gained from time to time by the juxtaposition of such themes as cricket and death:

> See the son of grief at cricket
> Trying to be glad.
> . . . .
> Try I will: no harm in trying.
> Wonder 'tis how little mirth
> Keeps the bones of man from lying
> On the bed of earth.

It is claimed by admirers of cricket and of war that Waterloo was won on the playing fields of Eton. If this may be held to be true, cricket did, on that occasion, bring a great many men to their death. But I do not think that Professor Housman has explained to us clearly enough how it is that cricket has saved men from dying. If he means us to understand that cricket, and cricket alone, has prevented men from committing suicide, then their continuation on this earth seems hardly worth while.

Professor Housman's poems show an obvious delight in

country pleasures, but little or no visual sense, or, in any case, no gift for illuminating or transmuting things seen. What, for instance, do the following lines add to our experience:

> And since to look at things in bloom
> Fifty springs are little room,
> About the woodland I will go
> And see the cherry hung with snow...

Nothing.

60. Chauncy Brewster Tinker, 'Housman's Poetry', *Yale Review*
September 1935, 84–95

Chauncy Brewster Tinker (1876–1963), scholar and critic. Educated at Yale University, he was Professor of English there from 1913 to 1945, and Keeper of Rare Books, Yale University Library, from 1931.

It is unusual for a poet to cultivate his reputation by a policy of silence. It seems strange that one should create an appetite for a particular kind of verse, and then deliberately refuse to gratify it. Nevertheless, in such a policy there may be a kind of weary wisdom, as of one who has apprehended the awful dangers of satiety. In the creation of a public demand for one's work – even for poetry – there is nothing very unusual. Many in this century, whose names still recur, have had their bright day, have formed their little circle, created a demand, satisfied it, and then passed into oblivion. Men in later middle age can well remember when the appetite for Mr. Kipling's poetry seemed insatiable. That demand was fully met, and the poet, whose collected verse now fills a stout volume of nearly a thousand pages, has passed into (perhaps temporary) eclipse. For the moment, nobody, not even his King, will do him any reverence. And those who remember the rise and decline of poor dear dead Stephen Phillips have a poignant theme on which to meditate: for what seemed fresher and more fragrant in its day than 'Marpessa'? But Mr. Phillips, alas, wrote himself out, and died, I make no doubt, of a broken heart. A dozen cases, nearer our own day, may be passed over in merciful silence. Poets give the public too much. Mr. Housman has followed the proud policy of giving too little.

When, in 1922, he put forth his second volume of verse, entitled 'Last Poems,' there were some among his readers who refused to take his implied threat seriously. This could not be the end. Can a poet, even a successful one, hold his peace? But those who knew the poet better realized at once that he would rather die than publish another line of verse. His career as poet was ended:

> To air the ditty,
> And to earth I.

Mr. Housman was sixty-three years old when that second volume, with its haughty preface, was published. He is now seventy-six.

His poetry, as one begins to see it in perspective, reveals an incredibly high level of worth. He is, *par excellence*, the poet who has produced nothing poor. His poems all measure up to a mark, and a mark which is set very high. He has no juvenilia; if he has preserved his first sketches, the work of his 'prentice hand, the world has been permitted to know nothing about them. They have, no doubt, perished in flames, so that the secret of his early training and practice may die with him. Hardly more than a hundred poems in all have escaped his ruthlessness: there are sixty-three poems in the first volume and forty-one in the second. Only one extends to more than a hundred lines; and the first of them betrays the same skilled hand that fashioned the last. All this gives the impression, as the preface of 1922 explicitly asserts, that he has written only when he felt the goad of the Muse. If so, his case is almost unique in the annals of poetry, for the very greatest poets have cluttered up their volumes with the second-rate and the trivial, in all honesty of conviction that they were still giving us of their best. What scoffing Mephistopheles has pointed his critical finger to Housman's worthless lines, and caused them to be blotted out forever?

Perhaps the poet guessed that the public, even such readers as are concerned for the good of poetry, could not bear too much of him. Fastidious as he is, Mr. Housman is often repetitious. One may assert too often that youth and beauty must presently lie down in the lonely grave. For, as we might easily have too long a 'Rubáiyát,' so we might speedily have too much of Mr. Housman and his lads. (The word 'lad,' by the way, occurs sixty-seven times in the first volume.) Terence, one remembers, is a performer on the flute, an instrument which, in a master's hand, utters a deliciously pure and limpid note, but one of which we presently grow weary. It is valued in proportion to its infrequency; so that we are not displeased when it is absorbed into larger harmonies.

He himself knows the folly of trying to prolong one's success unduly. With the bitter knowledge that comes only in middle age he realizes that the flowers from his garden may not always be 'the wear.' He is not the man to linger on the scene till his audience begins to melt away, but rather prefers to make an end before his admirers have realized their delight.

Characteristic of middle age, again, is the atmosphere of disillusion that prevails in his poetry. His are not the swift vicissitudes of joy and sorrow that mark a passionate youth; his moods are deep-seated, never to be changed. He ceases not to sing of the land of lost content and happy highways where he cannot come again. In all the endless road we tread there's nothing but the night. These are the expressions of a man who has long since settled his philosophy and taken his stand. There are moments when he recalls the work of an earlier bard who also knew that the world can give us nothing equal in value to what it takes from us:

> For the sword wears out the sheath,
>   And the soul wears out the breast,
> And the heart must pause to breathe,
>   And Love itself have rest ...
> So we'll go no more a roving
>   By the light of the moon.

These lines were written when the author, Lord Byron, was nearing his twenty-ninth birthday, the age at which Housman, if we may trust his dates, wrote the first poem in 'A Shropshire Lad'. The bulk of it, he says, was produced as late as 1895, when he was thirty-six; so that despite the perpetual assumption of the rôle of youth, the sentiments are actually those of middle age. It is all reminiscential. About that there is nothing incredible: a poet may sing of 'liquor, love, and fights' long after he has ceased to be a practitioner of the arts with which they are related.

It is not given to youth to speak with the professional skill of a Housman, whose manner, for all its apparent and engaging simplicity, results from a mature knowledge of the art of rhetoric (as it was once universally called, before modern colleges had brought it into disrepute), the French *éloquence*. Every phrase tells. His climax catches us unaware like a blow upon the mouth, a blow carefully placed, delivered, with full knowledge of its deadly force, by a professional. Not even in Browning can you find opening strains more blinding in their suddenness than

> Shot? so quick, so clean an ending?
> Oh that was right, lad, that was brave.

It is only when we turn to his scholarly prose, and particularly to his reviews of the publications of rivals, that we see how awful a power this may be when mercilessly applied. Professor Housman, who is professionally concerned with late Latin poetry, belongs to that extinct and evil school of reviewers, headed by Jeffrey and Brougham, who regarded the authors under their scrutiny as head-hunters do their captives. The wretched victims are neatly slaughtered, their heads cut off, and shrunken to the size and smiling contours of a wax doll's, and henceforward serve as trophies, proof of the artist's skill – *sein Hand zu weisen*. There are those who admire this art, and if they wish to study it in detail may examine Professor Ferguson's essay, 'The Belligerent Don.' He cites an example (which, I fear, he admires) of a poor devil who had ventured to publish a translation of the elegies of Propertius, or 'Cynthia,' as the first book of those somewhat artificial love poems used to be called. The translator modestly asked the reader's pardon for his 'bald' rendering. Rash man! Professor Housman (a student of that lyric poet who courteously referred to a rival as 'stinking Maevius,' and hoped that the ship on which he was putting forth to sea might go to the bottom) remarked in a review:

' "Scholars will pardon an attempt, however bald, to render into English these exquisite love poems." Why? Those who have no Latin may pardon such an attempt, if they like bad verses better than silence; but I do not know why bald renderings of exquisite love poems should be pardoned by those who want no renderings at all.'

Such blows are not unrelated to the art of the bully, nor are they unrelated to the art of the poet, as Horace and the Latin satirists have taught the Cambridge don. Those who enjoy British arrogance at its best may pursue this subject exhaustively in the classical and philological reviews to which Professor Housman has contributed.

I am not further concerned with all this than as it relates to the poet's very beautiful art, for, as I have said, the relation is there. The skill behind the savage prose and the force behind the poetry is the same shattering power. There is death in the words. In the simplest poems there is *passion* wound up to the intensest pitch. Take a poem like 'The New Mistress.' There is nothing really satirical about it, and a stanza chosen at random reads like one of the 'Barrack Room Ballads':

> I will go where I am wanted, to a lady born and bred
> Who will dress me free for nothing in a uniform of red;
> She will not be sick to see me if I only keep it clean:
> I will go where I am wanted for a soldier of the Queen.

This obviously is Tommy Atkins speaking, but there is a subtlety in the poem to which Mr. Kipling never attains, a recurrent *motif* of sickness, which extends from the scornful sweetheart's 'Oh, sick I am to see you,' all the way through to the final line with its insistence upon the theme,

> And the enemies of England they shall see me and be sick.

These verses are the product of a man who esteems workmanship as one of the best things to be found in poetry.

Mr. Housman is fond of writing about soldiers; but he is not forgetful of the bitterness in their lot:

> What evil luck soever
>   For me remains in store,
> 'Tis sure much finer fellows
>   Have fared much worse before.
>
> So here are things to think on
>   That ought to make me brave,

A.E. HOUSMAN

> As I strap on for fighting
> My sword that will not save.

It is perhaps natural that, among the elegies upon the dead who fell in the Great War none is so powerful as that of Housman, who realizes and stresses the unmitigated and abiding horror of it. No poem produced by that conflict sums up quite so well the terror and the grim realism, not of the battlefield, but of the cowering nations huddled watchfully behind their armies:

> These, in the day when heaven was falling,
>   The hour when earth's foundations fled,
> Followed their mercenary calling,
>   And took their wages and are dead.
>
> Their shoulders held the sky suspended;
>   They stood, and earth's foundations stay;
> What God abandoned, these defended,
>   And saved the sum of things for pay.

An 'epitaph on an army of mercenaries'! For sheer irony where shall be found anything superior to 'took their wages and are dead'? Pathos, pity, and all the fine sentimentalities about death on the field of glory drop out of mind and leave only the stark finality of dying. Were a soldier's wages a shilling a day? Yes, and death into the bargain. But compare it with the great Greek epitaph on the soldiers who fell at Marathon, and you shall see a difference: 'Traveller, go tell the Lacedemonians that here, obedient to their word, we lie.' It is no less forceful, but it is without bitterness.

Mr. Housman may idealize youth, but he never forgets its temptation to violence and even to crime; and this may account, in some degree, for his strange preoccupation with death by hanging. Nobody is likely to forget the pieces on this subject in 'Last Poems,' or that horrible burlesque of the Crucifixion in the earlier volume, entitled 'The Carpenter's Son,' a poem that I prefer to pass without comment. It is not the poet's only satire on the Christian way of life.

> And if your hand or foot offend you,
>   Cut it off, lad, and be whole;
> But play the man, stand up and end you,
>   When your sickness is your soul.

This simple counsel and the oft-repeated theme that, though death is cruel, life is more cruel still, accounts, I suppose, for the adjective 'pagan' that is so often applied to Housman's poetry; but this is hardly the correct term, for the pagan, properly so-called, is intensely religious in his way, 'other-worldly' in truth; and to religion and its consolations Mr. Housman never makes a concession. Yet I cannot convince myself that such poems as 'The Immortal Part,' 'The Carpenter's Son,' and the ones on suicide are a considered message that it is better to enter into death than to endure the ignominy of life. I cannot even believe that they are intended to overthrow a consolatory religion and set up a grim and tight-lipped stoicism in its place. Mr. Housman does not use his poetry for 'messages,' and I doubt whether it is intended to influence our conduct in any special way.

Poems of this sort have no ethical relations. If they were seriously intended as lessons of conduct, their author himself might reasonably be expected to apply them and make his stormy way to the grave. And we, the readers of this verse, can we be said really to have taken it to heart unless we too play the man and set the pistol to our head? However much we may admire this verse, our use of it is confined to the realm of the imagination, and never touches the more practical problems of conduct. If the function of a poem is merely to persuade the reader to mend his ways or to adopt some high principle or noble standard of living, such verse is of secondary import, nothing more, indeed, than means to an end, means which may very properly be forgotten when the end is attained.

Take such a type of verse, for example, as the hymn. It releases within us certain emotions and instincts, memories and pieties, which transcend poetry altogether and touch higher and more lasting concerns. A hymn which remains merely a poem, without influencing our walk and conversation, has not properly discharged its function. This is why it is impossible to evaluate hymns as literature; and it is also the reason why poetry that is employed for propaganda can never be of a high order. This is what is wrong with the lyrics that William Morris wrote for the socialist party of his day, and this is what is wrong with such a thing as Mr. W.H. Auden's 'Dance of Death,' because, effective as that satire on the modern world may be, it concludes with the triumph of Karl Marx and his young adherents. Like Mrs.

Browning's 'Bitter Cry of the Children,' it is dedicated to a cause and not to the Muse.

The cause served by poetry is a peculiarly elevated one, because it enriches our spirit by giving us vicarious experience, and so enabling us to understand ways of life that are never to be ours. Hence it is that among the hosts who have loved the 'Rubáiyát of Omar Khayyám,' few have tried to live by it, few have become winebibbers as a result of reading it, and fewer still have filled a drunkard's grave. We read Swinburne's most macabre ballads, without sinking into degeneracy. We may read and admire 'The City of Dreadful Night' without ourselves falling into melancholia, and may delight in the most sinister lyrics in 'A Shropshire Lad' without the temptation to make way with ourselves or even to embrace the austerities of the Stoic school. But we are wiser and more experienced for having read these things, and have a larger conception of the incredible variety and intensity of human life.

No critic has been more insistent upon the non-ethical view of poetry than Mr. Housman himself, who has gone so far as to say that poetry is not the thing said but a way of saying it. His lecture on the 'Name and Nature of Poetry,' delivered at the University of Cambridge two years ago last spring, is a highly characteristic utterance, designed to annoy as well as to invigorate – a perfect irritant. 'Meaning,' he asserted, 'is of the intellect, poetry is not.' He affects to be wholly serious about this, and blandly announces that poetry is frequently the product of persons who have gone mad. He seems, throughout, to be thinking (like Poe) of poetry as consisting exclusively of brief lyric poems, what used to be called 'ejaculations' or 'effusions.' Having told us that it is frequently 'inadvisable' to draw the meaning out of such poems, he leaves us to decide for ourselves what to think of such vast works as the 'Agamemnon' of Aeschylus, the 'Oedipus' of Sophocles, the sixth book of the 'Aeneid,' 'King Lear' and the 'Divine Comedy.' If these things be not poetry, and, moreover, poetry at its most majestic, what are they henceforth to be deemed? If they are what the world has thought them hitherto, we must find a place for them in some poetic category, and we shall find it both possible and highly advisable to draw a meaning out of them. Such things, as Mr. Housman's own career reveals, are worth the attention of a lifetime.

But all this is from the point. The significant thing about the lecture is its complete revelation of the personality of the author. It may be read with emotions similar in kind, if not in degree, to those awakened by his verse, and may, furthermore, serve as a commentary upon it. Like his poetry, the lecture is meant to startle and waylay. It succeeds in doing so. It proclaims that the effect of poetry is more physical than intellectual, that the seat of poetic sensation is the pit of the stomach, that poetry at its most intense makes the flesh creep and the hair of the head stand up. It is unwise to recite poetry to oneself while shaving. As for the act of creation, a certain deadening of the intellect is apparently desirable, and in Mr. Housman's case, at least in the days of the Shropshire Lad, the poet before composing drank a pint of beer at luncheon as a 'sedative to the brain.'

Those may take this seriously who can. For my part I cannot forget Housman's besetting temptation to jostle the Ark of the Covenant. I cannot forget that he must be aware of the activity in Cambridge of Mr. I.A. Richards and his young school. I can imagine his delight in telling the dons and the bluestockings in his audience how he had answered a foolish American who had asked him for a definition of poetry. (An English lecturer can always get a laugh by girding at Americans.) Housman replied that one 'could no more define poetry than a terrier can define a rat, but that I thought we both recognized the object by the symptoms which it provokes in us.' In which there is, of course, something deliciously unregenerate, something pungent and slightly sulphurous, highly amusing and quite unacceptable.

There is nothing in the lecture to indicate any waning of the poet's powers, so that the reader cannot but wish that instead of this vigorous and provocative lecture, we might have had another slender volume of perfect and provocative verse. But this is to cry for the moon. Housman has spoken eloquent words about the exhaustion that ensues for the poet upon the completion of his work: 'I can no longer expect to be revisited by the continuous excitement under which ... I wrote the greater part of my other book ('A Shropshire Lad'), nor indeed could I well sustain it if it came.'

That is his *apologia*. He has bidden us farewell in one of the most beautiful translations that has ever been wrought in English:

A.E. HOUSMAN

> We'll to the woods no more,
> The laurels all are cut,
> The bowers are bare of bay
> That once the Muses wore;
> The year draws in the day
> And soon will evening shut:
> The laurels all are cut,
> We'll to the woods no more.
> Oh we'll no more, no more
> To the leafy woods away,
> To the high wild woods of laurel
> And the bowers of bay no more.

Here is that power to pierce the breast with unutterable emotion of which Mr. Housman lectured so eloquently, and which he would, rather rashly, hold to be the sole and complete mark of poetry.

Whether it be so or not is a question that does not concern us here; if not the highest power possessed by poets, it is certainly among the highest. It is one which we shall, I think, seek in vain among other living poets in England. Who, now that Mr. Housman has fallen silent, stabs the heart with the sudden and unforgettable word? Who speaks the word that conquers and controls the breast, and gives utterance to the deepest emotions of the spirit, and so becomes a partner in the will of the Creator? Mr. Kipling has remarkable gifts – gifts which at the moment are perhaps too lightly esteemed – but this has never been reckoned among them. The Laureate has depended upon other means to touch the emotions and to hold the interest. The younger poets are preoccupied with their own emotions and their exciting programme, and are probably unaware that the public has a heart to stab.

Although Mr. Housman has condemned himself to silence, he has not been without his active influence upon the literary world. He has remained a symbol of sanity and intelligibility, and has reminded us that a poet may have a larger audience than his own narrow circle of personal friends. The enduring steadiness of his poetic reputation has served as a commentary on the rise and fall of the paltry poetic fashions of the day. As a poet he has displayed a becoming modesty in strange contrast to his native arrogance. He has never pandered to the public taste or solicited the discipleship of poets; but he has kept alive the notion that a poet has a profession to learn and a duty to fulfil. His pride in his craft has been contagious. Meanwhile he has been content to be Professor of Latin and an authority on Manilius. His activity in this chosen field he has been pleased to describe as his 'proper job'; posterity will remember him for a 'job' of a very different kind, but one discharged with no less professional skill.

OBITUARY COMMENTS
1936

61. 'Death of Professor A.E. Housman', *Manchester Guardian Weekly*
Friday, 8 May 1936, 375

Extract from an unsigned obituary.

We regret to announce the death of A.E. Housman, Professor of Latin in the University of Cambridge and the author of *A Shropshire Lad* and *Last Poems*. He died on Thursday of last week at Cambridge, aged 77.

Few poets have achieved so wide a renown upon so slender an output as A.E. Housman. As the author of *A Shropshire Lad* he was known to many whose interest in verse was slight and recognised as a voice unique for its purity and intensity by all to whom poetry was dear. This short and concentrated sequence of lyrics was first published in 1896. It was composed in about six months, and the strain of its creation was so intense that for nearly twenty years Housman could not bring himself to endure it again. In 1922, however, appeared *Last Poems*, breathing the same haunting desiderium, the same sweet bitterness, the same aroma of the English countryside, and all with that supple simplicity of diction and of form which expressed in itself a sort of fastidious stoicism. For the verse of Housman is so piercing and poignant in its appeal because its simplicity is the outcome of multiplied exclusions. All but the essence of his emotion has been pared away, and its expression, with its artifices of assonance and alliteration, its mingling of the choice word with the speech of every day, and its ironic, heart-breaking stabs, often at the conclusion of a stanza, is controlled with a rigid economy.

Critics have complained of his pessimism, as they have complained of Hardy's, have deprecated a view of life which never allows them the luxury either of vague hope or of vague despair. But a poet is to be judged rather by the sincerity than by the helpfulness of his vision, and it is exactly by its unflinching personal sincerity that Housman's vision, at once so stern and pitiful, differed from those moods of luxuriant melancholy of which so much of the poetry of the nineties was the mannered expression. His philosophy is never explicit as it is so often in the work of Hardy. The critical mind in him refines and crystallises with a relentless logic the heart-sickness of a sensibility wounded, we feel, by life to the quick, but it never itself generalises.

The emotion in which all his verse is rooted is too insistent to allow of that, and although his mood is always essentially the same and to this extent limited, it never grows monotonous because it is re-experienced and redefined in every lyric. The intensity, indeed, of the experience in which these poems originated may be judged by Housman's power to express it over and over again without once affecting us with a sense of formal repetition.

Such a pessimism as this is not depressing, because in its austere denial of life it is so passionately alive. Few poets, indeed, have expressed the injuries of existence with such emotional and intellectual integrity, and it is this integrity which ensures for *A Shropshire Lad* and its sequel not only the appreciation of an age which found in them a perfect articulation of its own perplexed and self-pitying temper but of a posterity which can still respond to the beauty of the tragedy of things.

62. E.L. Woodward, 'Les Lauriers Sont Coupés', *Oxford Magazine*

14 May 1936, 571–2

Ernest Llewellyn Woodward (1890–1971), historian, educated at Corpus Christi College, Oxford; Fellow of All Souls from 1919 to 1944 and from 1962 until his death; Professor of International Relations at Oxford, 1944–7, and Professor of Modern History there from 1947 to 1951. His publications included *Christianity and Nationalism in the Later Roman Empire*, *War and Peace in Europe 1815–70*, and (after

Housman) *The Twelve-Winded Sky*. He was knighted in 1952.

> Oh we'll no more, no more
> To the leafy woods away
> To the high wild woods of laurel
> And the woods of bay no more.

When a poet dies, there begins the dissection of his work, and the stir of the critics, eyed and eyeless, fretting their way through the flesh and the heart. Time passes, and good work stays. Time passes, and there comes the charm of the antique, the addition of strangeness to beauty; forgotten cadences, words that carry with them past centuries, and a pain that has become measured and more easily borne. Who can hear the three words *flammantia moenia mundi* [1] as a Roman first heard them? The language even of men of plain, direct speech takes this incrustation and change from bone to coral. Consider one sentence from *The Pilgrim's Progress*: 'let us here show the pilgrims the gate of the Celestial City, if they have skill to look through our perspective glass.'

If there be something of moonlight about all poetry belonging to the distant past, then a poet, like an actor, must take with him into the grave the peculiar and personal quality of his art. Yet he takes something more than this away with him. When a poet dies, an element in his humbler contemporaries dies with him. These tens of thousands never knew him. He might have disliked them, or wondered at the gloss which they put on his clear text. As for them, they have lost their herald. They are dumb.

The words of my own generation were written more sharply, more deeply, by Housman than by any other man save Thomas Hardy. These two men are now dead. Others have come since Thomas Hardy and A.E. Housman; if we can see their meaning, and understand the moods which they have set out in an older and perhaps a stronger English rhythm, we cannot share these moods, and we would not have chosen for ourselves this rhythm. No one else can speak for us.

> Nous n'irons plus aux bois
> Les lauriers sont coupés.

The technician will notice certain curious things about Housman:

his choice of metres; those very forms of assonance which give to English monosyllables something of the beat of Latin. The repetition of words and phrases, held back or remade after long intervals of time. The sudden inruption [sic] of terror at the prime movement and the darkness of the universe.

> The vast and moon-eclipsing cone of night.

Even with the sun at mid-heaven,

> The subterranean dark
> Has crossed the nadir, and begins to climb.

It is less than fifty years since the writing of one of the earliest of the poems in *A Shropshire Lad*, but already one could take lines and subjects from the book to illustrate the history of the later Victorian age. Housman, far more than Kipling, and more than Henley, has the real instinct, the real secret of English power. For this reason there is no talk of imperialism, no use of the word Empire, no *snobisme* about sahibs; but who would want more than this:

> And you will list the bugle
> That blows in lands of morn,
> And make the foes of England
> Be sorry you were born.

Or, again, who could choose eight lines on the soldiers of this country more true and more direct than the Epitaph on an army of mercenaries? (It is said that the term was never used by Germans in contempt of the English. The words may not have been used in 1914, but they were shouted up and down Germany throughout the Boer War. Housman had a long memory.) The justification of this response to the tramp of soldiers must be the knowledge and love of the world from which the soldier goes never to return. No man has described middle England with greater desire or more complete surrender to its light and shade. For us, in the flow of things, this England of the white main roads, with a dust on the wild roses in early summer, this quiet England, has gone. The large landscapes only are there; the coloured counties below Bredon Hill; star-filled seas beyond Portland; troubled woods along Wenlock Edge.

So strong, so consuming is this leisure of the eyes for the

hawthorn and the wild cherry, the farms and coppices and 'blue remembered hills', that it makes of itself the pattern of a philosophy. A philosophy which must hark back always to the past.

[quotes stanzas 1 and 2 of *A Shropshire Lad*, No. XXVII]

Yet it is a philosophy of action, hating bitterly that one must see injustice done on the earth; a philosophy of friendship, sudden friendship nobler than the universe which treads down good and evil in its aimless fulfilment of law. It is a philosophy of endurance, the measured endurance of one who, weaponless, tricked, and ambushed, watches a cowardly enemy creeping nearer to make an end. There is no flinching from the facts, no belief that a bad tale becomes good if it be told noisily, or that knowledge is not to be sought because it is painful, or that for ever men must joyfully throw themselves before Juggernaut. I have looked often for analogies to this grave philosophy of resignation which has no weak pretence that in things surrendered there is no loss. I have found one sentence written, like Housman's verse, by one of aristocratic temper and, curiously enough, a certain dryness of mind, not unlike Housman's writing apart from the hours of excitement and illumination; a sentence in which a great Jansenist considered the catholic church which, to religious minds in France, was the whole significant world ... 'Il me semble que je suis né dans une Eglise éclairée de diverses lampes et de divers flambeaux, et que Dieu permet que je les voie éteindre les uns après les autres, sans qu'il paraisse qu'on y substitue de nouveaux. Ainsi il me semble que l'air s'obscurcit de plus en plus, parce que nous ne méritons pas que Dieu répare les vides qu'il fait lui-même dans son Eglise.'[2]

NOTES

1 'The burning ramparts of the world'.
2 'It seems to me that I was born in a Church lit by diverse lamps and candles, and that God is allowing me to see them extinguished one by one, without the apparent substitution of any new ones. Thus it seems to me that the air darkens more and more, because we no longer deserve that God should repair the holes which he himself makes in his Church.'

63. F.L. Lucas, 'Mithridates: The Poetry of A.E. Housman', *Cambridge Review*
15 May 1936, 385–6

More and more it looks as if devils, mediums, pythonesses, and poets were in the same boat – or at least frequently travelled in it. So often they suggest cases of multiple personality; so often poets in the state we call 'inspiration', like mediums in their trances, seem to differ from their daily selves with a baffling completeness that recalls that strange plurality of souls which played hide-and-seek with one another in Miss Sally Beauchamp.

> They cease not fighting, east and west,
> On the marches of my breast.
> They kill and kill and never die;
> And I think that each is I.

A poet's dream-picture of himself – and yet even dreams do not come by hazard. The world, at all events, will not easily forget either Housman the Scholar or Housman the Singer.

They made indeed a strange combination – strange as Arnold's Scholar-Gipsy. For poetry of an over-erudite kind the Germans have coined (they would) a special term – *Professorenpoesie*. But it was not the kind of poetry that Professor Housman wrote. Familiarity stales all things; but, to the unblunted imagination, that the editor of Manilius should have produced *A Shropshire Lad* still seems a miracle as amazing as if Great St. Mary's turned overnight into a haystack, or an ink-well in the Examination Schools during the Tripos blushed into scarlet poppies; as if the Proctors were seen proceeding down King's Parade scythe on arm and straw in mouth, or a flock of sheep appeared (*mirabile dictu*) running to vote in the Senate House.

Perhaps I may be allowed to repeat a passage written a dozen years ago, since it did not, apparently, altogether displease the poet himself. For I remember finding myself shortly after, with some alarm, sitting next but one to him at a feast. During dinner I was protected by our common host, William Heitland (now, alas, both those editors of Lucan are gone together to converse with their poet in the Elysian fields); but when we rose, instead of the icy silence I was looking the other way to avoid, came a quiet voice: 'I have been battening on your flatteries in the weekly press'. (But then Housman is known to have been unexpectedly indulgent to bores, provided they did not try to edit the classics.)

[quotes most of paragraph 3 of 'Few, but Roses' (1923) – see No. 42 above]

How much his poetry was derived from a less conscious and more instinctive side of him (to which, no doubt, he also owed some of his inspired emendations – not the sort of thing that can be produced by long and solid sucking at a pen) he has himself recorded. We know his recipe – a pint of beer and an afternoon walk. But that was not all. He was no lisper in numbers. We know also that the strong sense of reality and logic, the insistence on hard thinking and clear thinking, which dominated the scholar in him, were not forgotten by this poet who did not flinch from rewriting a stanza twelve times in as many months. Only he kept these qualities in their place.

Housman is, in fact, an example of what I believe to be a general truth – the sort of truth which people pronounce obvious and then promptly go and do the opposite. Good poetry, I think, is most likely to be written, not by those (sometimes called 'Romantics') who live drunken with their own dreams; nor by those (sometimes called 'Classics') who consider that a gentleman should carry his liquor without a tremor, even on Parnassus; but by those who stand between. It was an evil day when neo-Classic critics got into their heads that poetry should be, not inspired, but 'painful'; painful it soon became. And it is an evil day when people begin listening to Surrealist critics preaching that the essential is to fling off all control of the Unconscious and produce, say, solemn films in which 'a flaming fir-tree, an archbishop, a giraffe, and some feathers are all flung out of a bedroom window'. There are always adventurous spirits who find something mean about the Golden Mean. Blake did. But there is nothing despicable about combining opposite extremes in perfect balance. And it is part of the strength of Housman's poetry that he was not only a Romantic, but a Classic also.

His ecstasies do not lose sight of the earth, nor his dreams forget reality.

THE CRITICAL HERITAGE

[quotes *Last Poems*, No. XXI]

If he had leanings, it was to the Romantic side. This became clear in that famous lecture on the Nature of Poetry, which so annoyed some 'experts' whose complete understanding of the subject was undisturbed by any distracting habit of writing it. Blake was for him 'the most poetical of all poets'. He dared to find most metaphysical poetry 'intellectually frivolous'; being too wise to overestimate a type of cleverness he could himself at need use so perfectly.

[quotes stanza 2 of *Last Poems*, No. XX]

He dared also the platitude of finding eighteenth-century verse sometimes fine, but mostly prosaic, even so. In his own work those who like tracing literary pedigrees and chasing echoes, can note a wide range of faint but unmistakable likenesses – touches of Homer, Theocritus, the Greek Anthology, Catullus, Horace, the Ballads, Shakespeare, Milton, Johnson, Landor perhaps, and certainly Heine. With these last and with Arnold he shares, despite his Romanticism, a strong and often bitter sense of fact, a disdainful distrust of what Landor has called 'the hot and uncontrolled harlotry of a flaunting and dishevelled enthusiasm'.

But after all it matters little whom he was like; what matters is how superbly unlike anyone but himself he remained, even while using some of the most hackneyed metres in English. He never fussed about originality, like those who have none. He could not touch a hymn-tune without setting his stamp on it. In his hands the brass tongs of Tate and Brady become a tongue of flame.

[quotes stanzas 1 and 2 of *Last Poems*, No. XIX]

Needing inspiration to write – an inspiration that often tore him in pieces – and extremely fastidious of what he had written, he naturally produced little. In that little it is not hard to pick certain holes. There is no doubt a sameness of tone; there is too much melodrama, throat-cutting and brain-blowing; too much about beer, soldiers, and hangmen; too much of that monotonously morbid death-wish which is a regular disease of

Romantics. His peasants, we may be told, are too unlike any modern proletariate [sic]; his imperialism too like many modern dictators. Again, I could never persuade Lytton Strachey that there could be much good in all this stuff about 'lads'.

Some of these charges, I think, stand; but so, fortunately, in spite of them all, does the poetry. For me, at least, it has stood the only test I know, that of time and change. That tiny volume, which cost me sixpence in 1913 and followed me to the War, and sent me, after it, on a Shropshire pilgrimage, where I discovered with deep disgust that there was not a single suicide buried north of Hughley steeple, will outstay many of its fatter and costlier fellows on my shelves. What makes the fascination of these poems? Not the characters they contain; those are vague and not very interesting, except for the author's own, glimpsed between the lines. Nor is it so much the bracing bitterness of that envenomed view of the world on which this Mithridates sustained life till he died old. His clear-sighted eyes lack a depth of human understanding which Hardy's, though equally without illusions, still possess. The spell lies rather in the imaginative power of these poems to induce in the reader, with the certainty of a drug, their own mood – a mood of melancholy that is yet not depressed, but intensely alive to the beauty both of the English country and the English tongue. They have the essential gift of saying things unforgettably, in phrases that become private quotations, rising silent and uncalled-for at unexpected moments in their readers' memories.

> But men may come to worse than dust.

> The troubles of our proud and angry dust
>   Are from eternity and shall not fail.

> The Spartans on the sea-wet rock
>   sat down and combed their hair.

> And the feather pate of folly
>   Bears the falling sky.

> But men at whiles are sober
>   And think by fits and starts,
> And if they think, they fasten
>   Their hands upon their hearts.

> Ay look; high heaven and earth ail from the prime

> foundation;
> All thoughts to rive the heart are here, and all are
>   vain:
> Horror and scorn and hate and fear and indignation ...

But one thing could make him forget the indignation – the English countryside. If it be the poet's business, above all, 'to make the much-loved earth more lovely', well he knew and minded it. His 'lads' may be mortal; his Shropshire lives – let us but pray that it may not outlive the lovely reality which our obscene generation is so fast destroying. From 'the blue and silver morning' to the hour when

> clear and wan
> Reach the gulfs of evening on;

from the days of the sloe's first flowering to those when 'north winds freeze the fir', these eyes which no leagues of print could dull, knew all her ways and changes.

> The chestnut casts his flambeaux, and flowers
>   Stream from the hawthorn on the wind away,
> The doors clap to, the pane is blind with showers.
>   Pass me the can, lad; there's an end of May.

It was on a May eve that he died, before on Wenlock Edge broom and hawthorn had bloomed again. Years before, he had written a farewell to Nature in which rings some of the bitterness of the dying Hippolytus towards the Maiden Goddess who is forsaking him, who among her young green leaves will so soon forget.

[quotes stanzas 1 and 5 of *Last Poems*, No. XL]

But though Nature in her witlessness may not know, it will be long before posterity while it roars along its roads past the forest-tower of the Wrekin or the peace of Clun, forgets whose footsteps walked there once; and among the dreary Roman tiles and drains and flues of the real Uricon, for long years yet, some will turn to remember him whose troubles are now ashes like the Roman's, where the calm of the eighteenth century broods over the greatest Roman city of the West.

64. Cyril Connolly on Housman, *New Statesman*
23 May 1936

Cyril Connolly (1903–74), educated at Eton (where he was a contemporary and friend of George Orwell) and Balliol College, Oxford; influential reviewer and critic from the 1920s onward, founder of *Horizon* and its editor from 1939 to 1950. At the time of his attack on Housman Connolly had just published his only novel, *The Rock Pool* (1935).

Connolly's article provoked defences of Housman, variously angry and magisterial, from F.L. Lucas, Martin Cooper, L.P. Wilkinson (Fellow of King's College, Cambridge) and John Sparrow, who scornfully noted that Connolly, though 'late for the funeral ... at least had the satisfaction of spitting on the grave before the mourners had departed'. These responses were printed in subsequent issues of The *New Statesman*. Connolly concluded his reply (6 June 1936) by stating: 'I think [Housman] will always have a place, for his good things, in late Victorian poetry, but I shall continue to maintain that he is greatly overrated.'

Nine years later, Connolly reprinted his views, and those of his opponents, in his collection of essays *The Condemned Playground* (1945), under the title 'A.E. Housman: A Controversy'. In his introduction, Connolly noted that it was a controversy 'in which I do not think I come out very well'.

The obituaries of Professor Housman have given us the picture of a fascinating personality and have made real, to an unscholarly public, the labour of an unrivalled scholar. But in one respect they seem to me misleading, that they all defer to him as a fine lyric poet, the equal of Gray according to some, acclaimed by Sir Walter Raleigh as the greatest living poet according to others. Now there are so few people who care about poetry in England,

and fewer still who are critical of it, that one is tempted at first to make no comment. But in case there are some fellow waverers, and in case we can be of small comfort to those whose ideas about poetry are the opposite of Professor Housman's, and whose success also varies inversely to that of the Shropshire Bard, I have made a few notes on his lyrics that may be of use to them.

It is the unanimous verdict of his admirers that Housman is essentially a classical poet. Master of the Latin language, he has introduced into English poetry the economy, the precision, the severity of that terse and lucid tongue. His verses are highly finished, deeply pagan; they stand outside the ordinary current of modern poetry, the inheritors, not of the romantic age, but of the poignancy and stateliness, the lapidary quality of the poems of Catullus, Horace, and Virgil, or of the flowers of the Greek Anthology. This impression is heightened by the smallness of Professor Housman's output and by the years he devoted to finishing and polishing it, and, not least, by the stern and cryptic hints in the prefaces, with their allusions to profound emotions rigidly controlled, to a creative impulse ruthlessly disciplined and checked. This theory seems to have hoodwinked all his admirers; their awe of Housman as a scholar has blinded them to his imperfections as a poet, just as the pessimism and platonism of Dean Inge have sanctified his opinion on topics which, in other hands, might suggest silly season journalism. The truth is that many of Housman's poems are of a triteness of technique equalled only by the banality of the thought; others are slovenly, and a quantity are derivative – not from the classics, but from Heine, or from popular trends – imperialism, place-nostalgia, games, beer – common to the poetry of his time. *A Shropshire Lad* includes with some poems that are unworthy of Kipling others that are unworthy of Belloc, without the excuse of over-production through economic necessity which those writers might have urged. Horace produced, in the *Odes* and *Carmen Seculare*, a hundred and four poems; Housman, not I think without intention, confined his two volumes to the same number. Yet a moment's silent comparison should settle his position once and for all. To quote single lines, to measure a poet by his mistakes, is sometimes unfair; in the case of a writer with such a minute output it seems justified. Here are a few lines from *A Shropshire Lad*, a book in which, incidentally, the word 'lad' (one of the most vapid in the language) occurs sixty-seven times in sixty-three poems.

Each quotation is from a separate poem.

(*a*) Because 'tis fifty years to-night
That God has saved the Queen.

(*b*) Clay lies still, but blood's a rover;
Breath's a ware that will not keep.
Up, lad ...

(*c*) I will go where I am wanted, for the sergeant does not mind;
He may be sick to see me but he treats me very kind.

(*d*) The goal stands up, the keeper
Stands up to keep the goal.

(*e*) And since to look at things in bloom
Fifty springs are little room.

(*f*) You and I must keep from shame
In London streets the Shropshire name;

(*g*) They put arsenic in his meat.
And stared aghast to watch him eat.
They poured strychnine in his cup
And shook to see him drink it up.

These are some of the verses that, we are told, could not be entrusted to anthologies because of the author's fears that they would suffer through incorrect punctuation! (*a*), (*b*), and (*c*) suggest barrack-room Kipling, (*d*) old-boys'-day Newbolt, (*e*) and (*f*) are typical of Georgian sham-pastoral, and (*g*) suggests non-vintage Belloc.

So much for a few of the bad poems. Let us now examine the better ones. There are two themes in Housman: man's mortality, which intensifies for him the beauty of Nature, and man's rebellion against his lot. On his treatment of these themes subsists his reputation for classicism. But his presentation of both is hopelessly romantic and sentimental, the sentiment of his poems, in fact, is that of Omar Khayyám, which perhaps accounts for their popularity; he takes over the pagan concept of death and oblivion as the natural end of life and even as a not inappropriate end of youth, and lards it with a purely Christian self-pity and a romantic indulgence in the pathetic fallacy. By the same treatment his hero becomes a picturesque outlaw, raising his pint-pot in defiance of the laws of God and man, running away to enlist with the tacit approval of his pawky Shropshire scoutmaster, and suitably lamented by him when he makes his final escape from society, on the gallows. In the last few poems it is his own mortality that he mourns, not that of his patrol, but here again his use of rhythm is peculiarly sentimental and artful, as in his metrically morbid experiments in the five-line stanza:

> For she and I were long acquainted
> And I knew all her ways

or

> Well went the dances
> At evening to the flute.

It must be remembered, also, that classical poetry is essentially aristocratic; such writers as Gray or Horace address themselves to their own friends and would be incapable of using Maurice, Terence, and the other rustics as anything but the material for a few general images.

> The boast of heraldry, the pomp of power
> And all that beauty, all that wealth e'er gave,
> Awaits alike the inevitable hour:
> The paths of glory lead but to the grave.

That is classical in spirit.

> Too full already is the grave
> Of fellows that were good and brave
> And died because they were

is not.

There are about half a dozen important poems of Housman, of which I think only the astronomical one (*Last Poems*, 36) is a complete success. Two were given us at my school to turn into Latin verses.

> Into my heart an air that kills
> From yon far country blows

was one, which would suggest to a Roman only a miasma; one has to put it beside 'There is a land of pure delight' to realize its imperfection in English, and the other was

A.E. HOUSMAN

> With rue my heart is laden
> For golden friends I had,
> For many a rose-lipt maiden
> And many a lightfoot lad.
>
> By brooks too broad for leaping
> The lightfoot boys are laid;
> The rose-lipt girls are sleeping
> In fields where roses fade.

This I have been told is the purest expression in English poetry of the spirit of the Greek Anthology – one of the few things that might actually have been written by a Greek. Yet the first line is Pre-Raphaelite; 'golden friends' could not go straight into a classical language, 'lightfoot lad' is arch and insipid. The antithesis in the last two lines is obscure. Once again it is a poem in which not a pagan is talking, but someone looking back at paganism from a Christian standpoint, just as the feelings of an animal are not the same as the feelings of an animal as imagined by a human being. The other important verses are in *Last Poems*. There is the bombastic epigram on the army of mercenaries, again with its adolescent anti-God gibe, and the poem which in texture seems most Horatian of all:

> The chestnut casts his flambeaux, and the flowers
>   Stream from the hawthorn on the wind away,
> The doors clap to, the pane is blind with showers.
>   Pass me the can, lad; there's an end of May.

The first verse, indeed, except for that plebeian 'can,' has an authentic Thaliarchus quality – but at once he is off again on his denunciations of the Master Potter – 'Whatever brute and blackguard made the world.' Even the famous last stanza,

> The troubles of our proud and angry dust
>   Are from eternity and shall not fail.
> Bear them we can, and if we can we must.
>   Shoulder the sky, my lad, and drink your ale

suffers from the two 'pass the cans' that have preceded it, and from the insincerity of pretending that drinking ale is a stoical gesture identical with shouldering the sky instead of with escaping from it. The poem does, however, reveal Housman at his poetical best – as a first-rate rhetorician. The pity is that he should nearly always have sacrificed rhetoric in quest of simplicity. Unfortunately his criterion of poetry was, as he explained, a tremor in the solar plexus, an organ which is seldom the same in two people, which writes poetry at midnight and burns it at midday, which experiences the sudden chill, the hint of tears, as easily at a bad film as at a good verse. Rhetoric is safer.

The Waste Land appeared at the same time as *Last Poems*, and the Phlebas episode may be compared, as something genuinely classical, with them. The fate which Housman's poems deserve, of course, is to be set to music by English composers and sung by English singers, and it has already overtaken them. He will live as long as the B.B.C. Otherwise, by temporarily killing the place-name lyric, his effect was to render more severe and guarded the new poetry of the Pylon school. His own farewell to the Muse reveals him at his weakest, with his peculiar use of 'poetical' words:

> To-morrow, more's the pity,
> Away we both must hie,
> To air the ditty
> And to earth I.

This is not on a level with Gray: it contains one cliché and two archaisms (*hie* and *ditty*), nor does it bear any resemblance to a classical farewell, such as Horace's:

> Vivere si recte nescis, decede peritis:
> Lusisti satis, edisti satis atque bibisti.
> Tempus abire tibi est, ne potum largius aequo
> Rideat et pulset lasciva decentius aetas.[1]

NOTE

1 The last four lines of Horace, Epistle II of Book II: 'If you do not know how to live rightly, give way to those who do. You have played enough, you have eaten and drunk enough. It is time for you to leave, lest, when you have drunk too freely, youth mock and jostle you, playing the wanton with better grace.'

65. Richard Rees, 'The Modernism of Housman', *Adelphi*

xii, June 1936, 177–80

To see Professor Housman, with his prim, grizzled countenance and his mincing gait, crossing the lawn of Trinity, you would hardly guess you were looking at a poet. Yet if he was not a great or a very original poet he was at least, after the deaths of Hardy and Lawrence, the best and most original poet in England. He was seventy-seven when he died and those who knew him in the latter part of his life, as Professor of Latin at Cambridge, tell us he was what is, perhaps unjustly, considered to be the typical don – fastidious, shy, almost a recluse. He shunned undergraduates and, for that reason, can hardly have been personally 'popular' with them. Indeed, he seemed to shun life. His bearing, half soldierly, half old-maidish, suggested aloofness, distaste and a prim resignation.

But, it may be said, the real man behind the stoic pose was given to the world in the two small collections of lyrics which made him world-famous. And that should be enough, it will be added.

Certainly there is a terrible completeness about the *Shropshire Lad* and *Last Poems*. Their narrow, limited, but exquisite art is often nearly perfect in its kind and the pessimism they express is also, in its kind, about as complete and profound as possible. But the tragic element in Housman's poetry is not great tragedy. And therein lies his inferiority to Hardy. The tragedy in Housman's poems is the crassest of crass casualty. He professes to show you the eternal injustice of a world which has 'much good but much less good than ill'; but in fact what he shows is more like a budding tulip broken by a hob-nailed boot or a wedding party run down by a lorry. His philosophy is inferior to the best quality of his mind. And those who think it an affectation to say that a man's poems are all we need to know about him will regret that a few dozen lyrics, a lecture, and some specialist papers are the only glimpses we are ever likely to have into the mind of a poet who wrote with intense and lovely feeling of the beauty of the countryside and of its youths and maidens, who displayed a rare generosity of passion and pity and yet continually lapsed into ungainly gestures of defiance at 'whatever brute and blackguard made the world.' The pessimism is not strange but, in such a sensitive being, its crudeness is.

Although, because of the smallness and unforgettableness of his output, his poems are well and widely known, the quality of his mind is often very superficially estimated. His love of the Shropshire landscape is emphasised and his sense of its history — the Welsh, Roman and Saxon blood warring in the veins of Shropshire yeomen; the sunset melancholy of the western hills; the preoccupation with the gallows and the grave; the sense of the enduring skeleton beneath the fleeting hues of health and youth; and the skilful blending of the simple English ditty with the epigrammatic Greek and the severe Roman notes. The yokel scholar, so to speak.

But though his subjects may be universal — death and unrequited love, bluebells and cherry blossom — and his epigrammatic style may be chaste and severe, there is nevertheless an obtrusive personal note in Housman's poems, a kind of fretful immaturity, which gives them their special quality. And here the image of the broken flower is seen to apply more aptly to Housman's brutal melancholy than to the humane pessimism of a Hardy or to the tortured intensity of a Lawrence or a G.M. Hopkins. Hardy might be compared to a gnarled and weather-racked tree bearing bitter-sweet apples and Lawrence to a rare and subtle plant, frail but tenacious and savage in its struggle for life, and Hopkins to a strong and lovely briar cramped between stones. But Housman is a flower blighted in its prime. From this point of view, and in spite of the vast difference between them, I should say that Housman had something in common with G.M. Hopkins. Both, though in different ways, lived monastically. If Lawrence and Hardy were mutilated by life, Housman and Hopkins were self-mutilated and there is a something like viciousness in Housman's black melancholy and a hectic feverishness in Hopkins' *desiderium* which may be 'unhealthy' but is closely connected with their poignant vision of natural beauty and their yearning towards the simple strength and goodness of unsophisticated human life. Certainly there is something which from a common-sense or 'normal' point of view would be called 'morbid' in Housman's attitude to the soldiers and shepherds and athletes who meet such violent and tragic fates in his verse; and its analogue could be shown in Hopkins, in the poem about the young soldier's first Communion, for example. It is utterly different from Wordsworth's feeling for the leech-gatherer and the country-folk of Cumberland and from Hardy's lament over Drummer Hodge, buried in the Veldt 'far from his Wessex home.'

In spite of his resolute conservatism of style Housman should really be placed with the 'modern' artists, in the sense that like other 'modern' writers as different from him and from one another as Whitman, Hopkins, Eliot, and Lawrence he seems to have felt shut out from the health-giving commonalty of human life, whereas poets like Wordsworth and Hardy were its natives. But Housman was not a 'rebel' like Whitman and Lawrence, nor did he surrender, like Hopkins, to an old religious communal discipline. He cut himself off stoically in his prime, wrapped himself in the toga of classical scholarship, and lived in seclusion.

So what does it all mean? When one is driven to use inverted commas for words like *unhealthy*, *normal*, *morbid*, *modern* and *rebel*, it is usually a sign that one's thoughts are groping rather than clear. Any point that this note may have will be blunted if it is maintained that poets and artists have always been isolated and socially mutilated beings and that therefore Housman and Hopkins and the other so-called modern poets we have been considering are in that respect no different from poets in other ages. But is it true? No doubt it is partly true. 'Lips only sing when they cannot kiss,' and if poets are the unacknowledged legislators of mankind it is because they are ahead of their age and therefore inevitably lonely. But I do not believe the isolation of the best and truest poets of modern times is of the same kind as the inevitable isolation of the exceptionally gifted man in all ages. It seems to me that the hectic strain of morbidity in Hopkins and of venomous hatred in Lawrence and of black vicious melancholy in Housman is symptomatic of a more disordered condition of general human life than was known to poets in previous ages. And if anyone thinks it strange that Housman's simple-seeming melancholy ditties should be compared in this respect with the metaphysical horror of some of Hopkins' sonnets or with Lawrence's tortured and tortuous sexology, let him ponder the overtones of these two verses from one of Housman's simple rhymes:

>   Her strong enchantments failing,
>   Her towers of fear in wreck,
>   Her limbecks dried of poison
>   And the knife at her neck,
>
>   The Queen of Air and Darkness
>   Begins to shrill and cry,
>   'O young man, O my slayer,
>   To-morrow you shall die.'

It would be interesting to know what this poem 'means,' though of course it will present no difficulty to those who like to give every discussion of poetry the fashionable politico-economic slant. But I will leave it to some orthodox Marxist to interpret the Queen as feudalism and the young man as Housman, representing the bourgeoisie and prophetically aware that he is destined to be slain by the proletariat. Poets, in their function as poets, cannot be political beings. We shall see the irrelevance of poets' politics if we reflect that of the modern poets considered here Housman was probably a High Tory, if anything, in politics and Hopkins was a Jesuit priest who in a remarkable letter expressed sympathy with Communism, and Lawrence and Whitman were rebels who would need to be thoroughly bowdlerised before they could be fitted into any contemporary political fold. The true measure of the seriousness of the contemporary crisis of the human spirit is not in the fact that spurious poets are deserting their function in favour of political propaganda. It is rather that true poets, the unacknowledged legislators of mankind and therefore infinitely more important than politicians, are increasingly rare and decreasingly productive; and when they do find utterance what they speak is often positively retrogressive in a much profounder sense than the political or else, as in the case of Housman, its tragic quality is merely suicidal, instead of selfless.

66. John Erskine, 'What is Contemporary Poetry?', North American Review (New York)

ccxlii, Autumn 1936, 171–80

John Erskine (1879–1951), educator. Born in New York City, he taught English at Amherst College from 1903 to 1909, and at Columbia University from 1909 to 1937. From 1928 to 1937 he was also president of the Juilliard School of Music. He was the author of *The Private Life of Helen of Troy*, *Jack in the Beanstalk* and *The Delight of Great Books*. The 'Great Books' Programmes offered by many American universities derived primarily from Erskine's views on education.

'A Shropshire Lad' appeared forty years ago. Having spent most of those decades in a conscious and systematic study of poetry, I am glad I met the little book first in the fresh ignorance of boyhood. I missed in it then the profound echoes of the centuries, the magnificent appropriations from Greece and Rome and the Middle Ages, and I fortunately did not know that A.E. Housman was a classical scholar, with a name in the universities of the world for meticulous and combative erudition. Unembarrassed by any preparation in me, the poems were free to make, as on new readers they still do, the poignant effect of immediate life. This Housman, whoever he might be, wrote about Shropshire, which I located on the Welsh border, and he must have lived there, and broken his heart over his girl and his friend, and he had got drunk, and had committed at least one murder, with consequent danger of hanging and a morbid interest in executions, and he had witnessed a suicide and served as pall-bearer at an athlete's funeral, and in his lighter moments he admired flowers and cherry trees and landscape in general, and was sorry boys die young or enlist in the army.

It had all happened to him, obviously. This haunting and essentially cheerful music was wrung from a tortured soul. I could see why, in the concluding poem, he offered the opinion that life is trying, and only a strong man can stand it. The odd thing was that though the flow of my own life had hitherto been smooth, I felt as if every one of these sorrows had happened to me.

When the 'Last Poems' were published in 1922, I sought their pages with conflicting zest and reluctance, having small faith that the early beauty could be repeated or extended, or that the illusion of personal experience would still convince, now that I had read much, and knew how much more Housman had read, and how respectable had been his conduct. But the magic was there undiminished. The same themes, the same regret for careless youth, the same harping on capital punishment, the same stoical advice to endure rather than hope to understand. I could trace these themes, if I chose, to Horace and Lucretius and other Romans, or to the Greek historians and philosophers, or to François Villon and later Frenchmen, and I could see a resemblance between the racy power of Housman's diction and the fiery, muscular speech of Catullus. But the poems in this second volume, as in the first, gave the impression of being anything but derivative. Their elements were completely fused in one very original personality, and the verse seemed spontaneous song.

In the *Cornhill Magazine* for April, 1901, Housman permitted to be published the 'Fragment of a Greek Tragedy,' one of the most brilliant parodies ever perpetrated. He considered it a negligible trifle, according to report, but once known to a few friends it could not be hidden, and it seems now an important clue to his methods and to at least the bookish sources of his inspiration.

He left us also the superb essay on 'The Name and the Nature of Poetry' delivered as the Leslie Stephen Lecture, May 9, 1933, at the University of Cambridge, where he was Kennedy Professor of Latin. His first impulse, as he tells us, was to speak on the Artifice of Versification, a subject on which few poets, even the successful ones, had in his opinion any precise instruction. A footnote of remarkable richness indicates the treatment he would have applied to this theme. But on further thought he concluded that such matters were unsuited to public discussion, and chose instead to define pure poetry, with illustrations, to remind us, in chief, that 'poetry is not the thing said but a way of saying it,' and to tell us, in a whimsical and tantalising passage, the conditions in which inspiration had come to him. It was as though he were burlesquing Wordsworth. 'I have seldom written poetry unless I was rather out of health, and the experience, though pleasurable, was generally agitating and exhausting. If only that you may know what to avoid, I will give some account of the process.'

We are to have shortly another volume, 'More Poems,' presumably a collection of gleanings. The four books and the parody are all the foundation we at present know of for a reputation in poetry which promises to rise steadily.

There is something magnificent in this fame, though it is so slenderly supported. Indeed, Housman's admirers already find it not disloyal to ask whether his place in literature, or the place he seems likely to occupy, can be explained by any of his poems, separately considered. Other poets of economical output, like Edgar Allan Poe, have at least produced single masterpieces. For purposes of immortality 'The Raven,' for example, is quite enough. Which poem of Housman's stands out? If you can name no one of them, then what is it in each of his charming lyrics which adds up to such a reverberating total?

I think Housman knew what it was, and studied to put it there. By genius no doubt, but also by forethought and self-criticism, he gives the illusion of being contemporary. After forty years his work remains not timeless but as true to the time as a mirror. To understand his art we should ask what is it that makes any poetry seem contemporary, even when it is first written – and what makes it continue to seem so; for the continued ability to speak to the condition, and with the accent, of succeeding moments, is what literary folk call immortality.

Every true poet, one may suppose, wishes to address his own people in his own day. He may also crave a hearing with those shadowy strangers, posterity, but this ambition is suspect, since it is liveliest among youthful versifiers, in whom the afflatus is as yet only a prickly stir, like a gathering sneeze, or among the elder and incompetent who having once spoken to deaf ears find consolation in a theory of postponed justice. The authentic talent is determined to have its say now and here. By instinct also, and with the aid of certain long-known rules, it tries to avoid a message or an accent which will date.

The secret lies partly in the choice of language, partly in the choice of theme. Though Housman is illuminating when he discusses language, he does not tell us where he found his themes. Surely not in his own experience, literally reported. To track him down we must use our wits, but since we know what his professional studies were, the hunt will not be difficult.

As to language, he follows the traditional rules of the classics. The art of poetry, he says in effect, is the art of calling things by their right names. Adam facing the animals was the first poet. Notice that Housman lectured on the Name as well as the Nature of poetry, beginning from the outside and working inward. In poetry as in life, that is the right order. In the beginning was the word.

The poet gives most of his attention, perhaps, to avoiding the wrong word which contemporary speech may offer him, or to avoiding the wrong use or the over-use of a good word. In the presence of an utterly new fact or experience, he must like Adam invent a new name. Housman illustrates from the less happy versifying of the eighteenth century, and from the linguistic achievements of modern science. I am tempted to quote liberally from one brilliant passage which conveys much of the wise humor we admire in the poems:

> Salt is a crystalline substance recognized by its taste .... It is not the private property of a science less than three hundred years old, which being in want of a term to embody a new conception, 'an acid having the whole or part of its hydrogen replaced by a metal,' has lazily helped itself to the old unsuitable word salt, instead of excogitating a new and therefore to that extent an apt one. The right model for imitation is that chemist who, when he encountered, or thought he had encountered, a hitherto nameless form of matter, did not purloin for it the name of something else, but invented out of his own head a name which should be proper to it, and enriched the vocabulary of modern man with the useful word *gas*.

The choice of the proper word in poetry is not a superficial exercise. You cannot proceed far in it without extraordinary feeling for the overtones in the common speech of man around you. You must have listened to the human heart, discovering that vital organ under whatever disguise the humdrum business of life imposes.

Moreover, the position of the word often transforms it. Much has been said wisely enough in praise of simple diction, but too often, especially in our prosaic day, the writer is satisfied with plain words taken by themselves, forgetting that language is formed of cadences, sentence-music, phrase-moldings, in comparison with which the single word is only a passing note. To speak to your contemporaries, you must master their way of shaping the curve of sounds when they are moved to love or anger or grief or dignity.

In this technique Housman was, it seems to me, a virtuoso. His ability to produce sincere effects by the manipulation of words and cadences is so highly developed that he can, when he chooses, project the same theme in a variety of moods or tones. The poems which stab us with the illusion of personal self-revelation turn out to be achievements in objectivity. Not exclusively that, but that among other things.

Sometimes I wonder whether he was poking fun at the theory of Benedetto Croce's which fascinated us thirty years ago. Croce thought that the poet's inspiration dictated the form, that whatever you had to say must be expressed, you being you, in one inevitable cast of language and meter. Whatever helpful truth the doctrine may convey, Housman certainly demonstrates his skill in saying the same thing several ways, each seeming inevitable.

Do you recall the poem numbered twenty-five in the 'Shropshire Lad'? It tells of two boys in love with one girl, two friends only one of whom can have his heart's wish. But the happy lover dies, and the girl gives herself to the boy who is still alive. Housman puts the cynical little story in the mouth of the second lover, who savors his luck but isn't proud of it.

> The better man she walks with still,
> Though now 'tis not with Fred:
> A lad that lives and has his will
> Is worth a dozen dead.

If we had only this treatment of the theme, we might say that here is the convincing, inevitable form of which Croce spoke. But in the next poem, the twenty sixth, Housman takes hold of the subject by another handle, and secures, as I think, a more tragic effect. The lover, walking out with his girl, recalls that a year ago he walked with a different girl, who is now in her grave; the circumstance suggests that in another year he may be dead and his new sweetheart may have comforted herself.

> When I shall sleep with clover clad,
> And she beside another lad.

But if we think the ultimate irony has here been extracted from the theme, we have only to read on into the poem numbered twenty-seven, in which the speaker is the dead lover, calling to his faithless friend. This version is so much more powerful than the others that we wonder why we were impressed by the first – that is, until we go back and read the first again. They are all three perfect, with the illusion of inevitability, but the drama is most stark in the third:

> 'Is my girl happy,
>   That I thought hard to leave,
> And has she tired of weeping
>   As she lies down at eve?'
>
> Ay, she lies down lightly,
>   She lies not down to weep:
> Your girl is well contented.
>   Be still, my lad, and sleep.
>
> 'Is my friend hearty,
>   Now I am thin and pine,
> And has he found to sleep in
>   A better bed than mine?'
>
> Yes, lad, I lie easy,
>   I lie as lads would choose;
> I cheer a dead man's sweetheart,
>   Never ask me whose.

These three poems illustrate as well as any Housman's mastery of the contemporary note, his way of persuading you that you hear a living voice. In the selection of language as well as of subject all writers are influenced by previous example, but for speech at least the model need not be bookish. A Matthew Arnold will advise you to carry on the grand style, with famous quotations in mind as samples. Housman, I fancy, would tell us rather to listen to our own speech in those moments when we are earnestly addressing our fellows face to face. If you can write as you talk, you can be contemporary. It seems that in the quotation from the academic lecture delivered and in the excerpts from the poems I hear the same man.

The themes which Housman treats are few, but they are imbedded in all experience, unanswerable and therefore permanent questions — the beauty and the cruelty of nature, the shortness of life, the passing of loves which swore to endure, the nearness of death, the injustice of the world, with desperate and witty counsel not to care too much.

> Malt does more than Milton can
> To justify God's ways to man.

All of these themes Housman found, I think, less by direct observation than by reading the minor poets of the Roman empire and certain medieval writers. Here is the sentiment of Catullus, and his despair; here is the stoic armor of Horace, transposed into idiomatic British; here is the weary sophistication of Tibullus; here, in the reiterated emphasis on death, especially on death by hanging, is our old friend François Villon. Some of the poems are frank translations, as in the echo of de Banville,

> We'll to the woods no more,
> The laurels all are cut.

Can a poet be contemporary who avails himself of old themes? The answer, I think, is that no other poet can be contemporary. The language must be of our own day, but the themes must belong to all our hearers, and since the race is not young, whatever is common experience is already very old. Leave out the themes which date, and you'll discover that all contemporary subjects are ancient and few. To recognize this fact is not to accuse literature of thinness but to pay homage to the depth of three or four unsatisfied hungers, the desire for beauty, the desire for loyalty, the desire for justice, the yearning to pursue these ideals with self-respect and dignity.

When I say that Housman learned these themes from old poets, I do not mean that having so learned them, he failed to recognize them in life. The old poets taught him, as he in turn teaches us, to see what is under our eyes. Nor do I mean that in order to grasp Housman's full meaning, we must first read the classics. The old themes interpret themselves in us. To understand the grand style of which Arnold was fond, you might need to know Homer; even more, you might need to hear Homer translated in the stiff bare English of the schoolroom. But though reading may provide you with extra pleasures, Housman's themes ask for no footnotes.

If I supply one now, it is to illustrate my point that the poems in themselves are contemporary. I have in mind the superb 'Oracles,' of the second volume. The oracle on Dodona is mute — and you needn't ask where or what was Dodona. The priestess with her cryptic answers is dead. But your heart answers your question, and when you ask your heart what your future will be, your heart says you must die. A good sensible answer, say you, trying to be brave; a good answer and an old one. Then for your comfort the poet adds this:

> *The King with half the East at heel is marched from lands of morning,*
> *Their fighters drink the rivers up, their shafts benight the air.*
> *And he that stands will die for nought, and home there's no returning.*
> *The Spartans on the sea-wet rock sat down and combed their hair.*

No reader fails to respond to the image of courage; we do very well with the poem even though we haven't read Herodotus, and therefore may not know that these were the Spartans who died with Leonidas at Thermopylae, and we may not have learned that the Spartans wore their hair long when they went to battle, and combed it carefully when they expected to be killed.

Xerxes had two and a half million fighting men; the Spartans dared to block the pass with three hundred. Not believing they could be so reckless, Xerxes sent to inquire what they were doing, and the spy reported that some of them were engaged in gymnastic exercises and others were combing their long hair. The occupation seemed effeminate, but a man in the army of Xerxes who knew the Spartan customs explained that the hair-combing was the usual prelude of battle to the utmost, with neither retreat nor surrender.

The acceptance of Housman by the readers of our time compels a reconsideration of much that has been said in favor of so-called modern art. He is in the tradition, but he seems contemporary. Perhaps any true poet will be in the tradition. If there is place for experiment in art, where should the experiment be made? In the language? In the subject matter? To invent an altogether new speech, or to use a bookish speech, cuts you off from your time, and in that case it's a shaky boast to assert that posterity will appreciate you. To avoid the themes which occupy our common fears and hopes is to throw away all chance of securing an audience.

MORE POEMS
1936

67. Raymond Mortimer, 'Housman Relics', *New Statesman and Nation*

xii (New Series), 24 October 1936, 631-2

Raymond Mortimer (1895–1980) regularly reviewed for the *New Statesman*, the *Nation* (of which he was for a time literary editor) and the *Sunday Times*. Among his own books were *Channel Packet* (1942) and *Duncan Grant* (1944). He was made a CBE in 1955.

Mr. Laurence Housman explains in his preface that he was permitted, but not enjoined, by his brother's will to publish 'any poems which appear to him to be completed and to be not inferior to the average of my published poems'. He has used this permission liberally, and printed forty-nine new poems. I think he was right to do so, for they will certainly give great pleasure to many. Moreover, we are glad of any scraps which fall from the desk of an important poet: his failures can on occasion illuminate and help us to appreciate his successes. And the opinion that Housman was an important poet is widely held.

The introductory poem seems to me a very fair example of the middling Housman:

[quotes 'They say my verse is sad', in full]

Here is the pessimism, so attractive to most fastidious persons, expressed in what seems an admirably lapidary style. But closer examination suggests, I think, that the trope in the second and third lines is not very felicitous. A sort of pun invites us to visualise the tears of eternity as a river, which, apparently, reading these poems will enable us to avoid. Further, the expression 'Unborn and unbegot', borrowed by Housman from *Richard II*, is appropriate in a dramatic vituperation, but in an epigram merely clumsy: 'unbegot' adds nothing to 'unborn' – it is there only to make a rhyme.

I pass over a number of poems which are written in a very monotonous metre. (Too often Housman's verses call irresistibly for the Hymns Ancient and Modern tunes used for *Jerusalem the Golden* and *The Voice that Breathed o'er Eden*). Then we come to this:

[quotes No. XXIII]

These lines seem to me admirable, and flawless, worthy, in fact, of Landor. How closely the versification follows the sentiment; the fifth line so quick and busy, the end so slow and spacious and serene! It is by a poet's best work that he must be judged, and the skill to write as well as this is rare.

A little later we come to a poem too long to quote, of which these stanzas are typical:

[quotes stanzas 1 and 4 of No. XLII]

One is irresistibly reminded of the famous review of *In Memoriam*: 'These touching lines evidently come from the full heart of the widow of a military man'. And the weakness, the sentimentality, of this poem, which is admittedly personal, brings us into rather ticklish territory. A ribald friend of mine once said: 'Professor Housman seems to have taken up first with a young man who committed suicide, and then with one who was hanged. No wonder his view of life is gloomy'. But the poet himself was at pains to explain that very little of *The Shropshire Lad* [sic] was biographical. At the same time, there can be little doubt, I think, that young men, especially young men in uniform, excited in the poet envy and a quite special solicitude. 'A soldier cheap to the King and dear to me', we read in one of the new poems, and the belted redcoat in his 'finery of fire' appears repeatedly in both the previous volumes.

[quotes stanza 2 of *Last Poems*, No. XXXII]

Housman's style is often very close to Kipling's, but when they write about soldiers it is with rather different emotions. One of the *Last Poems* contains repeated the lines:

A.E. HOUSMAN

> Says I, I will 'list for a lancer,
> Oh who would not sleep with the brave?

It is very dangerous to attribute to a poet all the sentiments he expresses in his work, but it seems evident that a passionate longing for the muscular and reckless company of soldiers, an envy of their rough and hazardous life, devoured Housman as a repeated daydream:

[quotes stanzas 1 and 3 of *A Shropshire Lad*, No. XXIV]

But it remained a dream.

> More than I, if truth were told,
> Have stood and sweated hot and cold,
> And through their veins in ice and fire
> Fear contended with desire.
> [*A Shropshire Lad*, No. XXX, stanza 2]

Fear was victorious, and Housman became the first Latinist in Europe; a professor; and a great authority on wine. 'Keep we must, if keep we can, these foreign laws of God and man'. It was his clear duty to resist these vagabond and antinomian longings, to stay at home, to use his prodigious talent for exact scholarship. And whenever this ark of refuge grew too chilly, there was a cosier way to escape – the pipe-dream of his verse. There was something at once sublime and ridiculous in the patience with which he edited Manilius, an astrological versifier, whose poetic talent was obviously inferior to his own. Scaliger and Bentley, it is true, had undertaken the same task, and no doubt Housman liked to measure himself against these heroes. But the futility of the work, judged by vulgar standards, may, I conceive, have added to its value for him, and he was able to vent upon other scholars the spite he felt against himself for not following his profoundest impulses. (Such was his delight in saying venomous and contemptuous things, his brother tells us, that he had his note-book stocked with phrases waiting for the appearance of appropriate victims.)

I have tried to elucidate this contrast between Housman's daydreams and his way of life because I believe it may explain the principal weakness in his poetry – a sentimentality due to a sort of insincerity. Scholarship was, by his choice, his real life, verse-writing a release, a fantasy. To describe as wish-fulfilment poetry so pessimistic may seem a paradox. But it is only too easy to luxuriate in gloom, and the Terence who speaks in many of the poems is, for all his gloom, a pretty dashing fellow who had not hesitated to follow his fancies. So I think it is not unreasonable to see in him a projection of what Housman regretfully suppressed in his own life. And those of his more devoted admirers, who may resent any suggestion of insincerity, are invited to peruse the hymn, printed in *More Poems*, which he so surprisingly wrote to be sung at his funeral:

[quotes stanza 1 of 'For my Funeral']

True, 'thou' and 'thy' are not honoured with capital letters, but these lines are an odd description of 'whatever brute or blackguard made the world.' Terence, it would seem, had been buried earlier, and presumably without the help of a hymn.

Some of Housman's best poems (such as 'The laws of God, the laws of man', and 'Others, I am not the first, Have willed more mischief than they durst') are expressions of the conflict which I have tried to define: others are more objective, like *The Merry Guide*, 'West and away the wheels of darkness roll', and 'We'll to the woods no more' – all of them admirable. In this sort too the new book contains a poem on Leander, an admirable translation of Horace's *Diffugere nives*, and a witty epigram on Noah, who fled the sinful cities of the plain only to fall, on a mountain, into incest. These are burnished and charming pieces, which are a valuable addition to our *Lyra Elegantarium*. But the high, and I venture to think, the exorbitant, claims made for Housman as a poet are not usually based upon such as these. Beneath an attempted stoicism, most of his poems are packed with self-pity, and with these it is all too easy to associate one's own emotions. The language is commonly very similar to, and presumably influenced by, Kipling's, but it is more scrupulously polished, and the pessimism of the poems makes them palatable to fastidious persons who are affronted by Kipling's heartiness. To some in each generation of adolescents, who are distracted by conflicts similar to his, Housman's poems, including the new volume, are likely to continue making a popular appeal. And where poetry is concerned, most men remain faithful to their adolescent taste. Those, on the other hand, who, growing older, reopen the volumes that once they bought from Mr. Blackwell or Mr. Heffer, and find much of the magic gone, are entitled to seek an explanation of this evanescence, to try to detect where and why these poems fail. And at the same time they can recognise that it is a great and honourable privilege for a poet to be much loved by very young men.

68. Ivor Brown, 'Poet and Scholar: the Last of the "Shropshire Lad" ', *Observer*

25 October 1936, 10

Ivor Brown (1891–1974), a prolific and various author, was dramatic critic of a number of journals, including the *Saturday Review*, the *Observer*, and (from 1919 to 1935) the *Manchester Guardian*.

Paragraphs 2, 3 and 4 of this review, concerned with A.S.F. Gow, *A.E. Housman: A Sketch*, are omitted.

When A.E. Housman died, the little burst of belittlement came from the little hands exactly as one knew it would. He had offended by writing poetry which scanned, made sense, and made music. Worse still, he had written poetry which pleased the previous generation. He had declared his faith in a simple philosophy of poetry; he followed his heart. But he knew also that composition of poetry involves technical study and deep practice. Few singers have achieved a greater air of spontaneity; yet he took pains on the grand scale, and would ponder for months on the turning of a line. The poets of our own day are mostly contemptuous of technique; they angrily reject what they cannot achieve. So Housman's sins were many in their eyes. On the other hand, those who felt the death of this remote, occasional singer as a direct personal loss were very many. His vein of melancholy had passed into their blood; his reply to the rhythms of the English landscape and the English tongue was rooted in their minds, their memories, and their affections. The growling on the Left was as mechanical as any result of a pressed button, as unimpressive as a fallen pin. In a comedy now running called 'After October', a woman who has been scolded at great length by a Communist poet for her life of bourgeois shams merely smiles at this petulant bore and says, 'When I saw your beard, I knew at once every word you were going to say'. This excellent remark may be applied with perfect aptness to the anti-Housman campaign. [...]

It was not, of course, to be expected that these last poems would enhance a name already great. They are his own rejected. But his scruples could dispraise his own work too easily. His will placed upon his brother Laurence a most embarrassing responsibility, which has been courageously and skilfully faced. Laurence was to select and to print verses appearing to him 'not inferior to the average of those already published';all others were to be destroyed. The editor knew both how exacting would be the poet's own standard of valuation and how eager would be the public appetite for more. He has saved from the flames close upon fifty pieces of varying length. 'Mainly workshop material', he admits the volume to be. Well, if all the chips on the floor of English poetry were of this quality, our wealth would exceed all bounds.

A considerable section belongs to the 'Terence' series of the Shropshire lad period; some such as the lines 'For My Funeral' (and who would not have them at his own) are later. The philosophy to be found is keenly individualistic as well as sombre in the extreme. Of a pocket-knife the poet sings: –

> I need but stick it in my heart
> And down will come the sky,
> And earth's foundations will depart
> And all you folk will die.
> [*More Poems*, No. XXVI, stanza 2]

The night without a star, the earth that crumbles, and the flowers that perish are the reader's continual companions. Once more we find the mood of the Greek anthology transmuted to the monosyllables of Saxon speech: –

[quotes *More Poems*, No. XXVII]

Continually the old magic leaps up and we are at large in the England of playing-fields as well as of churchyards, of lights in tavern windows, as well of [sic] darkness in the sky: —

> On miry meads in winter
> The football sprung and fell.
> [*More Poems*, No. XXXIV, ll. 9–10]

And

> I see the air benighted
>   And all the dusking dales,
> The lamps in England lighted,
>   And evening wrecked on Wales
> [*More Poems*, No. XXXIII, ll. 25–8]

'More Poems' are offered to the unhappy living from the happier dead: —

[quotes stanza 1 of Prefatory Poem]

Housman, tortured continually by the cruelty which somehow emerges from human and natural factors not seemingly or essentially cruel, conscious to the verge of agony of the error in earth's foundations which no human repair can fill, complaining that

> The toil of all that be
> Helps not the primal fault,

may seem in this last gathering of his infrequent song to be driving sadness over-hard. But what a twist of genius could he give to melancholy! Here is an epitaph: —

[quotes *More Poems*, No. XXXVI]

This is perfect Housman in form, cadence, and philosophy. All else is not so good, nor could it be. But our gratitude for what has been saved from a too-exacting self-criticism is great and will abide.

69. Peter Monro Jack, 'The Shropshire Lad's Farewell: A Distinguished Final Volume by A.E. Housman', *New York Times Book Review*

25 October 1936, 1

> This review was illustrated by a large reproduction of a drawing of Housman by John Rothenstein. The poem 'actually printed' for *Last Poems* (but not actually published) was *More Poems*, No. XLV.

So great a hold had 'The Shropshire Lad' [sic] over its generation that many were almost afraid to read 'Last Poems', doubting that the magic could still persist. But soon that volume had become as famous and sacred as its elder and there was nothing in it that one would wish away. And yet again the same trepidation awaits the opening of 'More Poems'. In the first place, we had no right to expect it. Housman died without having made up his mind whether to publish or not, and finally he had turned over the reponsibility to his brother, Laurence. For himself, we should have seen no more of his poetry. But his readers from all over the world were insistent, and he left them this loophole in his will, permitting, but not enjoining, his brother to publish, as he pleased.

In the second place, so widely has his style become known and imitated that when we open the book at random and read:

> From the wash the laundress sends
> My collars home with raveled ends;

we feel at first that we have stumbled on a parody. But no, it is an inferior poem, but it is Housman. No one else had the trick of style to give two short and homely verses the authenticity of poetry. The only difference is that we have to clear our minds of the penalty of greatness and forget his imitators.

Having decided to publish, Mr. Laurence Housman has wisely given us full measure. There are forty-eight poems, though some are no longer than a quatrain, two interesting complete variants, and a list of the datings of some of his earlier poems. This last reminds us that some of the 'Last Poems' narrowly missed going into 'The Shropshire Lad'. 'Yonder see the morning blink' is dated 1895, and 'The chestnut casts his flambeaux' (annoyingly misprinted here as 'the chestnut carts') is dated 1896, the year in which 'The Shropshire Lad' came out. In the same way, some of the poems here were expected to go into 'Last Poems'. One of them, says Laurence Housman in the Preface, was actually printed. Reading it now and pondering its exclusion, we can only feel again how fastidious an artist Housman was, how scrupulous a critic of his own work. Something must have irked him, perhaps the feeling that his style had not sufficiently controlled and enriched the banality of its theme – it is that sand castles, whether of nations or persons, are quickly washed away – and yet his themes have often been banal and his writing never commonplace, and this poem seems to us, though not astonishingly good, yet typically good. It *could* very well have gone into 'Last Poems', and it almost did, and now we have the feeling that it is a left-over. These mixed feelings prevent a fair estimate of the posthumous poems. But in any event the pleasure of Housman is in the memory. At first sight anyone, we might now think, might now write his poetry. It is only when we turn over in our memory its especial pleasure that we realize that no one can touch its relaxed perfection. It will take some time until these new poems become a quotable part of our experience.

Meanwhile this is the last we shall have of this gentle Victorian poet of despair whose work ought to frighten and demoralize us, and who succeeds in the end in charming and consoling us. His verse iterates the injustice of life, the futility of human endeavor, the oncoming of death. It has no hope of betterment and little of any sentimental prettiness to gild the ultimate silence. And yet it takes our intensest interest, so admirably is it realized, and it speaks for all of us, so far removed is it from the ordinary egotism of the complaining soul. By style and by sincerity – and without these nothing can be done – Housman has miniatured man's fate to the last twist of the knife, and still he has made it bearable with the demonstration that truth and beauty go with it.

[quotes Prefatory Poem in full]

This is the epigraph to the last of Housman's poems, and it is justly chosen. Here is a poem that tells of the Israelites guided by God's cloud and flame into Canaan, but as for the poet, he will tell truly that no prophet has ever guided him aright, and that the promised land is still a dream:

[quotes stanza 5 of No. II]

It will remind one of the poem (in 'Last Poems') of the Greek oracle that is also as silent as the Jewish God; it is not as good a poem, but it is still a good poem. Here is a poem from the sage to the young man assuring him that no endeavor of his will come to anything – and yet it may, by some miracle, and it is worth the trial. Here is a poem (there are too few) that reminds one of the famous beauty of the cherry tree in Eastertide, and again is not so good by comparison, but how lovely it is in its gentle music:

[quotes No. IX]

Here is a poem again of the unattainable where the ale is better and the girls are fonder, but

[quotes stanza 2 of No. XXXIII]

By what magic does this escape parody, and by what magic does even a parody of Housman read better than the average run of verse? Partly that Housman deliberately chooses simple rhythms and language, the stuff that endures in ballads, hymn tunes, nursery rhymes and folksongs, and then, with the art of a profound scholar, stylizes them into an exact acquiescence to his thought. His form is the last refinement of the commonest sort of poetry.

Only in one poem, I think – for it is time to be critical – is there a definite feeling that Housman is writing out of something that he has not made his own. Largely it is a matter of rhythm, a rhythm that Tennyson and Kipling have used; and then it becomes a matter of language, the language that Mr. Noyes uses; but it does not remind us of Housman:

[quotes ll. 6–8 of No. XLVI, 'The Land of Biscay']

This is literary commonplace, and it reminds us how narrowly

Housman holds his generally unassailable position. And here it is in its almost perfection, in the last poem of all.

[quotes No. XLVIII]

70. John Sparrow, 'A.E. Housman', *Spectator*

clvii, 30 October 1936, 756

John Hanbury Angus Sparrow (b. 1906), classical scholar, Fellow of All Souls College, Oxford, from 1929, and Warden from 1952. An authority on Housman's manuscripts, he contributed an introduction to the Penguin edition (1956) of Housman's *Collected Poems*. The conclusion of this review's final paragraph, concerned with A.S.F. Gow, *A.E. Housman: A Sketch*, is omitted.

More Poems should give pleasure to all Housman's many readers: to his detractors, because it contains several pieces to which they will be pleased to point, quite justly, as almost parodies of himself; to his uncritical admirers simply because they will find in it, beyond expectation, a further and not unworthy instalment of *A Shropshire Lad*; to those whose worship stops short this side idolatry, because it will afford them the opportunity of comparing Housman's less successful with his more successful efforts, and of speculating which pieces he excluded from his earlier books and why he did so; and because it contains not only several poems in which he is at once at his best and most characteristic, but also a few which are more intimate than, and in a way quite different from, anything published by him in his lifetime.

Almost all the new poems are entirely characteristic, full of the peculiar quality which invests everything that Housman published; for even his few failures are unmistakably his, and carry a charm which reconciles the reader to words, images, and turns of phrase not easily defended against the objections of an unsympathetic critic. It is this charm which captures the unliterary as well as the literary, and makes them admire all his work with equal fervour; it is a charm not unlike the charm of Fitzgerald's *Rubaiyat*.

What is its secret? Like all charm, it cannot be analysed; it is part of the man, and is not wholly explained by considering the mechanism of his verse or by recalling its themes – the passions and the moods that it expresses. To feel its force, one must read his poems at length: one likes them, or one does not; there is no more to say.

But it is possible to discuss, and should be possible to explain, the difference between the good and the less good; and it is interesting to read Housman's poems carefully, with an eye on his technique (he studied the craft of verse-writing very minutely, as appears from a note in *The Name and Nature of Poetry*), and to notice when his failures are due to mere exploitation of a knack or repetition of a formula – to a feeling too easily expressed – and when they are due to something not felt, or felt too easily.

A review does not afford space to do more than indicate the lines which such criticism might take: Housman's poetic genius cannot be illustrated by selections (he was quite right not to allow his poems to appear in anthologies), for an isolated stanza or two does not do him justice; nothing, on the other hand, is easier than by such a selection to exaggerate his weakness and to make what is in keeping in its context appear affected or ridiculous by isolation.

Some indication of the quality of the new book may be gathered, however, from the following:

> Bells in tower at evening toll,
> And the day forsakes the soul;
> Soon will evening's self be gone
> And the whispering night come on.
>
> Blame not thou the blinded light
> Nor the whisper of the night:
> Though the whispering night were still,
> Yet the heart would counsel ill.
>   [*More Poems*, No. XVII]

This is not outstanding in merit, but it is a good example of how economically and effectively Housman can convey a mood. We hear in the reduplicated 't' the measured toll of the bell, and the thin long 'a's' in the second line contrast with the deeper vowel-sounds that precede them, and suggest the dreary forsakenness which the line describes (substitute 'desert' for 'forsake' and see what is lost). Between stanzas 1 and 2 there is, as it were, a whole stanza in which nothing is said, but in which the word 'whisper' has acquired a sinister meaning. The strong alliteration in line 5 masks and makes more effective that in line 6; the last line is weak, for the last two syllables are cacophonous, and it may be that this cacophony led Housman to reject the poem.

This may be taken to represent the average of the poems: sometimes a poem falls below it because the artifice seems too easy –

> But now their coins are tarnished
> Their towers decayed away,
> Their kingdoms swept and garnished
> For haler kings than they –

sometimes because the verse itself does not convince us of the genuineness of the mood, so that an attitude seems merely a pose:

> Then came I crying, and today,
> With heavier cause to plain,
> Depart I into death away,
> Not to be born again.

Surrender to the music and accept the idiom, and the verse gives nothing but pleasure; but by a severer standard it is condemned, and Housman no doubt rejected such poems because he had done the same thing, and had done it more successfully, already. We should not, however, be ungrateful to his brother for now printing them, since, in this separate volume, they do not spoil his other work, and they afford material for an interesting comparison.

It is easy to illustrate these fallings away from Housman's supremely high standard, but harder to illustrate his successes by quotation. The opening poem deserves to be quoted, however, for it is one of several in which there sounds a note not familiar from his earlier work; it is called *Easter Hymn,* and this is the first verse:

[quotes stanza 1 of No. I]

It seems here as if the poet were speaking in a more directly personal tone, the rhythm and form are less epigrammatic, less lapidary than usual; the cloak of convention has been cast aside. This abandonment of convention shows most strikingly in the personal poems in this volume: in several of these we hear Housman speaking undisguisedly in the first person and not through the mouth of Terence; and the effect of these poems — for instance, XL ('Farewell to a name and a number'), LXII (headed with the initials 'A.J.J.') XLIV (addressed to 'Andrea') — is not to show that the Terence poems, with their 'my lads', their red-coats, their death in battle and their prison-yards, are unreal, but to demonstrate the depth and nature of the emotion which needed that imaginary setting and those half-real characters for its poetic expression.

These poems reveal pretty clearly (and those who care most for Housman will find the revelation least surprising) the spring of Housman's personal emotions.

71. Conrad Aiken, 'A.E. Housman', *New Republic*

lxxxix, No. 1145, 11 November 1936, 51–2

Conrad Aiken (1889–1973), prolific American poet and novelist, contemporary and friend of T.S. Eliot at Harvard, author *inter alia* of *Blue Voyage* (1927) and *Preludes for Memnon* (1931). He was a contributing editor of the *Dial* from 1917 to 1919.

The 'Last Poems' of Housman have now been succeeded by 'More Poems', chosen from among the completed verses which he left behind him at his death, and thus the total number of lyrics given to the world by this most reticent and self-denying of poets grows to the total of one hundred and fifty-three; but one can say at once that it is an addition which does not change, that the addition of the third volume, like the addition of the second, extends slightly, if at all, the range, does not alter the character, and that the three books are really one, are really 'The Shropshire Lad' [*sic*]. It is more or less true that the third collection is very slightly inferior to the second, just as the second was very slightly inferior to the first. The thinnesses and barenesses are more noticeable, the repetitions of theme and tone more staring, the genuine felicities are certainly fewer. Nor are there whole poems, as many of them, which attain to quite the cool completeness of the best in 'The Shropshire Lad'. Nevertheless, the best here are *almost* as good as ever, and admirers of Housman will find much here to please them; while for those whose admiration is more temperate the slight slackening of the fiber will itself be of interest, as so often it tends to lay bare Housman's essential limitedness.

That he is limited, no one in his senses would deny. The actual range, when one stops to consider it, is extraordinarily narrow, and the perhaps too-well-disposed critic wonders whether he is not wish-thinking in supposing that many of Housman's restrictions were self-restrictions. It is one thing – one may say – to be limited, another to *impose* limitations on oneself; and somehow or other the myth has grown up that Housman's limitedness, like the smallness of his output, was the result of an iron discipline or restraint, a process of selection and elimination at a very high degree of tension, and that the product was accordingly, *ipso facto*, severely and beautifully classic. Housman himself did a good deal to encourage the growth of this notion – the twenty-six years of silence with which he followed the tremendous success of the book which made him famous, years during which he allowed it to be supposed that he had turned his back on poetry forever in order to bury himself in scholarship, calculatedly or uncalculatedly were bound to impress his admirers with the extreme *preciousness* of his work; and to break the long silence at last with the publication of forty-one little lyrics, rather somberly and pointedly entitled 'Last Poems', as if to say 'this little parcel of verses is the work of a lifetime', was only to carry the process further.

Moreover, an idea got abroad, whether with his own imprimatur or not, that one reason for the extreme smallness of his output was that the intensity of the effort, as of the 'inspiration', for even the tiniest and most fragile of his verses, was too exhausting for him, could not more than occasionally be endured, an idea only partially offset by a sister rumor that it was really beer which was his inspiration – the often-celebrated 'pot' of the poems. Just the same, it is permissible to question whether the narrowness of the range and the smallness of the output were not actually implicit in the nature of Housman's talent, and imposed from within rather than from without; and to question in parallel fashion whether the often-praised 'classic' perfection and severity of his style might not more justly, now and then, be termed pseudo-classic.

And that, for better or worse, and at the risk of being considered guilty of something perilously like *lèse majesté*, the present reviewer has always thought, and still thinks, thinks more than ever after a rereading of the three little books. It is idle to deny the charm, the grace, the dexterity, the neatness, whether of form or thought, just as it is idle to deny the wistful and brave individuality which everywhere shows in these poems; but it seems equally idle to deny that the classic should be made of sterner stuff than this, and that if it is not to be profounder, then it must at least be more richly and variously wrought.

And even taken at its best, the texture of Housman's verse tends to be thin. Nor is this wholly a matter of choice. Simplicity is aimed at, to be sure, but there is always, also, a little *more* simplicity than was aimed at, and this looks as if it arose from the fact that Housman's sensory equipment for poetry was definitely somewhat arid. The range of mere perception is very narrow indeed – it is a world in which the grass is green and sheep are white, as simple a world as that of W.H. Davies, for example, but with almost nothing of Davies's sudden felicities of observation or quick aptnesses of statement. Housman conventionalizes, and that would be all right if the conventionalization were itself more interesting; but for this reader at least the constant reliance on a pretty threadbare and perhaps deliberately anachronistic kind of martial imagery, joined with a bucolic imagery just as deliberately 'quaint' or 'homely', becomes in the end both barren and defrauding.

That one should cease to believe might not matter, provided the *playing* at poetry, the playing at profundity or skepticism, were itself more rich and ingeniously managed; but this Housman only seldom achieved. The result is a charming but incomplete and essentially adolescent poetry – the questionings and despairs and loyalties are alike adolescent, and so are the thoughts and the bravenesses and the nostalgic gayeties; and what makes it sometimes worse is one's suspicion that this adolescent note, this boyishness, is a cultivated thing, a calculated falsetto. It has been pointed out that one of the longest of the new poems – Down the waterway of sunset drove to shore a ship of gold – is a little Kiplingesque. But the truth is that something very like the Kipling note is always lurking just round the corner, in these poems, both in the tone and the text. The slightly too dactylic dittylike use of the octosyllabic quatrains, coupled with the characteristically too-thumping [sic] use of Universals, an attitudinizing orotundity, produce now and then an effect perilously close to that of the 'Barrack Room Ballads'.

But no, that is perhaps being too hard on a very fine poet, and to overdo our point that at least a part of Housman's charm grew from his very limitations. Greatness? No. Epigrammatic, lovely, light-coloured, youthfully charming above all; but to quote a typical epigrammatic quatrain by a greater poet, Emily Dickinson, at once shows him up as a little bit thin:

> Lay this laurel on the one
> Too intrinsic for renown.
> Laurel, veil your deathless tree;
> Him you chasten, that is he.

Which is a real voice, and the real thing.

72. E.M. Forster, 'Ancient and Modern', *Listener*

11 November 1936, 921–2

E.M. Forster (1879–1970), one of the century's most eminent writers of fiction and essays, perhaps best known for *A Passage to India* (1924). After reading *A Shropshire Lad* in 1898, Forster became a strong admirer of Housman's poetry, writing in a private memoir (*c.* 1928) that 'this writer is my natural food'. His attempts at friendship with Housman brought him disappointment, however. Both the admiration and the disappointment were frankly described in a paper Forster gave (probably to the Bloomsbury 'Memoir Club') in the late 1930s. Forster concluded his paper by reading his *Listener* review (of Gow's *Sketch* as well as of *More Poems*), telling his audience that he had approached his task initially with hesitation, but had finally decided that 'I *ought* to write about Housman, because I should do it so much better than anyone else.'

A.E. Housman has been well served by his executors. Both these books are good, they will delight his audience, and he himself should tolerate them. The posthumous poems appear with his acquiescence; the sketch, delicate and firm, gives to his character an outline which he could not resent and atones for any excursions into intimacy by two erudite appendices. His shade can ask no more. It certainly will not want a favourable review. Even that flimsy creature whom he so much despised, even a literary critic, is not tempted to over-praise. His lofty shade advances over our eulogies, warning us to be clear in our thinking, precise in our diction, accurate in our punctuation and discreet in our sentimentality.

The sentimentality – that perhaps is the main problem. The passionate broodings, the indignations and devotions, the emotional reconstructions of an actual or imagined past: these, which lie at the heart of the poet, what place did they occupy in the man? He was an unhappy fellow and not a very amiable one. To his friends he accorded the measured intimacy well described by Mr. Gow; to his acquaintance he could be sardonic and (what was still more disconcerting) petty. Pettiness also disfigured his scholarship; his attacks on other Latinists in his prefaces to Manilius and to Juvenal are brilliant scathing and sound, yet they are in the last analysis undignified, for dullness ought to be reprimanded dully. He was too small to see this. What is the relation between all these tiresomenesses and the burning desire to help another which is so moving in his poems – the outstretched hand, the lifted brow, the beating heart, the faithfulness that shatters the gates of hell. What connection can be established between the stilted, uncertain-tempered don and the writer of:

> Ho every one that thirsteth
>   And hath the price to give,
> Come to the stolen waters,
>   Drink and your soul shall live.
>
> Come to the stolen waters
>   And leap the guarded pale,
> And pull the flower in season
>   Before desire shall fail.

The two books under review help to answer this question – a question to which no mark of interrogation has here been appended, as the proof-reader beyond the grave will observe. The 'sketch' helps most. Like Housman himself, Mr. Gow is interested in the truth, and, expounding it quietly, he brings his man alive.

The critic in whose eyes 'high heaven and earth ail from the prime foundation', the rebel forced 'by man's bedevilment and God's' into unwilling conformity with standards which he condemned, was marked for a life of discontents, and they were reinforced by the antinomies of his mental outlook. That his desire for friendship has been overborne by fear of what friendship might hold in store, has already been suggested, and his desire for fame was similarly counter-balanced by fear of the honours which in most men would have gratified it.

In passages such as these, Mr. Gow pulls Housman together, and connects his unamiability and his creative power. He emerges as a man who was difficult to meet but is not difficult to understand; the troubles of his angry dust are ours, though they took an unusual shape, and if we do care to give him a bad mark it is the mark which in one form or other stands to the discredit of us all: timidity.

The poems help, too. About half-a-dozen of them are marvellous, and purists may wish that these alone had been printed. His editor, Mr. Laurence Housman, has rightly taken another view, and has included several poems which are echoes, several which are imperfect, and a few weak ones. This is the proper way to edit a person who wrote living stuff. Fragments of what is merely scholarly or clever should be differently treated; they ought to be burned, and this indeed is the fate to which the Professor has consigned his prose remains. The poems, forty-nine in number, bring up the published total to a hundred and fifty-four, and one point which comes out in a general retrospect is the bizarre yet fertile alliance between the manner of them and the matter in them. The manner is scholarly and churchified; 'Ho every one that thirsteth': the dean might be giving out a hymn. The matter is blood-hot or death-cold. And the reader remains in an agreeable state of suspense and can never foretell how much he is going to feel. It is as if he took up a sampler to estimate its period-value and then observed, embroidered in it, some bitter and explosive truth. The sentiments mean more to him than if he had been prepared for them, as a result of which the whole sampler gains in importance. The 'antinomy' which Mr. Gow regrets in Housman's life is thus the mainstay of his poetry. The hymnal framework, the polished antithetical style of writing, increase the passion of the theme, and give it much more force than could be achieved through ruggedness and verbal daring.

The theme, like that of Shakespeare's Sonnets, involves a story. But, here as there, it is impossible to figure the story out and discover through what mutations it passed before the writer clamped it into print. We shall never know the name and number of the soldier 'cheap to the king and dear to me' who haunts the three volumes in so many uniforms. We shall never know why the account of a murder and execution, read by chance in a local paper, produced the Terence group. A poet hides things up and pares them away, not because he is refined, but because his method requires it. The living fact which he experienced was entangled in dead stuff which did not interest him: he has to isolate it before he can express it passionately, and because it is isolated it changes and is unrecognisable to his biographer. Of its bones are coral made. Matthew Arnold's 'Margaret' poems and Meredith's 'Modern Love' are other examples of the process, and the true reader of poetry is he who can detect when a poem is the result of the process and when it is merely an exercise. The late Sir Sidney Lee thought the Sonnets were an Elizabethan exercise, and his arguments are unanswerable. And some admirers of Housman have presented him as a sort of serious Austin Dobson, whose inspiration was the classics: Epicureanism and Stoicism for the sentiments, Horace, the Greek Anthology, etc., for the images and turns of phrase. Certainly the classics abound in the present volume (Sappho, Callimachus and other sources have been pointed out), and he loved his old stuff. But that, too suffers a sea change, and is subdued to the temper of his mind. The last verse of his translation of *Diffugere nives* imports a quality not to be found in the original, and when he summons the classical boat of Charon and the classical grammatical device of apposition, this is what he turns out:

> Crossing alone the nighted ferry
> With the one coin for fee,
> Whom, on the wharf of Lethe waiting,
> Count you to find? Not me.
>
> The brisk fond lackey to fetch and carry,
> The true, sick-hearted slave,
> Expect him not in the just city
> And free land of the grave.

Ancient has become modern. The tags and tricks of the past have been bent to his personal pain. He has written elsewhere that 'to transfuse emotion – not to transmit thought but to set up in the reader's sense a vibration corresponding to what was felt by the writer – is the peculiar function of poetry'. He practises what he preached. Whether the reader on his side vibrates accurately is another question, and the views put forward in this article may be queried. That his poems are *not* scholarly exercises; that is the only point on which one can dogmatise. They are what he says they are: the vibrations, the motions of his heart. There we must leave him.

Housman's handling of life – it is too sincere to be called a philosophy – is full of incongruities. He praised virtue, he praised license, too. He both denied and denounced God, and why denounce what does not exist? He laboured to build himself an abiding monument in scholarship, yet he knew that every building stands upon sand. Incapable of illusions, he pursued phantoms; convinced of treachery, he dreamt of affection. Unlike most of us, he would not tolerate the second best, and so was threatened with shipwreck unless the seas kept miraculously calm. His intelligence and sensitiveness imperilled him, shocks disturbed him which were imperceptible to coarser chaps. Things might have been much worse: he found an adequate haven at Cambridge, he was fortunate in making a quiet circle of friends who understood him, and outside the college gates an appreciative public cackled, not always unwelcome or unheard. He enjoyed a glass of port. That is something. One wishes he could have enjoyed the happy highways which he resigned in the body and possessed so painfully in the imagination, but he was not destined for vulgar pleasures. Perhaps he had a better time than the outsider supposes. Did he ever drink the stolen waters which he recommends so ardently to others? I hope so.

73. Edwin Muir, review, *London Mercury*

xxxv, November 1936, 62–3

Edwin Muir (1887–1959), Orkney-born poet and, with his wife Willa Muir, translator of Kafka. He published his earliest poems in 1925.

'This final selection of A.E. Housman's poems', says Mr. Laurence Housman in his Preface to it, 'is published by his permission, not by his wish'. It seems he left express instructions that all his prose manuscripts should be destroyed, but made the proviso that 'any poems which appear ... to be completed and to be not inferior to the average of my published poems' might posthumously appear. Mr. Laurence Housman confesses that he found this bequest a difficult one. The poetry in this volume certainly has not the intensity of the *Shropshire Lad* sequence, nor of *Last Poems*; but on the other hand nothing has been included which was not worth including for its own sake, or for the light which it throws on those other volumes. Housman's poetry at its best has two salient qualities: an evocative power and an epigrammatic power. The evocative power is almost completely absent from the present collection; but this throws into sharper relief Housman's essentially epigrammatic cast of thought, and shows how profoundly it determined the shape of all his poetry from the beginning. Mr.

Gow in his little sketch points out rightly that 'Housman the poet and Housman the scholar' were 'not so far apart as is sometimes supposed'; and many of the poems in this volume might pass as translations or deliberate imitations of classical epigrams. We know that they are not; nevertheless they show that the scholar pursued the steps of the poet in the most persistent way.

The epigrammatic cast of thought is so insistent in this volume that almost any verse one cares to select will illustrate it. It has become almost a principle of syntax.

> The toil of all that be
>   Helps not the primal fault;
> It rains into the sea,
>   And still the sea is salt.
> [*More Poems*, No. VII, ll. 5–8]

> Alas, the country whence I fare,
>   It is where I would stay;
> And where I would not, it is there
>   That I shall be for aye.
> [*More Poems*, No. VIII, stanza 2]

This last thought returns persistently throughout these poems. It is shown again in:

> The rainy Pleiads wester
>   And seek beyond the sea
> The head that I shall dream of,
>   That will not dream of me.
> [*More Poems*, No. XI, stanza 2]

It is shown typically in a poem on Hero and Leander, but also in chance verses such as

> All knots that lovers tie
>   Are tied to sever;
> Here shall your sweet-heart lie,
>   Untrue for ever.
> [*More Poems*, No. XXIV, ll. 5–8]

All these epigrams are at bottom variations on one epigram, the theme of which is separation. One might almost say that this is the sole subject of Housman's poetry, and perhaps its chief inspiration: separation in its various forms, between lover and lover, friend and friend, life and death, innocence and experience.

> He, standing hushed, a pace or two apart,
> Among the bluebells of the listless plain,
> Thinks, and remembers how he cleansed his heart
> And washed his hands in innocence in vain.
> [*More Poems*, No. XXVIII]

The keenness of the emotion in these lines comes from a sense of inevitable separation which nothing can prevent. Seen in this way, separation is a form of betrayal:

> Here shall your sweetheart lie,
> Untrue for ever.

For this sense of betrayal, which comes from an apprehension of the contrast between appearance and reality, hope and fulfilment, the natural form is epigram, a brief and surprising statement of an obvious incompatibility. This volume can still surprise us by the unabated ingenuity and sincerity with which Housman went on making that statement; but there are signs of merely mechanical construction, the reiteration has become a formula, and the diction as in all poetry written to formulae (Poe's, for instance), tends to become threadbare. We are interested in the thought merely, or rather in the ingenuity by which the poet reaches it, for it is always the same thought; and there are very few lines with the old power of evocation. The following verse has a far-off echo of it:

> The farms of home lie lost in even,
> I see far off the steeple stand;
> West and away from here to heaven
> Still is the land.

But this verse is used merely as a step to get to the last one, which repeats the old epigram again:

> The land is still by farm and steeple,
> And still for me the land may stay:
> There I was friends with perished people,
> And there lie they.
> [*More Poems*, No. XIV, stanzas 1 and 3]

The extraordinary inventiveness and persistence with which Housman reaches this point finally have the effect of withdrawing our attention from it to themselves, and of falsifying the poetry and making it in a sense provisional. This did not happen so obviously in *A Shropshire Lad*, for there the purely poetic impulse was much stronger. But it happened there too, and that probably helps to account for the unusual popularity which that volume once enjoyed. This is not to call into account its undeniable poetic power.

74. Geoffrey Grigson, review, *New Verse*
No. 23, Christmas 1936, 22–4

Geoffrey Grigson (1905–85), poet, was the editor of *New Verse* from 1933 to 1939. As well as many collections of poetry, he published books on John Clare and William Barnes; in 1974 he compiled the *Dictionary of English Plant Names*.

It seems to me that one of the best of these new poems by A.E. Housman is the ninth:

[quotes No. IX]

I should choose this not before, but at least with, such poems more perfect in Housman's own convention as No. 8 or No. 19, because it works, in the last line, up to an example of Housman's best virtue *as a writer*. Housman always describes softly (brevity should not be mistaken for precision); compare –

> And like a skylit water stood
> The bluebells in the azured wood

with

> And azuring-over greybell makes
> Wood banks and brakes wash wet like lakes.

He *sees* 'the purple crocus pale Flower about the autumn dale' and so on, objects entering his verse very little except as objects already reflected and blurred in literature. 'When roses to the moonrise burst apart' – the roses are the roses of poetry not the experienced roses; and green buds do not hang in the elm much like dust (they flutter round elms, as D.H. Lawrence said, like green snow) or sprinkle the lime much like rain. So Housman depended only (through literature) on himself. And his best virtue is to make the sound of his lines equivalent to his feeling. I think a fine example is the second line of the translation in *Last Poems*:

> We'll to the woods no more,
> The laurels all are cut,

in which a pause is forced after 'laurels' before the emphasis which must go on the open word 'all', a pause which I, at least, cannot come to without being much affected. So – though perhaps it is too near to type: Housman would repeat his best peculiarities – the pause before an open syllable, at the most emphatic, emotionally crowded point, 'are lying' – pause – 'about the world', seems to me extraordinarily well designed. I hope I do not underesteem Housman or exaggerate his worth. He was narrow, he was monotonous, he posed, he evaded, he knew only about literature and himself, and wrote foolishly when he wrote outside himself (as a man among other men), but he wrote poems and pieces of poems quite deeply affective. If his age clamped him about pretty securely, he was not too much taken in by its values, its liberating optimism, and the men of his own years who were its most passive reflections, He refused the O.M. because – excellent reason – it had been given to Galsworthy; and he was interested enough in life and its expression in younger poets even after the war, which, in spite of the cheap 'Epitaph on an Army of Mercenaries', must have confirmed in him all his bitterness about human nature, to buy their books and to subscribe to *New Verse*. For what he did and thought, and failed to do and think, he can be read now with profit. In this last book his faults are chiefly exemplified or his virtues repeated. But it is worth having, and not only because one or two poems e.g. No. 31 make the nature of his 'unlucky love' much more obvious.

75. Robert Hillyer, review, *Atlantic Monthly*
clviii, December 1936 ('The Bookshelf', n.p.)

Robert Silliman Hillyer (1895–1961), poet, educated at Harvard and from 1937 to 1945 Boylston Professor of Rhetoric and Oratory there. He later taught at Kenyon College, Ohio, and the University of Delaware, and became chancellor of the Academy of American Poets.

Another volume of A.E. Housman's delicate lyrics comes as a surprise in event rather than in matter. We know the mood and the voice; a continuation of them enriches us almost reminiscently. Housman's was a one-stringed lyre, but its clear melodic line has overtones wherein English folk poetry and the Classic pastoral are harmonized. The language is the simplest, almost the homeliest, English; the stanza form is based on the familiar ballad metre of our ancestors; but the refinement of phrasing shows the influence of the Classics, and the Shropshire lad's epitaph has already been written in the Greek Anthology. In general these lyrics belong in the class to which Gray's *Elegy* belongs, and which Fitzgerald's *Rubáiyát* just misses – high poetry that makes no concession to popular taste and yet is popular.

Housman's metric is based on the simplest of traditional forms, a four-stress or three-stress line or an alternation between them. He rhymes scrupulously. When he leaves the first and third line unrhymed, he substitutes for the missing rhyme another recurrent effect – a 'feminine' or two-syllable ending; as, for example, in poem XXXI. Frequently he makes this form richer by rhyming the feminine endings as well. We find other measures in this book, as in its forerunners. The 'Easter Hymn' is in loose heroic couplets, and the version of Horace's 'Diffugere Nives' is in heroic quatrains.

The fact that these two are among Housman's best poems leads to a consideration of his diction. The measured panoply of the five-stress line in English leads to a more rigorous selection of words. It is a paradox of our verse that the longer the line, so much less opportunity is there for looseness in thought and in phrasing or even in metre. Since the bulk of Housman's work is in the short line, he creates great lyrics only when his verbal attention is as alert as it should be for the longer lines. His diction is a strange mixture of the casual and the forced. He does not hesitate, at times, to employ shameless inversions of syntax to fit a metrical pattern, and many of his lyrics are spoiled by the mutual elbowing of colloquialisms and archaisms. A studied simplicity at times declines into mere prosiness. In his search for the simple phrase he is treading the tightrope Wordsworth trod, but when he falls the jar is lighter because the weight is less.

There are three reasons why I find Housman's *Last Poems* and this posthumous *More Poems* progressively inferior to the *Shropshire Lad*. In the first place, they are. Secondly, the poet is a man of one mood, and though any one of the aspects of that mood may be persuasive, in bulk they merely satiate. I find the same satiety in the endless discoveries of undiscovered poems by Emily Dickinson. She had her say, beautifully, and the rest should be silence but is, in fact, repetition. Thirdly, I do not find valid Housman's own contention (exquisitely put, by the way, in the introductory poem to this volume, as it was wittily put in 'Terence, this is stupid stuff') that his bitter melancholy is an antidote for the horrors of actual existence. For his pessimism is not the dainty melancholy of the Elizabethen lyric, nor yet the methodical doom of Greek tragedy. It is Hellenistic rather than Hellenic, and verges dangerously on romantic indulgence. It is the substitution of an artistic technique for a human technique – in other words, an escape. It comes from within. One feels that he worked much harder on his art than on his character. This suspiratory mood, so attractive to me 'when I was one and twenty', seems to me now, when actual despair looms on the horizons of the world, as rather a romantic luxury. As part of a larger whole, like the magnificent dirge in *Cymbeline*, it has its place; as the whole, it is artistically and philosophically inadequate. Therefore I prefer to think of Housman as the author of a handful of perfect lyrics, chosen from this book and its predecessors, rather than of three volumes, the major proportion of which falls beneath perfection.

In conclusion, I should like to point out the affinity between Housman and a greater poet, Thomas Gray. Their idioms, of course, are entirely different; but the circumstances of their lives and the temper of their natures were extraordinarily like. Surely the 'youth to fortune and to fame unknown' was the Shropshire lad; surely the Shropshire lad was the hero of 'Ode on a Distant Prospect of Eton College'. It might almost be said of Housman, as Matthew Arnold said of Gray, that 'he never spoke out'.

76. William Empson, 'Foundations of Despair', *Poetry* (Chicago)

xlix, January 1937, 228–31

William Empson (1906–84), distinguished poet, critic and scholar, educated at Cambridge while Housman was Professor of Latin there. He was, successively, Professor of English Literature in Tokyo, at the University of Peking, and (from 1953) at the University of Sheffield. At the time of this review he had published his first two critical books (*Seven Types of Ambiguity* and *Some Versions of Pastoral*), and *Poems* (1935).

It is long since I cut pages with more curiosity and expectation than I did these, and they are not disappointing. The editor says he will publish a chronology of the poems later; so far nothing has certainly been written after the preface to *Last Poems* except the hymn for Housman's own funeral. This curious document may have some bearing on a question one cannot help raising, as to how far the poet means what he says; but probably it only tells you that he took the same view of his church as Thomas Hardy and most Anglican atheists of that generation. The poems here were mostly rejected from the two earlier books, some for a flaw in the workmanship, some for making the stock situation of the poems too obviously a personal one, some for no clear reason. They have been kept back till the fashion that would have made them more obvious has gone.

It would be interesting to know why the stinging nettle one did not appear before. The lads are sowing, but it does not matter what they sow, because only one thing will grow:

> The stinging nettle only
>   Will still be found to stand:
> The numberless, the lonely,
>   The thronger of the land,
>   The leaf that hurts the hand.

It is first-rate Housman, both in the nostalgia and the power. It seems also to consist of remarkably untrue statements even for first-rate Housman. When I went to Japan as a teacher I chose the *Shropshire Lad* [sic] for detailed reading in my first term, and several of the class were drafted to Shanghai, where there was a row at the time. 'I think Housman is quite right', one of them wrote in an essay before starting, 'I will do no good to anyone by dying for my country, but I will be admired, and we all want to be admired, and anyway we are better dead.' I thought Housman would have been as much shocked by this as I was; it is a fishy game, to play the amateur of tragedy. A thing like the stinging nettle poem is splendid verse, therefore not fishy, but you would have to talk for a long time to give an adequate account of why not.

An attack on Housman by Cyril Connolly appeared in the *New Statesman* recently [see No. 64 above], and needs to be faced by anyone who feels the strength of this poetry, though it was an unfair bit of work. A curious muddle about classical poetry became prominent. Connolly said that no classical poet wrote about the lower classes, but when a correspondent mentioned Theocritus, he said that no classical poet had serious personal feelings about the lower classes, though they might be pegs for verse. Whereas Housman among his lads was a Scoutmaster. Very likely this complex insult will not seem blasting outside England. It is true I think that all Despair Poetry needs a good deal of 'distance' (of the poet from the theme); you can only call despair a profound general truth when you are looking beyond all the practical particulars, which might well have been more hopeful if the man had been stronger; and in a personal story, even a half-told one, you cannot do this easily. In the same way, on the face of it, the poem in *More Poems* about how the speaker will not enter the Promised Land but other people will, is a contradiction of the general poems which say that nobody will, and its statement is much smaller than theirs even if less untrue. But there seems no decent ground for calling all Despair Poetry about love sentimental, and then all tragedy sentimental, as Connolly is on the edge of doing. And granting the stuff can be good, it has a technical condition, whatever the personal background. It wants as its apparent theme a case of love with great practical obstacles, such as those of class and sex, because the despair has to seem sensible before this curious jump is made and it is called a universal truth. Of course the jump may be done badly, but Connolly found no argument to show it was done badly here, nor is it.

Housman himself gives this reason why this one of his stock themes can carry a large implication, in a poem that imitates Andrew Marvell, a pleasant thing to see in a man who despised the metaphysicals, even though he refused to publish it. 'All things may end, for all begin' [sic]

> But this unlucky love should last
> When answered passions melt to air; [sic]
> Eternal fate so deep has cast
> Its sure foundations of despair. [sic]

And indeed the foundations of all this narrow and haunting poetry seem to me very solid. But it is the only poetry I have yet seen having a pernicious effect on the young.

77. Earle Birney, 'Swan Song', *Canadian Forum*

xvi, January 1937, 23–4

Earle Birney (b. 1904), distinguished Canadian poet, novelist, and scholar. Among his collections of poetry are *David and Other Poems* (1942) and *Near False Creek Mouth* (1964). From 1946 to 1963 he was Professor of English at the

University of British Columbia, and from 1963 Head of its Department of Writing. The reference to 'Dr. Markowitz' alludes to a piece by J. Markowitz, MD, entitled 'A.E. Housman: A Dissection', which appeared in the *Canadian Forum*, xvi (October 1936), 19–21.

Housman's reputation will be little disturbed by these careful siftings from his literary ashes. Forty-eight short pieces – some only single quatrains – have been published by his posthumous 'permission, not by his wish'. Laurence Housman, his brother, has had the duty, not entirely enviable, of making the selection, and adding a preface.

Technically there is no development, no apparent lapse. Here is the same monotone of rhythm, and elaborate simplicity of phrase, the same sculptured nudity which, because its fashioner was in later life a Cambridge professor of Greek, has been too readily assumed to be 'classical'. Housman himself told us that before he wrote the Shropshire Lad he gave his nights to the lyrics of Heine and Shakespeare, and to the Scottish border ballads. Nor were his other literary preferences exactly in the tradition of Horace. He had as many good things to say about Campbell as about Arnold; he admired Christina Rossetti and seems to have imitated, occasionally and indifferently, her echoing music; he liked Bennett as well as Hardy and Austin; and though he was eccentric enough to consider Bridges' Shorter Poems the finest single volume of English verse, he still thought Shelley the greatest poet – and he much preferred detective thrillers to Galsworthy. Housman's austere brevity in image is more Anglo-Saxon than foreign, his laconic narrative is mediaeval rather than Greek; and his formal 'classicism' is only the stoicism with which he remains inside the narrow compass of these effects.

It is the very maintenance of this virtuosity which, in More Poems, allows us to see its limitations clearly. There is now a sufficient corpus of Housman's work to reveal, for example, that his simple vocabulary is a diction rather than a language, William Lyon Phelps to the contrary. 'Haven', 'distaff', 'fare', (for 'go'), 'tarry', 'bourn', are not the words of Shropshire 'lads' of the 1890's or of today. Nor did such country folk die from 'sabres', falling in battle with 'plumes… under heel'. This is the outworn language of an Oxford student who wrote from Highgate about imagined beings in a romantic western horizon of hills, hills which he did not even visit until after he composed the first six of the poems which fixed his style. The frugal clichés which consequently intruded are still here in these final verses, interfering not only with the language of men but also with those standards of the flawless miniature to which Housman aspired:

> On the far-beholding foreland
> Paced at even grief and I...
> O maiden, let your distaff be
> And pace the flowery meads with me.

Such staginess reveals how narrow a course Housman steered between pedantry and bathos. He has been proof against parodists only because by his faint lugubrious humor he parodies himself:

> From the wash the laundress sends
> My collars home with ravelled ends;
> I must fit, now these are frayed,
> My neck with new ones London-made.

The same parsimony is now as obvious in the metre and metaphor as in the diction. There is none of the 'harmonious madness', nothing of that companioned rush of thought and image which characterizes the great lyric poets. It is not without significance that Housman was unable to enjoy paintings or music. All poetic expression was to him a long mathematical labor – a final quatrain might be the work of three weeks. Ideas came to him rarely and painfully, with great physical disturbance. Though he began writing at eight, the best known of his published verses – and some even of this last volume – were the fruit of less than two years in the mid-nineties. That period of heightened consciousness began, he has solemnly told us, with a 'relaxed sore throat.'

Housman himself made a sharp distinction between this intense subjectivity of his poetic experience and his 'poetic attitude.' The latter, he insisted, was 'founded on my observation of the world, not on anything so trivial or irrelevant as personal history.' But how can one observe life without individual experience? Is it not permissible to suspect a connection between the sharp change in Housman's character, after he had failed his Greats at Oxford and had returned home to spend ten long years as an obscure clerk in the Patent Office, and the beginning of his austere despair in poetry? Laurence Housman is testimony to that sudden metamorphosis in his brother from the merry and energetic leader of a literary family circle to the 'silent and impenetrable recluse', a man almost proud of his reputation as a vinegar-tongued pedant. Dr. Markowitz, in a previous Forum, has suggested a connection between Housman's misogynous and sexless life, and the vulgar adolescence of his references, in poetry, to the intimacies between men and women. Later, when he had made a name in literature and achieved a chair at London, some of his affability returned. He wrote sprightly letters and nonsense verse to his brothers, he toured Europe to enjoy its wines, he lived comfortably without economic stress. But by then his poetic philosophy was fixed and his lyric impulse virtually ended.

The limitations of that attitude are also clearer, with More Poems. Here is the same brooding over death, a morbidity which is not pagan in quality but Anglican rather, because beneath the apparent serenity is a disturbed refusal to accept and by that means dismiss from the mind the inescapable mortality of man.

> The lad that hopes for Heaven
> Shall fill his mouth with mould.

The simplicity of the view conceals its contradictions. He believes that the addition of knowledge is man's only increasing pleasure – yet also that the clodpole and the sensitive soul are equally vulnerable to ill. Nor is there any poetic evidence that Housman did add to his knowledge with years; the face of the heavens do not bring to him new speculations upon the obscure magic of life on this planet, but only mediaeval warnings that the world rushes 'ruinward.' In fact Housman, for all his atheism, is as firmly convinced of original sin as Eliot. If no outside forces twisted us, 'yet the heart would counsel ill.'

> The toil of all that be
> Helps not the primal fault.

But he cannot, like Eliot, accept the surety of the waste land and prepare only to endure it in penance:

> Where trees are fallen, there is grief:
> I love no leafless land.

To others, however, he still counsels endurance, or suicide; he still regards his verse as an armour lent to 'ill-treated fellows' and a warning that achievement is difficult and vain. He reiterates his Spartan advice tirelessly, almost as if he fears none are listening, as if he realizes that those who elect to remain in life also elect striving and self advancement as a condition of life.

Most contradictory of all, perhaps, is his self-styled 'pejorism.' Life gets worse for each of us as we age; that is why young men, ignorant of the worst, dislike to die, and that is why Housman pities the shot soldier, but does not feel it worth while to bestir himself against the causes of his early death:

> Life to be sure is nothing much to lose;
> But young men think it is, and we were young.

Setting aside the questionable psychology here (is it not mature men who in general like least to perish and striplings who can be persuaded to throw their lives away for a drum-beat?), we must face the fundamental weakness in Housman which Flecker saw – that he was too indifferent to be either a significant teacher or a genuinely inventive artist. Laurence Housman apologizes for the 'bitterness' of his brother's verse on the grounds that Housman is expressing a desire that the 'laws of God and man' should be kinder than they are. But the point is that Housman is too inverted and apathetic to care. He never pauses to examine which of man's ills are innate, which are from temporary social causes. He was a sensitive but tired man, somewhat of a failure in human relations, desiring in his last years only to continue his inverted existence or to have 'sudden death' as life's best reward. The annihilation of a young soldier was not really to him the symbol of great human causes lost or achieved, or of a waste avoidable or certain, but simply, like the death of any other man, a turning 'to the thing He was born to be'.

Housman gazed in dignified pity from his study window, but only long enough to catch the fog and smoke of our era; and he too readily assumed that the light behind was sunset and not a dawn. Because of this, it may be that in fifty years More Poems, despite the apparent permanence of their technical achievement and the noble 'universality' of their thoughts, will be read but rarely. When they are I think it will be for casual lines like these:

> When green buds hang in the elm like dust
> And sprinkle the lime like rain,
> Forth I wander, forth I must,
> And drink of life again.

and not for Housman's 'criticism of life'.

78. Jacob Bronowski, review, *Criterion*
xvi, No. 64, April 1937, 519–22

Jacob Bronowski (1908–74), mathematician, biologist and author (of a book on Blake (1944), of *The Common Sense of Science* (1951), and of radio plays, after World War II). He was contemporary with William Empson at Cambridge, and co-editor with him of the avant-garde magazine *Experiment*. He was a scientific adviser to the government during the war; after it he held senior positions with UNESCO, the National Coal Board, and (1964–74) the Salk Institute for Biological Studies. His argument about, and against, Housman was developed at length in his first book, *The Poet's Defence* (Cambridge University Press, 1939, 209–28).

These poems from Housman's remains do not differ from the poems which Housman printed in his lifetime. They have the same thought and the same manner; and they have been chosen, as Housman asked that they should be, 'to be not inferior to the average of my published poems'. They are not new poems, but more poems, of a known kind. To judge them, therefore, is to judge the kind of poem which Housman wrote.

This kind is commonly taken to be spare and exact in manner, and stoical in thought. I am not the first to remark that it is neither. There are two poems in the book which seem to me to be equal to Housman's best. I quote the first verse of one,

A.E. HOUSMAN

> Tarry delight, so seldom met,
>   So sure to perish, tarry still;
> Forbear to cease or languish yet,
>   Though soon you must and will.
>   [No. XV, stanza 1]

and the last verse of the other

> The brisk fond lackey to fetch and carry,
>   The true, sick-hearted slave,
> Expect him not in the just city
> And free land of the grave.
>   [No. XXIII, stanza 2]

These verses have pathos and bitterness; but they are not stoical. Nor are they spare and exact. 'Cease or languish', 'must and will', 'fetch and carry', 'the just city and free land' all go to fill out vaguely to four lines what should be said exactly in three. Housman wrote short poems, but not spare poems. His poems are as wordy as the poems of Shelley or of Browning, because the ratio of words to thought in them is as high.

All this has been said before; and it is only the beginning of criticism. True, it shows that Housman's readers have misunderstood their taste. But so have the readers of Herrick and of Blake. And true, it stresses that Housman's thought and feeling are narrow. But so are those of Gray and of Wordsworth. We do not judge Housman until we judge the kind of thought and feeling on which he draws.

I have already used the word 'pathos' for Housman's feeling; and it is the key word to his poems. Housman's pathos lies in the to-and-fro of two sadnesses, which cannot be held together. One is the sadness of man in the world,

> The brisk fond lackey to fetch and carry,
> The true, sick-hearted slave.

The other is the sadness of losing the world:

> Tarry delight, so seldom met,
> So sure to perish, tarry still.

The first sadness makes him wish to die,

> Now who sees night for ever,
> He sees no happier sight:

> Night and no moon and never
> A star upon the night.
> [No. XXXVIII, stanza 3]

The second sadness makes him wish to live,

> Alas, the country whence I fare,
> It is where I would stay;
> And where I would not, it is there
> That I shall be for aye.
> [No. VIII, stanza 2]

No doubt all men feel one of these wishes at one time, and the other at another time. But Housman's poetry is solely spent in these two wishes, in trying to hold them together and at the same time. This irresolution gives his poems their air of stoicism. The stoicism is false, because it is got by judging life merely by the act of being dead. Death is not a standard, and it has no bearing on how we should live. It may be, as Housman thought, that man is helpless and worthless; but he is not helpless and worthless because he will die. Housman's poems are pathetic poems because they are poems which judge without standards.

It is part of this pathos that Housman should always hanker after and always belittle the standards of others. On one page he is glad that a young man has not outlived his honour; on the next he adds that death is sadder than dishonour. And always he tells us that he himself has chosen dishonour. Many readers dislike the self-pity of Housman's poems. But a fault which sits deeper is their self-belittling. The more moving are Housman's feelings the more surely he will ask the reader to despise them; and his writing is then most tender and most wry. I quote once again:

[quotes No. XXIII]

The effect of such writing becomes bewildering. It pits against one another the littleness of Housman's love, and the extravagance of the feeling which he draws from it. Thus it asks the reader to be sorry, not for Housman's suffering, but for the maudlin feeling which Housman draws from his suffering. Only one more bitter step is left: to ask the reader to like Housman for belittling himself, and for being little. Housman took this step – I quote from *A Shropshire Lad*:

[quotes stanzas 5-8 of *A Shropshire Lad*, No. XXVII]

The soft irony of 'I lie as lads would choose' is the high point of Housman's poetry. This is Housman's pathos; he is saying plainly 'Not only is this a sad and mean poem, but there remains the untold sadness that it should be moving.'

It seems to me that, in implying this, Housman's poetry condemns itself. In this his poems test themselves, and find themselves to be bad. For we may believe that life matters or does not matter. We may believe that honour matters, or does not matter. And it may be possible to write good poems in any of these beliefs. But it cannot be possible to show one's contempt for one's feelings, to ask the reader to be moved because they are contemptible, and to make good poetry of this. It cannot be possible to think poetry so unworthy, and to write worthy poems. Housman's poems do not believe it possible: and they judge themselves.

79. Eugene Davidson, 'The Span of Housman's Poetry', *Yale Review*
xxvi, Winter 1937, 404-6

Eugene Davidson (b. 1902), journalist, reviewer and poet. Born in New York, he was educated at Yale, and worked for Yale University Press in various capacities from 1919 onwards, becoming a director in 1938.

With the exception of two groups of people representing opposite ends of the spectrum of taste, Housman has appealed to a wider public than any other lyric poet of these times. Those extremists who have disliked him have been on one side the people who think poetry ought to be 'majestic like Tennyson's', on the other people who are aestheticians or even metaphysicians in these matters. But excluding these cabals, the reading public of England and America has read and bought Housman's poems in large and enthusiastic numbers. The outstanding reason for his popularity seems to be plain enough. The first is that he is writing about things important to our common humanity: youth and beauty and death and the perplexity of man. Secondly, he writes about these things with such purity of tone, such sharp-edged technique, that what he says is fresh and delightful even when what he is saying is neither the one nor the other.

These forty-eight poems do not make a book of the standard of excellence of the poet's other two volumes. But about ten of them could appear in *A Shropshire Lad* or in *Last Poems* and in no way detract from their perfection. For example, there is the first poem in the book:

[quotes 'They say my verse is sad' in full]

Observe the muted assonance of the first and third lines of these stanzas, the delicate counterpoint, the fact that no line fails to repeat a dominant consonant or vowel at least once, with the exception of the last line, which so to speak precipitates the poem and requires no melodic effect and would in fact suffer from having attempted one. That craftsmanship is completely absorbed in the run of the poem. It doesn't manifest its purposes; it is concealed in the texture of the poem itself.

Not all the poems are so good as this one, but every one of them is unmistakably Housman. There is always somewhere in them the characteristic accent and the perfect word. Even in the curious poem, 'The Land of Biscay', which has little of the compactness of the poet's other work and which sounds in part as though Masefield or Noyes might have written it, we come on the lines:

Grief and I abode the nightfall; to the sunset grief and he
Turned them from the land of Biscay on the waters of the sea.

And there through the foreign accent is the unmistakable voice of Shropshire and the clear song.

In some ways these poems take the place of Housman juvenilia. Only in this book is there to be found the clue to what the poet considered possible variants – there are alternative readings of certain lines and in one case two versions of an entire poem. There are also repetitions of phrases that Housman himself would undoubtedly have excluded, weak echoes of poems that have already appeared in other books and a few really poor stanzas. But he gave permission to his brother Laurence to make this selection after his death, and he has been, in general, well served. No one but the poet himself would be so rigorous in his decisions as to which of his verses were to be published, and we can only be grateful that Mr. Laurence Housman has not shared his passion for leaving nothing but faultless lyrics in print.

These poems are a worthy if unequal addition to the preceding volumes. It is true that the book contains a misprint, but it also has an excellent reproduction of the poet's portrait and a specimen of his handwriting. It includes enough of Housman's best work to enable it to stand alongside *A Shropshire Lad* and *Last Poems* and alongside, too, the poems of Catullus and Heinrich Heine and the English balladists with whom Housman had so much in common. He was a great poet. His range was limited, but there is not much reason for complaining that a violin has only four strings. Within that range he was very nearly perfect.

One thing characterized him more than love of beauty, or bitterness, or stoicism – that was compassion. Compassion for the lad who thought the fair was held for him, and for the army of mercenaries who saved the sum of things for pay; for courage and cowardice; the suicide and the young men playing games they would not play for long. Whether you think he observed truly the place of man in the world depends on your own *Weltanschauung*. But his importance as a poet has little to do with anyone's world view and still less with how one feels about social forces.

[quotes stanzas 3 and 4 of No. XXXII]

Lines like these are not dependent for their effect on whether or not the reader believes in kings or even whether there are any kings to believe in. They cut beneath social dogma and personal enthusiasm, they deal with the plight of man as it doubtless was seen in any season or in any country. And it is unlikely that the establishment of Utopia can dilute the importance of that marvellous singing.

80. Nevile Watts, 'The Poetry of A.E. Housman', *Dublin Review*

January 1937, 117–33

There are two absolute superlatives that may be applied at the outset to Housman's poetry: it contains more beauty, and at the same time more sadness, than any other poetry of modern times. That is why its own phrase 'angry dust' is its best epitome, for it expresses (and the generalization may pass, as nearly all the poems have this for their direct or implicit theme) the resentment of man at his mortality. Of man – for this poetry is not subjective; it does not 'parade the pageant of a bleeding heart'; it avowedly speaks for the race, and 'its narrow measure spans' not the poet's sorrow, 'but man's'. Tennyson wrote in *In Memoriam*:

> Thou wilt not leave us in the dust:
> Thou madest man, he knows not why;
> He thinks he was not made to die;
> And thou hast made him: thou art just

– basing man's immortality on the impossibility of conceiving that God would disappoint the aspirations God had implanted. Housman denies both God's justice and man's immortality, and uses that beauty which he apprehends so deeply to aggravate the charge against God and the wrong done to man.

This poetry is something of a phenomenon. Its author was a scholar, and not merely a scholar but, upon the lowest possible estimate, the second only among English classical scholars of all time in learning and eminence. Furthermore, not merely was he a scholar unequalled among his contemporaries in any nation, but his scholarship was of a kind that admitted no parley with the world; he was not a Murray or a Mackail, making the dull paths of learning glow with blooms to delight the common wayfarer. He scaled the most arid and craggy heights, devoting his life to a microscopic study of obscure and abstruse Latin poets, scorning either popularity or popularization, and writing introductions wherein he scarified with sarcasm such fellow scholars as failed to attain to his own rigorous standard of accuracy and acumen. And at two widely separated periods of his life this Jekyll transforms himself into a Hyde, and breaks into song so tender yet so fierce, so simple yet so penetrating, that it is as though the owl were suddenly to astonish us with the notes of the nightingale. This dry-as-dust professor sobs his heart out like a child; this bloodless analyst of yet more bloodless texts reveals a contact with elemental emotion closer than that of any professed poet of his day.

But an explanation of this mystery is forthcoming: Housman wrote these poems with his tongue in his cheek; they are a clever fake, a *tour de force*. The man who composed that diabolically smart parody of Greek tragedy would have had no difficulty at all in throwing off a few score of monosyllabic stanzas purporting to describe how sundry lads and chaps of a western countryside experience the tragic loves and friendships proper to rustics, and meet with properly tragic ends. It is the Dresden-china pastoralism of Spenser and Watteau in a new shape; the gibbet stands up instead of the maypole, the scene is the village churchyard instead of the village green. But the one picture is as false as the other; it is only the old convention inverted. The simplicity of the poems is only *simplesse*; their passion is only pathos.

If one has carried these poems about with one for half a lifetime, carried them not in the pocket alone but in the ears and head and heart, such a charge provokes deep anger, not merely because it is humiliating to be thought to have fixed one's trust upon a fraud, but at the bare suggestion that poetry which is a manufactured sham can have any lease of life at all. Poetry which is a sham has never lived, and can never live. Good pastoral poetry lives, for though it is a pretence it has never pretended to be anything but a pretence. But poetry which was a mere masquerade of truth could not live for a week, for poetry and falsity are incompatibles.

The hundred and four short lyrics which Housman published during his lifetime were given to the world in two instalments, the second twenty-six years after the first. In spite of world-shattering events that intervened, the second shows no development upon the first either in artistry or outlook, save that the later collection is more uniformly grave in tone and of more even workmanship, and is at the same time more introspective in themes and character. *A Shropshire Lad*, while it contains the most purely beautiful of all the lyrics, contains also some which fall below the level of any in *Last Poems*. Both volumes have this special distinction; that, composed though each was at a time when poetry had lost centrality and was either exotic or esoteric, the poems they contain are, with scarcely an exception, simplicity and centrality themselves. Their diction is that of every day, their metres are few and (save for variations of a five-line stanza) ordinary, and the alliteration which is their only apparent artifice is so unforced as to seem inevitable. Far better than Wordsworth's own verse they illustrate Wordworth's dictum: 'There neither is, nor can be, any essential difference between the language of prose and metrical composition.' The order of the words is almost always that of prose. Finally, whole stanzas are built of nothing but monosyllables:

> I know not if it rains, my love,
>   In the land where you do lie;
> And, oh, so sound you sleep, my love,
>   You know no more than I.

The lyrics selected by Mr. Laurence Housman for his posthumous gleaning, *More Poems*, add little to their author's previous achievement. They are, to a great extent, duplications of earlier themes; phrases familiar in the other two volumes recur; some of the poems read like self-imitation, almost self-parody. With full allowance for the appeal of old acquaintance, there are not more than two or three that haunt the mind with the irresistible melody of 'Into my heart an air that kills' or 'When I would muse in boyhood'. Some half-dozen, it must be said, seem to have been conscripted to make up a complement. The new volume will not supplant, or even accompany, its predecessors in our pockets or our affections. If in those Death was everywhere, Beauty and Joy walked everywhere at his side. But in *More Poems* the beauty is intermittent and the joy nowhere. If we had only this book whereby to judge of Housman, we might be prepared to allow his claim for 'steady' vision, but we should accuse him of blindness to a very large area of human life.

Housman was one whom the transient beauty of this world embittered, not into cynicism, but into a torturing acuteness of response to beauty. What private blows he had sustained from fate we do not know, and it would matter little should we never know. But one blow that fate dealt him we know, for it is the blow that fate deals to us all alike, save that some of us (like Mrs. Gummidge) feel it more than others – the sense that beauty, which should be eternal, turns to dust and ashes, and with it the heart that beats faster at the sight of beauty. Man is a baffled and frustrated creature, for his Maker has filled him with aspirations which are doomed to be defrauded:

> It is in truth iniquity on high
>   To cheat our sentenced souls of aught they crave,
> And mar the merriment as you and I
>   Fare on our long fool's-errand to the grave...
>
> The troubles of our proud and angry dust
>   Are from eternity and shall not fail.
> Bear them we can, and if we can we must.
>   Shoulder the sky, my lad, and drink your ale.

And since this frustration is part of the unalterable nature of things, a man's first duty is close-lipped endurance; and endurance is most easy if a man will shut out reflection. Life will not bear thinking about, and the fortunate are those who are born not to think about it, or who can deliberately stifle thought. And the figure under which Housman expresses this absence or refusal of thought is 'ale':

> Ale, man, ale's the stuff to drink
> For fellows whom it hurts to think.

But for himself not to think is unthinkable. He has looked upon the west, to look on which is to 'think eternal thoughts, and sigh'; he has given his heart away, and he cries:

> past the plunge of plummet,
>   In seas I cannot sound,
> My heart and soul and senses
>   World without end are drowned.

There is but one thing he can do – translate his gift into song to aid his fellows:

> 'Tis true the stuff I bring for sale
> Is not so brisk a brew as ale;
> Out of a stem that scored the hand
> I wrung it in a weary land.
> But take it: if the smack is sour,
> The better for the embittered hour;

> It should do good to heart and head
> When your soul is in my soul's stead;
> And I will friend you, if I may,
> In the dark and cloudy day.

Housman would probably have repudiated the idea that it is the duty of a composer of short lyrics to set forth a consistent philosophy. The short lyric is the mirror of a mood; and if a man's moods contradict one another – well, they contradict one another. But, even though it be with criticism thus disarmed, we may criticize thus: the poems dwell insistently upon loveliness, the loveliness of spring flowers, of young love, of the freshness and purity of youth, of the life of adventure, of friendship, of childhood's memories. But wherever beauty sits at feast, there also is the skeleton of transience and decay. And the poet turns to rail upon the gift of loveliness and the Giver who gives only to defraud the appetite He has engendered. He who has given us, in the past, Mays bright with hawthorn and the flambeaux of the chestnut is a 'brute and blackguard', for our twenty-third May has been ruined by wind and rain, and the twenty-fourth can never be what the twenty-third might have been. It is the cry of the spoilt child who stamps and sulks on the floor of a nursery littered with expensive toys. Housman typifies the outlook of those moderns who, having discarded the faith, grumble at the temporal measure of fun allowed to them, just because it is temporal. Because they no longer have the cake which they have eaten, therefore the gift of cake is an outrage.

Let us first take Housman's attitude towards nature. His touch here is most delicate and most true, with the truth and delicacy of an exile's memory. He is condemned to live in London, 'the town built ill', but his soul yet 'lingers sighing above [sic] the glimmering weirs' of the 'western brookland that bred him long ago'.

> Into my heart an air that kills
>   From that far country blows: [sic]
> What are those blue remembered hills,
>   What spires, what farms are those?
>
> That is the land of lost content,
>   I see it shining plain,
> The happy highways where I went
>   And cannot come again.

Each spring as it returns recharges his soul with yearning, for others 'possess as he possessed the countries he resigns'. And nature, which is transient as man, draws him by the fellowship of a common doom:

> bound for the same bourn as I,
> On every road I wandered by,
> Trod beside me, close and dear,
> The beautiful and death-struck year.

But here again, when he tells how in his own shire earth was his 'homely comforter', it is but the expression of a mood, and in *Last Poems* he rejects the Pathetic Fallacy, the dream that nature feels with man, as a fallacy indeed. Nature is heartless and witless, and cares nothing for her lovers:

> The sigh that heaves the grasses
> Whence thou wilt never rise
> Is of the air that passes
> And knows not if it sighs.
>
> The diamond tears adorning
> Thy low mound on the lea,
> Those are the tears of morning
> That weeps, but not for thee.

But the poet's love for nature is the more passionate for being unrequited, and there is no poet since Tennyson who has mirrored earth's moods so truly or in such clear outline. He does this not by detailed description, but by brief strokes in which a single epithet or verb reveals a whole landscape:

> On russet floors, by waters *idle*,
> The pine lets fall its cone;
> The cuckoo *shouts* all day at nothing
> In leafy dells alone;
> And traveller's joy beguiles in autumn
> Hearts that have lost their own.
>
> On acres of the seeded grasses
> The changing *burnish heaves*;
> Or *marshalled* under moons of harvest
> *Stand still* all night the sheaves;
> Or beeches strip in storm for winter
> And *stain* the wind with leaves.

But if man's life viewed in his relation to nature is a tragedy of unrequited passion and unfulfilled yearning, man's life in his relation to his fellow men is not less so. Love and friendship alike end in oblivion. Friendship alone is not wholly vain; it is hand reaching out to hand for a moment in the gloom:

> Now – for a breath I tarry
> Nor yet disperse apart –
> Take my hand quick and tell me,
> What have you in your heart.
>
> Speak now, and I will answer;
> How shall I help you, say;
> Ere to the wind's twelve quarters
> I take my endless way.

And friendship, in that lurid and powerful imaginative picture 'Hell-Gate', can defy and quell the powers of darkness itself:

> And the hollowness of hell
> Sounded as its master fell,
> And the mourning echo rolled
> Ruin through the kingdom old.
> Tyranny and terror flown
> Left a pair of friends alone,
> And beneath the nether sky
> All that stirred was he and I.

But, in general, friendship in the poems is a faded memory of youth, and the Shropshire Lad resigned all save that memory when he resigned his fields to others. The firmest bond is severed by death, and at last even memory fades from the living:

> Good-night, my lad, for nought's eternal;
> No league of ours, for sure.
> Tomorrow I shall miss you less,
> And ache of heart and heaviness
> Are things that time should cure.

Nature, love, friendship, all play a man false and leave him lonely. Can we then go through life resolved to admit no dependence upon these? Can we close the door upon them, and find satisfaction in a stoical self-sufficiency? Therein lies the irony of man's life. He must, if he is to find any measure of peace. But on the other hand he cannot, for earth and man grapple him to themselves with hoops of steel. He has given his heart away, and

> There flowers no balm to sain him
> From east of earth to west
> That's lost for everlasting
> The heart out of his breast.

But if neither response to the external world nor refusal to respond to it can satisfy, surely there remains action, with which a man may mix himself 'lest he wither in despair'. The instinct of youth and the brevity of life alike call for action before the night comes:

> Clay lies still, but blood's a rover;
> Breath's a ware that will not keep.
> Up, lad: when the journey's over
> There'll be time enough to sleep.

And the life of external action Housman has, after his fashion, allegorized in the figure of the soldier – a figure whereto he was moved in the first instance by the enlistment of a younger brother and later by his death in the Boer War. Action ends in vanity and oblivion, like the love of earth and of friends, but action is the destiny of the race. The roads of earth are filled with 'soldiers marching, all to die':

> Far the calling bugles hollo,
> High the screaming fife replies,
> Gay the files of scarlet follow:
> Woman bore me, I will rise.

And with action go ambition and the dreams of youth. As year follows year, and our hopes and our thirst for fame still remain unsatisfied, we comfort ourselves with the thought that 'the best is yet to come', till we wake to find that the life with which we had resolved to do so much lies behind us, and we resign our dreams at last:

> They came and were and are not
> And come no more anew;
> And all the years and seasons
> That ever can ensue
> Must now be worse and few.

The life of endeavour and the winning of fame calls to the lover who wanders maying 'in valleys green and still'. But the business and the dream alike close in long forgetfulness, and the loudest of actions does but 'walk the resounding way to the still dwelling'. 'When all is done,' says Sir William Temple, 'human life is, at the greatest and the best, but like a froward child that must be played with and humoured a little while to keep it quiet till it falls asleep, and then the care is over.'

> Lie down, lie down, young yeoman;
> The sun moves always west;
> The road one treads to labour
> Will lead one home to rest,
> And that will be the best.

Man then, is condemned to this tortured interval between two sleeps. How is he to bear himself, since all is vain? The poet imagines himself surveying a Greek marble athlete in the British Museum; they exchange reflections. Each feels himself uprooted and condemned to live among aliens. 'Courage!' the statue seems to say. 'Quit you like stone, be strong.'

The greatest poem in the three collections, greatest because it is conceived on the largest scale and is of a workmanship proportioned to that scale, is that in which the poet expounds his gospel of silent endurance:

> Now, and I muse for why and never find the reason,
> I pace the earth, and drink the air, and feel the sun.
> Be still, be still, my soul; it is for but a season: [sic]
> Let us endure an hour and see injustice done.

'Vanity of vanities,' says our poet-preacher, 'all is vanity.' But not quite all, for his poems may have some passing validity. 'Here and there' to cheer us 'will flower the solitary stars'. 'Ill-treated fellows' may read them 'when they're in trouble', and be friended 'in the dark and cloudy day'. And it may well be asked, how can we be friended by poetry which teaches that life and all that it holds end in dust and ashes, and that nothing is left to us save to endure? And if we reject Housman because he preaches 'the black negation of the bier', are we to reject the plangent sighs over mortality of the Greek Anthology and the book of Ecclesiastes, and the majestic sadness of Lucretius? Are we to cut the *Rubáiyát* from our anthologies, and banish Swinburne from our shelves?

No; for we value these poets not for their negations, but for their affirmations. Their negation is extraneous to themselves as poets, and if it is more than a prejudice or a by-product of experience it is an effluence of that theologian or that philosopher which is in every man, whether poet or not. But it is by virtue of his affirmations that Housman is a poet, for every several ingredient of his poetic product – rhythm, metre, diction, and that ultimate quality of magic which transcends all these – affirms that the essence of life, as apart from teaching and theorizing about life, lies beyond the philosopher and the teacher, beyond even the poet himself. How much richer than any philosophy or any theory is the poem 'Sinner's Rue'!

> By night I plucked it hueless,
>   When morning broke 'twas blue;
> Blue at my breast I fastened
>   The flower of sinner's rue ...
>
> Dead clay that did me kindness,
>   I can do none to you,
> But only wear for breast-knot
>   The flower of sinner's rue.

The same charity finds a voice in 'Hughley Steeple'; to the south lie the ranks of the respectable, while to the north, 'steeple-shadowed', sleep the slayers of themselves:

> To north, to south, lie parted,
>   With Hughley tower above,
> The kind, the single-hearted,
>   The lads I used to love.
> And, south or north, 'tis only
>   A choice of friends one knows,
> And I shall ne'er be lonely
>   Asleep with these or those.

This is Christian pity, and to be filled with the Christian pity without the Christian philosophy to sustain it must have hurt infernally. Most of the pessimism of modern literature arises from the fact that writers have discarded the second and retained the first. If they could discard both together, they would better consult their peace of mind; they could be gay as Horace or as Edward Fitzgerald is gay. But they are without the faith, and they will not have the fun, because they cannot, for they are committed inextricably to the Christian tradition of pity and they see too deeply into life; 'when they think they fasten their hands upon their hearts'. The one half of the world knows all too well how the other half lives. This infinite longing in the poet's finite heart makes him an alien in a strange land, a misfit, encompassed with powers that baffle and bewilder him:

> How am I to face the odds
> Of man's bedevilment and God's,
> I a stranger and afraid
> In a world I never made?

It does not invalidate a poet's work for us that he should fall short of 'the faith that looks through death'. It may even add urgency to his meassage, for his communication to us will gain in significance and effect from his persistent sense

> of Beauty that must die,
> And Joy, whose hand is ever at his lips
> Bidding adieu.

The heightened significance wherewith beauty is fraught for him from its inevitable and tragic brevity will be conveyed to us also, though to us the significance will come not from brevity, but from the knowledge that earthly beauty is a symbol and an earnest of the beauty that is eternal. This is the paradox of faith, that to survey our passing human griefs and joys in the light of eternity is not to reduce them to triviality, but rather to lift them up until they touch the everlasting heavens. The Lady Juliana of Norwich was made aware of this truth in a vision:

Also in this He shewed me a little thing, the quantity of an hazel nut in the palm of my hand; and it was as round as a ball. I looked thereupon with the eye of my understanding and thought: What may this be? And it was answered thus: It is all that is made. I marvelled how it might last, for methought it might suddenly have fallen to naught for very littleness. And I was answered in my understanding: It lasteth, and ever shall, for that God loveth it ... In this little thing I saw three properties. The first is that God made it, the second is that God loveth it, the third that God keepeth it.

A.E. HOUSMAN

The poetry of Housman, scholar and recluse, is, above any poetry of modern times, the poetry of the ordinary man who, having forgotten all that he learnt at his mother's knee about heaven, hell, the soul, and God, is stirred by a conviction of ultimate futility, not to cynicism, but to a torturing acuteness of sense in regard to immediate values. Life is vanity, and therefore life is desperately real and earnest. This poetry, beyond any modern poetry, is 'the still sad music of humanity'. And its simplicity – a simplicity achieved by long and difficult effort – is the outward sign and symbol of its close contact with fundamental humanity. We have learnt something, in the Leslie Stephen Lecture on *The Name and Nature of Poetry* and in Mr. Laurence Housman's memoirs of his brother, of the meticulous filing and hammering to which he subjected his work. And this process, it will assuredly be found, aimed always at heightening the energy of the product by simplicity; at stripping ornament away rather than adding it. It is the simplicity of consummate art which by every touch of the chisel brings the work into closer relation with life. Every word is carefully selected, with full regard to every vowel and every consonant, and so placed as to achieve the maximum of truth, that is to say approach to the subject. Analyse, for example, the stanza:

> On Wenlock Edge the wood's in trouble,
>   Its forest fleece the Wrekin heaves;
> The gale, it plies the saplings double,
>   And thick on Severn snow the leaves

and note in the first two lines (i) the $w \ldots f$ alliteration, (ii) the struggling agglomeration of $ts \ldots st$, and (iii) the repeated long $\bar{e}$s, all these materializing for us the tumult and persistence of the wind; in the third line mark the sequence $pl \ldots pl \ldots bl$, and the vowel chime rung on $\bar{a} \ldots \bar{\imath} \ldots \breve{a}pl \ldots \breve{u}bl$; while in the last the riot subsides into weaker vowels, as through the sibilants the leaves hiss down upon the stream. Not, of course, that the poet's art consists, save incidentally, in such minutiae, or that, in composition, any such synthesis took place as is suggested by this analysis: but a Bramante achieves an apparently effortless beauty only by a calculation of every detail of strain and stress; and, while a poet does not deliberately build a mosaic of imitative sound, yet the sounds are an essential element in the expression and in the ultimate *im*pression.

This poetry is the nearest of all poetry to the speech of daily life, the freest from literary device, of any in the language since Burns and Blake. And it is in the most unliterary of the lyrics that the greatest beauty is achieved. These have every quality of the greatest lyric poetry of England save one – that which for lack of a better word we may call Magic. It is the absence of this quality alone that debars Housman from a seat beside the two greatest of our lyrists – Shakespeare and Blake. Pass a few of these under review: 'Loveliest of trees, the cherry now', 'The time you won your town the race', ''Tis spring; come out to ramble', ''Tis time, I think, by Wenlock town', 'Far in a western brookland', 'When lads were home from labour'.

The final test of poetry is not popularity; if it were, then Martin Tupper in his day and Ella Wheeler Wilcox in our own would stand supreme. Nor is it a final test of poetry that it should be acclaimed by the pundits as work of indubitable genius; for work that has been so acclaimed, as was that of Alice Meynell, has become tarnished by time. But when the critics and the rank and file of readers are at one, and when those who taste the wine to assay it and those who quaff it for joy and refreshment both exclaim at its richness and power, then assuredly the vintage is undoubted. There is nothing 'high-brow' in the greatest art – the frescoes of Fra Angelico, the tragedies of Shakespeare, the symphonies of Beethoven; these draw alike the expert and the simple – unless, indeed, the simple taste has been vitiated and atrophied by the sentimental or the sensational. *A Shropshire Lad* was chanted or crooned by undergraduates when I was an undergraduate thirty years ago; the little volume was carried in the tunic-pocket by soldiers when I was a soldier twenty years ago; and it and *Last Poems* are part and parcel of the daily lives of thousands today.

These poems have their faults. They can be parodied; at their worst they parody themselves. We have all smiled at their predilection for suicide and for hanging; and it is perhaps comforting to reflect that in them the devil has all the worst tunes, for the poems which have these for themes sink below the mean level, and sometimes touch real badness, as in the appalling stanza:

> And naked to the hangman's noose
> The morning clocks will *ring*
> A neck God made for other use
> Than strangling in a string.

To ring a neck without a *w* in the verb is surely inadmissable in any writing not deliberately comic. And the poet's grievance against life leads him in one important context into a distressing anti-bathos. We deride Tennyson for letting us down with so graceless a bump in the last line of *Enoch Arden*; but the fault is as bad, thought it is the reverse fault, when Housman concludes a complaint against unseasonable weather with lines of gorgeous diatribe fitted for the colossal woes of a Lear or an Othello:

> The troubles of our proud and angry dust
> Are from eternity, and shall not fail.

This is, indeed, the mouse in labour bringing forth the mountain.

But the greatest poets are not the most faultess; and it is in his positive merits that Housman's greatness lies. There is first his limpid simplicity which often conceals great depths of thought; there are perhaps only two lyrics – both in *Last Poems*: 'Beyond the moor and mountain crest' and 'Her strong enchantments failing' – of which the meaning is obscured by abstruse metaphor. There is secondly his energy and passion, and his faculty of packing an infinite volume of thought and emotion into a narrow space. There have been three-volume novels that have said no more in four hundred thousand words than this poem says in forty:

> The sloe was lost in flower,
>   The April elm was dim;
> That was the lover's hour,
>   The hour for lies and him.
>
> If thorns are all the bower,
>   If north winds freeze the fir,
> Why, 'tis another's hour,
>   The hour for truth and her.

The bulk of Housman's work is so small that one hesitates to predict permanent pre-eminence for him; for those poets who are permanently pre-eminent have all ballasted themselves heavily. But, as no poet has ever said so much in so few words, so he will probably defy the prophets who judge by avoirdupois, and live by virtue of his intensity, as Simonides lives, and Sappho, and Catullus. It is with these poets of the older world that he holds kinship rather than with any other poet of English blood, for there is no native lyrist to compare with him in grave and austere beauty and concentrated passion. But in one quality he is peculiarly English, in that the glory of a landscape ardently cherished is entangled in his chords. The whole English countryside, not alone Wenlock Edge and the hills and woods of Clun and Clee, is fairer and sweeter for his music. He spoke of himself and his song as of things that fade – himself to be lulled in earth and his song to be lost upon the air. But what he spoke in bitterness we may receive as a joyous verity; for so long as the shadows lengthen eastward from his Shropshire uplands, so long shall he be part of 'this blessed plot, this earth, this realm, this England', and his song be wafted upon the air that fans English temples and fills English lungs:

> The lofty shade advances,
>   I take my flute and play:
> Come, lads, and learn the dances
>   And praise the tune today.
> Tomorrow, more's the pity,
>   Away we both – must hie,
> To air the ditty,
>   And to earth I.

81. Louis Kronenberger, 'A Note on A.E. Housman', *Nation* (New York)

18 December 1937, 690–1

Louis Kronenberger (b. 1904), American novelist, editor and reviewer. He was an editor with Boni and Liveright (1926–33) and with Knopf (1933–5). From 1938 onwards he was drama critic of *Time*, and from 1951 he lectured at Columbia University. Kronenberger's article was prompted by the publication (New York, 1937) of *Alfred Edward Housman: Recollections by Various Hands*.

Since Housman's death much has been written in the form of memoirs concerning a personality that had earlier seemed closed and inaccessible. All of us knew Housman's poetry; some of us knew a little about his scholarship – had dipped, it may be, into the prefaces to the 'Manilius' and both relished and recoiled from their just but unmerciful and even needless excoriations. None of us knew more about the man than might be contained in a page of 'Who's Who' eked out by half a dozen possibly apocryphal anecdotes. The man remained remote; and after reading what has been written about him since he died, one concludes that he was remote from almost everybody who knew him. He was not inhuman: he had an epicene sense of fun, a delight in good drink, a need though not a capacity for friendship, a delicate family sense; he had grieved over the death of his mother, and he must have known some more private grief which, we are half promised, will some day be explained. But he not only withdrew from what we loosely call the world; he withdrew hardly less from that smaller world of dons and scholars in which he made his home. I have neither the data nor the intuitions to trace out here the psychological reasons which caused him to live so inwardly. I want to speak only of the poet, and of those aspects of the man which the poet somehow revealed.

Housman's death, though it meant something sentimentally to those who had been brought up on his poems, meant almost nothing to the life stream of poetry itself. For what he wrote bore no acute relation to our own times; and though he had imitators, what they imitated was not new and was not susceptible of becoming new in their hands. *A Shropshire Lad* has a slight period air about it and seems, if it belongs anywhere, to belong to the 1890's; but that is quite a different matter from the strict relationship of creative activity to a particular age, and of that strict relationship Housman's poetry never partook at all. At its first appearance it was already a minor classic, not simply because it was faultless in its kind, but also because it adhered to a few unchanging moods, a few emotional rather than intellectual truths.

As a result, and in keeping with the nature of such poetry, we have ourselves responded to Housman wholly by way of the emotions. Much has been written about his verse, but very little that was more than a way of expressing pleasure in it – very little, that is to say, which was really critical in method. A knowledge of his limitations perhaps tempered but never extinguished the emotional enthusiasm of those who wrote; and after all, how much was there to say? One could hardly tie him in with anything very original concerning life itself, or explain at great length a philosophy that was almost self-explanatory, or find special meanings in him that the rest of the world had neglected to find. When one has said that Housman was plainly a perfect poet, and just as plainly not a great one, one has gone far towards characterizing him. As time passes, it is not so much with men like Heine and Hardy, whose feeling he shares, that he will be grouped, as with men like Campion and Marvell, whose charm and artistry he recaptures.

A few things, however, remain to be said. Not much concerning his art, since all that has been said before. Still, to maintain perspective, one must say again of his art how delicate and evocative it is, how scrupulous and sometimes magical in its use of diction, rhythm, and cadence; how austere when there is reason for austerity. But, to pass on, something might be said about Housman's aloofness and something about his reaction to life – as they are revealed in the poetry itself – since to assess them is to come closest to assessing his scale of values, to discovering what his stature is as opposed to his style.

His aloofness was, of course, a condition of temperament and persisted long enough to harden into a condition of mind. He lived what passes for an austere life because he enjoyed a few fine and simple pleasures intensely, and others not at all. He had a severe, or at any rate a fastidious, taste, which means that he would have protested against most of life because it seemed contaminating before he would have protested against most of life because it seemed unsound. His rejection of first-hand living must finally be set down to too much aesthetic sensibility, to a kind of squeamishness. It kept him, as a poet, whole, but it also kept him undernourished; his purity survived at the expense of his humanity. The familiar moods deepened as he grew older, the 'cello note which is fugitive in his first book is much better sustained in his later ones; but we are simply made conscious of an older man and a maturer artist, not of a profounder thinker or a more experienced human being.

This aloofness, this sealed personality, of Housman's has cost him some of our adult allegiance; one's delight in his poetry is apt to be in some sense a hangover, a sentimental prolongation from one's youth. Those to whom he means the most are people, I should guess, of facile emotions and too little toughness of mind: even people whose feeling for literature, though sensitive, borders on the superficial. For the rest of us he has been much more of a pleasure than a need. As a poet he has remained magnetic, but as a philosopher he has been increasingly less persuasive.

T.S. Eliot has discussed the question of how far we can acquiesce, for the sake of the poetry, in a poet's ideas which on other grounds we should disavow. The point is opposite with Housman, whose sentimental fatalism does not always ring true to begin with, and is furthermore too indulgently and even gratuitously applied. When we are young, the overwritten pathos in Housman seems the most tragic thing in the world; but as we gain experience of life it seems – so self-inflicted, so almost graceful it has become – scarcely tragic at all. (What seems tragic is the suppressed emotion in the poet, but that is another and purely inferential matter.) When I read Housman today, particularly *A Shropshire Lad*, I find so many lads lying in so many graves and so much mortal beauty doomed, page after page, to fade, that sometimes it is more than just unconvincing; it is a little distasteful. Housman seems dangerously thin, which is very different from seeming minor. It is only the graver mood of some of the later poems, where a note is struck at once ironic and moving, that restores my faith in the poetic soundness of his philosophy.

Poems such as these best ones show the mark of true poetry, which must always be an equipoise of sound and sense, and which is another and better thing than true lyricism. At such times Housman transforms a way of thinking about life into a way of experiencing it, so that in the grip of a strong emotion – to revert to the point raised by Eliot – you simply ask no questions. These best poems have the perhaps accidental virtue of being impossible to parody or imitate, whereas the lightfoot lads, the young man hanged by moonlight, the crowns and pounds and guineas, are easy to parody – not just because of their lilt or their simplicity but because they constitute a manner of poetry rather than poetry itself. Whenever Housman rises from the sentimental to the elegiac, from the rueful to the stoic, his philosophy and his feelings both regain their dignity, and are helped on their way by a very great tradition; he has ceased to write, however skilfully, the kind of verses schoolgirls sigh over.

> The troubles of our proud and angry dust
> Are from eternity, and shall not fail.
> Bear them we can, and if we can, we must.
> Shoulder the sky, my lad, and drink your ale.
> [*Last Poems*; No. IX, stanza 7]

There you have Housman's whole outlook upon existence – the pessimism, the stoicism, the cynicism all compact; what to expect from life, what response to make, and in what manner to make it. At least the first two lines of this are fine poetry; but a note creeps in in the last two I could wish left out, a faintly British note of playing the game and not giving in on the job, an equally British note of asking no questions about it all, of going in for that mindless and stolid acceptance of things which diminishes suffering by ignoring it. No doubt this is a Spartan or Roman attitude; it also smacks a little of Sir Henry Newbolt;* and it does not save Housman, for all his fine sensibility, from a kind of soullessness. It is not like Hardy's pessimism, but rather like Browning's optimism turned inside out.

But a more formidable objection lies in the general meagerness of the philosophy itself. It speaks not of the suffering of someone who has striven as a person and fought desperately and failed, but of defeatism tied neatly with lyrical knots and bows. From the immense height of Housman's aloofness it would be almost comforting to see everything foredoomed. That is the unintentional, as opposed to the conscious, sentimentalism in Housman's work, and the result is that after much iteration we take it intellectually with a grain of salt. It has become as much a habit with him as a conviction.

His stature, then, is not great. By virtue of a certain poetic accent he comes close at times to the mood of great poetry; but he never plunges us into a world more spacious than our own, never breaks the graceful lamp that guards the naked flame. His real place is perhaps less with the poets I mentioned earlier than with the epigrammatists of the Greek anthology. Like them, he is intense but remote, pathetic but impersonal. The revelations of greater poets who stand rooted in a sense of reality which Housman feared and so came to disdain, the insight and audacity of those who were men before they were poets – of these things Housman gives us nothing, because he had nothing to give. His is a special charm, very potent of its kind; but it must be seen in its proper perspective.

NOTE

* It is interesting to note (and I have noted it only *after* writing these words) that during the war Housman was a vigorous patriot, and gave every cent of his savings to the government.

82. Lawrence Leighton, 'One View of Housman', *Poetry* (Chicago)

lii, May 1938, 94–100

This article was presented as a review of A.S.F. Gow, *A.E. Housman, A Sketch*.

More than half of Mr. Gow's book is devoted to a bibliography of Housman's numerous writings, almost entirely on subjects connected with classical scholarship. The few pages that list his work on English literature or more general subjects do not profess to be complete. Of more immediate interest are the fifty-odd pages that contain a memoir of the poet-scholar. The two men did not know each other until Housman went to Cambridge, and the treatment of the early years is slight. In the account of the later years attention is chiefly paid to Housman, the scholar. There is consequently no homage paid to the vulgar taste that is more interested in poets than in poetry. Yet occasionally in this book and more particularly in the small volume of anecdote and reminiscence written by his relatives and friends we can see the beginning of a Housman legend, a new creation, neither the man nor the poet, a treatment that has affected posthumously the two Lawrences.

The result is plain. The problems that are posed, if we permit them to be, by this personality are so perplexing to amateurs of soul analysis that, just as early admirers of Housman's poetry confused that poetry with their own personalities, so their successors will now confuse the poetry with the poet's personality, finding elucidation for the one in the other and becoming bad scholars and worse critics. And yet there is some justification for this. Housman's poetry needs finally a key, a key which can come only from our knowledge of the poet. This is really an indictment of the poetry, but to Housman it would not have seemed a defect. His own taste in English poetry was plainly a preference for that poetry which might be interpreted as personal statement. His formula, 'transfusion of emotion,' implies a communication theory of poetry in its most inchoate form. But most of us for whom poetry is a making or a creation, and not a communication, will find flaws in his work arising from the effort to communicate, and what others regard as code or incantation will seem bad workmanship.

If we could, we would avoid recourse to consideration of the person in our effort to make judgments about the poetry. At first sight it seems possible. The poetry seems to be there, bare and plain, obvious to inspection, inviting a quick approval or disapproval. And usually when in our youth we first read this verse we gave our whole-hearted approval. The forms are simple and traditional; they do not contradict the subject matter that they carry, nor do they require any extension of the normal reader's sympathy. The subject matter is general to mankind, the familiar topics of centuries of human experience. The style is easy and chaste; Wordsworth and the simpler romantic poets have trained our sensibilities to its ready acceptance. The symbols are coherent and concrete without obscurity. They make little demand upon any reader's erudition or ingenuity. As a result, Housman's audience was as wide and as acquiescent as any in the last half century.

But repeated reading brings confusion and question. The forms are simple, to be sure, but they are also mechanical. Four and five line stanzas are reiterated and arbitrary; the iambic and anapaestic movement becomes perpetual and boring. The frequency of feminine endings and the tight and heavy rhyme-schemes produce a monotony which makes us question the poet's extent of talent in simple verse-handling . Working as Housman did in short breathed lyrics – his longer poems are always the weakest – he was unable to create much interest or value by the structure of the poem. There is always little interior direction or movement, the last stanza has usually seen no advance or change from the first, except where there has been the surprise twist of the conventional epigram.

The subject matter is general and at the same time remarkably limited: 'Gather ye rosebuds,' suicide, military glory, the transitoriness of beauty and love, nostalgia, the certainty of death – in general, the tendency of the earth to revolve. These banalities, expressed by a banal technique, have grown out of an attitude that must be described as adolescent. The embittered Epicureanism, the pessimistic conception of destiny, the whine about the laws of God and man, all seem somewhat less than half a philosophy. The order that Housman created in his own experience rested upon categories that deny admission to most of human life. His wisdom is trivial, tricked out with a self-advertising stoicism.

The style is easy, but its very ease betrays its essential carelessness. The word that might startle comes rarely. The precise and unexpected word that might define the poet's intention and compel a readjustment of the reader's expectancy never occurs. Perhaps *Bring, in this timeless grave to throw* provides the few exceptions. Normally the reader is never required to dissolve long united connotations nor to create new combinations. He merely has to follow the poet in a usual groove. The 'transfusion of emotion' is actually only a reimpression by stereotyped words, phrases and ideas.

The symbols of Housman's poetry are concrete and coherent, but meaningless without an act of faith on the part of the reader. The gallows, sunset, scarlet uniforms, clay, the perpetual 'lads' and the occasional 'lasses' are irritating and banal. They are cinema-stuff, the residue of the tedious books we read and dreamed about in childhood. They operate only if we are willing to assume their validity, if we surrender reflection and merge with the illiterate. Notably the religious symbols (as in *The Carpenter's Son* and *Easter Hymn*) assume an attitude of conventional belief, and the intended shock can be secured only in that case. One must cite as an exception to Housman's usual symbolism *The Welsh Marches*. Here the symbol of the Saxon and the ideas of early England and strife that are evoked develop, obsurely but interestingly, the theme of the poem, internal conflict. The reader's imagination has been released and permitted to respond without prejudice. But normally Housman depends upon just such prejudice and his poetry consequently depends for its popularity upon mere fashion.

The predicament of the simple reader is plain. Here is verse which can excite and move him and which makes large statements that claim his faith. If he submits, however, to these claims he is in the end baffled, for the poetry does not justify its statements nor for all its apparent effect does it advance his understanding. The simple reader is unwilling or unable to realize that Housman has merely imparted rhythmical form and conventionally poetic diction to the reader's own chaotic, limited and banal experience. Consequently he hopes that there is something more, that this is poetry *à clef*, and that a biography will help matters out. But unfortunately neither Mr. Gow's memoir, pleasant reading though it is, nor other works of testimony by friends and relatives really help. Housman was reticent and solitary. There remain the gossip that circulates in common rooms and reviewers' articles and the dark hints of eventual revelations. The simple reader must be content with these.

But another problem arises for other readers even though its final statement may be in terms of the same elements. Housman was not only a writer of poetry, he was also one of the first scholars of the world. The three books of verse may be disregarded but the prose that constituted the great bulk of his writing cannot be. The prefaces to his editions of Latin poets and even his casual articles and reviews are the work of one of the few contemporary masters of prose writing. Here is excellent witwriting, a disciplined style that was perfect for its purpose and which transcended its purpose so as to make the minutiae of an *apparatus criticus* matters of immediate concern and delight to the least scholarly by-stander. Here the living emotions of hatred, scorn and contempt that were blurred and reduced in his verse have received their fit exposition and by the excellence of their form have become general to mankind. Here also when Bentley or Heinsius is named is the honest expression of admiration and love which were furtive and indefinite and impersonal in the poems. The qualities that make a great classical scholar, such as accuracy and saturation in a language and literature, have no necessary relation to the qualities of a poet, and there is no reason to believe that Housman's scholarship had the slightest connection with his verse. But it provided the substance for remarkable prose.

Housman declared that he was not a literary critic and *The Name and Nature of Poetry* proved that he was right. It is neither incisive nor persuasive; it is merely personal. However, his fragmentary parody of a Greek tragedy is actually excellent criticism, in large part of English translations, but also, in part, of Greek tragedy itself. Its implications as to what we really understand and appreciate in Greek tragedy are unpleasantly satirical. It suggests, as does the tone and structure of much of his prose, that his literary genius found wit and satire natural forms of expresion, and that it was alien to the romantic lyric.

Such a judgment involves what one would wish to avoid, a judgment about Housman's personality. Yet recourse to such aid is inevitable when one contemplates the discrepancies of his achievement. His experience, which seemed to him to require a sentimental expression, became whole only when he secured the comparative detachment of prose and satire. Further than that there is as yet insufficient evidence for analysis, and it is doubtful whether in any case the problem would be one for a literary critic. He plainly suffered from his ability to live in compartments; his knowledge of Latin poetry ought to have shown him the weaknesses in his own. He suffered also from the fashions of his time. Henley's *Invictus* had established a mode of self-assertion which received only slightly less blatant expression from Housman, and what passed for a philosophy in Hardy was plainly congenial. But he did not have Hardy's poetic skill, and his verse must serve simply as a belated document to illustrate that once popular phrase, *fin de siècle*.

83. Carl and Mark Van Doren, 'A.E. Housman'
1939

Carl Van Doren (1885–1950), prolific author and editor. Born in Illinois, he taught English at Columbia University from 1911 to 1930. His biography of Benjamin Franklin (1938) won a Pulitzer Prize in 1939.

Mark Van Doren (b. 1894, and younger brother of Carl) taught at Columbia University from 1920 onwards. He was a prolific author and poet, and compiled *The Portable Whitman*, *The Portable Emerson* and *The Best of Hawthorne*. His *Collected Poems* (1939) was awarded a Pulitzer Prize.

Reprinted from Carl and Mark Van Doren, *American and British Literature since 1890* (1925), revised and enlarged edition (New York: Appleton-Century, 1939), 166–70.

In 1896, just ten years after the appearance of Kipling, another and very different poet appeared who was recognized at once as a classic. A.E. Housman's 'A Shropshire Lad' contained only sixty-three short poems, and for twenty-six years the public had nothing else from his pen. In 1922, however, came forty-one 'Last Poems' which followed the others as naturally as if all had been written together; in 1936, the year of his death, 'More Poems' were published by his brother Laurence; and now that their author's whole mind has been offered to the world, he can be discussed as if he actually were a classic.

Housman is indeed as firmly established as he would be if his books had been written in Greece or Rome. His subjects are often the same melancholy ones that occupied the other poets of the eighteen-nineties – the shortness of life, the frailty of beauty, the cruelty of time – but he stands detached from his period because of his invariable excellence and because of the timelessness of his style. His poems also are pastorals – concerned with lanes and brooks and lads and lasses; while there is much unhappiness in his voice, it is a calm, clear voice, and there is no trace of the modern fret which is heard in the works of his metropolitan contemporaries. His landscape and his mood are universal, as those of the ancient Greek lyric poets were universal; and this is not altogether an accident in view of the fact that he was a classical scholar, a well-known professor at the University of Cambridge, most of whose time was spent in editing and examining the great literature of the past.

Housman's style is so light and sure, and his stanzas are so perfectly finished, that a reader is likely at first to miss the meaning and the passion behind them. There is a great deal of both meaning and passion. The poet's consciousness of the ravages which time makes in youth and love has brought an ache into his soul which does more than inspire a commonplace complaint. It is almost intolerable for him to think of the friends he once had, or the places he once dwelt in; but he must write about them because the memory of them presses upon him continually.

> With rue my heart is laden
> For golden friends I had,
> For many a rose-lipt maiden
> And many a lightfoot lad.
>
> By brooks too broad for leaping
> The lightfoot boys are laid;
> The rose-lipt girls are sleeping
> In fields where roses fade.

A good many of the poems are concerned with soldiers who have left their farms and gone off to be killed. But where Kipling was blustering and patriotic when he treated of soldiers, Housman is softly ironic. He knows only too well that the lives of his young men have been wasted, and the pity of this waste is strong throughout his work. Irony also compels him at times to tell the strict truth about battles. In one poem, for instance, he represents a fighter as keeping his position in the lines not because he is brave but because he knows he must die some time, and if he dies in battle he will have the best possible funeral at home. But the subtlest expression of Housman's pessimism comes in those poems which declare the futility of thought. If thought could make life better, it would be well; but it only confuses the thinker further.

> Could man be drunk for ever
>   With liquor, love, or fights,
> Lief should I rouse at morning
>   And lief lie down of nights.
>
> But men at whiles are sober
>   And think by fits and starts,
> And if they think, they fasten
>   Their hands upon their hearts.

This is not gay, as may at first appear, but immensely bitter.

Housman has added to English literature a beautiful and classical note of elegy. He has also contributed a few ballads which hold their own with the famous established ones. Those who are acquainted with the old British ballad called 'The Wife of Usher's Well' will recognize a certain resemblance in the following, particularly in the last two stanzas, wherein the speaker runs over in his mind the familiar details of home which he is about to lose forever.

> Farewell to barn and stack and tree,
>   Farewell to Severn shore.
> Terence, look your last at me,
>   For I come home no more.
>
> The sun burns on the half-mown hill,
>   By now the blood is dried;
> And Maurice amongst the hay lies still
>   And my knife is in his side.
>
> My mother thinks us long away;
>   'Tis time the field were mown.
> She had two sons at rising day,
>   To-night she'll be alone.
>
> And here's a bloody hand to shake,
>   And oh, man, here's good-bye;
> We'll sweat no more on scythe and rake,
>   My bloody hands and I.
>
> I wish you strength to bring you pride,
>   And a love to keep you clean,
> And I wish you luck, come Lammastide,
>   At racing on the green.
>
> Long for me the rick will wait,

> And long will wait the fold,
> And long will stand the empty plate,
> And dinner will be cold.

Even with that resemblance, the poem is original and great because it is the sincerest and most concentrated utterance of a rare, accomplished spirit.

'More Poems,' the volume left for posthumous publication, was impressive for its consistency with its predecessors. No modern poet has struck so high an average as Housman; none of his pieces is bad, and most of them are good. And many of them are little masterpieces.

> Alas, the country whence I fare,
>   It is where I would stay;
> And where I would not, it is there
>   That I shall go for aye.
>
> And one remembers and forgets,
>   But 'tis not found again,
> Not though they hale in crimsoned nets
>   The sunset from the main.

There is Housman still magical with rhyme and idea; and there he is still preoccupied with the theme of death. In a lecture published in 1935 [sic] under the title 'The Name and Nature of Poetry' he made it clear that poetry for him had never been a matter of the intellect merely. 'The intellect is not the fount of poetry,' he said. It is something more 'physical' than that, a 'secretion,' something which 'sets up in the reader's sense a vibration corresponding to what was felt by the writer,' something which in his case had bubbled up at certain moments rather than come as a result of taking thought. The essay is a perfect statement of the quality to be found in his own poetry. For that poetry is spontaneous if any ever was, and the response of any reader is as immediate.

COLLECTED POEMS
(1939, London; 1940, New York)

84. Bonamy Dobrée, 'The Complete Housman', *Spectator*

clxiv, 5 January 1940, 22–3

Bonamy Dobrée (1891–1974), educated at Haileybury and Woolwich, was first a career army officer (1910–19), then, after a degree at Cambridge, became a university teacher and a prolific scholar, editor and biographer. He was Professor of English in Cairo (1926–9), and at the University of Leeds (1936–55). Between 1929 and 1936 he published nearly a dozen books, and many others later. He also served in World War II, ending as a lieutenant-colonel.

There is so much that is poignantly topical in Housman's poetry that it is hard to see it dispassionately as poetry. A great deal of it has, certainly, a moving quality, but is it the poetry that is moving or something else? The question would have appeared pertinent to Housman himself, since he wrote in his delightful, inadequate, and infuriatingly perverse Leslie Stephen lecture, *The Name and Nature of Poetry*:

> I am convinced that most readers, when they think that they are admiring poetry, are deceived by their inability to analyse their sensations, and that they are really admiring, not the poetry of the passage before them, but something else in it, which they like better than the poetry.

And, indeed, it is notorious that it is possible at any time to like *The Shropshire Lad* [sic] and to be impervious to poetry; how much the more today, then, with Housman's insistence on the fleetingness of life, on the gallantry of youth, on disillusion, the bullet, the lonely bed, the grave.

No doubt Housman dealt in commonplace; much great poetry

does – in the great commonplaces; but it is not the meaning that matters so much; it is the voice it is uttered in. 'Meaning is of the intellect, poetry is not', to quote him again; and 'Poetry is not the thing said, but a way of saying it'. These are dangerous half-truths, but they give us a clue to the interpretation of Housman's poetry, and warn us that we must look for the meaning behind the obvious symbol: what his poetry expresses, we find, is the immense nostalgia of the faithless 'nineties such as we get in Hardy, and the disillusion which began to emerge at the agnostic beginning of the century:

[quotes *Last Poems*, No. XXXV]

The tremor and the fear we get in Housman – the hanged man was his symbol – is very old: 'When men think they fasten, Their hands upon their hearts'; nor is this typical of the romantic only, of Keats with 'Where but to think is to be full of sorrow', but just as much of the poets on whom Housman, presumably, was nourished: we think of *Pallida mors*[1] and *nobiscum semel occidit brevis lux*:[2] it is the old haunting fear, the old stoicism, the old dignified way of saying, Gather we rosebuds while we may.

The question we have to ask ourselves is whether Housman expressed this memorably enough, poetically enough, not merely in the manner which

> though it may differ from prose only in its external
> form, and be superior to prose only in the superior
> comeliness of that form itself, and the superior
> terseness which usually goes along with it

is called poetry: and here one must state the personal opinion that he sometimes did, especially when he confined himself to the simplest vernacular, and to perfectly rigid forms, as in the poem quoted. Often there is padding, clumsy inversion, 'poetic' diction which dates the thing: which is not the same as giving it the temper of the age, which Housman did in his best work. For in him the sentiments are not mere repetition: they are personal, as well as of his time, as all good personal work is.

It is a pity that he padded and expanded: sometimes, by adding an otiose stanza, he spoilt a piece as clean and 'diaphanous' as an epigram of Landor's; sometimes he created a sentimentality by a veriation in the form, adding, perhaps, a redundant line with a tag. Indeed, it was only by being metrically as severe as a Professor of Latin should be that he avoided sentimentality. Possibly, one imagines, it was in his poems that the man took revenge upon the Professor of Latin, the renowned textual critic, the redoubtable satirist of the superb *Preface* to Manilius. The man betrayed the professor, in the main to the advantage of the poet, though sometimes to his undoing. For at all events something distinct emerges, something memorable, something which, as you read it, 'goes through you like spear', though the seat of this sensation is not, as Housman said it was, the pit of the stomach.

Admittedly the gems are few. In spite of his contrary views about poetry, his own came from the mind through some emotional process: it had to have a meaning which appealed to the reader's mind through some recognisable emotion and some common symbol; and the complex had to be worked up under enormous pressure to produce the work of art. His poems are artefacts, not organic things. Yet every here and there, in a metaphor, a rhythm, a sudden turn of phrase, he captured something of the other kind of poetry, as when he spoke of the dead youth who

>   Has woven a winter robe,
>   And made of earth and sea
>   His overcoat for ever,
>   And wears the turning globe:

where we receive something like the Blessed Damozel's vision of the earth spinning like a fretful midge: for there, with that touch of metaphysical wit he so much despised, Housman burst the bounds of his own convictions, which it is good for professors from time to time to do.

NOTES

1 'Pale Death', the beginning of stanza 5 of Horace, Ode IV of Book I: 'Pale Death knocks with impartial foot at poor men's hovels and the palaces of kings.'
2 'As for us, once the brief light has set', from Catullus, *Carmina*, V.

85. Peter Monro Jack, 'A.E. Housman's Lasting Art', New York Times Book Review
17 March 1940, 1/16

No literary reputation of our time is more certain than Housman's. No poet is likely to be better and more constantly remembered. His feeling has become a language, his words a style, his music an absolute pitch of the magic of poetry. It will not do to say, as his publishers say, that when he died in 1936 he was 'universally acknowledged the greatest English poet of our day'. Two of his contemporaries were Hardy and Yeats. But Housman was certainly better known than either of these more various and more excellent poets, and he had been from the first more clearly distinguished in subject and style. Nothing that he wrote could be mistaken. Novelists who were far removed from his limited experience went to him for titles that meant much to them: 'Brooks Too Broad for Leaping', 'Shoulder the Sky', 'A World I Never Made'. Housman belongs with the poets who said their lines at their best, and only at their very best. The least thing that he said is remembered with the pleasurable sense of the way that he said it. He was a scholar also, and a critic, and perhaps even a philosopher, and whatever he learned he made use of; but from the first and finally he is the Shropshire Lad, the perfect poet of an imperfect world.

This edition of his collected poems has been expected and it is as good as one would wish it to be. It contains *A Shropshire Lad*, *Last Poems*, *More Poems*, and the additional poems printed in Laurence Housman's 'My Brother', with two new poems from manuscript and others from periodicals, and three early translations from the Greek. The chronology of the poems, as far as his brother could determine, is reprinted. No editor is specified, but he has been a good editor since no misprints – possibly for the first time in a Housman volume – are to be found. The light poems and parodies and nonsense verse, and the burlesque of Greek drama – all in Laurence Housman's book – are omitted, rightly enough. They can be found in his brother's informal biography. Amusing as they are, they do not belong with the serious work.

This definitive collection comes at a moment when there is a radical disagreement among the younger poets as to the social value of Housman's poetry. His world has been called a 'fancy' world, not realistic, not properly aware of the class struggle. His introspection and outlook are disliked: his gentle pessimism, his acceptance of the injustice of things, his resignation, his attempts at reconciliation; above all, his *sub specie aeternitatis* attitude toward human suffering, where the young critic looks for the economic causes and cures of the moment:

> The troubles of our proud and angry dust
> Are from eternity, and shall not fail.
> Bear them we can, and if we can we must.
> Shoulder the sky, my lad, and drink your ale.

It is understandable how infuriating it must be to the young poets and critics hot with revolutionary certainties to be told to shoulder the sky and drink their ale when confronted with the iniquities of our social system:

> Iniquity it is; but pass the can.
> My lad, no pair of kings our mothers bore;
> Out only portion is the estate of man:
> We want the moon, but we shall get no more.

This could be called the very decadence of nineteenth-century *laissez-faire*, the last tired voice of private failure in a new and noisy public world of arrogant and intolerant demands. If the critical imagination is restricted to a handful of ideological jargon masquerading as literary criticism this will do well enough to ridicule Housman and intimidate his admirers. Criticism of this kind – and there has been an approach to it – is utterly and fatally wrong, the worst critical aberration of the century, and in the end the end of poetry.

And yet it is, incredibly enough, the younger poets who are throwing away this living and shining heritage and earnest of their art. Evidently because Housman was neither a current communist nor fascist, nor social credit man, nor fellow-traveler, new dealer, Spanish-sympathizer, appeaser, Catholic, atheist, humanist – not even a yogi-man – evidently because his views did not coincide with this or that group of organized and militant opinion, because his private life was private and his public life limited to the public responsibilities that he had assumed, his poetry is suspect. Readers used to headlines and symposiums on 'What I Believe' are confused by this unusual and to them by now unnatural reticence. They immediately suspect something wrong, something pathological, as they did, for instance, with Emily Dickinson.

This resentment came to a head in a reprehensible poem by Mr. W.H. Auden, who had once written that

> Private faces in public places
> Are wiser and nicer
> Than public faces in private places

but who seems now to have changed his mind. The poem begins, 'No one, not even Cambridge, was to blame' – as if to take for granted that Housman's life had gone wrong, that something was to blame for it (the *not even Cambridge* is interesting of course, and a sort of private game: Housman was an Oxford man rehabilitated by Cambridge; Auden, also an Oxford man, is good enough not to blame Cambridge for whatever he thinks is the deficiency in Housman) – and as if some explanation and apology were needed for the poet. Mr. Auden is an unusually good poet himself, obviously the best, at his best, of his younger generation. He would be a better poet, and our critics would be more critical, if they merely read once again Housman's poems in these new covers instead of being amateur detectives or professional ideologists.

For Housman's poetry speaks for itself, clearly, traditionally, musically, movingly, and if we put our temporary prejudices aside, it speaks for all of us. That it is an English traditional poetry is true, and I should think, considering English poetry, that is in its favor; but I do not believe its origins have been sufficiently realized. The old Scottish ballad, the most simple and direct expression of experience ever known, is a sure test of Housman's excellence. The ballad of Marie Hamilton,

> Ah, little did my mither think,
> That day she cradled me,
> What lands I was to travel ower,
> What death I was to dee,
> Oh, little did my father think,
> That day he held up me,

> That I, his first and fairest hope,
> Should hing upon a tree

should be compared with Housman's

[quotes stanzas 1–3 of *Last Poems*, No. XIV, 'The Culprit']

noting the original and astonishing effect of the addition of the fifth line.

Shakespeare is in Housman with his 'golden lads and girls all must, as chimney-sweepers, come to dust', and in his 'Care no more to clothe and eat' ('Oh often have I washed and dressed'). Wordsworth's 'Rolled round in earth's diurnal course, with rocks and stones and trees' is remembered in Housman's elegy on Dick who 'wears the turning globe'. And Dr. Johnson, the epitome of the English character, has contributed his wisdom (as Pearson and Kingsmill have pointed out in 'Skye High'). Johnson speaking: 'Sir, sorrow is inherent in humanity. As you cannot judge two and two to be either five or three, but certainly four, so, when comparing a worse present state with a better which is past, you cannot but feel sorrow'. And now Housman singing:

> To think that two and two are four
> And neither five nor three
> The heart of man has long been sore
> And long 'tis like to be.
> [*Last Poems*, No. XXXV, stanza 3]

This traditionalism, so far from being a fault, is the best of Housman. In his own way and with a new music he has added to and advanced the cause of English poetry, bringing to it the perfection of its [*sic*] art. It may be, for all I know, the last perfection of its kind; it may quite likely be, as young men say, that Housman's lovely lines are no more than a melancholy echo of the past and a prescience of the death of all of us. To these appalling reflections has the state of the world reduced us, to distrust even the greatest art of poetry with which our civilization is bound! But we are becoming altogether too timid if we deny the courage and integrity of Housman's imagination, the beauty and discipline of his art. His 'fancy' world, his world of old-fashioned soldiers, ill-fated lads, annual cherry trees and perennial doubts, despairs and desires, is the world we inhabit — how marvelously and movingly mirrored in his poetry!

86. Stephen Spender, 'The Essential Housman', *Horizon*
i, No. 4, April 1940, 295–301

Stephen Spender (b. 1909), distinguished poet, critic and man of letters; author of *Poems* (1933), *The Still Centre* (1939), and many other books. Co-editor of *Horizon* from 1939 to 1941; later co-editor of *Encounter*. Made a CBE in 1962; knighted 1983.

Here are the collected poems of Housman — one hundred and seventy-five poems, and three short translations of Greek Choruses. Of these, seventy poems were not published during the poet's lifetime, and one may guess that he would certainly have wished the greater number of his posthumously published poems to have been suppressed.

Anyhow, the publication of *More Poems* and *Additional Poems* disposes of any idea that Housman may have burned or concealed a great many poems that would have extended the range of his poetry. The posthumous poems are interesting, but on the whole they do him a disservice, because although they contain beautiful lines, and even whole poems as good as many he wrote, they say in a cruder form, which sometimes amounts almost to parody, what he had said before, and they do the one thing which Housman must have wanted to avoid doing — heighten the reader's curiosity about the biographical background to his poetry.

If one starts thinking of Housman's poems in this way, one can go on trimming and paring away poems around a fairly well-defined core which one might call the Essential Housman, of perhaps less than fifty poems, in which Housman really says all he has to say. The remainder of the poems are slight, or attempts to say something which he conveyed better in other poems, or else introductory ornaments, like the opening poems in *A Shropshire Lad* and *Last Poems*.

At his best, Housman is a poet of great force and passion whose music is quite unforced, combining sensuousness with a cold discipline which gives the poetry an almost anonymous quality of being something said rightly, rather than something said by someone:

> A Grecian lad, as I hear tell,
>   One that many loved in vain,
> Looked into a forest well
>   And never looked away again.
> There when the turf in springtime flowers,
>   With downward eye and gazes sad,
> Stands amid the glancing showers
>   A jonquil, not a Grecian lad.

When one recalls how this stanza is contrasted with the stanza that precedes it, nothing could be more admirable and yet spontaneous than the organization of these lines. The repeated word 'looked', the lingering of the fifth line, the effectiveness of 'downward' in the sixth line, and then the pause with the word 'stands' are all uses of language so appropriate that the lines seem to spring from the scene they describe. The same may be said of another poem in *Last Poems*, No. XXXIII, which begins:

> When the eye of day is shut,
>   And the stars deny their beams,
> And about the forest hut
>   Blows the roaring wood of dreams,
>
> From deep clay, from desert rock,
>   From the sunk sands of the main,
> Come not at my door to knock,
>   Hearts that love me not again.

To the end of his life Housman could write lines which have a resilient leaping quality, like 'The blue height of the hollow roof,' in poem XV of *Additional Poems*.

Housman wrote some great poetry if not great poems and no criticism can lessen the value of certain lines and whole poems which have an independent rightness and certainty which is beyond comment. All criticism can do is to attempt to define the range of his poetry, and say whether the pessimistic philosophy which he advances repeatedly in poem after poem is an adequate attitude towards life.

Housman's poems have properties as defined as the machinery of diabolism in Baudelaire: the countryside of Western England, the lads who are brave and true, the references to the ancient world, the stilted and firmly established imperialism. Within this environment, there springs a poetry which has three main sources of inspiration: a frustrated love, a passion for justice, equally frustrated, and the view that life is misery and that man is only happy when he is safely under the ground.

Ultimately, the whole of Housman's pessimism and sense of injustice springs from the idea of frustrated love:

> He, standing hushed, a pace or two apart,
>   Among the bluebells of the listless plain,
> Thinks and remembers how he cleansed his heart
>   And washed his hands in innocence in vain.

The young, the straight, the true, the brave, gain nothing from their virtue; they are shot just the same, and the world is so vile a place that they are happiest dead: 'Let us endure an hour and see injustice done.'

This frustration is best in its purest form when it expresses a complete despair, as in 'When the eye of day is shut.' At other times it is merely suicidal, as in dozens of these poems, and at others it becomes ludicrous:

> Now in Maytime to the wicket
>   Out I march with bat and pad:
> See the son of grief at cricket
>   Trying to be glad.
>
> Try I will; no harm in trying:
>   Wonder 'tis how little mirth
> Keeps the bones of man from lying
>   On the bed of earth.

If one compares Housman's love poems with those of Donne,

one sees how inadequate his rejection of love and hence life is. In Donne we feel that the poet has tasted deeply of life, and that while he is still tasting it, it turns to ashes. In Housman, we feel that he had a youthful disappointment on which he constructed an edifice of personal despair and bitterness which lasted a lifetime. For Housman himself this disappointment may have been tragic, but it is not valid as a judgement by which the whole of life, or even the life of the senses can be condemned. The effect of Donne's poetry is to make one feel that life is haunted by the sense of death and guilt; the effect of Housman's, after one has reached a certain age, merely to make one feel very sorry for Housman.

The nature of Housman's disappointment is revealed in these lines:

> Because I liked you better
> Than suits a man to say,
> It irked you, and I promised
> To throw the thought away.
>
> To put the world between us
> We parted, stiff and dry;
> 'Goodbye,' said you, 'forget me'.
> 'I will, no fear,' said I.
>
> If here, where clover whitens
> The dead man's knoll, you pass,
> And no tall flower to meet you
> Starts in the trefoiled grass,
>
> Halt by the headstone naming
> The heart no longer stirred
> And say the lad that loved you
> Was one that kept his word.

The idea of death simply as a negation of life is very strong in Housman. The idea of the city that is not, the young man who is not, the lover who is not,

> The pale, the perished nation
> That never see the sun,

recurs again and again in this purely negative form. For him there is just life and not-life. Death, as he points out in one of his poems, is the same as not having been born.

Death the negation of life, ill the negation of good, injustice the negation of justice, everything in Housman's poetry exists side by side in a pure and undiluted form, with the balance, of course, always on the side of the bad, because there is bound to be more death, more evil, more injustice in the world at any given moment than the reverse. He rather grudgingly admits:

> ... Since the world has still
> Much good but much less good than ill,

and in another poem, he sees everywhere the quantities of:

> Horror and scorn and hate and fear and indignation.

His puritanism is of a kind which is always very close to death not in a religious sense, like Donne or the Elizabethans, but in a pseudo-scientific sense, like Aldous Huxley's novels, simply because there is so much death and corruption about. But this means that life too ceases to be positive and becomes merely a feeble little effort to pretend, with cricket balls, footballs, sex, Shropshire, etc., that it is worth doing, when to the honest man it must be evident that nothing positive has any virtue because of the immense surplus of what is not which denies and frustrates it the whole time.

Housman once compared himself with T.E. Lawrence. One of the qualities he must have shared with that other great scholar – though he did not indulge it to the same extent – is surely a shrinking from publicity combined with an almost violently censured tendency towards exhibitionism. Both Housman and Lawrence throw out a kind of double legend which is probably the shadow of a double personality. The one legend is of a severe, puritanical, repressed, passionately single-minded, integrated personality, one who has looked evil fearlessly in the eyes, is master of his destiny. The other legend, of which Lawrence and Housman both disclaim all responsibility, is of a mysterious and withdrawn personality, who not only has a secret clue to his passional life, but to whom also something has definitely happened at some period in his life which will not happen again. Both writers evidently want the mystery to remain a mystery. At the same time they cannot help throwing out hints and using the second unofficial legend of the mystery-man to add intensity to the first legend of the man who is stifling his personality. One side of

Housman censured the posthumously published poems; but the other side scored a victory in writing them at all; moreover this second Housman managed to insert numerous dark hints to puzzle generations of Wykehamists in *Last Poems*, and even in *The Shropshire Lad* [sic] itself.

Why are there two sides to Housman's poetry? I think it may be that Housman recognized the inadequacy of his philosophy of life, and wished to reinforce it with special pleading in defence of his own personal situation. This opens out another possibility: that he might have thrown aside the role of repression altogether and written a poetry which explored his own personality. But this would have involved accepting far more of life than he was willing to accept.

There is another writer with certain affinities to Housman who did this; that is Gerard Manley Hopkins. He also was a writer who was for ever at war with one side of his personality, but he did not reject and disown it and condemn the whole of life on the strength of it as Housman did. Comparing Hopkins and Housman, one sees the superiority of the Catholic environment to the Protestant and Puritan. In Hopkins there is a continual struggle, there is not a blank refusal and an enforced silence. Housman had what is called 'integrity', Hopkins had honesty and audacity. Hopkins's poetry is that of a man who struggles with life and illuminates more and more life in the process. Housman's is that of a wonderfully mummified and preserved everlasting young man, like one of his narcissistic lads who stands for ever by the stream and looks at his image in the waters.

87. Louis MacNeice, review, *New Republic*
cii, 29 April 1940, 583

Louis MacNeice (1907–63), classicist and poet, son of a Church of Ireland clergyman who in 1931 became Bishop of Cashel and Waterford. His first volume of poems, *Blind Fireworks*, appeared in 1930. During the 1930s he was a

A.E. HOUSMAN

lecturer in Classics/Greek, first at Birmingham University, then at Bedford College, University of London. From 1941 to 1961 he worked for the Features Department of the BBC.

It is a great pleasure to have all of Housman's poems assembled in one handsome volume rather than dispersed in thin waifs of books whose very appearance exaggerated their author's aloofness and narrowness. The *Collected Poems* consists of *A Shropshire Lad*, published in 1896, *Last Poems*, published in 1922, *More Poems*, published almost immediately after the author's death in 1936, and 'Additional Poems', which had so far only appeared in Laurence Housman's memoir of his brothers [sic]; of work hitherto unpublished in book form there are three translations of Greek choruses (lapidary but Roman rather than Greek in tone) and one or two not very remarkable original poems. What is exciting about this book is its cumulative effect – Housman's verse throughout his life shows an extraordinary identity of mood. In 1905 he began a poem about a lover deserting his beloved for the wars; he finished it in 1922; the mood and attitude still held good for him and the poem is a unity. While technically he maintained a consistently high level, *Last Poems* is in my opinion a better collection than *A Shropshire Lad* because less dominated by the pseudo-pastoral element. His admirers still refer chiefly to these two collections, but the other two sections of this book make valuable additions to the picture. There is the same brilliance of phrase – 'lamps in England lighted, and evening *wrecked* in Wales', there are further fine examples of lyrical epigram, and there is one poem which, from a man who believed in slavery, is a welcome concession to social conscience – 'they're taking him to justice for the colour of his hair' [sic].

Housman was a paradox. An austere and uncommonly bitter recluse, he wrote verses which were uncommonly popular with everyday people, while it was his basic pessimism, his actual antipathy to life, which gave such life to his work. It is a mistake to think of him as a 'simple' poet; the simplicity is often bluff; his very directness, like his regular music, is ironic. There were already many examples in English of the poignancy of a statement so simple as to sound almost naive, in Cowper for example:

> But I beneath a rougher sea,
> And whelm'd in deeper gulphs than he.

Housman varied this naiveté with a grand manner – a more pompous metric and a diction involving archaisms and poeticisms – but this too was usually redeemed by the quality which the Romans called *salt*. In one respect the last of the Romantics, he was also, owing to his salt (more than a grain of it), a precursor of that new classicism heralded by T.E. Hulme, of a dry, hard poetry which should rely on fancy rather than imagination. Thus his trick of ironic juxtaposition, as shown in the poem 'The fairies break their dances' was an anticipation of what T.S. Eliot did on a wider scale with less deference to the reader.

Housman's own remarks about poetry in 'The Name and Nature of Poetry' (1933) were not only unsound but did not agree with his practice. In renouncing meaning and plumping for the magic of pure music and imagery he would have cut away the ground from the Shropshire Lad. Admittedly the meaning, the beliefs, behind *A Shropshire Lad* are a pretty thin meaning and rather reprehensible beliefs when abstracted from the poetry, but without them the poetry would be dead; even a poor spark will start a fire but you must have a spark of some sort. His example of Blake as a poet of magic and no meaning was badly chosen; Blake's lyrics have body just because he had so much meaning, though that meaning may not be logically formulated or always comprehensible by reason. And Blake, like Housman himself, had a strong strain of epigram (which is the distillation of meaning):

> The prince's robes and beggar's rags
> Are toadstools on the miser's bags.

Housman was also inconsistent both in attacking the 'wit' of the seventeenth century and in excluding the eighteenth century from poetry because it was too intelligent. His own work is full of play upon words or ideas and often has the varnish of Latin rhetoric.

Psychologists could discover a fascinating dialectic in him – stoic and epicurean struggling and canceling, the ascetic scholar dreaming of stolen waters, the rationalist fighting the nonsense poet. It is significant that he wrote nonsense verses (they are not represented in this book); Mr. Edmund Wilson in a very interesting article has put him in a group of English solitaries which includes not only Colonel Lawrence but Lewis Carroll; nonsense poetry was the last efflorescence of the Romantic nostalgia for the home we never had. The 'folk' element in *A Shropshire Lad* is a reflection of the same impulse; his Shropshire is largely myth. As for his soldiers they are on much the same plane as the figures in Yeats's twilight; the nineties had to look around for legend.

88. John Peale Bishop, 'The Poetry of A.E. Housman', *Poetry* (Chicago)

lvi, June 1940, 144–53

John Peale Bishop (1892–1944), American poet, educated at Princeton, contemporary and friend of F. Scott Fitzgerald. After service in World War I he became managing editor of *Vanity Fair* and, until 1933, divided his time between France and the United States. His *Collected Poems* were published in 1948.

I

Now that the *Collected Poems* are out, we have all we shall ever know of A.E. Housman's poetry. The long silence that followed *A Shropshire Lad* was broken by Housman himself in 1922, when he brought out his *Last Poems* while, as he said, he was still there to see them through the press. He died in 1936. And later that same year *More Poems* were published by Laurence Housman, who after a little decided that he could, without violating the wish of his older brother that nothing be printed after his death that was not up to the average level of what had already appeared, produce twenty-eight *Additional Poems*. Their number is now thirty-three, three of them rescued from old magazines, two from the poet's papers. To these have been appended three translations from the Greek, made long ago for an anthology of odes from the Greek dramatists. The remaining manuscripts and notes have been destroyed. The way in which Housman's poetry has been published is marked throughout by his passion for distinction, his craving to be famous, his equally strong and perverse dislike of being known.

The posthumous poems will not much change the estimation in which Housman has been held. They are work worthy of that proud mind. The *Additional Poems*, while they increase the sum of his poetry, add no poetic quality that was not there before. This they could hardly do, for it is apparent from the list of dates, incomplete as it is, which Laurence Housman has allowed to be included in the present volume, that they were composed along with the poems we already know. Some of them are contemporaneous with *A Shropshire Lad*; the latest, as far as anyone knows, is from 1925. What they do is to let us see the poet plain. Now that we have his poetry whole, we know what his personal plight was, and that is bound to affect our reading of all the poems. To know 'Oh who is that young sinner with the handcuffs on his wrist?' is to know something that we should have known all along about those culprits of *A Shropshire Lad*. We have known and long known those hanged boys who hear the stroke of eight from the clock in the tower on the market place and never hear the stroke of nine. We know now for what crime all of them have been condemned. We have known when the noose went round their necks, but not whose head stood above the rope. They have many names and all have one name. Their features are not beyond recognition. The head is A.E. Housman's.

Romantic poetry as Housman received it was in need of correction. He corrected it. The romantic conflict of man against society, of man against immutable laws is still there, but presented by a man who had the classic craftsman's respect both for himself and his craft. The form is concise and accurate; but for all their lightness, his poems never lose the sense of earth, for all their grace, they are tough enough to sustain a considerable irony. The limits within which Housman was able to feel at all were strict, but within them he felt intensely, and both strictness and intensity are in his verse.

His style has in it nothing strange. It is not conventional; it is extremely careful never to affront conventional ideas of what a poetic style should be. The truth was quite strange enough. Poetry that pardons the poet nothing less than the truth, once the truth is assured, pardons him everything. The passion for truth was in Housman. He could, in his poetry, condemn himself as contemporary opinion – in the very year *A Shropshire Lad* was written – had condemned Wilde. When almost all others had abandoned him, Housman sent Wilde a copy of *A Shropshire Lad* to prison; Wilde's answer was *A Ballad of Reading Gaol*. But it was not only on account of the poet that Housman had to consider prison; there was someone else, whom he had known more closely, confined. His death is recorded in *The Isle of Portland*. Housman could go beyond imprisonment; not once, but many times, he sent his culprit straight to the scaffold. For whatever was will and conscience in Housman was conservative. It was on will that his career was founded and it was continued with a conscience as scrupulous as it was churlish, so that he could end, Kennedy Professor of Latin at Cambridge, all honors at his disposal and all declined. He was quite ready, if not willing, in his career as in his style, to conform outwardly to convention. For both career and style are masks.

'While I was at the Patent Office I read a great deal of Greek and Latin at the British Museum of an evening. While at University College, which is not residential, I lived alone in lodgings in the environs of London. *A Shropshire Lad* was written at Byron Cottage, 17 North Road, Highgate, where I lived from 1886 to 1905.'

This, as it stands, is honest enough; but, as so often happens in what Housman wrote, behind the straightforward statement there is much that is not said. In 1892, Housman had been able to return to that academic career, from which he had been uncomplainingly banished ten years before, when, at Oxford, he had failed to obtain honors in the final School of *Literae Humaniores*. Alone he had done it. His gifts that were to make him the most formidable Latinist in England had never been in doubt, not even as a boy, when he had been the terror of his classical masters lest he should ask them some questions they were not prepared to answer. By his studies published in learned reviews, he had made himself known as he was willing to be known, as a scholar with that minute and accurate knowledge of the classical tongues which, as he said, affords Latin professors their only excuse for existing. He was not yet the great scholar he was to become, but the greatness of his qualities had been recognized wherever men cared for these things and, what is perhaps more important, he had himself already correctly appraised them.

About this time something happened to Housman that was not in accord with his will. What that was, there is no way of knowing, or even when it happened, unless from his poetry. *A Shropshire Lad* includes no poem written before 1890; the greater part of it was written in the first half of 1895. Whatever that experience was, whether he had been prepared for it at Oxford, as there seems some reason to suppose, or whether it came to him unexpectedly in London, it was profound and fatal. It was followed, as we know, by great emotional perturbation. It left Housman a poet. 'And I think that to transfuse emotion – not to transmit thought but to set up in the reader's sense a vibration corresponding to what was felt by the writer – is the peculiar function of poetry.' Alfred Housman in 1895 was thirty-six years of age.

II

No matter where we open Housman's poems, we are almost sure to be struck with how young are those who suffer in them, how brief and sure their suffering, its course predictable, since all has been known before:

> These, in the day when heaven was falling,
>   The hour when earth's foundations fled,
> Followed their mercenary calling
>   And took their wages and are dead.
>
> Their shoulders held the sky suspended;
>   They stood, and earth's foundations stay;
> What God abandoned, these defended,
>   And saved the sum of things for pay.

Whatever the occasion that gave rise to them, these moving lines can scarcely be read without bringing to mind the part played by the professional soldiers of the British Army in the retreat from Mons. They are called, however, simply *Epitaph on an Army of*

Mercenaries, and as they stand are as applicable to the soldiers of some desperate and remote army in some forgotten war of antiquity as they are to the men of 1914. Here, a particular situation has produced a tragic emotion; whatever is lacking we can supply, so that the event behind the lines is adequate to the emotion. But this is not always so in Housman. If – to follow Joyce's excellent and convenient definitions – pity is present in poetry whenever what is grave and constant in human sufferings is united with the human sufferer; terror, whenever what is grave and constant in human sufferings is united with the secret cause; then pity and terror should scarcely be lacking from anything that Housman wrote. And pity and terror do not lack in this noble and completely successful poem. And yet, in Housman's poetry as a whole something is lacking. Despite an apparent clarity such that almost any poem seems ready to deliver its meaning at once, there is always something that is not clear, something not brought into the open, something that is left in doubt. Housman knew very well what he was doing. He could always put himself in the reader's place. You must, he wrote his brother, 'consider how, and at what stage, that man of sorrows is to find out what it is all about. You are behind the scenes and know all the data; but he knows only what you tell him.' What Housman told the reader is clear. But there is much that he would not, and while he lived could not, tell him. Of the suffering we have no doubt, but something it seems has been suppressed that it is essential to know of the particular situation of the human sufferer. There is an emotion here that is unaccounted for. It is apparently united to the secret cause.

> Ay, look: high heaven and earth ail from the prime foundation;
> All thoughts to rive the heart are here, and all are vain:
> Horror and scorn and hate and fear and indignation –
> Oh why did I awake? When shall I sleep again?

There is much here that is moving: but again the essential is not evident. Sophocles also believed that a man's best fate would be never to be born and, failing that, it were best for him to perish young. But Sophocles' pessimism does not, as Housman's seems to do, exist in a void.

The passion of the lad on the scaffold is made appallingly present to us; but for what crime he is being punished is not, in any of the poems in which he occurs, made clear. What had he done, that other lad who lay dead, never to rise, never to stir forth free, to be sent to the island where

> Black towers above the Portland light
> The felon quarried stone?

Or those lads so in love with the grave, why are they so attracted to that unfeeling solitude? It is not enough to blame the primal fault. Death has its attraction, and it is possible for a poet to put it in a moral framework so that we know, not only how strong it is, but its motivation. Yeats has done it, not once, but many times. But in Housman we move so rapidly from the personal situation to an impersonal despair that we cannot but feel that something has been left out. What has been left out is his personal plight, which did not find a perfect solution in poetry and probably could not, so long as no place could be found for it in any moral scheme of which Housman's mind could approve. The facts are clear; the meaning is not. 'Even when poetry has a meaning, as it usually has, it may be inadvisable to draw it out,' Housman wrote. 'Perfect understanding will sometimes extinguish pleasure.'

It is possible that Housman did not want his meaning drawn out; but about that I am not certain. Perfect understanding of his poems depends upon knowledge of his personal plight, for until that is known, the emotion must seem in excess of its object. Now that we know from the posthumous poems what that plight was, all slips into place. The despair is explained; the scholar's abandonment of Propertius for Manilius; the reticence that at last seemed to fix his mouth in a perpetual snarl; the churlish silence which made the poet who had written the poems which above all others in our time have been loved into the least lovely of men. There is point to his philosophy. And we are at last in a position to understand the special pathos of *A Shropshire Lad*.

III

What Housman did in *A Shropshire Lad* was not to create an object of desire. That he had found, presumably in London, and none can doubt the intensity, the reality, the impossibility of his love. What he did was to make himself into a proper lover, or at least into one of an appropriate age, and to create in a country called Shropshire conditions where that love – without ceasing to be what it was – could come into its own. He became young, but with such a youth as he had never known. The hands which for almost twenty years had scarcely left their Greek and Latin texts, were put to the plow. He was a young yeoman, complete with an ancestry which Housman made up, perhaps without knowing it, since he seems presently to have persuaded himself that it was his own. The heart of the youth was his, the temper was his own, and, what is most remarkable, the voice he found for him had the vibration of very youth.

The country of *A Shropshire Lad* is so created that it is with surprise that we learn, not only that Housman was not native to Shropshire, but that he had seldom been there. But once we begin to think about it, we see, not only that no such countryside exists in England, but that there could have been none like it in the last century. It is a country that belongs to the dead. What was important to Housman about Shropshire was that it lay on the western horizon of the Worcestershire in which his own boyhood was passed. The West has long been in popular imagination where the dead dwell, and, at the very time that Housman was writing, English soldiers did not die – they went West.

> Comrade, look not on the west:
> 'Twill have the heart out of your breast;
> 'Twill take your thoughts and sink them far,
> Leagues beyond the sunset bar.

It is the underworld. And to Housman with his mind on the classical poets, it is probable that the West is identified, not only with their underworld of the nerveless dead, but also with a classical world, long dead, in which loves such as his would not have found all the laws of God and man against them:

> Look not in my eyes, for fear
>   They mirror true the sight I see,
> And there you find your face too clear
>   And love it and be lost like me.
> One the long night through must lie
>   Spent in star-defeated sighs,
> But why should you as well as I
>   Perish? gaze not in my eyes.

If we love at all, it is because our bodies, if not we, anticipate death for us. But in this poem of Housman's it is to be noticed that the loved one can, like the lover, love himself and that if he should once be attainted by that desire, he would perish. In the two lovers identity of desire is possible, but the identification of love with death is prompt and precise. Just as in *A la Recherche du Temps Perdu*, Proust's narrator has never such conviction of completely possessing Albertine as when he sits motionless by her side and looks at her lost in sleep, so, in Housman's poetry, there is no complete consummation of desire until the lad he loves lies dead. The body that lust demanded must be all bone and contemplation before he is finished with fear and condemnation. Even then, Housman cannot delude himself into believing that any love, least of all a love like his, can long survive on the contemplative satisfactions of the grave.

> Crossing alone the nighted ferry
>   With the one coin for fee,
> Whom, on the wharf of Lethe waiting,
>   Count you to find? Not me.
>
> The brisk fond lackey to fetch and carry,
>   The true, sick-hearted slave,
> Expect him not in the just city
>   And the free land of the grave. [sic]

To Housman, all loves are frustrate or faithless. The best a girl can do is to listen to a boy's lies and follow him into the leafy wood; the best the boy can do there is not work her ill. The conception is, of course, prejudiced. Still, what Housman sets down is not so far from the actual conditions under which love is made in youth. The youth Housman reverted to was an imaginary one, and it is precisely because he was true to the imagination that he seems so often to speak, not merely for himself, but for all who are, or have ever been, young. What we should know from our own responses to Housman's poetry, if we have not already learned it more explicitly from Proust's prose, is that such desire as his, while it differs from others in its object, is most painfully distinguished from them by the brevity of time in which it is possible, even as unrequited desire. The youth's garland is always briefer than a girl's. And it is this constant presence and inescapable pressure of time that constitutes the special poignancy of Housman's poetry.

But if his personal plight is responsible for much of the poignancy of the emotions that went to the making of Housman's poetry, it also placed serious limitations on his emotions. And what nature had not limited, Housman himself thwarted. He is the poet of the end of an age in England and he is the best poet that could be produced at the end, as he is probably, in England, the purest poet of the whole age. His range is small. We have only to look largely at poetry to see that there is an honesty, a humanity, that simply is not in Housman, any more than it was in the world that made him. What was left in that world was enough for him to perceive how impossible is the achievement of all desire, how vain the search for honor and happiness, and yet what pathos, what beauty, what grandeur even, man releases in their vain pursuit.

89. Morton Dauwen Zabel, 'The Whole of Housman', *Nation* (New York)

cl, 1 June 1940, 684–6

Morton Dauwen Zabel (1901–64), scholar and critic; associate editor of *Poetry* (Chicago) (1928–36). From 1929 to 1946 he was professor and chairman of the English Department of Loyola University, Chicago, and from 1947 Professor of English at the University of Chicago.

The letter quoted at the beginning of Zabel's essay (A.E. Housman to Laurence Housman, 14 December 1894) can be found in Henry Maas (ed.), *The Letters of A.E. Housman* (London, 1971), 31–4. Zabel's page numbers, later, indicate the following poems: *A Shropshire Lad*, Nos. XV, XLIV,

XLV; *Last Poems*, No. XIV; *More Poems*, No. XXVIII; 'Additional Poems', Nos. VI, VIII.

In 1894 A.E. Housman, having been given a manuscript of his brother's poems to read, sent that prolific author a minutely detailed criticism that included the following sentences:

What makes many of your poems more obscure than they need be is that you do not put yourself in the reader's place and consider how, and at what stage, that man of sorrows is to find out what it is all about. You are behind the scenes and know all the data; but he knows only what you tell him. It appears from the alternative title 'Heart's Bane' and 'Little Death' that in writing that precious croon you had in your head some meaning of which you did not suffer a single drop to escape into what you wrote: you treat us as Nebuchadnezzar did the Chaldeans, and expect us to find out the dream as well as the interpretation.

The irony here requires no italics. Two years later Housman published the book that sped his fame through the English-speaking world. *A Shropshire Lad* caught the pathos of its generation; its accents of loss and regret are fixed in the consciousness of all modern readers, and its croon has been judged sufficiently precious; but the grimly disciplined poignance that forms its claim and appeal to the world, though sometimes quavering towards intimacy or revelation, remained to the end of Housman's life masked and inscrutable.

That inscrutability was the mark and habit of his character. By the age of thirty-seven he had set his back implacably on the vivacity of spirit that had once made him a stranger to his relatives. Ten years of drudging service in the Patent Office had passed like a slow purgatory, varied only by solitary labour under the gas lamps of the British Museum, where he won the mastery of classical texts that was rewarded in 1892 by the Latin professorship at the University of London. Long before he reached the middle of his road, Housman had withdrawn into the secret fastness of his nature. Robinson alone among modern poets offers a comparable figure of mute austerity; Conrad's abrupt check to intimacy or confidence in his personal writings becomes almost genial by contrast. 'Can you get him to talk? I can't!' cried Robert Bridges on one occasion; and when Housman was told that

A.E. HOUSMAN

Wilfrid Blunt, speaking in his diaries of a visit from the poet, had said, 'He would, I think, be quite silent if he were allowed to be', he answered, 'That is absolutely true'.

Silence is the initial condition of Housman's poetry, as it was the token of a painful diminution of personality that befell him at the outset of adult life. His verse was set from the beginning, by an almost violent mandate, in a fixed and deliberate mold. It offers no characteristic modern pattern of growth, experiment and discovery. Only Hardy's shows as undeviating an identity from first to last. His distance from the great poets of tragedy or pessimism – agonized, rebellious, impressionable – is great: not only from Baudelaire, Verlaine and Villon, for whom he expressed a distaste, or from Heine, whose continuous influence brought so little of the German's critical wit and exhilaration into his lyrics, or from Arnold and Hardy, whom he admired above all his contemporaries, but from Pascal and Leopardi, those two stricken witnesses of the dark abyss and the frightening heavens, whom he 'studied with admiration' and whose anguished vision and starlit shudders are sometimes caught in his own finest songs. Beyond any of these brothers in darkness he stifled his agony before the mystery and fatality of life. His lyrics speak from the threshold of silence itself. Had their discipline become as absolute as the one he imposed on his practical emotions, his poems would have receded wholly into the reserve that marked Housman's outward character.

That discipline was as final as any poet, short of the defeat of his gifts, could make it. Housman's first problem as a lyrist was to perfect a form and language exactly expressive of the extreme mandate of will he imposed on his sensibility. He once admitted Heine, Shakespeare's songs, and the Border ballads as his models but was 'surprised' at the imputation of Latin and Greek influences. But these cannot be slighted. Housman's whole temper, recognizing its suspension between an active poetic impulse and a willed surrender of it, between an instinctive fervor for life and a tragic denial of its value, sharpens toward irony, seeks resolution in the ambiguity of epigram, and tends to express the ingrowth of its forces and the tension of its faculties in a salient virtue of the Latin lyric style – its integrity of structure, its verbal and tonal unity, its delicate stasis of form. What it gave him – as did the Elizabethans, among whom he once called Jonson his master – were the interlocking balances and inversions of phrase, the distributed reference in nouns and pronouns, the hovering ambiguity of particles, the reflexive dependence of verbs and subjects that give his stanzas their tightness and pith. Had he coerced a purely modern and explicit English into these structures he would have produced a language continuously – instead of intermittently – stilted. But here one of his strongest sympathies came to his rescue – his love of folk speech. The aphoristic tang and irony of peasant idiom, grafted to the sophistication of the Horatian style, relaxed his temper, freed it from formulated stiffness and cliché, and gave Housman his true and single medium as a poet – a verse style marked by a subtle irony of tragic suggestion, a tensile integrity of phrasing, a sense of haunting human appeals played out against the grim inexorability of law. In that medium, rising above the inertness of a formula and the desperate repression of his impulses, he wrote his finest poems.

These, now that his work stands complete, now appear in some of his most quoted lyrics, those that cast his thought into the inflexibly didactic form that is always the bane of a negative temperament. The lesser Housman, the one most vulnerable to parody, imitation, and personal attack, is seen wherever his lyric style hardens into such inflexibility and his pessimism into the hortatory despair that becomes by inversion sentimental. Originally, it appears, Housman had an extremely uncertain taste in words and meters. He was fond of the singsong lilt or chant used in rather tawdry and superficial poems like Atys, The Land of Biscay, and 'Far known to sea and shore'. Of Atys ('Lydians, lords of Hermus river, Sifters of the golden loam') he once said that he was so fond of the rhythm that he always doubted the merit of any poem in which he succumbed to its attraction. He came to guard himself from that music as he guarded his emotional impulses from the appeals of common life and friendship. At both ends of his narrow lyric range, as at both ends of his emotional character, he exercised a ruthless vigilance: here from the spontaneity of feelings that had to be canceled, there from the violence of a censorship so strong that it could end not merely in silence but in emotional paralysis and the logic of suicide. Recoiling from instinctive music or feeling, he produced poems of an opposite extreme: of a deadly and inverted romanticism, of a pessimism so imperative and bare of realistic qualities that they produce a repellent travesty of his talent. Here the Latinized concentration bristles with guards to emotion, and starkness of vision becomes as cloying as the lines in which he rings changes on the ale, the lads, the night, the noose, and the gallows to the point of comic surfeit. It appears at its worst in 'Think no more, lad', The Welsh Marches, 'Say, lads, have you things to do', 'Others I am not the first', 'The Laws of God', 'Yonder see the morning blink', The Immortal Part, and The Culprit. The authentic part of his talent demanded escape from confines as laming as these, and it is only when he gives some voice to the instinctive delight of his senses, to memories of lost youth, or to responses to nature, that he arrives at the finer sincerity of 'With rue my heart', 'On Wenlock Edge', 'Far in a Western brookland', and The Merry Guide. He succeeds best of all when the repressed emotion becomes externalized, released from an iron-clad vigilance, adopts a dramatic mask or situation, and so takes on the life and pathos of genuine lyric realism: when, in Bredon Hill, Hughley Steeple, 'Is my team plowing', 'To an athlete', ' I to my perils', 'In valleys green and still', and 'With seed the sowers scatter', he resolves the hostilities of his nature to their finest delicacy and harmony, avoids both the curt asperity and the occasional Aeschylean pomp of which he was capable, and contributes exquisite poems to the English lyric tradition.

They succeed, moreover, in revealing and relaxing the enigmatic nature of the man who wrote them and in dissolving the contradiction that gave him his quality as a character. They make credible the tyrant of Latin texts who could flay rivals or sycophants alive, yet who led a life of painful loneliness and who, given evidences of affection, described their effect as 'almost overwhelming'; the solitary who called himself a Cyrenaic but who favored Epicureans above Stoics; the critic who disliked democracy and defended slavery but who protested the tyranny of the laws of God and man and pleaded for the felon taken to prison 'for the colour of his hair'; the man who enjoyed bitterness and kept notebooks carefully indexing his vituperations but who saw himself in T.E. Lawrence's words as stricken by 'a craving to be liked – so strong and nervous that ... the terror of failure in an effort so important made me shrink from trying'; the recluse who was contemptuous of comfort and flattery but who told a young American admirer, 'Certainly I have never regretted the publication of my poems. The reputation which they brought me, though it gives me no lively pleasure, is something like a mattress interposed between me and the hard ground.'

He was complex obviously and an eccentric certainly, a personality of laming deficiencies and self-persecuting logic; a lyric artist of the most limited order. He lends himself almost naively to J. Bronowski's attack (in 'The Poet's Defense') as a victim of inverted sentiment from whose 'welter of standards' little emerges but a cancelation of feelings almost antiphonal in regularity and as a self-belittler who took evasive refuge in negations of life, of emotion, of the nature and meaning of poetry itself. Housman's admirers have done him the disservice of blind adulation; his detractors, with the added cooperation of his own perverseness and inconsistency of temperament, will go to inevitable extremes. There are even severer measures of his stature. The cry of despair has sounded in modern poetry, as in ancient, with an anguish but also with an illumination that Housman seldom or never attains. 'Wer wenn ich schriee, hörte mich denn aus der Engel Ordnungen?'[1] 'Selfwrung, selfstrung, sheathe- and shelterless, thoughts against thoughts in groans grind.' 'I must lie down where all the ladders start In the foul rag-and-bone shop of my [sic] heart'. 'L'Irréparable ronge avec sa dent maudite Notre âme.'[2] Of the protest, intensity, and courage of these castings down of spirit he dared little, and his loss in range and force of character is inevitable.

Yet as we now see Housman in his full stature, as the obscurity of his temperament begins to wane, so also the exacerbation of his emotion and his evasion of responsible feeling begin to take on the alleviation of what at its best becomes a subtle and ennobling lyric dignity, a mastery of selfhood and of style that surmounts the imposed denials of his life and the implacable tragedy he saw there but, having seen and faced it, refused to disguise from himself. What the tragedy was is too much a part of the complex of his nature and his poems to bear crude expression, but this much he makes unmistakable: it was his realisation that he was destined to live a life deprived of human love. That fact, implicit everywhere, is written clearly enough into the poems on pages 28, 66, 68, 114, 187, 221 and 233. Whatever irresolution exists in his book is a reflection of the contradiction imposed on his faculties by nature itself; the pervading frustration resulted from an intelligence that permitted no blinkers before the fact. But concealed in Housman's nature, masked by his forbidding exterior and his scholarly isolation, existed the true stuff of the poet, once free and impulsive but surviving even its later curtailment, and he was strong enough to make of that conflict the strength and charm of his poems. The science and realism that permit us to see the errors or defects of men also impose the responsibility of understanding them. Outside his poems Housman made that understanding difficult enough, and even inside his verse the slightest comparison with Baudelaire and Hopkins, Yeats and Rilke, immediately gives the measure of his lower station. Yet if he ate of the shadow so long that he became something of a shadow of a man, he at least refused to lapse into sullen silence over the whole wretched business of existence. His endurance was the sign of his character, and the lyrics he wrested from grief and discipline are the marks of his true, if minor, genius. He is one of the most complete instances in literature of the man determined to live by will alone, and his lyrics too often reveal what the discipline of will does to a poet. Yet the discipline was real, and its reward came when his suppressed forces broke from him in the form of an exact and exquisite art. It saved him from languor and annihilation, and in the complete book of his songs, standing between the perils of sense and insistence of death, are the lyrics that hold their permanent beauty. They sufficiently redeem his title as a poet and bring to mind what his friend A.C. Benson once said in assaying the talent of Edward Fitzgerald, a fellow-sharer with Housman of the melancholy shadows of life:

The process of estimating the character even of the best of men must be of the nature of addition and subtraction. It is the final total that is our main concern... There can be little question on which side the balance lies. We may regret the want of strenuousness, the overdeveloped sensibility, which led him to live constantly in the pathos of the past, the pain of the contemplation of perishable sweetness. But we may be thankful... that the long, quiet years were not misspent which produced, if so rarely, delicate flowers of genius. To enrich the world with one imperishable poem, to make music of some of the saddest and darkest doubts that haunt the mind of man – this is what many far busier and more concentrated lives fail to do... To touch despair with beauty – this is to bear a part in the work of consoling men, of reconciling fate, of enlightening doom, of interpreting the vast and awful mind of God. Truth itself can do no more than hint at the larger hope.

NOTES

1 'Who if I cried out would hear me from the orders of angels?'
2 'The Irreparable gnaws our soul with his accursèd tooth.'

90. Benjamin Gilbert Brooks, 'A.E. Housman's Collected Poetry', *Nineteenth Century*

cxxviii, July 1940, 71–6

It is unlikely that A.E. Housman will make anything like the appeal to present-day youth that he made to the youth of 1900 or of 1914. But why? What contributed in the first place to the really startling enthusiasm which *A Shropshire Lad* seems to have aroused during the two decades that followed the first printing of 1896? It certainly was not at all the same feeling as that which led the young bloods of *New Verse* to search their souls, or at least their hearts, during his obituary period, in justification of a writer whom one would so easily have expected to find them treating with contempt. Housman's verse seems to have had the happy knack of supplying the critics and readers of several generations with just some special detail of their own particular confection, always in such restricted proportions as never really to queer his chances with the next comer, but yet sufficiently to make them feel that they lose no standing by accepting him as an ancestor.

The 'poetic' reasons for accepting Housman seem to have died away with the Georgians: but apparently the personal and psychological reasons made him of even greater interest to the later schools. It is hard not to feel kindly towards a man who, however reactionary and woolly his technique, was actually known to have bought copies of modernist magazines, and the inner conflict which raises its head everywhere, and which finds explicit expression in *The Welsh Marches*, was bound to endear him to our modern collectors of case-book items. Perhaps on the whole, both for those who remember it, but still more, I believe, for that incredibly large number of people who actually suffered from it, that early enthusiasm remains a mystery. I recollect being myself charmed by a vigorous appraisement of the poems towards 1916, and yet feeling uneasily at the time that they must have in them, apart from their actual obvious content, something, some power of suggestion, some consonancy in mood with that of the critic, which might explain what he said. There is no doubt that among the influences which served to stiffen the rather vague poeticality of the Georgians lay very firmly that of Housman. So that, if it is not blasphemy to set these names in juxtaposition, he seems to have occupied the place, along with Bridges and Hardy, now accorded to Hopkins and Mr. T.S. Eliot.

Housman, on his appearance in the 'nineties, presented a special and unusual combination of the elements of poetical life then current. His classical training gave to his poems a certain rigidity and formality of construction, a power of compression, and at the same time of conveying elaborate situation within such compression, that belongs to Latin verse. This tendency, reaching his contemporaries through the less direct tradition of French poetry, had with them become modified on the way to an intense concentration on a small and neat perfection. But Symons, Dowson, and even Lionel Johnson, generally associated it with material or mood which had too local a colour to carry its readers outside the decade itself. The influences of the *fin-de-siècle* fashion for painting delicately idealised pleasures of the town, or for exploiting and echoing the faint nostalgias of the Symbolistes, of Swinburne, or of O'Shaughnessy, were of the past rather than of the future. But while the turn of the century took away any meaning *they* might have had for new poets, Housman's complete lack of charm and his relative directness acted as a preservative.

He also appealed to the current mood of pessimism that demanded for its full expression the adoption of some unfortunate local area such as Wessex, or in this case Shropshire, and the forcing upon it of an unhappy pastoral convention. In doing this he had at his call the growing public which was admiring both the imitation Maupassants of the period, and the native-bred novelist of the calibre of Hardy, and which had been previously taken with 'the laureate of pessimism' – James Thomson, the author of *The City of Dreadful Night*. What made his pessimism the more acceptable to a generation which was already coursing afar under the bright but varied banners of Kipling, Shaw, Wells, Chesterton and Belloc, was probably not these associations, but the fact that, like Leconte de Lisle, Housman drew his pessimism in draughts from the fountain of the Classics, and that, like Baudelaire, he wrote at times with a harsh and rhetorical vigour. And both these things fitted in quite reasonably with that deference to French taste that characterised the period generally.

Finally, in phrase, he appealed to the ears that first licensed that peculiar deformation of the written language which is associated with cheap newspaper journalism, and which had already been giving its distinctive colouring to the verse of Kipling. He seems often to go out of his way to use always the less living words, those that have been most smeared over, as if he found, indeed, in the absorption of cliché into his texture, or in the invention of phrases which have just the right non-conducting unsuggestiveness of cliché, the very best material for some of his most typical effects. 'The hilly brakes,' 'the forsaken west,' 'the woodland brown,' 'the autumn dale,' 'blowing realms,' 'high-hilled plains,' 'trefoiled grass,' 'whispering night,' 'sceptre-shaken world,' 'the sands of eve' – all these are picked at hazard from well-known poems that have made Housman's reputation. But what do they mean? They, and a host of others, are just things talked about, not impressions conveyed. And it is to be noted that this employment of cliché has not the artistic justification of the younger modern poets, who reflect with these blemishes their own impatience with a world which can present itself to their consciousness only as cliché. It is simply, as style, second-hand. A generation that has absorbed the technique of the Imagists cannot away with it. Yet Housman's classical training encouraged him in this very mannerism. For it demanded what seemed to him the same sort of generalisation of experience.

The style, then, depended very little on that keen sensibility to the sensuous aspects of nature which gave its peculiar and enduring tone to Victorian poetry. Although simple in some ways, it has none of the limpid and fluid simplicity of Swinburne's long lines, except for No. XLVIII of *A Shropshire Lad*:

Earth and high heaven are fixt of old and founded strong.

Historically it seems to be more definitely connected with the Church hymn, and it is quite conceivable that he was unconsciously directing himself at the one form of non-utilitarian literary expression through which it was possible to assail that new and strange reading public of the 'yellow press' of the 'nineties.' Some of his most striking poems seem indeed, from the technical point of view, to depend upon nothing more than the deft balancing and forceful organisation of what in isolation might have been thought very conventional phrasing. But what such unpromising elements could be made to achieve is well illustrated by the famous *Epitaph on an Army of Mercenaries*, grandiose in its rhetoric, capable of producing an unforgettable effect, and undeniably great.

The spiritual world of A.E. Housman behind this carefully constructed façade is at times strangely unsophisticated. For him as an artist, whatever he may have believed as a scholar, a tragedy is simply a sordid or catastrophic happening, and to invest his incidents with sufficient atmosphere he works up an elaborate and artificial pastoral terminology of 'lads' and 'carts' and 'cans' and 'gallow-trees,' a society whose denizens go 'listing for a Lancer,' or knife each other gloomily, with a short abrupt line at the end of each stanza to make their dismissal more brief. His greatest success is in conveying, in spite of these artificialities, the crisis or pith of the story in the very minimum of words. All through, the essential thing is the presentation of the people and their actions. There is the same epigrammatic clarity about the story in *The Fairies Break Their Dances* as in No. XXV of *A Shropshire Lad*, where we have sufficient detail respecting Fred, Rose Harland, and 'I' for us to be able to develop a genre novel out of the situation. Here, indeed, the colloquialism, often presenting an unhappy and false note in Housman, does just what is required – indicates the social milieu, and hardens the emotional tone.

The concentration on murders and hangings and sudden deaths belongs very definitely to the world of the uneducated sensationalists for whose pleasure the new journalism of the 'nineties' catered. Housman, in these poems, may be considered as giving some sort of acceptable art form to the popular taste in news, much as Coleridge did to the broadside ballad, Kipling to the Music-hall ditty, and Masefield to the Salvationist's 'testimonial.' Actually the passion for the sordid was one which declared itself quite strongly in the 'nineties' and had the sanction of Zola and Verlaine. Most of the poets kept it for their lives, or better still their legend, and wrote the delicate music for their poems. Only Wilde and Housman touched on really sordid aspects of human nature, and by comparison one must concede that the latter did not fall into the defect of romanticised sentimentalising. *Eight O'Clock*, No. XV of *Last Poems*, is worth pages of *The Ballad of Reading Gaol*. Neither have any significance beside Villon, but in the former we have a complete mastery of the technique of words and rhythm, used for a single dramatic moment, and freed for once of the artificiality that mars the poems on similar melancholy themes in the more characteristic metre.

It is an unlucky business for a poet when he happens to have laid down with some cogency a general theory of his art. He perhaps feels it to be very sound in his own case, and his readers may feel it to have an added value as coming from one who has himself struggled through to some recognisable public success. But it frequently comes about that by his own standard he is condemned. In all its detail one would not apply this comment to Housman. But there is no denying the fact that the term 'glorious words' as a justifying summary of the essential element in song, and the idea that song might normally take its rise in that rather equivocal moment when the physical heaviness of a digesting meal and the glowing and mellowing haze of the postprandial pint have combined with the regular rhythmical surge of the motions of walking, are suggestions that contain in themselves material for the complete cancelling-out of his own inspiration.

For the words are, on the whole, not 'glorious.' They are at best but a classically trained writer's threadbare imitations of words which he realised once to have been 'glorious.' Housman in *The Name and Nature of Poetry* quoted several of those more or less meaningless wonders which stand near the highest points of English literary expression. By comparison, phrases such as 'The chestnut casts her flambeaux,' 'The half-moon westers low, my love,' 'Wake not for the world-heard thunder,' 'West and away the wheels of darkness roll,' 'By shores and woods and steeples,' 'Delight it is in youth and May to see the morn arise,' are recognisably 'pseudo.' On the other hand, if the 'song' owes its inspiration to a certain state of the digestive system – and, within certain limits, one is not averse to accepting the possibility in a general sense – then, what becomes of all the importance Housman attached to the philosophical aspect of his poems? That Housman did attach such importance is clear from the Baudelairean moment when, after the prim wit, the artificial almost Georgian colloquialism and the strained phrasing of the concluding references to Mithridates in 'Terence this is stupid stuff,' he proceeds in No. LXIII of *A Shropshire Lad* to give just the same subject-matter – the justification of his method – in the very tone of the French poet, even to the use of the flower imagery.

Housman provides a type of poet in some respects out of the ordinary. In his earliest work he presents his material in an undifferentiated form. His characteristic dramatic situations, his emotional atmosphere and his philosophical thought co-exist in practically all the poems of his first volume. Normally one expects the poet to synthesise the elements of his art as he develops greater control. But here we have an increasing differentiation, until in the later books we find a very clear-cut division between certainly the emotional and the philosophic elements. On the one hand we have work which is purely lyrical, and which exhibits that playful and frivolous handling which one expects in the lyric. An outstanding example of this is *Fancy's Knell*, No. XLI of *Last Poems*. Here, there is the delicate and light touch of the pastoral symbolism, the neat lilt of the old-fashioned air and the ripe and easy perfection which sets it with Blake's *The Echoing Green*. On the other hand we have an increasingly numerous development of the gnomic type of verse, a type which with Housman conforms definitely to Classical model. It is probable that among the latter are to be found most of the poems that receive admiration to-day, since Housman seems to have replaced Kipling as the poet of the Traditionalists. But the former, beautiful as they sometimes are, and shot through with his pessimism, seem to reveal a freedom of mood and an artistic responsiveness to emotion far enough away from the sort of poetry that originally gave Housman his fame.

91. Cleanth Brooks, 'The Whole of Housman', *Kenyon Review*

iii, Winter 1941, 105–9

Cleanth Brooks (b. 1906), distinguished 'New Critic', author of such classic texts as *Modern Poetry and the Tradition* (1939) and *The Well-Wrought Urn* (1947). He taught at Louisiana State University from 1932 to 1947, when he became Gray Professor of Rhetoric at Yale. From 1935 to 1942 he co-edited, with Robert Penn Warren, the *Southern Review*.

The reference to Randall Jarrell at the end of Brooks's review is to Jarrell's article 'Texts from Housman', published in *Kenyon Review*, i (1939), 260 – 71: it closely analysed *More Poems*, No. XXIII, and *A Shropshire Lad*, No. XVI.

The appearance of the *Collected Poems* provides an occasion for making some tentative generalizations on the total value of Housman and his work, though a note so brief as this can hardly pretend to go beyond suggestion.

First, there is the matter of Housman's basic attitudes, his world view. Actually, I believe that the pessimism of Housman's poetry is pretty closely related to that of Bertrand Russell, his Cambridge contemporary – say, to that of the famous purple patch in Russell's 'A Free Man's Worship': 'Brief and powerless is Man's life; on him and all his race the slow, sure doom falls pitiless and dark. Blind to good and evil, reckless of destruction, omnipotent matter rolls on its relentless way, etc., etc.' Here are to be found all the elements of the Romantic despair which possesses Housman's young soldiers, shepherds, and athletes: the helplessness of man in an alien universe, the stoicism, the Spartan courage, the Romantic bravado.

Frank Harris records in one of his essays that Housman protested that he had not meant '1887' to be taken as irony at the expense of Queen Victoria and Victorian imperialism. It is possible that he did not (though it will be impossible for most readers of that fine poem not to feel such irony as a necessary and valuable ingredient of the experience). If Housman's poetry seems to show a continual thrusting at Victorian optimism and conventionally held ideals, there are still other poems sufficient in number to indicate that Housman had no special animus against the commercialism and imperialism of his times. The Shropshire lad, far from teeming London, finds evil all about him, the necessary accompaniment of human life.

Yet a rereading of the mass of Housman's poetry indicates that Housman had no ambitious or even passionately held world view to set up. Intellectually, he has not moved far past an austere scepticism; emotionally, one feels that he has a special and 'literary' interest in the pathos of the passing of first love, the parting of friends, the loss of youth, the unpredictable and meaningless death – he is interested in them for their own sakes. Indeed, the intellectual fabric is so slight that one feels that his impulse borders on the literary and his performance occasionally hovers on the verge of the sentimental. In any case, one can understand why his *Name and Nature of Poetry* should have turned out to be a rear-guard action fought against the modern enemies of Romanticism, with some not very carefully disguised thrusts at Cambridge contemporaries like I.A. Richards and F.R. Leavis.

The late professor of the classics is essentially a romantic poet, and no amount of talk about classic influence, classic lucidity, etc., should delude us into thinking him otherwise. It is no accident that another Cambridge contemporary, F.L. Lucas, in his *Decline and Fall of the Romantic Ideal*, should again and again put Housman's poetry within what he calls the magic triangle bounded by Romanticism, Classicism, and Realism.

It is not difficult to see why Housman should appeal to Mr. Lucas. The difficulty is in explaining why some of his poems should also appeal to us. I think that we can bound his talent with a different set of terms: (1) his irony, when it commits itself firmly as in '1887':

> To skies that knit their heartstrings right,
>   To fields that bred them brave,
> The saviors come not home to-night:
>   Themselves they could not save...

(2) his understatement, when it does not degenerate into self-

conscious smirking; (3) his use of symbolism, when timidity does not force him to label the symbol; and (4) his use of metaphor, when he will use it wholeheartedly.

Suppose we state Housman's essential method as Mr. Lucas might have stated it for him: 'Housman takes the ordinary theme, and then, by a faultless choice of words and by the practice of a beautiful simplicity, makes us fasten our hands upon our hearts.' Fair enough. But on what principle is the selection based? And may not the simplicity be more exactly stated as 'economy' and a 'sense of understatement'? The selection is 'faultless' just in proportion as it succeeds in dramatizing the theme with sharp contrasts, revitalizing it with fresh perceptions (inevitably by means of metaphor). And as for economy – is not the essence of economy in poetry the exploitation of metaphor?

If these propositions are true, one is allowed to see how much handicapped was the poet who distrusted irony and wit as smacking of the unpoetic intellect (see *The Name and Nature of Poetry*), and who distrusted the obscurity of metaphor to the point of reducing it to the clarity of abstraction. That is why Housman, in his weaker poems, is flat and thin. Even so fine a poem as 'Bredon Hill' is flawed by Housman's fear of the obscurity inherent in metaphor. In this poem, death is described as a bridal – and effectively. Yet even here, Housman finds it necessary to explain the metaphor to his reader:

> They tolled the one bell only,
>   Groom there was none to see,
> *The mourners followed after,*
>   And so to church went she,
>   And would not wait for me.

It is in the bolder poems, where the poet triumphs over the restrictions of Victorian decorum, that one finds the Housman that will endure. Consider the following passages: Poems XXV of *A Shropshire Lad* ends thus:

> Fred keeps the house all kinds of weather,
>   And clay's the house he keeps;
> When Rose and I walk out together
>   Stock-still lies Fred and sleeps.

Poem XX of *Last Poems* ends:

A.E. HOUSMAN

Fall, winter, fall; for he,
Prompt hand and headpiece clever,
Has woven a winter robe,
And made of earth and sea
His overcoat for ever,
And wears the turning globe.

Both poems attempt to accommodate the grave to the commonplace and the domestic, and thus their irony. But in the first the explanatory 'And clay's the house he keeps' comes perilously near robbing the fine 'Fred keeps the house all kinds of weather' of its effect. The second passage with its full commitment to the metaphor and its triumphant assimilation of the domestic and realistic 'overcoat' is rather unusual for Housman. The first passage is nearer his norm.

If Housman's desire for simplicity sometimes makes him flat and obvious, the fault is frequently of a different kind: a too self-conscious archness. But like the first, it too is an aspect of Housman's difficulty in handling the witty and the ironic. Many of Housman's poems seem to be epigrams softened in the direction of the romantic and the 'poetic.' As a consequence, a number of his poems are oddly suggestive of Dorothy Parker or Edna St. Vincent Millay. This is especially true of some of the poetry which Housman did not choose to publish in his life time, but which has been included in this volume. Consider, for example:

> From the wash the laundress sends
> My collars home with ravelled ends;
> I must fit, now these are frayed,
> My neck with new ones London-made.
>
> Homespun collars, homespun hearts,
> Wear to rags in foreign parts.
> Mine at least's as good as done,
> And I must get a London one.

Even the poems which aim at an effect of laconic understatement sometimes fail in the same way. For all their surface hardness and toughness, they discover themselves, on second glance, to be pretty and at worst sentimental. 'With Rue My Heart Is Laden' is 'pretty' – in the bad as well as the good sense of this word. Or, consider 'Could Man Be Drunk Forever.' The poem ends thus:

> But men at whiles are sober
> And think by fits and starts,
> And if they think, they fasten
> Their hands upon their hearts.

Obviously, the poem works by insisting on a studied understatement. The men on whom the melancholy impinges are not mooning sentimentalists – they are lusty, red-blooded fellows, no strangers to 'liquor, love, or fights.' They betray their feelings by no outcry, no lamentation – only by the almost instinctive gesture, made before their self-possession masters their actions once more. But if the reader is not too easily beguiled, if *he* thinks, he will find the gesture not an understatement at all, but melodramatic and theatrical; and this effect is not softened by the choice of the word 'fasten' and the emphasis which the poet places upon it.

Housman is not the perfect minor poet. Real poetic power he undoubtedly possessed; and he has left us a small number of fine lyrics. But everywhere upon the body of his work is the evidence of limitations imposed upon his essential genius by a conscious aesthetic which was crippling to it. The proof of this, it seems to me, is that you cannot defend the best effects of his poetry in terms of the critical position laid down in *The Name and Nature of Poetry*. Those effects can best be described in terms of the wit, irony, and even 'conceit,' which Housman consciously repudiated; or in terms of such 'ambiguities' as Mr. Jarrell has ably discussed in an earlier issue of this *Review*. We must be grateful for good poetry, however it is come by. Some of the poems that Housman wrote are very good indeed. But the best of his poetry seems to me poetry achieved in spite of the immediate tradition out of which he wrote.

92. George Orwell on Housman
1940

George Orwell (1904–50), born Eric Blair, was educated at Eton, and served in the Indian Imperial Police in Burma from 1923 to 1928; journalist, essayist, novelist, most famous for *Animal Farm* (1945) and *Nineteen Eighty-Four* (1949).

An extract from Section II of 'Inside the Whale', first published in *New Directions in Prose and Poetry* (1940). Reprinted from *The Collected Essays, Journalism and Letters of George Orwell* (Penguin edition, 1970), i, 550–4.

When one says that a writer is fashionable one practically always means that he is admired by people under thirty. At the beginning of the period I am speaking of, the years during and immediately after the war, the writer who had the deepest hold upon the thinking young was almost certainly Housman. Among people who were adolescent in the years 1910–25, Housman had an influence which was enormous and is now not at all easy to understand. In 1920, when I was about seventeen, I probably knew the whole of *A Shropshire Lad* by heart. I wonder how much impression *A Shropshire Lad* makes at this moment on a boy of the same age and more or less the same cast of mind? No doubt he has heard of it and even glanced into it; it might strike him as rather cheaply clever – probably that would be about all. Yet these are the poems that I and my contemporaries used to recite to ourselves, over and over, in a kind of ecstasy, just as earlier generations had recited Meredith's 'Love in a Valley', Swinburne's 'Garden of Proserpine', etc. etc.

> With rue my heart is laden
> For golden friends I had,
> For many a rose-lipt maiden
> And many a lightfoot lad.
>
> By brooks too broad for leaping
> The lightfoot boys are laid;

The rose-lipt girls are sleeping
In fields where roses fade.

It just tinkles. But it did not seem to tinkle in 1920. Why does the bubble always burst? To answer that question one has to take account of the *external* conditions that make certain writers popular at certain times. Housman's poems had not attracted much notice when they were first published. What was there in them that appealed so deeply to a single generation, the generation born round about 1900?

In the first place, Housman is a 'country' poet. His poems are full of the charm of buried villages, the nostalgia of place-names, Clunton and Clunbury, Knighton, Ludlow, 'on Wenlock Edge', 'in summer time on Bredon', thatched roofs and the jingle of smithies, the wild jonquils in the pastures, the 'blue, remembered hills'. War poems apart, English verse of the 1910–25 period is mostly 'country'. The reason no doubt was that the *rentier*-professional class was ceasing once and for all to have any real relationship with the soil; but at any rate there prevailed then, far more than now, a kind of snobbism of belonging to the country and despising the town. England at that time was hardly more an agricultural country than it is now, but before the light industries began to spread themselves it was easier to think of it as one. Most middle-class boys grew up within sight of a farm, and naturally it was the picturesque side of farm life that appealed to them – the ploughing, harvesting, stack-thrashing and so forth. Unless he has to do it himself a boy is not likely to notice the horrible drudgery of hoeing turnips, milking cows with chapped teats at four o'clock in the morning, etc. etc. Just before, just after and, for that matter, during the war was the great age of the 'nature poet', the heyday of Richard Jefferies and W.H Hudson. Rupert Brooke's 'Grantchester', the star poem of 1913, is nothing but an enormous gush of 'country' sentiment, a sort of accumulated vomit from a stomach stuffed with place-names. Considered as a poem 'Grantchester' is something worse than worthless but as an illustration of what the thinking middle-class young of that period *felt* it is a valuable document.

Housman, however, did not enthuse over the rambler roses in the week-ending spirit of Brooke and the others. The 'country' motif is there all the time, but mainly as a background. Most of the poems have a quasi-human subject, a kind of idealized rustic, in reality Strephon or Corydon brought up to date. This in itself had a deep appeal. Experience shows that over-civilized people enjoy reading about rustics (key-phrase, 'close to the soil') because they imagine them to be more primitive and passionate than themselves. Hence the 'dark earth' novels of Sheila Kaye-Smith etc. And at that time a middle-class boy, with his 'country' bias, would identify with an agricultural worker as he would never have thought of doing with a town worker. Most boys had in their minds a vision of an idealized ploughman, gypsy, poacher, or gamekeeper, always pictured as a wild, free, roving blade, living a life of rabbit-snaring, cock-fighting, horses, beer and women. Masefield's 'Everlasting Mercy', another valuable period piece, immensely popular with boys round about the war years, gives you this vision in a very crude form. But Housman's Maurices and Terences could be taken seriously where Masefield's Saul Kane could not; on this side of him, Housman was Masefield with a dash of Theocritus. Moreover all his themes are adolescent – murder, suicide, unhappy love, early death. They deal with the simple, intelligible disasters that give you the feeling of being up against the 'bedrock facts' of life:

> The sun burns on the half-mown hill,
> By now the blood is dried;
> And Maurice amongst the hay lies still
> And my knife is in his side.

And again:

> They hang us now in Shrewsbury jail:
> The whistles blow forlorn,
> And trains all night groan on the rail
> To men that die at morn.

It is all more or less in the same tune. Everything comes unstuck. 'Dick lies long in the churchyard, and Ned lies long in jail.' And notice also the exquisite self-pity – the 'nobody loves me' feeling:

> The diamond drops adorning
> Thy low mound on the lea,
> These are the tears of morning,
> That weeps, but not for thee.

Hard cheese, old chap! Such poems might have been written expressly for adolescents. And the unvarying sexual pessimism (the girl always dies or marries somebody else) seemed like wisdom to boys who were herded together in public schools and were half-inclined to think of women as something unattainable. Whether Housman ever had the same appeal for girls I doubt. In his poems the women's point of view is not considered, she is merely the nymph, the siren, the treacherous half-human creature who leads you a little distance and then gives you the slip.

But Housman would not have appealed so deeply to the people who were young in 1920 if it had not been for another strain in him, and that was his blasphemous, antinomian, 'cynical' strain. The fight that always occurs between the generations was exceptionally bitter at the end of the Great War; this was partly due to the war itself, and partly it was an indirect result of the Russian Revolution, but an intellectual struggle was in any case due at about that date. Owing probably to the ease and security of life in England, which even the war hardly disturbed, many people whose ideas were formed in the eighties or earlier had carried them quite unmodified into the nineteen-twenties. Meanwhile, so far as the younger generation was concerned, the official beliefs were dissolving like sand-castles. The slump in religious belief, for instance, was spectacular. For several years the old-young antagonism took on a quality of real hatred. What was left of the war generation had crept out of the massacre to find their elders still bellowing the slogans of 1914, and a slightly younger generation of boys were writhing under dirty-minded celibate schoolmasters. It was to these that Housman appealed, with his implied sexual revolt and his personal grievance against God. He was patriotic, it was true, but in a harmless old-fashioned way, to the tune of red coats and 'God save the Queen' rather than steel helmets and 'Hang the Kaiser'. And he was satisfyingly anti-Christian – he stood for a kind of bitter, defiant paganism, a conviction that life is short and the gods are against you, which exactly fitted the prevailing mood of the young; and all in charming fragile verse that was composed almost entirely of words of one syllable.

It will be seen that I have discussed Housman as though he were merely a propagandist, an utterer of maxims and quotable 'bits'. Obviously he was more than that. There is no need to under-rate him now because he was over-rated a few years ago. Although one gets into trouble nowadays for saying so, there is a number of his poems ('Into my heart an air that kills', for instance, and 'Is my team ploughing?') that are not likely to remain long out of favour. But at bottom it is always a writer's tendency, his 'purpose', his 'message', that makes him liked or disliked. The proof of this is the extreme difficulty of seeing any literary merit in a book that seriously damages your deepest beliefs. And no book is ever truly neutral. Some tendency or other is always discernible, in verse as much as in prose, even if it does no more than determine the form and the choice of imagery. But poets who attain wide popularity, like Housman, are as a rule definitely gnomic writers.

TWO POST-WAR SUMMINGS-UP

93. ' "A Shropshire Lad" at Fifty', *Times Literary Supplement*
30 March 1946, 145-6

This unsigned front- and second-page article was prompted by the publication of the Jubilee Edition of *A Shropshire Lad*, with notes and introduction by Carl J. Weber (Waterville, Maine: Colby College Library).

The 'acute literary critic' of paragraph one was Cyril Connolly, whose 1936 article on Housman (No. 64) had been reprinted in 1945 in Connolly's *The Condemned Playground: Essays: 1927–1944*.

A 'Jubilee' edition of *A Shropshire Lad* – garnished with adulatory tributes, few of which will increase respect either for the worshippers or for their idol – has appeared in the United States. In this country an acute literary critic has just reprinted (with some disarming prefatory words of self-depreciation) the challenging essay with which ten years ago he commented upon the news of A.E. Housman's death. *Manibus date lilia plenis,* he seemed to say, *purpureos spargam flores,*[1] as he laid among the sickly profusion of lilies on the tomb, his darker tribute of deadly nightshade, not unmixed with garlic.

A Shropshire Lad is as old today as 'In Memoriam' was in 1900. The moment is perhaps not inopportune for a review of Housman's standing as a poet, and a glance at the controversies which his verse seems destined perpetually to provoke. Was Housman, even at his most successful, truly a poet – or was he merely a writer of accomplished verses? What, after all, is poetry? Wherein is the secret of the effectiveness that distinguishes it from verse? What should be, and what in this case was, the relation of poetry to the poet's experience?

A much greater range in what may be called the substance of literature has latterly been vindicated for writers. Verse and prose are made the vehicles not merely of rational discourse, not merely of articulate emotion, but of picture, idea, image, so disposed as to reproduce the phantasmagoria of the writer's own sub-consciousness or to evoke emotion in the reader by touching directly, or with the least possible mediation of the intellect, springs which lie below the level of the conscious mind. Mr. T.S. Eliot and James Joyce have been among the pioneers, in prose and verse, of writing of this kind in England. There is still dispute whether some writers have not pushed unprofitably far their experiments along these lines, but there is no denying that they have opened up new and fruitful fields for literature, and revealed much that was hitherto imperfectly understood about the effectiveness of writings in more familiar kinds.

The main issues in the current phase of this perennial debate were very justly and very strikingly summed up by Housman himself in the lecture on 'The Name and Nature of Poetry' which he delivered before the University of Cambridge in 1933. Poetry, he says in effect, usually (though it need not always do so) takes the form of verse; its main function is to communicate, or at least to arouse, emotion, and its effectiveness varies ordinarily with the quality and depth of the thoughts and sentiments which it conveys. But not only in accordance with these; there is an element in poetry, and it is the essentially poetic element, that consists not of thinking and sentiment, but of ideas and images, and works through their purely suggestive power. If that element is lacking, no utterance, however sublime, however deep, however moving, can be deemed truly poetic.

Many lines and stanzas, and even whole lyrics, which are among the most moving in our poetry (and the same is true, though less often, of snatches of prose) appeal to us solely by virtue of the second of these elements – the mysterious effectiveness of words and images which act not merely as sounds, still less as elements in a complex of thought, which make no appeal to the intellect but that it should recognise the meaning of words and grasp the structure of simple sentences, and which possess no emotional significance other than that somehow inherent in certain ideas as symbols or sources of suggestion.

The best examples of such poetry in English are the lyrics of Blake, though the Symbolist school in France and their English disciples have exploited more fully the possibilities of *la poésie pure*. In Blake we find poetry, in Housman's words, 'disengaged from its usual concomitants, from certain things with which it naturally unites itself and seems to blend indistinguishably,' from nobility of sentiment, for instance, and depth of thought. 'Blake again and again, as Shakespeare now and then, gives us poetry neat, or adulterated with so little meaning that nothing except poetic emotion is perceived and matters: –

> A fathomless and boundless deep,
> There we wander, there we weep;
> On the hungry craving wind
> My Spectre follows thee behind.

'I am not equal', Housman declared, 'to framing definite ideas which could... correspond to the strong tremor of unreasonable excitement which [such] words set up in some region deeper than the mind.'

Hence follows the conclusion that poetry is 'more physical than intellectual', which Housman sought to confirm by a striking account of this reaction to others' poetry and of his method of composing his own. The 'symptoms' – the bristling of the skin, the 'precipitation of water to the eyes', the shiver down the spine – will be familiar to readers of poetry; the method of composition – 'there would flow into my mind, with sudden and unaccountable emotion, sometimes a line or two of verse, sometimes a whole stanza at once, accompanied, not preceded, by a vague notion of the poem which they were destined to form part of ' – though unusual, particularly in a poet whose work is so intellectually precise as Housman's, is, of course, by no means without parallel.

Some words of warning should, we think, be added to what Housman and others have written on this subject. Recognition of the non-intellectual element in poetry and of the physical effect of poetry upon a sensitive organism must not mislead us into attributing undue importance to that element, or exalting the physical test into a criterion of what is poetry and what is not. Even lyrical poetry – and, far more, poetry of the dramatic, tragic and reflective kinds – may demand the co-operation of the reader's mind for its appreciation. As for the physical criterion, it is no test of the 'purity' of poetry – for a complex and reflective poem may equally bring tears to the eyes; nor even of aesthetic quality – for tears may be evoked in the most fastidious of judges by cheap melodrama or oratory, by the strains of military music, or by a sentimental situation in the theatre or in real life. The physical criterion is so obviously subjective (being at the mercy of circumstance, of mood, and the idiosyncrasies of the individual reader) that it cannot be appealed to in any field, however limited, as a sovereign touchstone. Above all, familiarity blunts this particular edge, and a poem is liable to lose this special magic, while retaining its other effective qualities, when one knows it well.

How far, then, did Housman respond to the influences – evidently well understood by him – which were at work in the field of poetry during the half-century before his death? And to what extent did he himself contribute to them? The answer to both these questions is, unambiguously, not at all. Thoroughly conventional in form, in diction, in substance, the verse he published in 1922 was the same as the verse of *A Shropshire Lad*, and there was no difference, in these respects, in any of his posthumously published poems. Though now and again a young admirer paid him the tribute of imitation, he cannot truthfully be said to have exercised any influence on the poetry of his day. As a poet he lived in a vacuum, shut off from the developments of his time; one need only consider Gerard Manley Hopkins and Mr. Eliot to appreciate, by contrast, the completeness of his isolation.

The tests suggested by Housman in his lecture may, however, without difficulty and not without profit be applied to his own poetry. The strong appeal that it makes to his admirers is not derived from its intellectual or its moral content. Housman is not a philosophical or an imaginative poet: he displays no Wordsworthian insight into the deep springs of human sympathy, no Shakespearean understanding of the range and intensity of human passions. Nor is his an example of the 'pure' poetry with which his lecture was so much concerned and towards which so much of contemporary poetry seems to be aspiring: it is not difficult to understand, but it must be understood if it is to be felt. Housman's poems are likely to suffer more than most from the application of the physical tests which he himself described; with a few notable exceptions they are devoid of that element of strangeness which is an almost necessary constituent of the poetry that evokes the shiver down the spine. Moreover, they gain their effects rather by the description or expression of recognisable emotions than by reliance on the suggestive properties of image or idea: his sentiments are precise, not only in the centre (so to say) but round the edges; his arrows are sharp and do not quiver in the wound.

> Ay, look: high heaven and earth ail from the prime foundation;
> All thoughts to rive the heart are here, and all are vain:
> Horror and scorn and hate and fear and indignation –
> Oh why did I awake? When shall I sleep again?
> [*A Shropshire Lad*, No. XLVIII, stanza 4]

Housman's method is well exemplified in that third line: even when he feels most deeply, he tries to tell us exactly what it is he feels.

That Housman is a 'pure' poet, therefore, will scarcely be suggested. Whether he is a 'classical' or a 'romantic' poet, whether he is a 'great' poet, whether he is, properly speaking, a poet at all – these are questions which have been hotly and, we think, fruitlessly debated.

A Cambridge mathematician once observed that too many philosophical controversies could be reduced to the following form: A: *I went for a walk to Trumpington this afternoon.* B: *I deny it: I did nothing of the sort.* So, many of the arguments about Housman's claim to the title of a poet, and about the merits of his work, when they are not quarrels about the definition of terms, are really but statements of the predilections of the participants, cast in disputatious form. Housman's work is particularly liable to provoke such disputations because he inspires very strong feelings, of admiration and the reverse, and the best service that the critic can perform is to attempt not to assess his claim to literary ranks and titles but to throw some light on the qualities of his poems and to suggest what it is in them that provokes such diversity of opinion.

Housman spoke of the 'narrow measure' of his verses, and the epithet is just in more senses than one. He published in his lifetime only a hundred or so short lyrics; about seventy more were brought out by his brother after his death. Almost all are concerned with a few familiar themes: passionate affection for the living –

[quotes stanzas 2 and 3 of *A Shropshire Lad*, No. XIV]

desiderium for the dead –

[quotes stanza 1 of *Last Poems*, No. XX]

the brevity of human life, and the vanity of human wishes. *Immortalia ne speres*[2] is his recurrent message, and a contemptuous but dignified acquiescence in the 'foreign laws of God and Man' is his counsel to the reader who resembles him in being

> a stranger and afraid
> In a world I never made.

Such comfort as he finds has two sources: pride in the maintenance of an unfaltering attitude in the face of destiny and pleasure in the beauties of nature as displayed in the countryside he knew. In life, no doubt, he had other resources, chief among which was the pursuit of classical learning; but this was a distraction rather than a comfort. While it may have helped him to forget his inner unhappiness, it cannot actually have diminished it, and it finds no place in his poetry.

Almost every poem bears the impress of his personal idiom in diction and versification, not least in the score or so in which, speaking in the character of a country boy, sometimes in his native country and sometimes exiled in London among crowds of 'men whose thoughts are not as mine', he describes romantic situations which involve not infrequently death in battle or at the hangman's hands. Such poems have attained celebrity and praise out of proportion to their number and their merit: some of those in which this convention plays the largest part are among his unquestionable failures:

[quotes *A Shropshire Lad*, No. LVIII]

There is Housman at his most easily recognizable and at his worst – the familiar ingredients displayed almost with the effect of self-parody. But in many of his finest poems he draws upon this stock-in-trade hardly at all – whether he is inspired by his consciousness of human destiny:

> When I meet the morning beam,
> Or lay me down at night to dream,
> I hear my bones within me say,
> 'Another night, another day.'
> [*A Shropshire Lad*, No. XLIII, stanza 1]

or by personal affection:

[quotes stanzas 1 and 3 of *A Shropshire Lad*, No. XXXIII]

or by external nature:

[quotes stanzas 11–13 of *A Shropshire Lad*, No. XLII]

These examples are all drawn from *A Shropshire Lad*, but equally moving poems are to be found throughout his work, and in a large majority of them the 'bucolic convention' plays no part whatever.

Those who do not care for Housman's poetry, however, will hardly like his successes better than his failures: the finish, the accomplishment, the clearness of the cut, which delight his admirers, and the charm which makes them uncritical in their admiration – these will only increase the distaste of those to whom Housman's voice is distasteful; for that voice is audible in every line, and there is nothing so repellent as the charm that fails in its enchantment, particularly if it is as insistent as Housman's. And I, says Tennyson,

> And I – my harp would prelude woe –
> I cannot all command the strings;
> The glory of the sum of things
> Will flash along the chords and go.

There are no such wild reliefs for Housman or his readers – no flashes or gleams from another world; he commands perfectly his strings and himself, and himself is all he has to offer.

This intransigence limits his effectiveness. Housman, like Gray (and no doubt for a like reason), 'never spoke out'; heartfelt as his lyrics are, they are never *cris de coeur*; he can never forget the man in the poet; among the children of unhappiness his kinship is with Heine, not with Emily Brontë. Poetry did not free his spirit; it was a key for the locking, and not for the unlocking, of his heart.

In his own words, his poems were to him what the pearl is to the oyster – a morbid secretion. Such models, such sources of inspiration as he had were indeed (we have his word for it) of the most 'romantic' kind – the Bible and the old ballads; and the feelings which forced him to write were deep and painful and 'romantic' too; but they were defined and cut into 'polygons with hard edges' before they became matter for his verse – at what deep level, often below consciousness, we know from his account of his method of composition already quoted.

A good deal has been written, by those to whom Housman's poetry is uncongenial, about his 'pose of pessimism', his 'faked emotions', his 'sham pastoral convention'. Such criticism springs, we may suspect, from the desire of those who do not like black pearls to condemn all black pearls as artificial. That Housman's verse lacked spontaneity – or rather, often lacked the appearance of it – is undeniable; many of his poems, indeed, are clearly the fruit of a process (never, we suspect, deliberate, and often quite unconscious) of self-dramatization. Yet only a superficial critic will stigmatize this dramatization of self as 'insincere', or suggest that it leads of necessity to aesthetic defects in the poems themselves. Those who are concerned with literary quality will rather ask simply whether the process was, poetically, a success – a question which cannot be answered without a detailed examination of Housman's poems, which it is the object of this essay to suggest, not to supply. It is not often that his poems receive such an examination at the hands of an impartial judge, for those who 'like the taste' of Housman's poetry will swallow with delight even the draughts, with their overdose of sentiment and bravado, provided in his least successful poems – poems which so nauseate readers to whom that taste is uncongenial that they too readily deny any merit to him even at his best: for them (to employ a metaphor which may reveal more clearly the defect in their critical approach) all Housman's pearls disclose that sable tinge which marks them as 'artificial' and so condemns them as worthless.

To discount Housman's habit of self-dramatization as a 'pose' betrays a misunderstanding of his personality, which, though it might have been defensible fifty years ago, has no excuse since the publication of the posthumous poems. Several of these make very plain the nature of the emotions which were evidently his strongest source of inspiration, and among them their editor, Mr. Laurence Housman, draws particular attention to the following –

> Ask me no more, for fear I should reply;
> Others have held their tongues, and so can I;
> Hundreds have died, and told no tale before:
> Ask me no more, for fear I should reply.
> [*Additional Poems*, No. VI, stanza 1]

The 'reply' is found in the succeeding stanza, and most clearly in the indignant outburst beginning,

> Oh who is that young sinner with the handcuffs on his wrists?

of which Mr. Laurence Housman declares that 'it says something which A.E. Housman very much wished to say, but perhaps preferred not to say in his own lifetime.'

'Friendship', says Housman's biographer, 'had once meant for him a whole-hearted devotion which its objects were not always able to repay in kind', and which, one may add, it was not easy for a reticent man to express in poems meant for publication.

> Because I liked you better
> Than suits a man to say,
> It irked you, and I promised
> To throw the thought away.
> [*More Poems*, No. XXXI, stanza 1]

Herein lies the reason for Housman's use of a bucolic convention and his persistent dramatization of himself. The convention enabled him to express emotions which he shrank from exposing undisguised; the imaginary or the internal drama was the expedient by which a frustrated nature sought unconsciously to compensate itself for the lack of those emotional contacts – the life and adventure of the heart – for which the lyric impulse craves, so that it may have the matter that it needs if it is to fulfil itself.

The distinction between 'sincerity' and 'artificiality' is not appropriate to such a case. It is enough to say that, re-reading *A*

Shropshire Lad in the light of 'The Name and Nature of Poetry' and of its author's own posthumously published verses we may learn an interesting lesson about the varieties of inspiration and poetic method.

NOTES

1 'Keep on giving lilies from full hands, I shall bestow purple flowers.'
2 From Horace, Ode VII of Book 4: 'The year and the hour that rob us of the gracious day warn thee *not to hope for immortal joys*' (Loeb translation, 1914).

94. John Crowe Ransom places Housman
1951

John Crowe Ransom (1888–1974), distinguished and influential poet and critic, the leading member of the 'Fugitive Group' of southern American poets and leader of the 'New Critics'. He was Professor of English at Vanderbilt University, Nashville, Tennessee; then at Kenyon College, Ohio, where from 1939 to 1959 he edited the *Kenyon Review*.

An extract from Ransom, 'The Poetry of 1900–1950', *ELH*, xviii (June 1951), 160–1; this article is the slightly altered version of a paper read by Ransom at a meeting of the Ohio College English Association, 6 April 1951.

I now go on to a judgement so presumptuous that I must insist it is tentative, it is anything but dogmatic. I name the poets of 1900–1950 who seem, at least as of this moment, to have established themselves, and to have good prospect of surviving in our literature for a few half-centuries. They are British and American indifferently. I cannot make speeches for these poets, though at another time I should delight in arguing their merits. And since I understand that even a prose discourse should be in the ascending or climactic order of interest, I begin with naming ten poets in an inferior category, denominated Minor Poets. The order is that of seniority

> Robert Bridges;   Ezra Pound;
> Walter de la Mare;   Marianne Moore;
> John Masefield;   E.E. Cummings;
> Vachel Lindsay;   Hart Crane;
> William Carlos Williams;   Allen Tate.

It will be noticed that there are fine poets junior to these who fail to make my list. I do not feel able as yet to rank them. As Solon said, we must wait to see how they finish. But in any case it is more likely than not that posterity, or for that matter any of my critical contemporaries, must find errors in my listing. I am afraid there may be errors of inclusion. I shall be happy if there are more errors of exclusion.

Now I come upon an embarrassing predicament. I have to name four poets of whom I cannot determine whether they belong with the Minor Poets just named or with the Major Poets to be named finally. In thinking of a poet as Major, I mean to assume only the criteria which will occur to everybody. His deliverances should be of vital human importance, and produced rather consistently in some volume; but freshly rather than repetitiously, so that he will need the largest resources, imaginative and technical too. The four poets who are hard for me to classify may fail of having this sufficient range of interest, though they will have their assured brilliances; or they may have veered from one kind of poetry to another kind without as yet making their second poetry decisive. As follows:

> A.E. Housman;   Wystan Auden;
> Wallace Stevens;   Dylan Thomas.

There remain the five poets whom I think a common consent will rank as the Major Poets of our period:

> Thomas Hardy;   Robert Frost;
> William Butler Yeats;   T.S. Eliot.
> Edwin Arlington Robinson;

These poets need no recommendation of mine. [...]

Select Bibliography

This bibliography is limited to items which relate to the growth or state of Housman's reputation as a poet.

ANON., '"A Shropshire Lad" Bibliography', *Times Literary Supplement*, 30 March 1946, 156: useful brief history of the early printings and reviews of *A Shropshire Lad*.

CARTER, JOHN, and SPARROW, JOHN, 'A.E. Housman: An Annotated Check-List', *The Library: A Quarterly Review of Bibliography*, Fourth Series, xxi, No. 2 (September 1940), 160–91: invaluable inventory of works by Housman, which includes details (for some of the volumes of poems) of the number of copies printed. A second edition (revised by William White) appeared in 1982.

EHRSAM, THEODORE, G., *A Bibliography of Alfred Edward Housman* (Boston, F.W. Faxon Company, 1941): lists (11–17 and 21–44) an enormous number of reviews, articles and book-excerpts on Housman published between 1896 and 1940.

HABER, TOM BURNS, *A.E. Housman* (New York: Twayne, 1967): Chapter 8 (170–8) deals briefly with Housman's reputation during his lifetime and after his death.

LEGGETT, B.J., *Housman's Land of Lost Content: A Critical Study of 'A Shropshire Lad'* (Knoxville: University of Tennessee Press, 1970): includes in its Selected Bibliography a sizeable number of articles on Housman published after 1945.

MARLOW, NORMAN, *A.E. Housman: Scholar and Poet* (London: Routledge & Kegan Paul, 1958): Chapter VIII (159–70) deals with 'Contemporary Criticism of Housman', and responds with particular trenchancy to critics hostile to him.

RICHARDS, GRANT, *Housman 1897–1936* (Oxford University Press, 1941): Chapter I mentions the early response to A Shropshire Lad (6–16); Chapters XXXIX and XL (351–75) deal respectively with 'Eulogy' and 'Detraction' of Housman. Chapter XXXVIII (342–50) is concerned with parodies of

Housman. All three chapters are of especial value in that they quote at some length from the material on which they comment.

RICKS, CHRISTOPHER (ed.), *A.E. Housman: A Collection of Critical Essays* (Englewood Cliffs, NJ: Prentice-Hall, 1968): brings together various poems and articles on Housman, and a parody of him; most of these items were published between 1936 and 1968. Professor Ricks's comments in his introduction are useful and lively.

STALLMAN, ROBERT WOOSTER, 'Annotated Bibliography of A.E. Housman: A Critical Study', *PMLA*, lx, No. 2 (June 1945), 463–502: a collection of, and a commentary on, 'all evaluations of Housman's poetry and poetic theory' published between 1920 and 1945. It includes some seventy-five pieces not listed in Ehrsam's bibliography.

Index

The index is arranged as follows: I Newspapers and journals; II Critics and reviewers; III Writers compared with A.E. Housman; IV References to A.E. Housman's poetry.

I NEWSPAPERS AND JOURNALS QUOTED FROM OR REFERRED TO

Academy No. 7, discussed 8, 82; No. 13, discussed 13–14; 13
Adelphi No. 54, discussed 33; No. 65, discussed 35
Athenaeum No. 15, discussed 11
Atlantic Monthly No. 75, discussed 41

Bookman (London) No. 5, discussed 7–8; No. 14; No. 29, discussed 24; 11, 19
Bookman (New York) No. 39
Boston Evening Transcript No. 56, discussed 33; 39
British Weekly No. 4, discussed 6

Cambridge Review No. 24, discussed 21; No. 63, discussed 36
Canadian Forum No. 33; No. 77, discussed 40
Chap-Book (Chicago) No. 8, discussed 10
Chapbook (London) 22
Christian Science Monitor No. 57, discussed 34

Citizen (Philadelphia) No. 10, discussed 9
Criterion No. 58, discussed 34; No. 78, discussed 40

Dalhousie Review 27
Dial No. 41, discussed 26–7; 9–10
Dublin Review No. 80

English 40
English Review No. 28, discussed 20
Essays and Studies 46

Fortnightly Review No. 11, discussed 11–13, 81, 84, 192–3; No. 34, discussed 25, 192

Guardian No. 6, discussed 8

Horizon No. 86, discussed 46–7

Idler 7, 13

Kenyon Review No. 91, discussed 43, 44

INDEX

Listener No. 72, discussed 39–40
Literary Review No. 31
Literary World (Boston) No. 9, discussed 9
Literature No. 16, discussed 13
Living Age 41, 44
London Mercury No. 26, discussed 24; No. 32, discussed 22–4, 192–3, 201; No. 51, discussed 32–3; No. 73; 34

Manchester Guardian Weekly Nos. 24, 49, 61
Le Mois 35

Nation (New York) No. 37, discussed 26, 194–6; No. 81; No. 89, discussed 44
Nation & Athenaeum 25
National Review 35
New Age No. 2, discussed 8–9
New Republic No. 38, discussed 22; No. 71, discussed 41; No. 87, discussed 47
New Statesman & Nation No. 42, discussed 27–8, 36; No. 50; No. 64, discussed 36–7, 40, 329–30, 415; No. 67
New Verse No. 74, discussed 41
New York Times 24
New York Times Book Review No. 69, discussed 41; No. 85, discussed 45
Nineteenth Century No. 90, discussed 47
North American Review No. 66, discussed 35–6

Observer No. 68
Outlook No. 12; No. 30, discussed 22
Oxford Magazine No. 62, discussed 36

Poetry (Chicago) No. 76, discussed 41; No. 82, discussed 43–4; No. 88, discussed 44–5; 20
Poetry Review No. 36, discussed 24, 25; 37

Queen's Quarterly No. 44, discussed 23, 28–9

Review of Reviews 10

Saturday Review (London) No. 17, discussed 11, 14
Saturday Review of Literature (New York) No. 55
Scribner's Magazine 29
Scrutiny Nos. 52 and 53, discussed 1, 33; 32
Sewanee Review No. 35, discussed 22
Sketch No. 3, discussed 6; 13
Spectator No. 27, discussed 24; No. 70, discussed 40–1; No. 84
Sunday Times No. 23, discussed 21, 25

Times, The No. 1, discussed 6; 2, 31
Times Literary Supplement, The No. 22, discussed 23; No. 93, discussed 47; 38, 39, 45–6
To-day No. 20, discussed 18, 192

429

INDEX

Virginia Quarterly Review 32
Week-end Review 31

Yale Review No. 40; No. 60, discussed 34, 37; No. 79, discussed 41–2

II CRITICS AND REVIEWERS QUOTED OR REFERRED TO

Abercrombie, Lascelles No. 49; 94
Adcock, St John 18
Aiken, Conrad No. 71; 41, 42
Archer, William No. 11; 12–13, 30
Auden, W.H. 46

Bayley, John xv
Benét, William Rose No. 39
Binny, Daphne 37
Birney, Earle No. 77; 40
Bishop, John Peale No. 88; 44–5
Bland, Hubert No. 2; xiv, 8–9, 42
Blunt, Wilfrid Scawen 16
Boas, Guy 40
Bronowski, Jacob No. 78; 41–2
Brooke, Rupert 16–17, 27
Brooks, Benjamin Gilbert No. 90; 47
Brooks, Cleanth No. 91; 43
Brown, Ivor No. 68
Brown, Stuart Gerry 48
Bullett, Gerald 31
Burdett, Osbert No. 45; 29

Clarke, George Herbert No. 35; 22

Davenport, Basil No. 55
Davidson, Eugene No. 79; 41, 42
Davis, H.J. No. 33
Dobrée, Bonamy No. 84

Dodd, Lee Wilson No. 31
Eliot, T.S. No. 58; 1, 26, 33–4
Ellis, Stewart Marsh No. 34; 25, 30
Elvin, René 35, 41
Empson, William No. 76; 41
Erskine, John No. 66; 35–6

Firkins, O.W. No. 44
Fitzgerald, Robert 41
Flecker, James Elroy No. 19
Forster, E.M. No. 72; 39–40
Freeman, John No. 29; 19

Gale, Norman No. 7; 8
Garrod, H.W. No. 47; 30, 46
Gawsworth, John 38–9
Gosse, Edmund No. 23; 21, 25
Grigson, Geoffrey No. 74; 41
Guiney, Louise Imogen No. 8; 10, 11, 30, 45
Gurney, Ivor 18
Gwynn, Stephen 27

Harding, D.W. No. 52
Hardy, Thomas 15–16
Harper, George McLean 29
Hillyer, Robert No. 75; 41
Holmes, John 39
Housman, A.E. xvi, 2, 3, 6, 20, 28, 30, 31, 34–5, 37–8, 42

Jack, Peter Monro Nos. 69, 85; 41, 45
Jackson, Holbrook No. 20; 18

INDEX

Jones, Howard Mumford 19–20, 22

Knights, L.C. No. 52
Kreymborg, Alfred 44
Kronenberger, Louis No. 81

Leavis, F.R. 33
Lee, Lawrence 43, 44
Le Gallienne, Richard 5, 7, 21, 24
Leighton, Lawrence No. 82; 43–4
Lucas F.L. Nos. 42, 63; 27–8, 31, 36, 37

Macdonald, J.F. No. 44; 23, 28–9
Macdonnell, Annie [?] No. 5; 7–8
MacNeice, Louis No. 87; 47
Marlow, Norman xiii–xiv, xv
Meredith, George 15
Monro, Harold No. 20; 19
Morley, John 5
Mortimer, Raymond No. 67; 40
Muir, Edwin No. 73

Newman, Ernest 18–19
Nichols, Wallace B. No. 36; 24, 25
Nicoll, William Robertson No. 4; 6
Norris, William A. No. 38; 22

Onions, Oliver [?] No. 3; 13
Orwell, George No. 92; 47, 48
Owen, Wilfred 18

Payne, William Morton 9–10

Percival, Alicia 37
Peters, E. Curt 43
Postgate, R.W. 25–6, 30
Priestley, J.B. No. 32; xiv, 22–4, 29
Putt, S. Gorley No. 53

Ransom, John Crowe No. 94; 48–9
Rees, Richard Nos. 54, 65; 33, 35
Richards, Grant xiii, xvi, 10–11, 19
Richards, I.A. 32
Ricks, Christopher xv
Rope, H.E.G. 28

Sapir, Edward No. 41; 26, 27
Schriftgeisser, Karl No. 56; 33
Sitwell, Edith No. 59; 34
Sorley, Charles No. 18; 17–18, 46
Sparrow, John No. 70; 37, 40–1, 47
Spender, Stephen No. 86; 46–7
Squire, J.C. Nos. 26, 43, 51; 24, 28, 32–3
Stonier, G.W. No. 50

Tinker, Chauncy Brewster No. 60; 32, 34, 37

Van Doren, Carl & Mark No. 83; 44
Wain, John xiv, xv
Ward, Thomas Humphry No. 1; 6
Watts, Nevile No. 80
Wilde, Oscar 15
Williams, Charles No. 48; 260
Williams, Iolo No. 46

Williams-Ellis, Amabel   No. 27; 24, 35
Wilson, James Southall   31–2
Wood, Clement   No. 37; 26, 27, 29
Woodward, E.L.   No. 62; 36
Woolf, Virginia   1–3
Yeats, W.B.   4
Zabel, Morton Dauwen   No. 89; 44

III   WRITERS AND WORKS COMPARED WITH HOUSMAN OR MENTIONED IN CONNECTION WITH HIM

'Adonais' (Shelley)   245
Alice in Wonderland (Lewis Carroll)   74
'Ancient Mariner, The' (Coleridge)   121
Arnold, Matthew   32, 46, 72, 100–1, 180–1, 198, 242, 279, 297, 319, 328
Auden, W.H.   267, 374
Aurelius, Marcus   127

'Ballad of Marie Hamilton, The'   374–5
Ballad of Reading Gaol, The (Oscar Wilde)   15, 386, 403
Barnes, William   64, 144
Baudelaire, Charles   191, 378, 394, 398, 401, 404
Beaumont, Francis   73
Beddoes, Thomas Lovell   141, 181
Belloc, Hilaire   283–4
Benson, A.C.   10, 398
Blair, Robert   141
Blake, William   177, 196, 232, 253, 278–9, 353, 383, 404, 417
Book of Nineties Verse, A   (ed. A.J.A. Symons)   3
Bourdillon, F.W.   196–7
Bremond, Abbé   253
Bridges, Robert   3, 37, 82, 100, 121, 212, 393, 400
Brooke, Rupert   46, 242, 411

Brown, T.E.   144
Browning, Elizabeth Barrett   268
Browning, Robert   184, 264, 336, 359
Burns, Robert   76, 88, 144, 161, 196, 353
Byron, George Gordon Lord   35, 157, 223, 263

Callimachus   320
Campion, Thomas   64, 193, 357
Carroll, Lewis   384
Carman, Bliss   65–6
Carter, John   42
Catullus, Gaius Valerius   248, 279, 283, 293, 297, 340, 355
Chatterton, Thomas   154
Chesterton, G.K.   138
Child's Garden of Verses, A (R.L. Stevenson)   69, 71
'City of Dreadful Night, The' (James Thomson)   88, 268, 401
Clare, John   90, 144
'Clark Saunders'   146
Coleridge, Samuel Taylor   32, 117, 177, 184, 245, 403
Collins, William   115
Constant, Benjamin   127–8
Cory, William Johnson   10
Cowper, William   382–3
Croce, Benedetto   296

432

INDEX

Dante Alighieri 204, 231
Dauber (John Masefield) 164
Davidson, John 4, 82, 99
Davies, W.H. 315
de la Mare, Walter 121, 151
de Quincey, Thomas 245
Dickinson, Emily 41, 316, 327, 374
Disenchantment (C.E. Montague) 128
Dobson, Austin 319
Donne, John 378–9, 380
Dowson, Ernest 4, 258, 400
Dryden, John 164
Duck, Stephen 90

Ecclesiastes, Book of 108, 349
Eliot, George 28
Eliot, T.S. 1, 26, 32, 241, 252, 254, 258–60, 290, 333, 358, 383, 400, 416, 418
Emaux et Camées (Théophile Gautier) 100
Emerson, Ralph Waldo 198
England's Helicon 71
'Erectheus' (Swinburne) 98

Fitzgerald, Edward 24, 45, 95, 131, 398
Flecker, James Elroy 242, 334

Galsworthy, John 201, 325
Goethe, Johann Wolfgang von 221
Gray, Thomas 45, 115, 196, 205, 282, 285, 326–7
Greek Anthology 102, 207, 279, 283, 286, 319, 326, 349, 360

Hamlet (Shakespeare) 121
Hardy, Thomas 12, 13, 15, 35, 64, 76, 101, 156–7, 184, 205, 226–8, 244, 272, 274, 288, 290, 328, 357, 359, 364, 372, 394, 400
Harris, Frank 405
Harvey, F.W. 18
Heine, Heinrich 9, 13, 50 note 22, 66, 77, 84, 86, 92, 117, 161–2, 171, 177, 181, 191, 279, 283, 340, 357, 394, 422
Henley, W.E. 60, 275, 364
Henry, O. 162
Herrick, Robert 167, 182
Homer 246, 279
Hopkins, Gerard Manley 258, 289, 290, 381, 398, 400, 418
Horace 279, 283, 285–7, 293, 297, 303, 319
House of the Seven Gables, The (Nathaniel Hawthorne) 173
Housman, Laurence 15, 17, 38, 42, 81–2, 137, 318, 340, 343, 352, 372, 423
Hulme, T.E. 383
Huxley, Aldous 380

Ionica (William Johnson Cory) 71

Jarrell, Randell 409
Job, Book of 121
Johnson, Lionel 4, 400
Johnson, Samuel 247, 279, 375
Jonson, Ben 394
Joyce, James 416

Keats, John 29–30, 108, 140, 154, 157, 164, 227, 370
Kipling, Rudyard 3, 35, 78, 104, 261, 265, 270, 275, 283–4, 301, 303, 309, 316, 366, 401, 403
'Kubla Khan' (Coleridge) 164

Landor, Walter Savage 99, 148, 181, 232, 279, 301, 370

INDEX

Lawrence, D.H. 35, 288–91, 325
Lawrence, T.E. 380, 396
Leavis, F.R. 406
Leconte de Lisle, Charles-Marie-René 401
Le Gallienne, Richard 7, 20–1
Leopardi, Giacomo 394
Lovelace, Richard 161
Lucretius 76, 108, 161, 251, 293, 350
Lucas, F.L. 406–7

Manilius 25–6
Mantuan 220
Marvell, Andrew 167, 247, 258, 330, 357
Masefield, John 17, 96, 205, 270, 339, 403, 412
Massey, Gerald 71
Maupassant, Guy de 173
Meleager 92, 184
Men and Women (Robert Browning) 18
Meredith, George 96, 319, 410
Millay, Edna St. Vincent 205, 408
Milton, John 71, 140, 153, 173, 184, 231, 236, 279
Morris, William 267
Murray, Gilbert 98

Nashe, Thomas 227
Newbolt, Sir Henry 4, 104, 284, 359
Newman, John Henry 185
Noyes, Alfred 309, 339

Oxford Book of Modern Verse, The (ed. W.B. Yeats) 4

Parker, Dorothy 408
Pascal, Blaise 394
Pater, Walter 108, 208
Patmore, Coventry 130
Phillips, Stephen 82, 262
Pindar 196
Poe, Edgar Allan 162, 294, 323
Poetry of the 'Nineties (ed. R.K.R. Thornton) 4
Pollard, A.W. 5
Pollet, Maurice 6
Pope, Alexander 164, 220
Proust, Marcel 391

Richards, I.A. 269, 406
Rilke, Rainer Maria 398
Robinson, Edwin Arlington 393
Rossetti, Christina 331
Rubáiyát of Omar Khayyám, The (Edward Fitzgerald) 18, 106, 108, 110, 121, 128, 132, 191, 263, 268, 311, 326, 350
Russell, Bertrand 405

Sandburg, Carl 195–6
Sappho 133, 184, 196, 246, 320, 355
Shakespeare, William 10, 69, 94, 164, 227, 279, 300, 319, 353, 375, 418
Shelley, Percy Bysshe 146, 152–3, 157, 336
Sidney, Sir Philip 32
Skipsey, Joseph 71
Sophocles 388
Spenser, Edmund 73, 173, 220, 342
Stevenson, R.L. 24, 46, 92, 224
Strachey, Lytton 280
Swift, Jonathan 185, 217
Swinburne, Algernon Charles 140, 157, 167, 181, 208, 268, 350, 402, 410

INDEX

Symonds, John Addington 208
Symons, A.J.A. 400

Temple, Sir William 349
Tennyson, Alfred Lord 96, 144, 172, 178, 309, 341, 346, 354, 421
Theocritus 279, 412
Thompson, Francis 258
Thomson, James 184–5
Tibullus 297
Trench, Frederic Herbert 15

Ulysses (James Joyce) 26
'Ulysses' (Tennyson) 98
Underwoods (R.L. Stevenson) 69

Verlaine, Paul 220, 394
Vigny, Alfred de 35
Villon, François 220, 293, 394, 403

Virgil 283
Voltaire 179

Waste Land, The (T.S. Eliot) 26, 32, 287
Watson, William 82
Webster, John 141
Wells, H.G. 135
Whitman, Walt 106, 290–1
'Wife of Usher's Well, The' 367
Wilson, Edmund 384
Wolfe, Humbert 214
Wordsworth, William 83–4, 92, 144–5, 153, 199, 223, 290, 343, 361, 375, 418
Wylie, Elinor 248

Yeats, W.B. 4, 35, 44, 95, 121, 151, 231, 258, 372, 384, 389, 398

IV DISCUSSIONS OF INDIVIDUAL VOLUMES BY HOUSMAN (LISTED IN ORDER OF PUBLICATION), TOGETHER WITH REFERENCES TO, AND SIGNIFICANT QUOTATIONS FROM, INDIVIDUAL POEMS

A Shropshire Lad (1896) Nos. 1–10; 5–11, 13, 21, 81, 86, 88, 90, 115, 124, 130, 155, 159, 168, 186, 208–9, 223, 272–3, 308, 365, 386–7, 379, 415

A Shropshire Lad (1898) Nos. 11–21; 14–19, 21–3, 26, 28, 32–3, 36, 38, 42, 47, 112–3, 116–7, 119–20, 126–8, 132–3, 135, 136-7, 139, 141–52, 156–7, 161, 162, 166, 170, 174–6, 188, 191–2, 193–4, 198, 199, 202, 205, 210, 212, 220, 224, 226, 229, 236, 242, 243, 258, 260, 263, 277, 283–4, 288, 301, 307, 310, 314, 321, 324, 327, 329, 331, 339-40, 353, 356, 358, 369, 377, 381, 382–4, 385, 389–90, 393, 410, 423; Individual poems: I ('1887') 95, 406; II 60, 141–2, 210, 227, 261, 353; III ('The Recruit') 73, 104–5, 275; IV ('Reveille') 79, 94, 100, 106, 199, 211, 247, 348; V 67, 147; VI 67; VII 94, 349; VIII 74, 146, 367–8, 412; IX 60, 75, 95, 102, 354, 412; XI 73; XII 80, 95, 102, 207, 222; XIII 79; XIV 141, 181–2, 420; XV 73, 99, 377, 390; XVII 74, 82, 93, 227, 260, 378; XVIII 61, 198; XIX ('To an Athlete Dying

435

Young') 72, 148, 166–7, 219, 353, 396; XXI ('Bredon Hill') 64, 80, 97, 99, 111, 151, 396, 407; XXII 95; XXIII 72, 79, 105; XXIV 302, 396; XXV 296, 402, 407; XXVI 7, 69, 94, 166, 296; XXVII 16, 79, 84, 276, 338, 396, 414; XXVIII('The Welsh Marches') 77, 85, 94, 99, 108, 277, 363, 396, 400; XXIX ('The Lent Lily') 353; XXX 87, 302, 303, 396, XXXI 71, 85, 96, 140, 352, 396; XXXII 85, 347; XXXIII 421; XXXIV ('The New Mistress') 265; XXXV 95, 222–3, 348, XXXIX 62, 73, 147, 210, 353; XL 83, 141, 155, 197, 345, 414; XLI 64, 232, 324; XLII ('The Merry Guide') 90, 99, 169, 303, 396, 421; XLIII ('The Immortal Part') 259, 267, 396, 421; XLIV 218, 264; XLV 78, 89, 266; XLVI 362; XLVII ('The Carpenter's Son') 266–7, 363; XLVIII 71, 78, 88, 94, 141, 349, 388, 402, 419; XLIX 396, L 62, 78, 89, 91, 150, 152, 193, 196; LI 78; LII 155, 353, 396; LIII ('The True Lover') 146; LIV 48, 106, 147, 218, 285–6, 366, 396, 408, 410–11; LV 96; LVI ('The Day of Battle') 79; LVIII 420; LIX ('The Isle of Portland') 389; LX 100, 197, 232; LXI ('Hughley Steeple') 64, 350, 396; LXII 66, 73–4, 77, 107, 148, 169, 212, 327, 344, 404; LXIII 404

Last Poems Nos. 22–41; 19–29, 35, 38, 42, 47, 179, 180, 192, 193–4, 198, 199, 201, 208, 224, 226, 229, 236, 243, 260, 262, 273, 275, 286–7, 288, 293, 307, 308, 321, 327, 339–40, 346, 353, 365, 377, 381, 382, 384, 418; Individual Poems: Prefatory Poem 116, 130, 156, 163, 269–70, 303, 325; I ('The West') 123, 156, 160, 163, 176, 390; II 156, 265–6; III 163, 291; VI ('Lancer') 171, 302; VII 158, 396; IX 127, 131, 163, 194, 286, 344, 354, 359, 373; X 135, 170, 175, 367, 408–9; XI 127, 153, 199, 375, 396; XII 114, 131, 156, 164, 228, 303, 351, 396; XIII ('The Deserter') 133, 156, 173, 183; XIV ('The Culprit') 153, 170, 171, 200, 375, 396; XV ('Eight O'Clock') 122, 156, 170, 175, 200–1, 403; XVIII 157, 170, 347; XIX 163, 279; XX 118, 150, 183, 279, 371, 375, 407–8, 420; XXI 133, 164, 231, 248, 279, 402; XXII 354; XXIII 117; XXIV ('Epithalamium') 133, 173, XXV ('The Oracles') 164, 169, 201–2, 299, XXVI 343; XXVII 122, 123, 128, 346, 412; XXIX 163; XXX ('Sinner's Rue') 119, 158, 171, 350; XXXI ('Hell Gate') 119, 133, 160, 187–8, 203–4, 229–31, 347; XXXII 141, 203, 301; XXXIII 163, 377; XXXV 123, 248, 370, 375; XXXVI ('Revolution') 170, 200, 285, 303; XXXVII ('Epitaph on an Army of Mercenaries') 22, 133–4, 164, 266, 275, 325, 387–8, 402; XXXVIII 163;

XXXIX 119–20, 125, 156, 202, 348; XL 113, 122, 123, 125, 134, 162, 183, 189, 281, 346; XLI ('Fancy's Knell') 121, 125, 134, 147, 170, 183, 190, 204–5, 287, 353, 355, 404

The Name and Nature of Poetry Nos. 49–58; 31–4, 37, 45, 46, 47, 293, 295, 311, 352, 364, 365, 368–9, 383, 403, 406–7, 409, 416, 423

More Poems Nos. 67–79; 38–42, 43, 294, 343, 423; Individual Poems: Prefatory Poem 300, 306, 308–9, 327, 339; I ('Easter Hymn') 39, 312–3, 363; II 309; III 312; V ('Diffugere Nives') 39, 303; VI 396; VII 306, 322; VIII 322, 324, 337, 368; IX 309, 324, 335; XI 322; XII 330; XIV 323; XV 303, 336; XVII 311; XIX 324; XXII 318; XXIII 301, 320, 391; XXIV 322; XXV 312; XXVI 305, XXVII 306; XXVIII 323, 378; XXIX 307, 332, 408; XXXI 325, 379, 423; XXXII 329, 340, 396; XXXIII 309; 336–7; XXXIV 306; XXXV 303; XXXVI 306, 334; XXXVIII 336–7; XL 313; XLII ('A.J.J.') 301, 313; XLIV 39, 313, 395; XLVI ('The Land of Biscay') 309, 339, 395; XLVII ('For My Funeral') 303

Collected Poems Nos. 84–91; 38, 42–7; Individual Poems: 'Additional Poems' I ('Atys') 43, 395; VI 423; XII 43; XV 377; XVIII 382, 385, 396, 423; XXI ('New Year's Eve') 67; XXII 43

For Product Safety Concerns and Information please contact our EU representative GPSR@taylorandfrancis.com
Taylor & Francis Verlag GmbH, Kaufingerstraße 24, 80331 München, Germany

www.ingramcontent.com/pod-product-compliance
Lightning Source LLC
Chambersburg PA
CBHW070749020526
44115CB00032B/1415